CW01622144

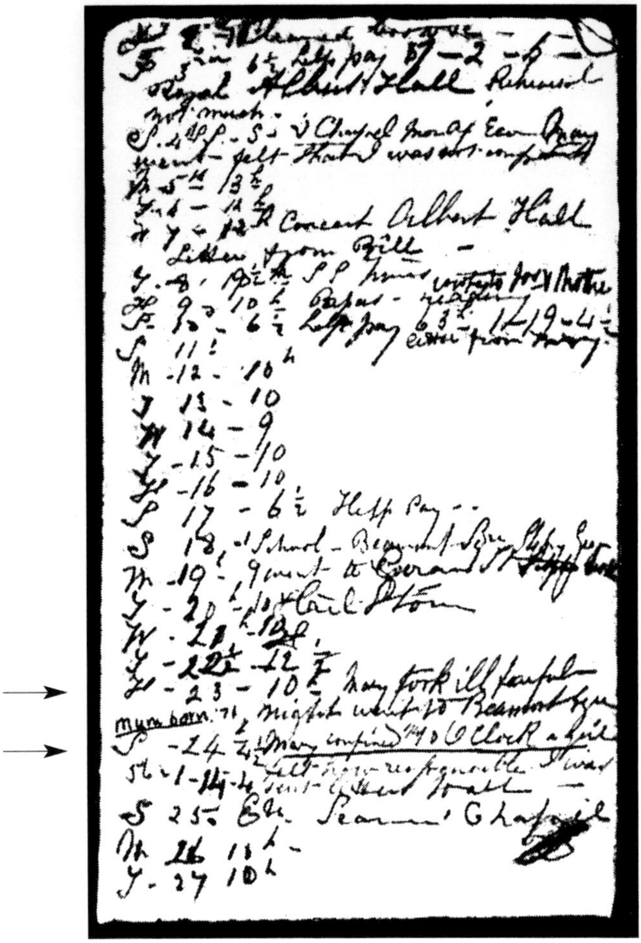

A page from the diary of Matthew Timberlake (Annie's father) for 1871. The entries arrowed announce Elizabeth Annie's birth:

F[riday] 23 [June] 10½ [hours worked] Mary took ill / fearful night / went to Beaumont Square [Wesleyan chapel].

S[aturday] 24 [June] 4½ [hours worked] Mary confined ¼ to 10 o'clock a girl / felt how responsible I was / sent letter to all.

Marion Flint, Annie's daughter, has annotated the entry, "Mum born '71" and has underlined it. On the following page an entry says:

M[onday] 17 [July] 10 [hours worked] Registered Elizabeth Annie [at Mile End, London] / wrote to Mother.

This page (written in pencil) is reproduced at the actual size of the original.

ANNIE'S LETTERS

"You've Come a Long Way, Mum"

THE LETTERS OF ELIZABETH ANNIE KIMPTON WRITTEN FROM CANADA AND THE UNITED STATES TO HER FAMILY IN ABBOTS LANGLEY, 1937-38

EDITED BY ROGER B FLINT AND DAVID A FLINT

2000

HALF DOME

First published in Great Britain by Half Dome,
38(B) Abbots Road, Abbots Langley,
Hertfordshire WD5 0BG
2000

Copyright © Roger B Flint, 2000

All rights reserved. No part of this publication may be reproduced, stored in a retrieval system, or transmitted in any form or by any means, electronic, mechanical, photocopying, recording or otherwise, without the prior permission of the Copyright owner.

The right of Roger B Flint to be identified as the author of the Editorial matter in this work has been asserted by him in accordance with the Copyright, Designs and Patents Act 1988.

British Library Cataloguing in Publication Data
A catalogue record of this book is available from the British Library

ISBN 0 9538513 0 3

*

The cover illustration shows a pencil sketch of Annie Kimpton drawn by her daughter, Marion, in 1926; it is reproduced at half size

*

This book was designed by David A Flint; the typeface is 1929 Monotype Bembo issued in digital form by Atomic Type; it was typeset by Ria L Flint using QuarkXpress; and it was printed by CLE Digital Print, St Ives, Cambridgeshire

For Annie Kimpton's great grandchildren:
Christine & Andrew; Rachel & Laura; Shani, Ria & Matthew

ACKNOWLEDGEMENTS

If any copyright material is included for which permission has not been sought through inability to trace the present copyright holders, apologies are hereby tendered to them and to the publishers concerned.

The following sources of Abbots Langley history have been used:

The enumerators' returns for the censuses of 1841, 1851, 1861, 1871, 1881 and 1891;

Peacock's Directories for Watford and District, 1890-1908;

Kelly's Directories for Watford and District, 1905-1938;

Abbots Langley by S G THICKNESSE, published by Staples Press Ltd in 1946;

The Endless Web: The History of John Dickinson & Co Ltd 1804-1954 by JOAN EVANS, published by Jonathan Cape in 1955;

The Church and Parish of Abbots Langley by the Rev R S WILKINSON, published by the Parochial Church Council in 1962;

Abbots Langley, A Hertfordshire Village by SCOTT HASTIE, published by the Abbots Langley Parish Council in 1993;

The "Newfangled Scheme" The First Hundred Years, A Centenary History of the Abbots Langley Parish Council 1894-1994 by C W CLARK, published by the Abbots Langley Parish Council in 1994;

Hastoe near Tring, Recollections of life on the Rothschild Estate in the time of the first Baron Rothschild by R R TIMBERLAKE, published in *Hertfordshire's Past,* issue 39, Autumn 1995.

Abbots Langley Then 1760-1960, Two hundred years in the development of the village and five miles around by C W CLARK, published by Clive Clark, in 1997;

Victorian Sanitation in Abbots Langley, A step forward in public health by CLIVE W CLARK, published in *Hertfordshire's Past,* issue 43/44, April 1999.

Thanks are expressed to VERA HODSOLL, Hon Secretary of the Eastbourne Local History Society, who located the monologue *Beachy Head*; and to RICHARD FOSTER, maritime bookdealer of Fareham, Hampshire, who located a reference to the fate of the SS *Manchester Regiment* in the book titled *60 years on the Western Ocean* by R B STOKER privately published by Manchester Liners Ltd, circa 1958.

Quotations are included of *Beachy Head*; of *O Canada!* by ROBERT STANLEY WEIR; of *Mornin' on the Desert*; of *The Passing of the Old Backhouse Seat* by JAMES WHITCOMB RILEY; of *The Old Time Religion* by Dr HARRY EMERSON FOSDICK; of *The Groves* by L L LOOFBOUROW; and of an extract from *A Christmas Sermon* by ROBERT LOUIS STEVENSON.

Drawings are included of the Funnel and House Flag of MANCHESTER LINERS LTD, adapted from *All About Ships & Shipping* drawn by F B HARNACK, published by Alexander Moring, 4th edition 1934; and of St Albans Abbey from *Wesley His Own Biographer, Selections from the Journals of the Rev John Wesley*, published by C H Kelly in 1891.

CONTENTS

LIST OF ILLUSTRATED PLATES

★

Between pages 240 and 241:

17a & 17b. Annie Kimpton's postcard of the *SS Manchester Regiment,* sent in May 1937 whilst it sailed along the Manchester Ship Canal at the start of Annie's voyage.

18. Ted Southam and his wife, Lizzie, with Annie Kimpton sitting between them in May 1937 at the back of their house at 13 Ida Street, St Catharines, Ontario, Canada.

19. Lizzie Southam née Hawkins and her brother, Jim Hawkins, with Annie Kimpton beside Jim's car in May 1937 at St Catharines, Ontario, Canada.

20a & 20b. Annie Kimpton with her cousins and other members of the Women's Auxiliary of "The Church of the Good Shepherd" at Niagara Falls, Ontario, Canada, in May 1937.

21. Alice Hawkins with Annie Kimpton in Victoria Park, Niagara, Canada, in May 1937.

22. A studio wedding photograph of Joe Kimpton in 1932, aged 34.

23. A studio wedding photograph of Alta Kimpton née Farthing in 1932.

24a & 24b. Alta Kimpton sitting in Annie's favourite chair and Joe Kimpton with the "denizens of the deep" at 400 Duboce Avenue, San Francisco, USA.

25. A pencil sketch of Annie Kimpton drawn by a young Italian or Mexican street artist on Olvera Street, Los Angeles, USA, in October 1937.

26a. The 1937 Christmas dinner with the Balzars in Oakland, California, USA.

26b. The message in Annie's 1937 Christmas card to the Botwright family at 56 Adrian Road, Abbots Langley, Hertfordshire.

27a. Joe Kimpton, Alta Kimpton and Wally Balzar picnicking on the beach at Russian River, California, USA, on their holiday in May 1938.

27b. Annie Kimpton, Alta Kimpton and Kitty Hotchkiss beside the table made from a section of a redwood tree, Sacramento Park, California, USA, in April 1938.

28. Constructing the Noren's new frame-house near Point Reyes, California, USA, taken on Sunday 28 August 1938.

29. An enlargement of the group of people in the window frame in Plate 28.

30. The last photograph of Joe, Annie and Alta Kimpton in August 1938 taken near Point Reyes, California, USA, on Sunday 28 August 1938.

31. Annie Kimpton's bedroom during her stay with Joe and Alta Kimpton in 1937 and 1938.

32. The headstone on the grave of David and Annie Kimpton in the parish churchyard of the Church of St Lawrence, Abbots Langley, Hertfordshire.

Every person mentioned in this book was real, their real names have been used and they are listed in the Index of Names. Some people who knew Annie Kimpton survived to a great age and provided background information. This has been acknowledged wherever possible at the appropriate point.

INTRODUCTION

ANNIE (ELIZABETH ANNIE) KIMPTON was highly amused whilst passing through Montréal in 1937, shortly after the Coronation of King George VI, when she saw written across a shop window: "KING GEORGE PEAS IN TWO QUART CANS". She quoted it as a postscript to one of her letters home.

Annie was my maternal grandmother. She was the eldest of the seven children of Matthew Timberlake and his wife Mary Ann (née Gates). Annie was born on 24 June 1871 and her growth from childhood paralleled the growth of the village of Abbots Langley. In 1868 the village was still only a hamlet with the Church of St Lawrence, several very large mansions with extensive grounds, the village schools, and the cottages between Langley House and the old Kings Head. There were also neighbouring hamlets of Kitters Green and Trowley Bottom. In 1868 construction began of the Leavesden Asylum for over two thousand inmates and of the St Pancras Industrial (later called, Residential) Schools for nearly seven hundred orphan children, both near Trowley Bottom. In anticipation of the number of staff that would be coming into the area, the BRITISH LAND COMPANY bought 96 acres of land in 1868 from the Estate of Sarah Smith of the Abbots House and began to lay out the roads which would form the new Abbots Langley. Further information and extracts from the Ordnance Survey maps 1873-1938 are given in Appendix IV : *Annie's Abbots Langley.*

Matthew Timberlake was a bricklayer by trade. He was born in 1845 in the hamlet of Nash Mills in the Gade Valley, three miles from Abbots Langley but within its parish at that time. Mary Gates was born in 1846 at the hamlet of Astrope, by Puttenham near Tring, Hertfordshire. They most likely met through their Wesleyan Methodist connections, for Matthew recorded in his diary that a Mr Gates preached at Nash Mills. (Matthew Timberlake's surviving diaries for the years 1869-1876, 1912-1919 and 1924-1933 are still in the possession of the family - but they are in three closely written volumes and difficult to decipher). Mathew recorded in his diary that he was bricklaying the low wall under the iron railings in front of Leavesden Asylum from February to March 1870. Matthew then moved to London and his diary indicates that he was working there and living in Stoke Newington. Matthew recorded that he was visiting Mary Gates. Matthew and Mary subsequently married on the 31st December 1870 at the Wesleyan chapel, High Street, West Hackney. Matthew wrote in his diary: "*Married / determined to serve God / brother Joe came, John Gates, Eliz Criddle / came to Langley, Mother's / all the family, Mr and Mrs Gates and Esther.*" Their wedding certificate states that Mathew was living on the High Street, Stoke Newington, and that Mary was living in Pembroke Square, Kensington. She was probably in service like many girls at that time. John Gates and Esther were Mary's brother and sister; John and Elizabeth Criddle were the witnesses at the wedding. Matthew later recorded that they moved in April 1871 to Bow in the East End of London. Annie was born on 24 June 1871 at 9 Silas Street, Mile End, according to her birth certificate.

In 1872 Matthew, Mary and baby Annie came to Abbots Langley where Matthew worked as a self-employed master bricklayer. In September 1872 his first job was the building of The Lodge, Langleybury, which he recorded in his diary by sketches and calculations of the quantities and costs of the brick and flint work. They lived initially somewhere in Adrian Road, probably renting one of the first houses built at its upper end. The Deeds of 54 Adrian Road show that on 30 December 1878, whilst resident in Adrian Road, he bought the plot of land for 54 Adrian Road from Joseph Chalk (the local builder) and on 17 June 1881 he bought the adjacent plot for 56 Adrian Road from Arthur Durrant. Both these plots had been originally bought at auction from the BRITISH LAND COMPANY by Joseph Chalk on 12 July 1876. Matthew Timberlake wanted to build No 54 for his family and No 56 to rent out. He probably designed, directed and did the bricklaying for their construction himself, for the Deeds do not include any record of the purchase of the houses. He took out a mortgage on them after their construction from the Watford and West Herts Permanent Benefit Building Society for £164. 1s. 10d on 21 July 1881. This was paid off by 9 December 1892. The two houses are distinct in their cream brick with decoration picked out in red.

Matthew Timberlake became one of the founders of the Wesleyan Methodist Society in Abbots Langley in 1878 and the driving force behind the establishment of the Wesleyan Methodist chapel. "The Society of the People called Methodists" was a revivalist movement within the Church of England started in 1743 by the two brothers the Rev John Wesley and the Rev Charles Wesley. After John Wesley's death in 1791, the movement broke away from the Church of England and subsequently split into various sects. The nine founding lay members of the Abbots Langley Wesleyan Methodist Society in 1878 (as recorded in the Society Class-Book) included Matthew Timberlake, his wife Mary, and her sister, Esther Hawkins née Gates. The Wesleyan Methodist chapel and its schoolroom were built in 1881. Matthew Timberlake was choir master, boys' handbell ringers' master, and Sunday school Superintendant at the Abbots Langley Wesleyan Methodist church; and was also a lay preacher. Much later the Wesleyan Methodist Church, the Primitive Methodist Church and the United Methodist Church re-combined in 1932 to form the Methodist Church of Great Britain.

*

ANNIE was only 2 years old when her brother, Matthew Henry, died at the age of 13 weeks (described by Clive Clark in *Abbots Langley Then 1760-1960,* based on an entry in Matthew Timberlake's diary). When Annie was 13 her sister, Edith Marion, died aged 8 months. When she was 18 another sister, Marion Dowse, died aged 3. And when she was 27 her surviving sister, Fanny Dorrofield, died aged 15. Only Annie and her two brothers, Joseph and another Matthew, survived to adulthood.

Following Wesleyan Methodist tradition, Annie and Joe were the first to attend the new Sunday school in 1879 in Joseph Chalk's old builders' shed, behind the site of the future Wesleyan Methodist chapel. Annie also went to Abbots Langley Girls' School where, amongst other things, she was taught needlework. Examples of her sister Fanny's needlework at this school were kept by Annie and are in the possession of the family. Every stitch was hand-done and is microscopic in size. It is probable that Annie's needlework would have been of similar quality.

Annie married David Kimpton who came from Leavesden where she was apprenticed as a dressmaker. David was apprenticed as a blacksmith at Ganders Ash, near Leavesden. He later worked as a blacksmith at the St Pancras Industrial Schools and at Leavesden Asylum. After the birth of their first child, they came to live at 56 Adrian Road (see Appendix I : *The Kimpton Family*). Annie and David had three children: Joe (Joseph Matthew) born in 1897, Marion (Marion Timberlake) born in 1902 and Fred (Frederick David) born in 1905. Both Marion and Fred were nicknamed "Kim". Matthew and Mary Timberlake and their younger children lived at No 54.

David, Annie's husband, suffered from pernicious anaemia which is associated with inadequate absorption of the vitamin B12. Although he was treated with a diet which included eating raw liver, he died in 1913 at the age of 41 leaving Annie with three young children aged 8, 11 and 16. Today, this form of anaemia is readily treatable and is rarely fatal. Annie's mother, Mary, died in 1914. She had left her handbag on the bus whilst going with her husband from Hunton Bridge to Watford, for there were no buses from Abbots Langley before 1920. Mary Timberlake, probably much aggitated by the loss of her handbag, had a heart attack after getting back and died during the night. Annie's father, Matthew Timberlake, whom Annie looked after in addition to her children, died in 1933.

Times were hard for Annie Kimpton, but she was a strong-spirited lady and a good needlewoman. She became well known in the village for the quality of her sewing, whether simple dressmaking and repairs or elaborate wedding dresses and gowns. In 1998 Dolly Brownsell née Cox (who had been born at 12 Adrian Road and who later lived at 58 Adrian Road) recalled that Annie had made her bridesmaids' wedding dresses; and Ciss (Doris) Smith of Abbots Langley (who was 88 in 1999) recalled Annie's large chest of drawers, full of dressmaking materials and patterns which were often borrowed.

Annie was only about 5ft tall and she had red hair when young. Her daughter, Marion, recorded that Annie was: "*lively, talkative, honest, immensely interested in people and things, and fun*". Being a lady of strong nonconformist opinions, her political leanings were towards the Liberal Party. She was greatly admired for her keen mind, her ability to get on with life and not complain, and her great sense of humour which was quite risqué for a Victorian lady and chapelgoer. She frequently arrived late for Sunday services and entered with much huffing and puffing. She was not slow to tell the preacher out loud to, "Get on with it," if he was rambling or failing to get to the point of his sermon. Her daughter, Marion, recalled that on one occasion when sitting in a pew next to her, Annie gestured as if to pull a handle to open an imaginary trapdoor in the pulpit to make the preacher disappear. This caused Annie and Marion to burst into such giggles of laughter that they had to leave the service for a time.

Like most Abbots Langley folk in those days, Annie did most of her shopping in the village. But she also shopped at the NORTH WATFORD CO-OPERATIVE SOCIETY Store. The CO-OP reimbursed a dividend varying between 3 and 4 pence in the pound (when there were 240 pence to the pound) to their customers. She saved her CO-OP "divi" and it gradually built up over the years into a little nest-egg.

*

JOE KIMPTON, Annie's eldest son, was very headstrong. After leaving Watford Grammar School and starting work initially at JOHN DICKINSON & CO at Nash Mills, he decided to enlist in the army. Annie was very upset and he was under-age. Joe's reaction was to tell his mother that he intended enlisting regardless of his age, and that if she attempted to stop him then she wouldn't see him again. Matthew Timberlake recorded in his diary that Joe enlisted at Hertford on 15 September 1914, soon after the declaration of the First World War on 14 August 1914. This was 15 months before his 18th birthday (the official minimum age of enlistment) when Joe was still only 16 years old. Matthew also recorded that they received a letter from Joe posted in Exeter on 11 December 1914 saying that he was off to India.

It is almost certain that Joe was transferred to the newly formed 2nd/4th Battalion (Territorial Force) of the Devonshire Regiment. By this time the British Expeditionary Force of professional soldiers had suffered catastrophic losses at the first battle of Ypres. New recruits were being sent to India to release professional soldiers from there, for service on the Western Front. This Battalion joined the Devon and Cornwall Brigade of the 2nd Wessex Division and sailed from Southampton on 12 December 1914, bound for India where they arrived in January 1915. Joe probably served in a mounted transportation unit. Subsequently, the Division left Bombay for Suez in Egypt in 1917 where it was disbanded in August 1918 and where Joe was transferred to Mesopotamia. He did not return from overseas service until September 1919. Matthew Timberlake recorded in his diary on September 9th, 1919: "*Saw Joe first time 5 years / looking well / am hopeful*". But after all the excitement and comradeship of army life abroad, Joe must have found Abbots Langley very dull.

In February 1924, after he had saved sufficient money whilst working as a plumber, Joe got a passage on a cattle-boat to Canada. After less than a year there, he "jumped" the border into the United States of America and hitch-hiked to California. An entry in Matthew Timberlake's diary on 2 March 1925 says: "*Cabled money to Joe / California*". In San Francisco, Joe met Alta Farthing who came to stay at the same boarding house. They married and set up home in August 1932.

By May 1937, Annie's other two children were off her hands: Marion, her daughter, had trained as a teacher from 1921-1923 at the London County Council Furzedown Training College in Welham Road, London. She first taught for four months in Abbots Langley School and then taught from 1923-1932 at the LCC Girls' School, Shepperton Road, Islington, London. She had then married Bert (Bertram Arthur) Flint of Abbots Langley. Bert was a Sunday school teacher, a Trustee and a Society Steward at the Abbots Langley Methodist chapel. Marion was a Sunday school teacher too and the chapel organist at that time. They had two children: David (David Arthur) born in 1932 and Roger (Roger Bertram) born in 1934. Annie's younger son, Fred, had also just married Muriel Turner who lived in the village. They were married at the Church of St Lawrence in Abbots Langley.

Marion recorded that, after a seemingly "impossible invitation" from Joe and Alta and despite comments that she was "a silly old woman", Annie decided it was time to use her CO-OP nest-egg and visit her son and daughter-in-law in San Francisco. She also had friends and relatives in Canada and just across the border in New York State,

USA, some of whom she had not seen for 30 years. She would visit them first and then travel by train across North America to San Francisco to stay with Joe and Alta and return by sea via the Panama Canal. She would write frequent letters and notes to her family giving details of her travels and her impressions. Annie would use the contents of these when she returned as the basis for talks to the Women's Meeting at the Methodist church in Abbots Langley.

Annie embarked on her journey on Friday, 7 May 1937 from Manchester having travelled there by train the day before with her brother, Joseph Timberlake of Hastoe Farm, near Tring. She stayed with relatives and friends in Canada and with relatives just across the border in Rochester, USA, for four months from May to September 1937. She then spent nearly 12 months living with her son, Joe, and his wife, Alta, in San Francisco. In June 1938, she extended her United States visa and intended coming back to England in the spring of 1939 but, sadly, never returned. Annie had a heart attack whilst visiting the Point Reyes lighthouse near San Francisco on 28 August 1938 and died shortly afterwards.

⋆

IN ALL, Annie Kimpton wrote 67 letters starting with a postcard sent from on board the SS *Manchester Regiment* as the ship sailed along the Manchester Ship Canal. Her last letter was sent from San Francisco on 23 August 1938. At Annie's request, they were put together, numbered and kept by her daughter, Marion Flint. The letters are given here in chronological order and annotations are given to explain them or provide background information. Annie was 65 years old when she left for North America. It was a time when the links between England and the early emigrants were still strong.

Annie had been brought up as a child in Victorian England. The farthest she had probably travelled previously would have been to the South Coast of England and to Bradford on Avon, Wiltshire, where relatives lived - a maximum of 100 miles from home. To Annie, life revolved around her family, her friends and the chapel. Her interest in news of the village provides a glimpse of life in Abbots Langley at that time, when families in the village were still very interrelated.

It had been Marion Flint's wish to have the letters typed out because many of them were written in pencil on poor quality paper. This was done in the 1950's by Joan Kimpton née Sheppard, Fred Kimpton's second wife. I have now reproduced them using a word-processor whilst referring back to the original letters as a check. Fortunately, Marion had also kept some of the photographs that Annie either sent back or that were returned by Joe Kimpton after Annie's death. Some of these and others of her family or associated with them are shown in the illustrated plates. No attempt has been made to alter Annie's words, apart from inserting paragraphs and punctuation (understandably omitted from Annie's "scribbles"). Her occasional archaisms have been left unchanged. Nothing has been left out and all the rude stories have been left in. I apologise for the occasional use of terms which are derogatory.

Reference to the Family Trees in Appendix II : *The Family Relationships* may be helpful when names of friends or relatives are mentioned. These show the relationships of some of the people in Abbots Langley that Annie mentioned, or that she stayed with or visited during her time in North America. Information about Abbots Langley Methodist church social life in the 1930s is also given in Appendix III : *The Wesley Guild.*

Annie's idea that the letters might be used as the basis for talks to the Women's Meeting at the Abbots Langley Methodist church did materialise. Over the 30 years or more following Annie's death, Marion Flint gave talks on Annie's travels in North America by reading extracts from her letters. Marion spoke at these meetings of her farewell on Kings Langley and Abbots Langley station platform: Marion said that she liked to think that even had she known of the outcome, she would not have kept her mother from such a wonderful adventure. As recently as 1997, Flora Botwright, Mabel Botwright, Dolly Brownsell and Daisy Greeves (who were former members of the Women's Meeting) recalled memories of the "gems" they heard from her letters and recounted how much they looked forward to each episode.

*

I SPENT my working life at KODAK LIMITED, Harrow, England, and on a number of occasions visited the EASTMAN KODAK COMPANY at Rochester, New York State, USA. Over a number of years, I became very close friends with an American couple, Carl and Nan Oster, and frequently stayed (together with my wife Mary) at their home in the town of Greece, near Rochester, not far from Lake Ontario. Carl Oster was by profession a scientist and worked for the EASTMAN KODAK COMPANY. By chance, they lived just a stone's throw from the intersection of West Ridge Road with Long Pond Road, which runs down past Long Pond itself to Grand View Heights where Annie stayed in 1937 with her cousins, Ben and Alice Hawkins. Whilst in Rochester I made several visits to Letchworth Park (the "Grand Canyon of the East") which Annie found so impressive. More recently, in the summer of 1996 whilst visiting Nova Scotia, Canada, with my American friends, I looked out from Cape North, the northern-most tip of Cape Breton Island, across the Cabot Strait towards Newfoundland. With some feeling, I recalled that nearly 60 years earlier my grandmother, Annie Kimpton, had passed through this channel on her way to the St Lawrence River on board the SS *Manchester Regiment.*

I should like to express my thanks to my brother, David, for the typographical design and layout of this book. Thanks also to his daughter, Ria (who produced the document ready for printing by working at weekends through the courtesy of BANG, Graphic Designers, of Basingstoke) and to her colleague, Sheila Duggan. A thank you too to my wife, Mary, for her support, suggestions and words of encouragement over the several years it has taken to put it all together. It would have been a great pity if this little treasure of family and village history had been consigned to the waste-bin.

Roger B Flint

ANNIE'S LETTERS

ANNIE'S LETTERS were addressed to either Marion and Bert Flint at Conway, Marlin Square, Abbots Langley, or to Fred and Muriel Kimpton at 54 Adrian Road, Abbots Langley. Only one envelope was kept so the actual addressees can only be ascertained (sometimes) from the letters themselves. The letters were intended for both families to read.

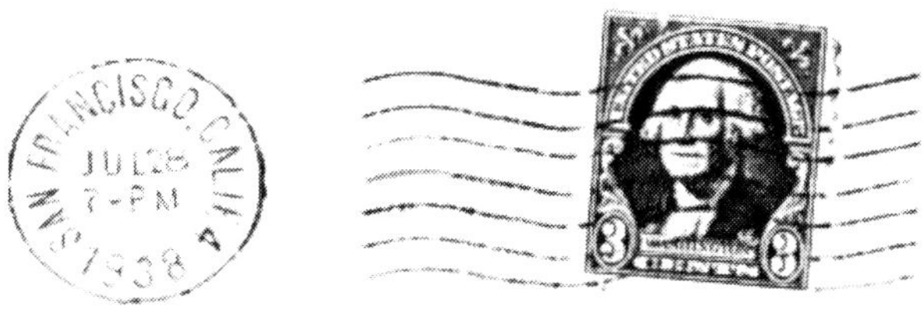

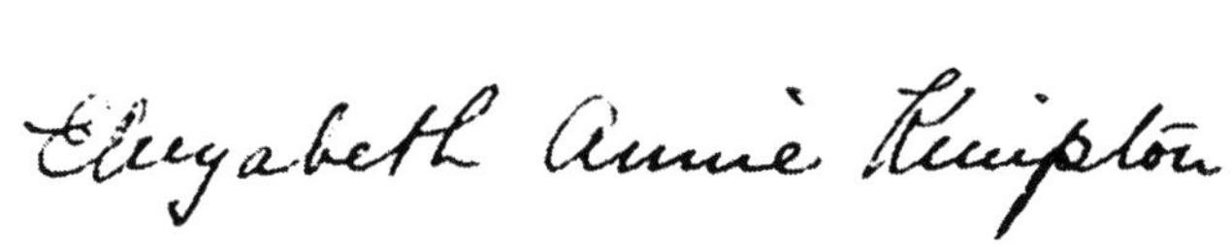

Annie Kimpton's signature on the Conveyance (to her) of 56 Adrian Road, Abbots Langley, from the Estate of Matthew Timberlake. The document was dated 6 January 1934 and witnessed by her brothers, Joseph Timberlake and Matthew Timberlake, Junior.

"Let Marion keep my scribbles till I return"

*

Crossing The Atlantic

Germany led the way with airship travel across the Atlantic Ocean between Berlin and South America in 1930. Airship travel from Europe to North America began in 1936 with the German airship "Hindenburg", the biggest flying machine ever built. A single fare was £80 and the flying time was 60 hours. On the first flight of the second year, 6 May 1937, whilst docking at Lakehurst Naval Station, New Jersey, USA, the hydrogen-filled "Hindenburg" burst into flames, killing 35 of the 97 people on board. All further airship flights ceased. Passenger travel by the flying-boat "Yankee Clipper" across the Atlantic began in 1939 but stopped within a few months following the outbreak of the Second World War. Passenger flights (this time by aeroplane) across the Atlantic did not begin again until 1946.

The tourist route to North America in the 1930's was by passenger ship, Cunard White Star Line, taking 5 days from Southampton to New York. These ships were great liners carrying many hundreds of passengers and Annie Kimpton probably preferred a smaller ship direct to Canada. So in 1937 she chose a Manchester Liners Ltd merchant ship, the SS "Manchester Regiment", sailing from Manchester for her journey across the North Atlantic to Montréal; the single fare was about £25 and the voyage took 10 days. Manchester was a straightforward journey by the London, Midland and Scottish Railway (LMSR) from Kings Langley and Abbots Langley station via Euston station, London.

The first communication received from Annie was a picture postcard of the SS "Manchester Regiment" (built in 1922) in which she was going to Canada. The postcard is shown in the illustrated plates; it was sent to the elder of her two grandsons, David Flint:

[LETTER 1 - *A postcard date-stamped Liverpool, 9 May 1937*]

Dear David,

This is a picture of Grandma's ship which she is now on going over the sea. My best love and a kiss to my dear little boys.

Grandma

* * * * *

[LETTER 2]

"Of course not . . . . . . we aren't moving yet"

SS *Manchester Regiment*, Manchester Liners Ltd
Friday, 7 May 1937

My Dears,

I am getting on quite well as yet, for we are not out of the Canal [*the Manchester Ship Canal*] and are now collecting coal at one of the locks. It is said we are to be coaling all night, so probably we shall be noisy. My cabin companion is Mrs Blakeman, a Canadian from Ottawa, who has been back and forth several times. There are twelve passengers, four of them ladies and two children. I don't know how I'll get on when we move as to eating and drinking but we seem to have done very little beside. We had dinner at 12 noon of soup and fish, which I did not have. I had lamb cutlet and mashed potatoes, apricots and cream. The steward comes round with a menu to see what we would like next. We had coffee and cheese. Then about an hour or so afterwards came, "Tea is served in the dining room," and we had tea and biscuits. I wondered in my own mind whether that was the high-tea promised but at 5 o'clock we had another dinner: soup, joints, fish, three or four vegetables, pudding, fruit, and coffee if we wished.

I am writing this in the nice little lounge. Some of them have gone off the boat to a village nearby. There is a bookcase full of books, the key kept by the steward. The cabin I share is No 1 and (I think) the largest. We have two portholes up high, a settee and basket-chair, and a writing cabinet with four drawers. There are large drawers under the settee and a wardrobe with more drawers. There is room under the berth for my and Mrs Blakeman's cases. She has plenty to tell me about Canada. There is only one other lady who has never been. She is a thin person uncommonly like Mrs Riddoch [*a Methodist chapelgoer*] but talks, talks, talks. She is also like Beattie Ellwood in many ways [*also a Methodist chapelgoer, and a very prim and proper spinster, who lived in Tibbs Hill Road, Trowley Bottom, Abbots Langley.*] We are unbending towards each other a little. Some of the 12 think they are tin gods - you can see.

Uncle Joe [*Joseph Timberlake, Annie's brother from Hastoe Farm, near Tring, Hertfordshire*] stayed a long time with me and treated me to everything: dinner, hotel, buses and trams. I would not live in Manchester for any money - it's so black and depressing. There was only one beautiful thing there - in the Market Square - a huge sunken garden with large, square flowerbeds of gorgeous shades of tulips, green grass and paths, and seats everywhere. Every flowerbed had an electric light and I should think that when floodlit it must be a wonderful sight [*Piccadilly Gardens*].

Tell David [*her 5 year-old grandson*] that when I got my seat in the train at Euston, a big black dog with a curly coat came and rubbed himself against everybody's knees. He had a brass box strapped upon his back and was collecting pennies for the Railway Hospital and sick people [*railwaymen*]. He got lots of pennies. There was one old chap in our carriage who had just caught the train, having come in from St Pancras [*station*] and landed that morning from Australia, going home to Manchester.

"It's a funny thing. Wherever I go about the world, in any town, I find somebody who knows me," he said.

"Well," I said, "that's not to be wondered at for I shall know you again, wherever I meet you."

He took it as a great compliment and laughed a lot. He talked, laughed and told us all his business and kept the carriage alive.

We have been discussing the Duke of Windsor and Mrs Simpson, and all agree that the Duke is a wash-out and Mrs Simpson a bad one. Every now and again a huge rumbling is heard and a quantity of coal tumbles down a chute into the hold. One gentleman has been pulling the boy's leg about not being seasick yet. "Of course not," says the boy, "we aren't moving yet." I don't know if I'll sleep if this huge noise keeps on all the time and some say they keep on all night long till late tomorrow. How is my poor old Topsy? [*Annie's cat*]. It seems a long time since I left home. Take care of yourselves, my dear ones, so that you are all the same when I get back. The berths look very small, Marion [*Marion Flint, Annie's daughter*], I hardly know how I'll get in. It looks such a cubby-house [*a child's play-den*] that I feel the top will seem to be pressing down on me. Will close with my love to you all. I had your telegram, Fred and Muriel [*Annie's younger son and his wife*] and one from all at "Langley". It was dear of you to think of it. I think Uncle Joe wants me to see the Timberlakes, so I shall see when I go to Jennie's. [*Jennie Stanton's in Ottawa - not too far from Montréal and the children of Annie's uncle, the Rev William Timberlake.*] P'rhaps I will, p'rhaps I won't.

Goodnight,

Your loving Mother

* * * * *

[LETTER 3 - *Annie wrote and dated separate installments of this letter, which could not be posted until she reached Québec. She also adopted this practice in many of her later letters.*]

"I shall get fearfully fat!"

SS *Manchester Regiment,* MANCHESTER LINERS LTD
Monday afternoon, 10 May 1937

MY DEAR MARION AND ALL,

We are having lovely weather and have been sitting out in the sun on deck-chairs with rugs. They charge 2/6d each for these [*two shillings and six pence, or half a crown, in pre-decimal coinage*]. The wind is now blowing a bit chilly and I have come into my cabin. My room mate, Mrs Blakeman (a Canadian), is a very up-to-date woman. There are also Mr and Mrs Coleman, Mr Hamilton, Mrs Johnson and two children, Mr Gill, Miss Wood, Mrs Chatengye, and a stout man whose name I've not heard.

My cabin is nice. We are in the front of the boat in No 1 State Cabin. It has a closed-in wash-basin with glass above and cupboards below, a nice cushioned settee, and book shelves above a dressing-chest and below the two portholes. Then come the berths and (behind the door) a wardrobe with a long mirror in mahogany with chrome fittings, a basket-chair, and a waste-paper basket all in cream. There is a pull-out writing table in the dressing-chest, an extra blanket for each berth, coat-hangers in the wardrobes, and a bedside lamp.

We have three tables in the dining saloon and I am at the table which the Chief Officer heads. One of the others is headed by the Captain. The Chief Engineer sits by me. We are fed well. A cup of tea at half past seven and breakfast at half past eight: grapefruit, porridge, etc, followed by bacon and eggs, fish, toast and heaps of things. Lunch at half past twelve: soup, fish, various meats, three vegetables, salad, coffee, biscuits and cheese; and with all the accessories on the table and beautifully set out. Then at 6pm another spread: soup, fish, joints, etc - almost a replica of the midday meal but all different dishes. Then at 9pm: tea, coffee, Bovril or beer, etc, sandwiches and toast and biscuits. It's early days yet but I've not missed a meal and (though it's hard to keep my balance) I feel all right. I slept like a top last night for the sea just rocked me to sleep. I and Miss Wood and Mr Gill are the only English people on the boat and I am

[LETTER 3 CONTINUED]
the only one taking a first ocean trip, for Miss Wood has been to Algiers where she has a missionary sister. We listened to the Archbishop on the wireless on Sunday - it seemed a queer day. [*Edward VIII had abdicated on 10 December 1936 to marry the twice-divorced Wallis Warfield Simpson, an American; George VI was proclaimed King two days later. On Sunday 9 May the Archbishop of Canterbury, Dr Cosmo Gordon Lang, broadcast his message to the world on the spiritual meaning of the Coronation which was to take place on 12 May 1937; this was the date originally planned for the Coronation of Edward VIII. The title Duke of Windsor had been conferred on Edward by the new King. The Duke of Windsor subsequently married Mrs Simpson on 6 June 1937.*]

There seems to be nothing to do but eat and drink for there are no gay [*lively*] young sparks among us. The stewards and crew are very obliging and the captain makes a pet of the little girl.

* * *

Tuesday, 11 May 1937

THE morning is wet so most of our time is spent in the cosy little lounge reading and talking. We had a typed, double-sheet of paper on the breakfast table sent from Rugby and headed THE MARCONI CABLE CO, etc, etc, with the news of the Coronation. I had a good breakfast and (so far) still feel all right. They tell me I may be all right. It is now 11am by ship's time and 2pm in England. They put back the clock each day so that people are continually altering their watches. We have two stewards who wait at table and they are very efficient and obliging. The Captain is a stout, white-haired man with immense, bushy-white eyebrows. He comes and tucks our feet in our rugs in our chairs, evidently looking upon the passengers as his charges but I wouldn't like to be in his black books. He has just come up to me and said:

"Writing up your diary?"

"Yes," said I, "I'm saying that it's raining" (etc, etc). How glad I am that there are plenty of books.

* * *

Tuesday afternoon, 11 May 1937

HAVE just listened to the wireless news from England - that today has been very wet there. We have laughed about the two ladies who have already installed themselves to see the Coronation, since it is 3.25pm ship's time and 6pm in England. I did not go out, the wind is so rough. I had soup, cod-fillet, potatoes, pudding, biscuits and cheese and coffee for my lunch - and I am still feeling full. Mr Hamilton tells me that I've probably got past being ill unless very bad weather ensues. In a few minutes we shall go to afternoon tea with cakes handed round and, at 6 o'clock, to dinner. I shall get fearfully fat! We have travelled over 300 miles [*a gross underestimate*] and by the route map in the dining room look to be in the middle of the Atlantic.

* * *

Wednesday, 12 May 1937

WE are nearing Newfoundland and it is very cold. Everybody says we have had an exceptionally calm crossing. Mrs Blakeman and I walked round and round the lower deck, keeping as far as we could from the wind this morning. Then after lunch, which consisted for me of soup, fish, fruit, biscuits and cheese and coffee, I sat with others in a screened corner of the upper deck and read, wrapped up in my blanket. We have beautiful extending chairs - white wood and cane. Then it grew cold and we had afternoon tea, toast and scones. Then I sat in the lounge until dinner: soup, fish, chicken with potatoes, peas and cauliflower, apple pie and cream, and coffee and (again) reading in the lounge.

The Captain told Mrs Chantengye this story tonight:

A very stout old lady died and was cremated. The next day her relatives called for the ashes and were told:

"There are no ashes but there is about 6lb of dripping".

We have not been able to have our portholes open at night for the wind. Mrs Blakeman is a fresh-air fiend so she sleeps with the door wide open and the curtains across. I go to bed first and do not hear her come for I sleep like a log all night until the steward brings tea. Mrs Coleman and Mrs Blakeman, the two Canadian ladies, are quite genial but wish us to understand what wealthy families they come from and their very influential positions in their towns. They dress well and (according to their talk) do no work nor ever have done. They play golf, swim and drive, etc, etc, etc, and of course I am greatly impressed. They know how to order the stewards!!! Mrs Johnson and Mrs Chantengye are English-born and are much simpler.

They have to leave tons of cargo at Québec and if the weather continues favourable we will reach there at 8 o'clock next Monday morning and will not move off until 6 o'clock at night. We may thus be able to go ashore for the day and sightsee. I hope so. We shall not reach Montréal until next Wednesday.

* * *

Friday, 14 May 1937

LAST night the sirens were going after all were in bed. Then the boat seemed to stop altogether for a long time. Then the sirens were on again in the early morning. We heard that ice and fog were met in the night and the ship slowed down to about three and a half miles per hour. The Captain has not been in evidence today. I guess he's sleeping.

We have passed a steamer quite closely, the *Regatta* - an Irish boat. Now we are going much quicker. I've been pacing the upper and lower decks with Mrs Blakeman in the sun today. But it's cold so I'm now inside again, writing this. The First Officer says the temperature is 33F, nearly freezing-point. No waves, only swell that looks like burnished pewter. We have seen several icebergs today in the distance. One of them went close by - a huge heap of snowy-white ice. Then we thought we saw the light from Cape Race and we are to look out for Bird Rocks - a sanctuary where birds go to breed. We have another 600 miles to go before we reach Father Point so

[LETTER 3 CONTINUED]

they tell me. [*The ship was passing south of Newfoundland, through the Cabot Strait towards the Gulf of St Lawrence. Father Point is now known as Pointe-au-Père and is on the St Lawrence River estuary, about 185 miles before reaching Québec.*]

I think this is a very old story, but it was told today:

A bishop on board a ship which encountered very bad weather continually asked if there was any danger. At length, one officer took him to the stokers' quarters and told him to listen.

"They are swearing most horribly," said he.

"That's all right," said the officer, "when there is danger they pray."

Later, the officer was amused to see the bishop steal away to the engine room and listen intently.

"Thank God they are still swearing," said the bishop.

For dinner tonight I had soup, halibut with anchovy sauce, roast pork with apple sauce, baked potatoes, carrots, spinach (which I don't like), chocolate pudding with a sweet sauce, and coffee - and I ate it all. There was stewed lamb, etc, but I liked the pork. I've had a warm sea-water bath and am just writing this before getting into bed feeling beautifully warm. Last night was bitterly cold and I wish I'd asked the steward to fill my hot-water bottle. My cabin companion [*Mrs Blakeman*] is going to play cards for a time. She has just been for her cigarettes.

* * *

Saturday, 15 May 1937

I SLEPT like a log all night and this morning walked the lower deck with Mrs Blakeman after breakfast. Saw land upon the horizon, St Pierre so I was told [*the French islands of Saint-Pierre et Miquelon*]. This afternoon we saw a little fishing boat just like those at Lowestoft and tonight Mr Keating says he has seen the lights of a lighthouse. We shall reach Father Point on Sunday night. The Chief Engineer who sits beside me at meals told me there were two large icebergs before us during the night and they had to divert the course of the boat.

We had the wireless news from Sydney [*in Nova Scotia, Canada*] and from Newfoundland that the bus strike was still on and that Lord Snowdon was dead [*formerly Philip Snowdon, Chancellor of the Exchequer in the first Labour Governments of 1924 and 1929-1931*] and that there had been several deaths at the Coronation. I hope Muriel got home safely. [*Muriel Kimpton, Annie's daughter-in-law, had been to see the Coronation procession in London.*] I've had soup, creamed cod, roast lamb with greens, carrots, potatoes and as I did not like the look of the coconut-sprinkled tart, I had biscuits and an apple and coffee. For supper I've had a cup of tea and sandwiches and am now going to bed at 10.30pm.

* * *

Sunday, 16 May 1937

THIS morning we saw land, Gaspé Point [*Québec Province, Canada*], miles and miles of rocky hills tipped with snow and snow in all the hollows. Then the slopes looked greener and trees could be seen. Mrs Blakeman tells me they are all wooded hills and that, very soon, small French villages will be seen, each with a big Roman Catholic church and a priest's house. The Captain declares that many families have 18 to 20 children! The sea is now a peculiar deep green like the olivine stones in artistic jewellery.

Mr Keating (the stout man) has found his tongue. He comes from Newfoundland and has really travelled everywhere and can speak personally of everything. We were discussing drinks and he said vodka is completely colourless, like water. He has been right across Russia and Siberia.

Have again been walking the deck this morning and looking at the shores of Canada which are now plainly visible. [*The ship was now entering the mouth of the St Lawrence River.*] We passed miles and miles of villages which looked like wooden hen-houses and in the distance and behind them great dark hills all powdered with snow like castor sugar. The sun is out but the wind is very cold. We reach Father Point tonight and Québec tomorrow morning - where I hope to post this and get my money changed.

My dearest love to you all,
Your loving Mum

* * * * *

FUNNEL: RED, WITH BLACK TOP AND ONE BLACK BAND

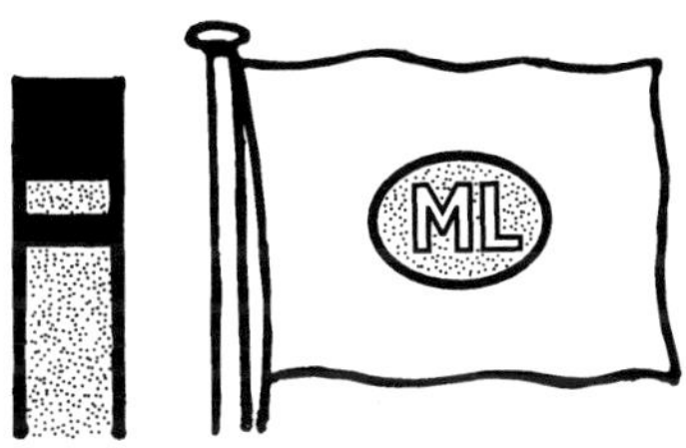

HOUSE FLAG: WHITE, WITH "ML" ON A RED OVAL

MANCHESTER LINERS LTD

The Manchester Ship Canal was opened by Queen Victoria in 1887 and it ran 35 miles to the River Mersey estuary, turning Manchester into a major sea-port. MANCHESTER LINERS LTD was established in 1898 as part of the FURNESS GROUP to operate between Manchester and North America - particularly Canada. All the Company's ships' names were prefixed "Manchester" and all these ships had funnels and masts which could be lowered to pass under the bridges on the Manchester Ship Canal.

THE ST LAWRENCE RIVER, CANADA

THE ST LAWRENCE RIVER in eastern Canada is the principal river of North America. It is the chief outlet of the Great Lakes and flows from Lake Ontario to the Gulf of St Lawrence at the Gaspé Peninsula and then to the Atlantic Ocean. It is some 744 miles long, increases gradually in width to 90 miles, is tidal below Québec and forms part of the border between Canada and the United States of America. The principal cities on its banks are Québec and Montréal. In 1937 it was navigable for ocean-going vessels to Québec and Montréal but no further. Annie had to complete her journey to St Catharines on the shores of Lake Ontario by train from Montréal.

When Europeans first reached North America, every part of it was occupied by long-established native peoples. Jacques Cartier first landed at the sites of Québec and Montréal in 1565, but they were not visited again until the arrival of Samuel de Champlain in 1608 who established fur-trading settlements. By the eighteenth century, "New France" extended from Newfoundland west to the Rocky Mountains and south to New Orleans, excluding the Atlantic seaboard. "New France" in Canada and east of the Mississippi River, was ceded to Britain in 1763 after the Seven Years' War. By the Québec Act 1774, Britain approved the French-Canadians' rights to their own language, to the Roman Catholic Church and to French civil law.

Québec lies at the confluence of the St Lawrence and St Charles Rivers, and the Old City is the only walled city in North America. Annie had time to go sightseeing there when the SS "Manchester Regiment" docked to unload some cargo. Montréal is built upon the slopes of Mont-Royal on an island in the St Lawrence River. Annie Kimpton simply disembarked at Montréal and made her way by bus to the Grand Parcs railway station. She caught the overnight train to Toronto where she changed for St Catherines:

[LETTER 4]

"Hello London, London calling"

SS *Manchester Regiment*, MANCHESTER LINERS LTD
Sunday evening, 16 May 1937

MY DEARS,

Have passed Father Point with its lighthouse and the tugboat *Rapello* has come alongside and the pilot has come aboard from it. He was dressed up with a bowler hat and gloves. The Captain said, "You should see him in his fur coat!" He is a French-Canadian. I hear they come to examine our passports tomorrow morning. It is in connection with that long paper I had to fill up. And the Customs officials examine luggage on board on Tuesday - which will be a good job. I've never seen a lovelier sunset: gold and pink and all the hills dark purple-mauve and the water deep green. The stars and moon look brighter than at home. They explain that it's because of the clear atmosphere.

* * *

Monday evening, 17 May 1937

THIS morning the officials came to examine our passports. We had to go one by one into the dining room to be questioned and to receive a yellow landing-ticket. Mr Gill (an old man from St Anne's near Blackpool) who was first said, "Now then, coom on. In thou goest. A've confessed." Then we dressed and went off to see the sights of Québec. Mr and Mrs Coleman were the guides to Miss Wood and I.

It's a strange city: French names and speaking everywhere though they speak to you in English. The lower part of the city is purely French and is built all higgledy-piggledy - stone buildings stories high or wooden houses like chalets. We saw the Château with its innumerable little gabled windows all with pointed cupolas [*the Hôtel Château Frontenac, built by the CANADIAN PACIFIC RAILWAY in the French baronial style in the late nineteenth century*] and went over the Ursuline Convent Chapel [*built in 1717*] and the Roman Catholic cathedral. Then into a company's offices, who allowed us to go up 14 stories in the lift and to go out of a little kind of window with steps, up and out onto a balcony from which we had a wonderful view of the city. I forgot to say that we went by one of those railways (like there are at Folkestone) to the Upper Town [*the funicular to the Old City - Vieux Québec*].

I went to the bank and changed my money; to the post office and posted my letter; and to the telegraph office to send my cable home. Also went to another place for postcards, round an antique shop, and got on a tram with cane seats where (by a queer arrangement) the driver gets you your ticket automatically and the driver gongs all along. The trams make the most hideous row. All drive on the wrong side and every one looks huge to me. We rode by this tram till we came to a railroad track. Then the tram kept on along it past queer foreign-looking houses to a very beautiful house in which the Duke of Kent, Queen Victoria's father, once lived. It is now used as a summer resort for moneyed people. We went down a winding wooden stairway to the Montmorency Falls which are much higher than Niagara Falls but, of course, not so vast and wide [*274ft high compared to 160ft*]. They are very lovely and go into the St Lawrence River. I've never before seen such a vast mass of water.

I must tell you about the lunch we had in a restaurant in Québec. They served soup in small basins and each had a queer plate with one big and two small compartments for meat and vegetables, and little round dishes with butter, and plenty of ice-cold water. My companions had cake with maple syrup, but I thought it too mawkish. I don't know if I'll ever get used to this money. It takes me an awful time to calculate my change when they say $1.30 and I only have a $5 bill.

One of the men passengers, old Mr Gill, was brought by two policemen just in time for getting on board again at 6pm. He had been imbibing too freely. He said, before starting, that Canadian beer was only mouthwash and I think his companions proved him wrong. The Captain said, "Shove him forrard," [*forward, the foremost-part of a ship, pronounced "forrard"*] and himself put him to bed, found his passport and rail tickets but did not know where to look for his wallet. We all hope he has not lost it. The view of Québec from the boat when we steamed out of the dock with the Citadel [*the old fort*] and Château was wonderful. We passed under the Québec suspension bridge on the way to Montréal. I have nearly packed my bag.

[LETTER 4 CONTINUED]

I must tell you that the passport official wanted to know if I had any money and how much, nosey lot - though he was much nicer than the American Consul.

* * *

Tuesday, 18 May 1937

I AM writing this in the Grand Parcs railway station in Montréal. The time is now 3pm and I have to wait until quarter to eleven. The Customs officials came on board and did not bother to examine my luggage. A short little maiden lady, Mrs Huff, met me on the boat and we came up into the town by bus about half past eleven this morning. She helped me check my luggage, etc, then took me and Mrs Chantengye (who is going to Ottawa) to a place where you mount a stool (where my legs dangled) and we had chicken and barley soup, jellied meat, potato salad and a cup of tea. I paid for her lunch and she made an awful fuss about my courtesy. Then she left us and now Mrs Chantengye has gone on her train and I am in an immense waiting room for ladies, all alone. There will be another lady on duty in the evening who will meet me at 9 o'clock. I travel all night to Toronto, then change for St Catharines - getting there at half past nine tomorrow morning. Euston Station is a mere fleabite to this great place. The porters are called Redcaps and they are all black men. The lavatories are queer, for you can see people's feet as they are in the enclosures. This place is so big and empty that when I cough it echoes like a gun.

I've had a bit of bother with one of my eyes that had something blown in it two days ago. I think I scratched the eye for ever since it has been inflamed and this morning it felt like a knife. The Captain said there was nothing in it but thought it was inflamed from the scratch. I think it feels a bit better so am hoping for the best.

The old man Gill was all right this morning but had lost his wallet and about £10 in money. "Ne'er mind the money so long as I have my watch. The money's nowt," says he. His son met him with a great car so he will now be looked after.

* * *

Wednesday morning, 19 May 1937

HERE I am in a huge train. I got very tired of waiting at Montréal from 3pm until nearly 11pm. Another Travellers' Aid (TA) lady came and saw me on to the train. I got on at 10 o'clock as it was more comfortable to sit in it. A young girl (a Pole) got on with me. She spoke to the lady, evidently knowing all about them and the TA lady said, "Here you are, this is Nellie Taroski who is going to Toronto". The child told me she had travelled alone all day from Shawinigan Falls [*near Québec*] and was leaving her aunt, who was very rich and had three farms - but who worked so hard herself and wanted her also to work very hard. She had been there three months and did not like it, so was going home again. I had not taken a sleeping-car as we thought of travelling by day but the boat was delayed by being unable to enter the dock as they were dredging or something. I had a pillow from the attendant and have slept, though I feel dirty. The train rumbles and roars and seems to be continually hooting like a fog siren. It is early daylight and we have stopped at a station, Trenton, and taken on a few passengers from a wooden platform beside a road. We are passing isolated houses and wooden huts, now and then farmlands and cows. Everything a lovely, tender green and trees coming into bloom and miles and miles of spruce-trees. Here we stop again at Cobourg to take on two men. It is about half past five by rail-time, an hour earlier than town-time. [*The railway passed through Standard time zones which occur at 15° meridian intervals from Greenwich (corresponding to one hour differences) and probably chose to keep its own time.*] The telegraph wires follow the railway and every now and then follow a road. I could see the lights on every pole twinkling away for miles and they are on all night. This town or village looks much prettier - not like large hen-houses. The grass does not look like ours, it's so fine and mossy. We have come by the side of an enormous lake. It looks like the sea, for you cannot see the other side [*Lake Ontario*]. Past a station, Great Hope Point, then a few more tiny ones where two or three smart, grey-hatted men get on. The conductor calls, "Dart Station," and everybody puts on their hats - so I do also. Then he comes calling, "Change for Hamilton and Baltimore," and says, "This is Toronto". A lady directs me where to go. The courtesy and particular verbal directions here are wonderful.

* * *

[*A little later on Wednesday morning, 19 May 1937*]

NOW I have found my connection. One part of my ticket was CPR [*CANADIAN PACIFIC RAILWAYS to Toronto*] and the other CNR [*CANADIAN NORTHERN RAILWAY from Toronto to St Catharines*]. I am now sitting in a long car (three times as long as an English one) with beautifully sprung seats of grey velvet which reverse if necessary and with radiators that go along the floor at the sides. I've said goodbye to Nellie Taroski and shall soon see Lizzie.

The conductor on the last train said, "Are you a stranger, lady?"

"Yes," I said.

"From the Old Country?"

"Yes."

"Did you see the Coronation?"

"No, I was on the boat."

"Oh, too bad. Do you live near London?"

"Yes."

When I got off the CPR the conductor said, "Where are you going lady? How do you like Canada?"

"I don't know yet," I said, "but I don't like your trains."

"Why not?" said he.

"Too much hooting and bell ringing to say nothing of the jolts when you start off."

He thought it very laughable. Everybody thinks I'm a Londoner. One or two of the boat officers when they met me said, "Hello London, London calling," [*a radio call sign*] thinking to chaff me. I saw a man on duty in Montréal with high, white

[LETTER 4 CONTINUED]
rubber boots, long white coat and flat white cap. Tell David [*Annie's grandson*] that I saw lots of black men with red round hats on. One carried my bag at Montréal Station. They have queer, soft voices and bow and act as if they are royalty in disguise. [*Annie had probably never met black people before.*]

* * *

Thursday, 20 May 1937 [*The day after reaching St Catharines*]

I FORGOT to mention the tall coloured man who passed up and down the CNR train in a long white coat and apron, black trousers and little black bow tie, with snowy white hair and spectacles. He looked like a parson calling, "Sandwiches, carfee and ices". After I had been on the CNR for an hour or so I began to listen intently for the queer calls of the conductor and (when he observed me) he said, "Caa'm yerself lady, another hour yet". So I caa'med myself until he said, "St Catharines next stop," and began to take special notice.

We passed a station called Vineland and you never saw such miles and miles of pink blossom. I thought it was almond blossom but I find they are peach-trees. Then thousands of apple, plum and cherry-trees. But everything here is in squares and lines. Each orchard seems to have ditches of water inbetween. We went by the shores of a great lake [*Lake Ontario still*] and then I saw a town appearing and a wooden platform (all are made of wood), then several people and then Lizzie, Rose and Betty peering at the train. [*The sisters, Lizzie Southam and Rose Cherry, were first cousins of Annie. Betty Outram was Rose's daughter.*] I tapped the window and they came running alongside. We got my case, left my trunk to follow, took a tram or streetcar and came home.

Lizzie's house is a pretty bungalow with a veranda in front and greensward right to the road. The front door is a double-door and each door and window is fitted with another filled with fine-mesh wire to keep out the flies and to keep cool. The lounge has a large partition down the middle which can be curtained off - but Lizzie makes it one big room. Two bedrooms go off from this and the kitchen is behind, and a larder and bathroom and lavatory go off from that. There is a washhouse with gas stove and washing machine at the back and then a garden with fowl-houses. All rooms are green and primrose with brown doors. I've a nice little room and a comfortable bed as you can guess when I tell you that I went to bed at 10.30pm and did not wake until 2.30pm the next day. I was dead-beat. I'd had a hot bath, a good meal, met Ted Southam [*Lizzie's husband, Edwin Southam*], young Ben Southam's girl, Marguerite [*Lizzie's son's girlfriend at the time*], Fred Cherry [*Rose's husband*], May [*May Love, another sister of Lizzie and Rose*] and one little girl, Elizabeth [*May's third daughter, Elizabeth Love*], and in the evening Jeanne, May's second daughter [*Jeanne Miles by May's first husband, William Miles*]. She is really beautiful and what with laughter and talk and all the journeying, I was about done-in when I got to bed.

Lizzie has altered the least of all here. I think the others look much older and they think I'm much the same only, of course, older. Ben and his wife are coming here Sunday [*Lizzie's brother, Ben Hawkins, and his wife, Alice, from Rochester, USA*]. Jim is coming for the weekend [*another of Lizzie's brothers - Jim Hawkins from Toronto, who was a bachelor*] and young Ben, Lizzie's son, also coming. All to meet me. The three sisters will be put to it to house and sleep all the guests.

An insurance agent called on Lizzie today:

"This is my cousin just from England," said she.

"Glad to meet you. I hope you will like St Catharines. You must get around and see the sights. Perhaps you and Mrs Southam will take a ride with me one day soon and see them?"

"Sure," said Lizzie.

"Let me know when," said he, "I'll be happy to do so" (!)

Esther [*Miles*], May's eldest girl, has been in to see me. She is not so lovely looking as Jeanne but is bonny-looking. Many think her nicer looking than Jeanne, Lizzie says, because of her beautiful disposition. Of course, I can only go by features. There was a letter from the bank telling me of the arrival of my money at the Canadian Bank, so that is all right. I must now call at the post office to see about my pension.

Your loving Mum

* * * * *

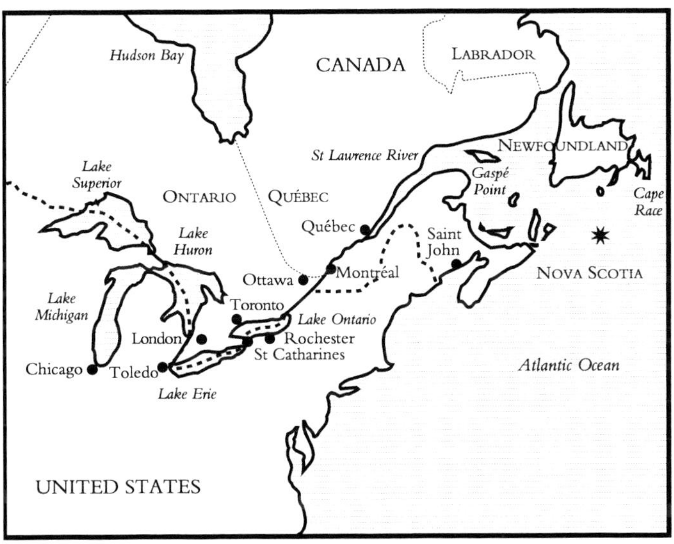

The parts of Canada and the USA visited by Annie Kimpton on her way to San Francisco in 1937.

✱ *Here two years later on 4 December 1939, the SS "Manchester Regiment" bound for Saint John, New Brunswick, with general cargo was in collision with the SS "Oropesa" of the PACIFIC STEAM NAVIGATION CO and was abandoned at 40°50′N, 55°30′W.*

AT 13 IDA STREET, ST CATHARINES, ONTARIO

ANNIE KIMPTON'S COUSINS, the Hawkins, originated from Redbourn in Hertfordshire (see Appendix IV: Annie's Abbots Langley). Benjamin Hawkins (Senior) was a soldier from the age of 14 until he was 30, and served in Ireland and Canada against the Fenian Irish revolutionaries. He left the army in 1875 to marry Esther Gates (the sister of Annie's mother). At the time of the 1891 census they lived in Breakspear Road, Abbots Langley, and Ben worked in Leavesden Asylum. His sons, Jim (James) and Ben (Benjamin), emigrated to Canada in 1904 followed by Lawrie (John Lawrence). Benjamin (Senior) and his wife, Esther, and their daughter, May, joined them in Canada in 1908 at a house bought by his son, Jim, at 9 Ida Street, St Catharines. His other daughters, Lizzie (Elizabeth) and Rose (Rosalind) followed in 1910.

Annie was staying with Lizzie Southam, daughter of Benjamin Hawkins (Senior). Lizzie was married to Ted (Edwin) Southam and they had a son, "Young" Ben. Lizzie's sisters, Rose and May, also lived in St Catharines. Rose was married to Fred Cherry and they had two sons, Fred (Frederick) Junior and Jimmy (James), and a daughter, Betty (Elizabeth) divorced and newly married to Larry (Lawrence) Outram. May was married to Frank (Francis) Love and they had four daughters, Esther and Jeanne Miles from May's first husband, William Miles, and Elizabeth and Pat (Patricia) Love from her second marriage to Frank Love. May Love later married Ted Southam after Frank Love and Lizzie Southam had died.

St Catharines lies on the southern shore of Lake Ontario, at the entrance to the New Welland Ship Canal. The Welland Canal opened in 1887 and was a link for vessels between Lake Erie to the south and Lake Ontario to the north, bypassing the Niagara Falls. In 1932, the much enlarged New Welland Ship Canal was completed to accommodate the Great Lakes grain carriers. St Catharines had grown to become the centre of the Niagara fruit belt.

[LETTER 5]

"Come Day, Go Day, God Send Sunday, sort"

13 Ida Street, St Catharines, Ontario, Canada
Friday, 21 May 1937

MY DEAREST MARION, BERT, FRED AND MURIEL,

Your letter arrived this morning while I had gone round to May's house. Her window looks onto a large green playground in front of a great school. I watched the children rehearse the Maypole, saw them line up to listen to a man speaking and then sing *God Save the King* in readiness for Monday (Empire Day). They sang a third verse to the national anthem. I must get it.

It seems so long since I had news of home and you all, almost as if I'd been away a year. The Rev Jones [*the Rev Albert Jones, Methodist Minister at Abbots Langley*] might have known when I'd go but he's what Mother used to call a, "Come Day, Go Day, God Send Sunday, sort". [*This was the title of an old street ballad. Annie's mother probably meant that he was rather unworldly.*] I may go to see his sister. They tell me I'm to stay the summer but my card is marked three months (although that is taken no notice of) and I expect it will be quite long enough. Lizzie says, "You see, Nance, maybe I'll never see you again. So do stay". [*Nance is a diminutive of Nancy, a variant of Ann. Annie was originally a diminutive of Ann but became a popular girls' name in England in the late nineteenth century.*] They are all very smart and young-looking around here, hair permed and colour on their cheeks and lips. I don't care for the children. Their manners are so abrupt. They never say "please" or "thank you". They are very dominant and overbearing. Lizzie tells me that Ben [*Benjamin Hawkins, Junior, the brother of Lizzie, Rose, May and Jim*] will wish me to go to Rochester, USA, and see him. He is coming here to meet me on Sunday.

Am glad that Fred and Muriel are settling in. I knew there would be a whole heap of things to bring down at the last. [*The recently married Fred Kimpton, Annie's son, and his wife, Muriel, had moved into Annie's home at 54 Adrian Road, Abbots Langley, whilst she was away.*] We heard that a stand had collapsed at Charing Cross [*at the Coronation procession*]. I hope all went well with Muriel's trip. Lizzie says all the churches and chapels here were decorated for Coronation Day.

I heard on the boat that there were earthquakes in San Francisco but nothing serious and that the new bridge had to be tested nut by nut for fear of damage. [*The Golden Gate Bridge was opened on 27 May 1937.*] I am writing to Joe today to tell him of my arrival and welfare. It seems to me that my trip divides itself up: first my boat journey . . . then my train journey . . . now at St Catharines . . . then to Detroit . . . then to California . . . and then on home. [*Annie changed her plans later and started her transcontinental train journey from Rochester, USA, instead of Detroit, USA.*] I want to go and see Joe but, as Lizzie says, it is not as if the warm weather will be gone in California. So I don't know what I'll do. Kiss my darling little boys from Grandma. Will be sending on another batch of scribble ere long.

My dearest love to you all,

Your loving Mum

* * * * *

[LETTER 6]

"The number of electric lights here astonish me"

13 Ida Street, St Catharines, Ontario, Canada
Saturday morning, 22 May 1937

MY DEARS,

I have just been into town with Lizzie to do her shopping. Ted started with us for I understand he receives a pay cheque on Friday and has to cash it at the bank. He works Saturday nights so is home on Saturdays. I saw many interesting things. The shops amaze me with the diversity of goods. The open-air flower market is wonderful - many strange flowers but also all the English ones. We went into WOOLWORTHS for some pins and sat on a tall stool and drank ginger ale (with ice floating on it) through a straw. It is what we call a Flag Day for the Salvation Army and its officers are at

[LETTER 6 CONTINUED]
every street corner and they say, "Can I tag you?" and for a small coin, or whatever you care to give, they pin a little red paper shield on your coat. I saw in a shop window, "PLAIN LADIES COATS CLEANED TWO FOR 85 CENTS". I thought it funny.

It seems very warm here to me, though they tell me it is not. "Wait until later," they tell me. Many of the houses here have coloured tiling made of non-inflammable roofing, a kind of rubber or asbestos in tile shape. I passed some on the street in a big bale, green and blue-shaded. They look very effective. Lizzie has a nice strip of grass lawn by the side of the house. It goes right out to the pavement with no fences, as do all the premises here. The street is quieter than Adrian Road and all the side streets have trees each side of the road. Up the street this afternoon is an auction sale of an old man's household effects. They put out a red flag on the sidewalk to tell folk about it. The buses pass the top of the street and you immediately turn into the busy shopping centre. On one of the verandas I saw a queer arrangement on wheels looking like a large oblong meat-safe. It is to hold a sleeping baby in the open air and a cover is placed on top so that no flies (or "bugs" as they call them) can get to the child. It looks just like a meat-safe on wheels. The baby carriages here are made of wicker - all colours, like Lloyd Loom chairs [*made of painted imitation cane*]. They do look nice.

People here say "Sure," and "Er'er," or "Ummm," a kind of grunt - like an [*American*] Indian. They tell me I'm sure to do the same. Lizzie and Ted both said my voice is just like Rose Cherry's. Could not tell who was speaking until they came in the room and looked. We went to see a friend of Lizzie's, a Mrs Aitkin, and sat out in her sun-porch in rocking-chairs. "How much your cousin's voice is like Mrs Cherry's," said she. So I suppose it is not Lizzie's fancy. Lizzie opened a jar of sweet pickles. I was dubious about them but they are good: onions, cucumber and cauliflower in small chunks - no mustard and not sweet or vinegary (it looks like white vinegar). We have breakfast and, when Ted is away, a light lunch meal and what they call "supper" about half past six and no more till the next morning. It is different to the five repasts per day on board ship but I like it just as well and with the heat (which I already feel) I'll get lighter in weight. I put on 3lb on the boat. They are busy tonight putting in the screen doors - that is taking out the centre of the door fitted with glass and putting in doors fitted with fine-meshed wire to keep out the flies and keep the room cool. This is done every summer.

Don't forget to use the apples and pears in the shed. If you or Marion don't want them, give them to someone so they don't go rotten. I've taken a note of the Rev Albert Jones's sister's address but don't know if I'll go. There is plenty of time yet. They tell me they will not let me go for a long time. I was weighed in town and weighed 148lb. So figure that out in stones!

* * *

Sunday, 23 May 1937

I WENT to bed late last night for Ted was working last night and Lizzie's boy, Ben, was expected to arrive about half past two in the morning. He works in a hardware store in Stratford [*about 100 miles away*] and comes in his car. I am in his room so his mother made him a camp-bed in the sitting-room and I met him this morning. He is a good-looking fellow, full of noise and jollity, tall and fair. Puts me in mind of Walter Cox on a better-looking scale [*a family friend from Abbots Langley*].

I went to church this morning. It was a Presbyterian church and very handsome. The parson wears a gown with a red and white hood. The organ has two sets of pipes in huge recesses on each side of the choir stalls and the organist sits behind the rostrum before an instrument looking like a large American organ, semi-circular in shape with three keyboards and foot arrangements. The church has three aisles but all the seats together form a slight half-circle round the rostrum and the sides look like Kings Langley church. [*The sister Methodist church across the Gade valley from the Methodist chapel at Abbots Langley. Annie's cousin Albert Timberlake, a bricklayer and builder like his father - Joseph Timberlake, gave the land on the outskirts of the village on which the Kings Langley Methodist church was built in 1935.*] All the seats are of maple, a very pretty wood, and the roof is in pine. The number of electric lights here astonish me. There is a shaded, reading lamp from the wall in all four corners of Lizzie's lounge and three from the centre - and all are often on together. Electricity is cheap here.

* * *

Sunday evening, 23 May 1937

AFTER church, we were starting for a little walk when we met Esther Miles and her fiancé [*Bruce Honsburger, who later married Esther Miles*] in his car, coming to take us for a ride. Ted, Lizzie and I sat in the back. It is a large car and he took us to Niagara (to the Falls) to see the coloured floodlighting. There were hundreds of cars and people. There is an immense power station and colours are thrown on the Falls from rows and rows of powerful lights. They are a million candle power! It's no use trying to describe the immensity of the Falls. Words are useless and we stayed watching them until 10 o'clock. Then drove home another way, making a circular tour through Queenston, Stamford, Chippawa and Pauls View to Niagara Falls and back to St Davids and St Catharines. We could see a vast city across the Falls - Niagara, in New York State, USA. There are no skyscrapers here in St Catharines.

* * *

Monday, 24 May 1937

THIS morning, Cousin Jim came [*Jim Hawkins, Lizzie's brother*]. We expected him yesterday but he has been ill or "sick" as they say here. We have been up to the principal street - among the crowds of people lining the pavement and the side-grass of the streets to see numbers of men in shorts, etc, running in a ten-mile race. The cars kept running just the same speed and "speed cops" (as they call them) on huge motorcycles kept riding up and down on each side the length of the road, hooting to keep the people back. Three prize-winners and lots of side-prizes are given. Fred Cherry was a prize-winner one year as the first veteran [*First World War ex-serviceman*] in the race. He received a bag of flour, etc.

This afternoon, Jim took Lizzie, Ted and me for a long ride. We went to Queenston Heights where there is a fine park, all wooded with places to picnic and very fine walks. There is a huge column with a figure of Admiral Brock [*Major-General Sir Isaac Brock*] who won battles here. There is also a monument erected by the Canadian Government to the memory of Laura Secord who saved the life of her husband at that spot and who walked many miles through the bush to give information to General Fitzgibbon and enable him to win the Battle of Beaver Dams. They mark slanting white lines on the road all around these sort of places for cars to draw-in and (if all are full) one circles slowly round till an opportunity occurs. There is a continual stream of cars coming and going today as it is a general holiday (Empire Day). [*The USA siezed Queenston Heights in 1812 expecting a welcome from the population and a swift victory whilst Britain was fighting Napoleon Bonaparte, but they were repulsed. Many Canadians were Loyalists who had left the USA at the time of the Revolution. Major-General Brock was killed on Queenston Heights. Laura Secord, the wife of a wounded Canadian soldier, overheard American troops who were billeted in her home in 1813. She walked 20 miles cross-country to warn the British troops of a pending surprise attack.*]

We came back down the Heights by a road alongside an immense river, Niagara River, and on the other side we could see Lewiston, New York State. For one shore is Canada and the other side USA. We passed by a beautiful botanical garden kept up by the Government - went in and admired the flowers [*the Niagara Parks Commission School of Horticulture Botanical Garden*]. The rock gardens are fine and the colours of the tulips beyond description. All are named and I saw two or three that I coveted - Zulu, Parrot and Narcissus. There is a stand there for people to peep through a frame of wood and glass: two pieces of glass to form a V and filled with water to form a wonderful prism. I saw a pair of Golden Oriole birds with black wings and golden bodies. The robins here are big as thrushes. [*The Golden Orioles were probably Baltimore or Northern Orioles because Golden Orioles are specific to Western Europe. There are no European Robins in North America. American Robins are members of the Thrush family; the adults have orange breasts and they are slightly larger than the European Song Thrush.*]

Then, when we got home to supper about 6pm, we had potato salad, cheese, bread and cups of tea. I am allowed to have a cup of milk and a little snack before I go to bed! After supper we went round to May's house to see some fireworks let off for the benefit of the two little girls, Pat and Elizabeth, aged 8 and 4. They are bonny girls but, oh dear, their behaviour - it is atrocious. I'm not in love with Canadian children at all, but these two take the cake above all I've seen. Their father [*Frank Love*] is a thin dark man who rarely speaks - an Irishman. I think May is a bit of a shrew. Poor old Jim [*Jim Hawkins*] looks ill. He has an attack of congestion of the kidneys. He is very thin as are many men here. The women are plump as a rule.

I heard the word "hitch-hike" and asked the meaning.

They said, "Can you cock your thumb back?"

"Yes," I said.

"You'll make a good hitch-hiker then." We passed two youths in shorts and knapsacks on the road and when they saw a car with two people in it they held up their hands and cocked back their thumbs at the riders. Car after car passed them but Ted said they would be sure to get picked up before long. It's a sign you want a lift.

* * *

Tuesday, 25 May 1937

LIZZIE has been washing today. She has a large electric washer and pulley-lines so that she can peg-out clothes indoors, open a large shutter, pull them out - and pull them back in again when dry. Several of the neighbours round here have sent invitations for Mrs Southam [*Lizzie*] to bring her cousin from England for tea. I'm not very keen but Lizzie says it's the usual thing so . . . . . .

Ben [*Southam*] and his girl went riding out at a farm where Marguerite's people live. She brought back a huge branch of Dogwood. Evidently it is a tree covered with large, white flowers with green centres and five pure-white petals about 3in across. It looks like giant cherry-blossom save that the flowers are flat, not like a bell. I'm very well and am hoping for a letter to tell me all the news of home.

My dear love to you all,
Mother

* * * * *

[LETTER 7]

"I had my teacup read the other day . . . . . ."

13 Ida Street, St Catharines, Ontario, Canada
Thursday, 27 May 1937

MY DEARS,

I am still well and having a nice time. The people here astonish me by their friendliness. We have had people here most evenings and all say: "Come and have lunch with me," or "Come and have tea with me". Lizzie tells me that this is usual. We went to see Mrs Wenham, a nice little English woman who has lived here many years. Her daughter [*Renée Wenham*] is getting married shortly and I had to see the contents of her "oak chest" as they call it - not "bottom drawer". She had the most lovely needlework and quilts all made by hand.

Yesterday, we went to Rose Cherry's and took tea. She lives quite a way out, over by the old Welland Canal which has been diverted and is now quite swampy in places. Betty [*Outram née Cherry*] lives near her mother, both in the usual wooden houses with cellars underneath. We are to take tea with Betty next week. The huge stoves look queer to me - larger editions of the one in our church schoolroom! [*An upright, cylindrical stove, with a lid at the top for putting in the coke.*]

Last evening, George Threader came to see me [*Lizzie's son by her first husband, George Threader, Senior*]. He is very like his father and an extremely nice fellow. His wife sent an invitation for me to go over to his place for the day. He has two children, Jackie aged 9 and Barbara aged 4. He thinks a lot of my Joe. Would you believe they all agree that Joe has no temper? At least they never saw it and George was with him all the time whilst they were in Manitoba and they speak so highly of him.

They have wild canaries here in the woods and often they come round the houses. I saw one on the clothes-line today - yellow with black-tipped wings. [*American Goldfinches, most likely, which are common in flocks in that area and one of the only two, all-yellow birds with black-tipped wings found in North America.*]

* * *

Friday, 28 May 1937

I'VE had a most interesting afternoon. Rose called to ask me to go to her house to stay for a week - so I am to go the week after next. Then an old Scots woman called - a Mrs McShane. She told me that she had been cured of arthritis in her neck, arms and feet by faith-healing and described it in full. I had to listen most intently to understand her broad Scottish accent. Then Lizzie and I went to a Mrs Pocknall for tea on her veranda. She has a two-storied wooden house - all very beautifully furnished. I had to go upstairs to see her rig-out for a wedding tomorrow - dress, hat, gloves, etc, etc. Ted [*Southam*] is working till midnight tonight so we came home and had supper. Then Mrs Pocknall (with her son and his fiancée) called unexpectedly to ask if we would like a car ride. They took us to Port Dalhousie to meet the Toronto boat. They are huge boats and during the summer they are crowded to capacity. The lake is a wonderful sheet of water and it takes two and a half hours for steamers to cross to Toronto. At Port Dalhousie there are all kinds of amusements: swings, water-cycles, airplanes, merry-go-rounds, stalls with ices, pies and hot dogs, water-chutes, children's pools and wide stretches of sand. They say that in the summer there is hardly room to move. There are hotels and tourist accommodation (which look like bathing-huts) which hold two bunk-beds. The bungalows there fetch $25 to $50 a month so many go just for the bathing.

The boat *Dalhousie City* came in without Mrs Pocknall's daughter on board. She is a nurse in Toronto and her husband is the caretaker of the biggest nonconformist church in St Catharines and he shewed me over it. It is an immense place with huge basement rooms and about 14 classrooms, galleries, a badminton room, a primary room, a babies' room, a great kitchen with automatic washer-up and kitchen ranges, large men's and women's wardrobes with cupboards - with individual places for mortar boards and hangers for gowns. Their minister gets $3,000 per year and the organist $100 per month. I saw the city fire engines racing to a fire. Loud sirens on two cars all loaded with men in helmets and a huge one loaded with ladders. Every car and tram parked themselves at once and (as the streets are always busy with immense cars) there is always a scramble. We are expecting Ben Hawkins and his wife [*Alice*] from Rochester tomorrow. It is over 30 years since I saw him.

I have been looking for a letter or paper from home all this week. Do hope you are all well. If one of you will write each week - so that I can have a letter regularly - my mind will be at rest about you all. My letters will be very rambling but I write them at odd times - often when I go to bed.

My dear love to you all,

Your loving Mother

PS. I had my teacup read the other day and I was to hear news of an animal. I hope my Topsy is all right.

A man asked me yesterday, "What sort of arithmeticians are you in England?"

"As good as other lands," I said.

"No, no," said he, "we take five from one this side, over here in North America!" [*The exchange rate was $5 to the £1 in both Canada and the USA.*]

* * * * *

[LETTER 8]

"Their iced drinks are lovely"

13 Ida Street, St Catharines, Ontario, Canada
Sunday, 30 May 1937

MY DEARS,

Ben [*Hawkins, Junior*] and his wife, Alice, came from Rochester [*New York State, USA*] last evening. He seemed so pleased to see me, put his arms around me and kissed me. I am the first relation they have seen and it's 32 years since he left [*Abbots Langley*]. I should have known him although he has lost his hair. He said he was surprised to find I was such a short woman. He had always pictured me a good bit taller. His wife is a very nice person, very beautifully dressed and very friendly. They immediately invited me to Rochester. They have a summer-cottage by the lake. He thought I might go from his house to Joe and looked at my passport and (would you believe it) that American Consul only issued my passport for three months. I had not noticed the three instead of a six. I shall probably stay there till July and then Alice will see me on the train to San Francisco. I have written to Auntie Jennie [*Stanton*] and Lois Harris [*née Munt*] but don't know, of course, when I'll go there. I am going to Rose's [*Rose Cherry's*] to stay on Monday until the next Monday.

I have had a Sunday of picnicking. Ben [*Hawkins*] has a wonderful car. It's an Oldsmobile, 90 horsepower and safe-riding at 60mph. Jim [*Hawkins*] and he brought round their cars this morning and took us and May's [*May Love's*] family to Niagara, to picnic. There are acres of grape-vines near here on the way to Niagara and (as we neared the city) lots of huts like bathing-huts to accommodate tourists - each to sleep two. I had seen the Falls by night but to see them in the sun is beyond description. Tomorrow is a public holiday in the [*United*] States and hundreds of cars were pouring into the beautiful park from Ohio, Michigan, New York State and even North Carolina. The wide roads were lined with cars parked each side and two rows of cars continually passed up and down the centre. There are pools, rock-gardens, trees, shelters, fountains - many called "bubblers", a white pedestal with a bowl on top and a sort of chrome tap from which a little stream of water continually bubbles up - and you put down your face and open your mouth and drink. May and Lizzie are used to picnics and each cut sandwiches and packed salad and cakes, lemonade and tea. At each open-air shelter there are tables and seats and a sink where boiling and cold water run to make tea and wash-up. We walked down the long parade to where the spray came over us. It looks like a huge smoke cloud. Over on the American side we could see crowds of people on the points of the islands opposite. There was a parade of hundreds of Rovers, Scouts and Guides there.

Ben and his wife, Alice, have a little white dog just like a woolly lamb which they adore. They have had it eight years. It certainly is a cute little thing. It got lost in the great park and we were all agog until Alice found it. Then May's girl, Pat, strayed and there was another shemozzle. She is a little devil. May is an indulgent mother and, of course, has to pay the penalty by being harassed to shreds. She says it's the Irish blood in them. I saw a queer contraption that sweeps and damps the road all at once - a huge machine driven by one man up-aloft (behind) looking like a threshing machine with a tank arrangement at the back. It's really a huge vacuum cleaner. Takes half the street at a time, removes all litter and sprays at the same time. It did away with 50 men's work and cost a huge sum. We are having lovely weather, warm and sunny. I get very scorched.

* * *

Monday, 31 May 1937

I'VE just received Marion's letter and the two lots of newspapers. Was so glad to know all is well with you all. I've not heard from Joe yet nor have I heard anything of my pension [*Annie's Widow's Pension*]. I hope it gets through before I leave here so that I can draw it. Am afraid it will take me some time to get used to spending dollars. The money goes such a little way. I am going to Niagara to see the American Consul tomorrow. I want to find out about my visa.

* * *

Wednesday, 2 June 1937

I WENT to the Canadian emigration office on Tuesday and found everything right. The three months is for Canada and they tell me my passport will be right for the USA for 12 months. So that is all right. Have been to Betty Cherry's [*Betty Outram's*] home to tea today. Very nice inside but looks a queer place outside. When wooden houses get shabby they look awful. I've been to George Threader's house to lunch and tea yesterday [*Lizzie's Southam's son*]. His wife is very smart - also his home. The little girl is very plain but the boy is bonny. He seems to be Lizzie's darling. Up in the streetcar [*the tram*] was a notice that said children in arms went free and that children under 51ins in height went half-fare and those over 51ins pay full-fare. I thought that queer. I've had my first taste of pumpkin pie and don't think much of it. The food here is not a patch on English food. Only the bread and butter and water are good. So much is tinned goods. Their iced drinks are lovely. The children here are all running round in bathing-suits and sunsuits, hardly a stitch on. I get scorched but am not too hot yet.

I was so glad to get Marion's letter and to hear about the Coronation. You all seem so far away. Don't forget that poor Topsy will have her kittens in my birthday week, 24 June. So leave her box (that's under my bed) so that she can get to it. Everyone thought Abbots Langley did well with their Coronation gifts to the children. [*Each child was given a Coronation mug.*] Ask Teddy Beaumont to let you have the *Pictorials* for me please [*the "Sunday Pictorial" newspaper*]. I soon had an applicant for the stamps with the King and Queen on the newspapers Marion sent [*the Coronation postage stamp*]. I'd like a letter from Fred and Muriel. Perhaps there is one in the post. Give my kind remembrances to all my friends. My love to Marie and the Misses Harris. [*Marie (Mary Ellen) Kimpton was the wife of Jim (Henry James) Kimpton who was a nephew of David Kimpton, Annie's late husband. They lived at 19 Adrian Road, Abbots Langley, in 1937. The Misses Harris lived in Abbots Road.*]

My dearest love to you all and a kiss for my little boys,

Your loving Mum

PS. Marion will keep my rambling epistles till I return.

The King George VI and Queen Elizabeth Coronation postage stamp, 1937.

* * * * *

[LETTER 9 -*This letter was pinned to the previous one*]

"Stockings are cobwebs"

[*neither addressed nor dated*]

DEAR MARION AND MURIEL,

I want you to get 3yds of Dorcas Radiant (I believe it is called that) in pale green. It's the same stuff that Mrs George Flint used for the knickers I bought - just like my knickers. Mrs George Flint knows [*Edie (Edith) Flint, wife of George, Bert Flint's uncle*]. Also I want Bert to get and send to me a cyclist's cape to fit and cover a man as tall as himself and waterproof leggings - also to fit himself [*Bert Flint was over 6ft tall*]. I want them so they would be good weather-proof ones to last a season or so. And send two pairs of ladies' stockings about I/II pastel shades. The cape and leggings are never seen here and stockings are cobwebs. I don't know what the cost will be but it can come out of the money Bert holds. I may just as well give my gifts now as wait until I leave for

San Francisco. I do hope you will like the rambling epistles I'm sending. I write at odd times and anywhere and pencil is handiest. I'd like the parcel sent as soon as possible.

My love to you all and give a kiss to my precious David and Roger,

Your Mum

PS. Let Marion keep my scribbles till I return. There are Canadian violets here so large but with no smell. To my way of thinking, none of the scented flowers are as sweet as ours. Just as the birds appear to have no song.

* * * * *

[LETTER 10]

"A wooden thing with a tin on it"

13 Ida Street, St Catharines, Ontario, Canada
Monday, 7 June 1937

MY DEARS,

It is Monday afternoon and Lizzie and I have been up the city all morning. I have bought myself a white felt hat to be like everybody else. I still cannot get used to the money yet, but I think it is because I have none coming in (in Canadian money) and only know the value of mine in English money. There are very few drapers' shops here (or stores). I'd like some of the folk to see Watford. There is one very long street (St Pauls) and a few leading from it with all the shops - but that's all. St Catharines stretches out miles and then there are miles of land and woods before the next town.

Yesterday was a big day here, Decoration Day. Uniformed men with bands and a contingent of Scotsmen and a band of pipers came from all parts for a grand parade and service at the Cenotaph. Uncle Ben [*Hawkins*], Larry Outram [*Lawrence, husband of Betty Outram née Cherry*] and May's first husband, Will Miles, wore decorations and had been soldiers or in the Territorials [*First World War volunteers*]. Then they got in cars or streetcars and came to the cemetery. Every soldier's and veteran's grave is decorated with a little Union Jack on Saturday and with a pot with red geraniums on Sunday. The bands play, the soldiers march, the naval cadets also and the pipers in full dress with the drum major in front and huge drummers with leopard skins down their backs. There were two microphones so that the crowd could hear the psalms and the prayers said by the Roman Catholic priest. Then they played *The Dead March* and went slow march through the cemetery. It seemed to me as if they were following corpses and then, at last, the veterans marched (men with rows of medals) and the pipers played *The Lament*. Jim drove me to the cemetery where everybody meets everybody. Betty Outram (née Cherry) lamented that it was the first year that she had not a new frock for the first Sunday in June. (But she is now Mrs Outram!)

Some friends of Lizzie's came back for tea and then we went back with them to their farm to look around. I rode with Jim [*Hawkins*] who went also as it was on his way back to Toronto. Mr and Mrs Tancock and their daughter, Ivy, and son, Leslie, have a fine place - thousands of grape-vines, a number of fruit-trees, cows, etc. We had supper with them: sliced beef and some sort of cold sausage, potato salad, green salad and pickled green tomatoes; then cherries and cream, chocolate cake, lemon tarts, and tea with cream in it. Mr Tancock then took us for a ride in his car for miles and miles up narrow tracks and very high hills - nothing but woods, trout streams in the valleys and the occasional farmstead with fields of tomato plants on almost vertical slopes. Also big fields of cabbages, lettuce, Indian corn and vineyards. All seemingly miles from anybody, no made-up roads - just tracks. The air here is so balmy and mild and on many days you can see 30 miles distant. Then home to Ida Street. I was tired. We are to spend another day at the Tancock's farm when Mr Tancock brings milk to the city in the morning. I saw a bluebird on the Tancock's farm [*either an Eastern Bluebird or a Blue Jay*]. A very beautiful blue, just like the pictures we see at home. Did I tell you of the queer contraptions every house outside the city has? As we went along the miles of road I noticed a thing here and there - a wooden thing with a tin on it. It is where the mailman leaves letters, etc, and where there are two or three houses near each other (although you can't actually see the houses) a row of these things is by the roadside.

A Mr and Mrs Webb called last week and took Lizzie and me to see the filtration-plant where Ted works [*Ted Southam, Lizzie's husband*]. It is seven miles away and he cycles there and back in all weathers. On the way is an immense hill over two miles long. These people (the Webbs) live on the place and have a nice home. It belongs to the city so is, of course, up to date. The plant is a vast place, immense engines, etc, everything spotless. Millions of gallons of water are filtered here to supply the whole of the city. I saw the tanks where the water is so clear that one does not know where the stairs start to enter the water. Unless you are told to look out for wet feet, you could walk right down into it. There is a laboratory where everything is tested for bugs!!! Alum is put in the water. It is filtered through sand and stones and so on until I couldn't grasp it all.

I went to a draper this morning. By the way, they never say material here - they call it "goods". They don't know a reel of cotton but think you mean calico - they call it "a spool of thread". The shopman said, "Are you from England?"

"Yes," I said.

"Do you know Whitechapel? It's my home. I was born there and when I think of London and the theatres and Hampstead Heath and all where I loved it so, I feel so sick for it. I could just fly there." He was evidently a Jew and had never been home since he was a young man, poor chap. "Oh, you are so lucky to be able to come and go back," said he. I don't realise how far I am from you all.

I go to the Cherrys tonight for a week so that I can talk England with them, for Rose says Lizzie will hear all and she none. Lizzie says she feels like Simeon: Lettest now thy servant depart in peace, etc [*the Bible, Luke 2:29, Simeon, having seen the Lord, could now die in peace.*] May does not care so much for England. The thought that the Plantation, Watford Wood and Gullet Wood are no more appals everyone and they don't want to see the houses and the bypass roads. [*Until about 1928, the Plantation was a narrow strip of woodland in Abbots Langley extending from Langley House, behind the buildings on the south-east side of the High Street and down Langley Road; Gullet Wood became the new North Watford Cemetery. The new A405 Watford North Orbital Bypass and the new A41 Western Avenue were under construction.*]

I've heard from Auntie Jennie [*Stanton*] telling me to go whenever I like, though to send my letter saying when early in the week so that it gets to Ottawa by Thursday or Friday. They only call for their mail once a week in town. It is getting so warm that I shall not need my warm clothing here but perhaps it will be cooler in Frisco. I am making a bag which a lady shewed me how to do and I will send it off to Bert's mum in case Marion is on holiday - for a stall at the Fête. [*This was the Methodist Church Fête held annually in Abbots Langley. Mabel Botwright née Funnell, aged 92 when she died in 1998, had kept her husband Jack Botwright's copy of the programme. The cover and some of its advertisements have been used as illustrations in this book.*]

I had a notice about my pension and have to wait for a communication from the Ottawa office about it, where I will have to fill up forms, etc. I shall have eight or nine weeks to draw!!! Tell Fred I want to hear from him. Everybody was so interested about Abbots Langley and the Coronation and we all turn up our noses at Mrs Simpson, etc. Some reckon it is foolish to give so much money to royalty but I say that they would have quite as heavy taxes with a dictator and they have to agree. Lizzie's dog, Lady, has adopted me as her aunt. She is old and her eyebrows and muzzle are growing grey. How's my Topsy? I do hope she'll be all right till I come home. Give my love to Mrs Brown and all the ladies. [*Mrs Brown, who lived in Abbots Road, was the leader of the Women's Meeting (about to be re-named the Women's Own) at the Methodist church in Abbots Langley.*] Kiss my David and Roger for me.

My dear love to you all,
Your loving Mother

* * * * *

METHODIST CHURCH **FETE** ABBOTS LANGLEY

IN AID OF THE MATTHEW TIMBERLAKE MEMORIAL

to be held in the

ABBOTS ROAD MEADOW (Opposite the Methodist Church)

(by kind permission of MRS. NEISH)

on

SATURDAY, 26th JUNE, 1937

To be opened at 3 p.m. by **Miss E. C. PERKINS**

Chairman: ARTHUR FLINT, Esq., J.P.

Admission 3d.
Children over
3 years of age 2d.

Price: SIXPENCE
(Returnable in Goods
as per Coupon inside)

The front cover of the 1937 Methodist Church Fête programme.

A WEEK WITH THE CHERRYS IN ST CATHARINES

ROSE AND FRED CHERRY with their baby daughter Betty (Elizabeth) emigrated to Canada in 1910, travelling with Rose's sister, Lizzie Threader née Hawkins - a widow with her 8-year old son George, and with Lizzie's future second husband, Ted (Edwin) Southam. Annie recalled in LETTER 20 that Rose (Rosalind) Cherry née Hawkins had been in the Sunday school class that Annie taught at the Abbots Langley Wesleyan Methodist church.

In 1978, Rose Cherry aged 93 presented the Abbots Langley Methodist church with a pulpit fall (a blue cloth which was later embroidered with a gold cross) as her contribution to the centenary celebrations of the founding of the Wesleyan Methodist Society in the village:

[LETTER 11]

"Auntie Annie is funny - she says tea for supper"

13 Sherbourne Street, St Catharines, Ontario, Canada
Friday, 11 June 1937

MY DEARS,

I am staying for a week with Rose and Fred Cherry. Rose and I get along admirably. Betty [*Outram née Cherry*] lives down the road - just one house between them. Each house has grass plots and all are wooden two-storied houses and bungalows. Outside is rough-looking meadow land and in the distance, factories and chimneys. The meadow is where the old Welland Canal ran. Only a few years ago it was diverted and it is now a wonderful Ship Canal with huge locks, etc, a little distance away. We can see the huge bridge opening up to let big boats through from our window here.

The people here are a mixed lot: next door - Irish and English; next door to them are from Finland; next - Russian Poles and at the back Ukrainian; opposite, the man is Austrian - his wife a Pole; the grocer's shop is kept by Italians or, as they say, "Eyetalians"; many are coloured people; there's a German family; a Norwegian, Jan Jansen; a family of Romanians; a Cosssack; a Polish family named Lewitski; and a Dutch family named Spillinger. Jimmy's last year's teacher at school is Miss Paladichuk, a Russian Pole. There is a small church for the coloured people, a small Baptist church, and a place where the Roman Catholics go. Rose and her family go to a Mission church connected with a larger one in the city and ministered to by the curate.

This is a two-storied home and I have a small room to myself. There is another bedroom and Fred [*Cherry, Junior*] sleeps on the landing. They make me most welcome and Fred tells me he wishes I'd stay for months and months. He would never grow tired of hearing me talk. But I reckon it's because I'm a good listener as well as a talker. Betty is very well, thin and dark; her husband is tall and fair. I hardly understand him for he is pure Canadian. They talk very quickly and do not open their mouths. Jimmy Cherry is the boy who was born after the Cherrys returned from England. [*Rose and Fred Cherry, along with daughter Betty and son Fred, had come on holiday to England in 1923.*] Their son, Fred, was 14 years old then and, of course, Jimmy is spoilt.

[LETTER 11 CONTINUED]

Fred Cherry (Junior) is a big fellow. He left school at 16 and was top of his form but wanted to leave. The children all do as they please here. He had a job of work but could not get apprenticed to a carpenter as he desired. Then came the years of the depression which certainly were worse here than at home. I've heard of people who lost their homes, etc, and people got down to their last penny. Then, after five years of idleness, he asked if he could return to school to try to become a teacher. He is now just taking his exams. He then has to go for two years to Collegiate School and then one year to normal school which, I believe, is like our student teachers. Lizzie thinks it a mad scheme but he is certainly not fit for manual labour. He is slow and awkward and wears glasses, takes no interest in games - but is a grand talker. A very plain chap, has two big teeth protruding each side of his mouth and a very little chin - but I like him.

Fred Cherry (Senior) comes home each day covered to the eyes in yellowy brick-dust. He wheels bricks at the brickyard all day. Each barrow carries 165lb of bricks and has a wheel and one leg only - so the men have to run with it. He has to strip and wash each night on his return and has clean socks and vest each day. He works in running shorts, singlet and canvas shoes. Many men only wear shorts and are barefoot. It's very hard work but they make good money as it's only summer work. This house is their own and one can see the effect of the depression in the many things that need to be done and the sparseness of the furniture and bedding, etc. Also, when Betty married she took all the things she had collected for years.

I went to the ice-cream parlour and had ice-cream soda in a tall glass with straw and a spoon. It was good - so cold - and it had a lump of ice-cream in it. I'm sending you one of their lists that I prigged [*old English slang for thieved*]. Did I tell you that every hostess cuts up the meat on a dish and everybody helps themselves to the quantity they want to eat? As for quantities eaten, I've not yet seen a dinner table like our English ones and we only have three meals a day here at Sherbourne Street. We have a little "lunch" they call it, before going to bed - a slight concession for someone from England. Young Jimmy says, "Auntie Annie is funny - she says tea for supper". They have no real teatime. Sometimes afternoon tea is handed around if guests arrive, but it's "supper" at half past six when the men come home. I have bought myself a white felt hat. It cost $1.49 but I can't figure it out yet. I pay by faith.

I have had a letter from Alta. She says: "Stay as long as you wish in Canada," though they are looking forward to seeing me. I was so glad when Lizzie brought Marion's letter down. Don't ever think your letters are dull or rubbish. I want to hear all the gossip and details. I am still looking forward to a letter from Fred. I shall send letters to both addresses but the contents are for all and Marion will store them. Tell Bert I don't think I am getting any heavier. The women weigh themselves each week, religiously. I've been the same weight for two weeks, 143lb. I detest the wireless out here. It's so blatant and loud and the advertising is awful.

I looked through Joe's bags today. His clothing is all moth-eaten but he has a lot of fine tools and some nice photos of Minnie carefully put away [*Minnie Mackay was Joe Kimpton's previous girl-friend back in England according to a note made by Marion Flint on the back of a photograph of Minnie with Annie Kimpton at the British Empire Exhibition,*

Wembley, 1924] and a beautiful letter from Grandma Kimpton [*Annie's mother-in-law, Emma*] and Grandad's [*Matthew Timberlake's*] photo.

I must close now and post this letter. I will soon be writing again. So glad my Topsy is all right. It is good of Marion to go round to feed her. We have a sandy dog and a sandy cat here - Browny and Sandy! I don't think I'll ever get used to the coinage here until I've drawn some cash. Remember me to Fred and Flora [*Fred and Flora Botwright who had been renting 56 Adrian Road from Annie since 1930, shortly after their marriage*] and Mrs Bull [*Mrs Bull was a near neighbour in Adrian Road*].

My dear love to you all,

Auntie Rose also sends her love to you all

* * * * *

An advert from the 1937 Methodist Church Fête programme. The wedding of Charles John (Jack) Botwright and Mabel Cissy Funnell, daughter of Ernest Joseph and Elizabeth Martha Funnell, on 14 September 1929 was the first marriage to be held when the Abbots Langley Methodist chapel became a Registered Building for the Solemnisation of Marriages. The first register indicates that these weddings followed up to 1938:

2nd : 21 June 1930, Arthur James Mansfield and Beatrice Charlotte Herring;
3rd : 25 April 1931, William Arthur Jelly and Lois Eunice Cox;
4th : 6 June 1931, Lewis (Lew) Brownsell and Dorothy (Dolly) Alice Cox;
5th : 1 August 1931, Harold Arthur Flint and Violet (Vi) Florence Sleap;
6th : 12 September 1931, Bertram (Bert) Arthur Flint and Marion Timberlake Kimpton;
7th : 30 July 1932, Frederick William Shephard and Ruby Emily Funnell;
8th : 4 December 1935, Victor George Arnold and Nellie Lilian O'Dell;
9th : 14 December 1935, Roland Ernest Funnell and Isabella Christie Anderson;
10th : 11 April 1936, Percy William Utting and Marjorie Edith Funnell;
11th : 21 November 1936, Frederick James Foster and Audrey Emma Staines;
12th : 30 July 1938, Levi John Cox and Ellen (Nellie) Lavinia Dando.

The ten Funnell children - Marjorie, Mabel, Edgar, Alice, Ruby, Roland, Amy, Bernard, Basil and Geoffrey - were all born over the shop at 22 High Street, Abbots Langley, Hertfordshire.

Back Again At 13 Ida Street

After the week with the Cherrys, Annie Kimpton returned to stay with Lizzie and Ted Southam again in St Catharines. Annie went on a picnic to the United States but was not as successful in "jumping" the border as her son, Joe, had been in 1925. She also went on a trip to Toronto to meet old friends.

Toronto, originally called York, was founded in 1793 by Lieutenant-Colonel John Graves Simcoe, Governor of Ontario. It was attacked and burnt down by the Americans in 1813. In retaliation, the British attacked Washington in 1814 and burnt part of it. Reputedly, the smoke damage on the Presidential residence was covered up by white paint which gave rise to its name - the White House:

[LETTER 12]

"If I had been 50 years younger with my boyfriend . . . . . ."

13 Ida Street, St Catharines, Ontario, Canada
Friday, 18 June 1937

My Dears,

I returned to Lizzie's on Monday and was glad to get back to my comfortable bed. Wednesday was Lizzie's birthday. I asked what she needed and I bought her knickers.

I went on Sunday evening with all the Cherrys to a queer little wooden church called "The Church of the Good Shepherd". About as big as our schoolroom with plain wooden seats and little ledges that were turned up or down as we entered or left the seats - to kneel upon. A mixed choir, all wearing surplices and the girls wearing queer black berets with corners, and a small pipe organ just a few feet from us with a great fat man playing. There was a bell over the porch clanging like a sheep bell. I got on quite well with the church service thanks to the training at Bradford on Avon. [*Annie had relatives there, believed to be her cousins on the Gates side of her family.*]

Jim [*Jim Hawkins, Lizzie's brother*] came down in the afternoon and took me and the two Freds and young Jimmy [*all three of whom were Cherrys*] for a short ride. In the street he saw the janitor of the Collegiate School that young Fred attends and introduced me with the usual, "Mrs Kimpton - my cousin - on holiday from England," and immediately everybody goes out of their way to interest me. He was going out but gave Jim his master-key telling him where to put it when we left and gave us free entry. It's a marvellous college, both educational and vocational. What we call a Technical College for girls and boys. They seem to have a room for everything. A great deal of it is much like our Grammar Schools but there are rooms full of machinery which greatly interested Jim. He said it must have cost a mint of money. Also a huge room with sewing machines, electric irons and all the equipment for dressmaking and tailoring. Another with scores of typewriters where they often learn to type to music. A great kitchen with electric cookers, grills and white tables where the girls learn to cook and to keep sinks and taps, etc, etc, clean. And a bedroom and lounge beautifully furnished to learn housewifery. White overalls and caps are worn while working and there are tall narrow metal cupboards - one for each pupil arranged round and across the middle of the room for them to keep their clothes in. Lastly, because I can remember no more, a room where they can learn poster drawing.

We were asked out for the day to Mrs Tancock's farm at Louth. Ted would come when he left work. Mr Tancock called for us when he brought milk to the city. It was a lovely morning and we had a good ride back together with four milk churns and some lengths of wood which here are called "lumber". All varieties of wood are called the same - lumber. I had such a pleasant day. Two years ago Mr Tancock picked 10 thousand baskets of grapes. Last year very few, since most were destroyed by hail. They are hoping for a good crop this year. The farmhouse is a two-storied wooden or frame-house with a verandah at the back. The barns and many houses here have specially shaped roofs. They call them barn-roofs and are built so that snow cannot pile up too high. Mr Tancock takes milk to a town dairy and his churns are then filled up with boiling water in the dairy and he takes this back home for his wife to use. She often does her washing with it.

I never saw such huge cooking stoves as the ones there. All houses have doors made double, the outside one half-glass for winter and the inside one screen-mesh for summer - to keep flies out. Windows also have screens for summer so that both windows and doors can be left open all day for air circulation. There is only one house in sight at the Tancocks even though the road passes it - "highways" they call them here. We had dinner at half past twelve: beef, potatoes, spaghetti, a tiny cabbage, a banana pie (which I liked) and the inevitable tea. This pie had the pie-plate lined with pastry and baked, then a thick layer of bananas cut in rounds, then a custard and (on top) meringue lightly browned in the oven. It was good. Then afternoon tea: just a cup handed round and cake, followed by supper at six: cold meats, two kinds of salad, fried potatoes, jelly with bits of oranges and strawberries with whipped cream and, again, tea.

After supper we sat outside and then came the surprise. In the distance came a car and in it were Betty and Larry Outram, Esther Miles and Bruce Honsburger. Then came another car with Mr and Mrs Webb who had a large bunch of roses and a box with a pretty cup and saucer in it for Lizzie. Finally another car came with Mr and Mrs Catt and their little girl. It appears they had planned a "Weena Roast" in honour of Lizzie's birthday and for me. We all piled into the cars and rode along fearfully rough tracks to the scrub where wood was gathered and a huge fire made. We sat upon logs and had Weenas which are a kind of long sausage [*Wiener or Vienna sausage, pronounced "Weena" in Canada*] placed inside long, buttered rolls - like our bridge-rolls but much bigger and longer. They put mustard into the hot dogs if you wanted some. They served hot coffee and lemonade in cups with doughnuts and butter tarts and we told stories and sang. It was weird: the trees, the fire and all the people - and I'm glad I've seen one but, to me, both the hot dogs and the rest are overrated. They are for youngsters and if I had been 50 years younger with my boyfriend (we are all men friends over here) I'd have been in my seventh heaven.

While I'm writing this, a firm of undertakers are advertising on the radio and at intervals soft organ music is played. "We shall know each other better, when the mists have rolled away," is just finished - played in funeral time [*from the Sankey and Moody hymn, 1883*]. This comes from Hamilton and anyone can send a request that some song, etc, be played on their birthday and this is announced with great gusto. Everyone is quite sure that English radio and music cannot be compared to this since they can't imagine how we can have good programmes without money obtained from advertising. "Why," say they, "these companies pay fabulous sums to the singers and advertisers."

I've never heard men talk so fast. I tell them I know they must be foaming at the mouth by the end of the advert. They have only a few moments to tell the public such a lot. To me it is absurd!

I've been asked if I saw the ice hockey match in England:

"No," said I.

"Didn't you listen to the radio?"

"No, ice hockey does not interest everybody in England!"

They nearly lose their breath but regain it to ridicule the English commentators saying, "Deah, deah, mahvellous shot, mahvellous shot!"

I laugh and imitate some of their queer expressions but have to be careful for, although Canadians are proud to belong to England still, they (as well as the Americans) think they are God's chosen. [*The British Ice Hockey team won the Winter Olympics gold medal in 1936 at Garmisch, Germany, in a historic victory over Canada who had won every previous Olympic ice hockey tournament. Britain was helped by fielding two Canadians who had not been selected for their own team. It was against the rules but, because England was not expected to stand a chance anyway, the authorities had not bothered to disqualify them. In 1937, Britain retained the European ice hockey title in London (the match that Annie was probably asked about) and went on to become World Champions.*]

We are having rainy weather. Though it is warm, it's dull. People say: "You've brought your dreadful English weather". I walked up to the town with Rose and Fred [*Cherry*] on Saturday evening. Fred said, "Want your boots cleaned?" and I saw a shop with a row of men and women cocked up on seats - high up on the wall. Men stood before them and blacked their boots. This establishment also cleaned your hats - topped and tailed you in fact. I thought it very funny. To look in the barbers' shops and see the men reclining in full view, being shaved and having face massages, etc, is to me most amusing. It is a queer thing to me that with all the thousands of miles of land outside the city, they call every bit of ground with a rockery, a seat or a monument - a "park".

We went to some friends of Lizzies, Mr and Mrs Bunting, for supper and cards last evening. We sat on the veranda and I must have attracted the gnats (mosquitoes) for I have a good array of blisters round my ankles. They are just like the ones I get at home down by the tennis courts. [*Abbots Langley Methodist Church tennis club laid out a pair of grass courts opposite the end of Popes Road (between there and Tanners Wood, where Nos 1 and 3 Greenways now stand), on land belonging to Arthur (Reuben Arthur) Flint. Chapel families - the Flints, the Kimptons, both the Botwright families, the Dunns, the Pratts and others, played there on Saturday afternoons during the summer. Dress was strictly "whites"; pails of water were carried from Hempton, Greenways (the home of Arthur and Ethel Flint), for making tea and for washing-up in the wooden pavilion; the young children played in the long grass which was full of wild flowers and butterflies. The "Stop-me-and-buy-one", WALL'S ice-cream tricycle man would call by. Only the Elsan outside toilets marred the idyllic setting.*]

I've heard from Lois Munt (Mrs Harris) and she is eager to see me. So Lizzie, Rose and myself are going next Saturday. It's a two-hour journey by boat across Lake Ontario. Also I shall probably go to London [*Ontario*], which is 150 miles away going via Hamilton, before I go to Jennie [*Stanton*] in Ottawa which is a day's journey. The travelling facilities are nothing like those in England - far, far behind. But when you consider the vast distances, it is understandable.

Probably, Marion and Bert will have gone to Broadstairs by the time this reaches you. If so, keep my letters so that Marion can let me see them to refresh my memory when I return. Do hope your face is quite better, Fred [*it is believed he had Bell's Palsy*]. I saw that one or two of my newspaper bundles were addressed in Fred's handwriting but I'm still looking for a letter from Fred or Muriel. I must write to Uncle Joe and Auntie Elsie but my days simply fly by. [*They were Annie's brother - Joseph Timberlake, and Elsie - the wife of Annie's other brother, Matthew Timberlake.*] All here send their love to you all. I see from the *Abbots Langley Parish Magazine* that old Mrs Grant has died. I wonder what her niece will do? So glad my Topsy is all right.

My dear love to you all and my darling little boys,

Your loving Mum

PS. Tell Bert that, here, Church members pay for their offertory envelopes. They all say that 25 cents is not missed and an expense is saved for the Church. I wonder what we would say if asked to subscribe to such a thing? [*In the Methodist Church it was customary for Members to give a regular weekly offering and to place it in a small, sealed, specially printed and identifiable envelope and put it in the collection plate.*] Did anybody see about the cape and leggings, etc, that I asked about? I'm hoping so.

* * * * *

[LETTER 13]

"You see, this is an old Indian trail"

13 Ida Street, St Catharines, Ontario, Canada
Sunday, 20 June 1937

MY DEARS,

It is Sunday evening and I've just come in from church. There was a thunderstorm and some kind man brought Lizzie and me home in his car through the teeming rain. We went to church this morning and then four families took quantities of food, teapots, cups, etc, and went picnicking to Niagara Glen. It's a most lovely place (not far from the Falls) kept up by the Government with tables and seats, an open-air kitchen with boiling and cold water, sinks and draining-boards, and bins for rubbish. We had a fine spread of good things. There were Mr and Mrs Tancock and family, Mr and Mrs Catt and family - they are farmers, Mr and Mrs Webb who are at the filtration-works, Ted [*Southam*] and Lizzie, Jim [*Hawkins*], me and the dog.

After lunch, Jim took me down the Glen. The others have been before and gave me to understand it was a dreadful undertaking though lovely to see. It has been made easy for people to get down to the river's edge by a mixture of steps cut in the rocks, wooden stairs and pathways. Now and then we crept under great rocks (with just room for one person) to where the river boils and races by as it flows between the Falls and the Rapids. The Glen is covered with trees and plants and foliage of inumerable kinds and the sides are hundreds of feet in height. Jim told me that the escarpment runs for many miles up the river. Mr Tancock and Mr Catt took me (in a car) round to see the aerial car going across just below the Falls on wire cables. They say that we have all the beauty spots on this side and that the Yanks have to come over here to see them. We then had tea, which was a replica of lunch and then got into the four cars and so home. The two farmers had cows to milk. Mr Webb was on duty and at 6 o'clock Jim started back to Toronto - a 75 mile journey. At 7 o'clock Ted, Lizzie and I went to church.

* * *

Tuesday, 22 June 1937

ON Saturday evening, Jim [*Hawkins*] took me for a ride around part of the countryside I had never seen - along King's Highway No 8. We came across a big board by the roadside saying, TRUTHVILLE WELCOMES YOU and, GOODBYE, COME AGAIN on another board at the end of the small town. The same welcome and farewell boards are seen at most towns and villages.

This was Lincoln County so, of course, we went through Grimsby! I saw miles and miles of vineyards and a small farm with a huge barn and upon each, four or more wires sticking up on the roof. I understand that these are lightning conductors and most necessary in these isolated spots. You can ride along a 40-mile stretch of road not seeing a single pedestrian, just cars. There are no sidewalks (pavements) since the distances are too great for walkers. Jim says the coming of cars and radio has meant new lives for many of these isolated farmers. We passed a little church and school here and there and I'm told that the local people gather there even now as it provides the only means of social intercourse - and that only once a week. The "kids", as everybody calls them, walk miles to school. One of the places we went through was called Winona (a Red Indian name) and whenever we drive on a street with bends in it they say rather apologetically, "You see, this is an old Indian trail".

It rained all day yesterday (though it was warm) and everyone called it a dreadful day and said, "What about the berries?" which means strawberries which should be picked and are being spoilt. We see cars and lorries packed with women and girls going berry-picking. Apparently, a farmer puts in an advert for pickers on a certain date and time and says he will meet them on such-and-such a street corner. I'm told that if the farmer is homely or not a good-looker and has a shabby car, he will get no girls to go with him. The men laugh about this.

Lizzie has an electric washer and it gets the washing done in no time and with very little trouble. She is washing this morning. Then we are going into town this afternoon. Tomorrow, we go to a picnic at Niagara and then cross the border to some army manoeuvres on the USA side. Some of the party we are going with go shopping there and smuggle back any goods bought. I am going to Toronto on Saturday to see all the folks there. There are four different lots of people to call on: Mrs Harris (Lois Munt), Mrs Perry (Nell Flint), Mrs Hearnden (Ruth Hitchinson's daughter) and Mrs Brodie (Mrs Adkins' aunt).

I had hoped for a letter this morning, since I want to hear what you are all doing. Do hope you are all well. I am keeping very well. Had a few mosquito bites around my ankles the other night - just like the gnat bites we get at home so I'm not worrying about them. Give my love to Marie and Jim [*Kimpton*].

My dear love to you all,

Your loving Mother

PS. I forgot to say that I found it no trouble getting up and down the ravine save that my face got red with the heat, for it was like a hothouse down there. Nobody walks anywhere here if they can avoid it and for someone to walk a mile or two is wonderful.

MURIEL, MARION AND MARIE

This is a recipe for lemon pie and is very good:

> Make some pastry and line a deep pie-plate and bake it. Take the juice and grated rind of one lemon, two egg yolks, a cup of granulated sugar, one tablespoon of cornstarch (cornflour) slaked down with a little water. Mix together with two cups of boiling water and boil until it thickens. When it's cooled slightly, fill the pastry. Make a meringue of whisked egg white, add a tablespoon of castor sugar and pile on top and brown lightly in the oven.

These can be eaten hot or cold and can be made also in tartlet form and look lovely and taste better. [*Lemon meringue pies were new to Annie.*]

* * * * *

[LETTER 14]

"Don't speak, Nance, and you'll go over with us"

13 Ida Street, St Catharines, Ontario, Canada
Sunday, 27 June 1937

MY DEAR MARION, BERT, FRED AND MURIEL,

I was so glad to get letters from my two daughters [*Marion and Muriel, Annie's daughter-in-law*]. Muriel's budget was read by Jeanne Miles and Betty Outram, and her description of the sightseeing was greatly enjoyed. Ted [*Southam*] told Jim [*Hawkins*] I'd had a letter of 20 pages. "Dear me," said he, "I get stumped for matter to write about just to fill one page."

I am thinking of Marion and her dear ones at Broadstairs today. I do hope they have good weather. [*The previous summer in 1936, Annie went on holiday to Broadstairs with Marion and Bert Flint and their children.*] I had a lovely birthday [*on 24 June when*

[LETTER 14 CONTINUED]

Annie was 66 years old]. Before I had my breakfast a lady called with a lovely bouquet of roses and white scented peonies. Then came a card from another lady and her husband followed by the cable from you all. The next-door lady, Mrs King, came with flowers from her garden. Lizzie gave me a little brooch made of rock from Niagara Falls and asked a party of her lady friends and her sisters round for afternoon tea. I told them I'd never had such a fuss made about my birthday before.

I went with a picnic party to Niagara on Wednesday last and we all went over the bridge [*Rainbow Bridge over the River Niagara, the border between Canada and the USA*]. Rose said, "Don't speak, Nance, and you'll go over with us". There were about 30 women in the party but by some mystic sense the customs man smelt me out and asked how long I'd been in St Catharines. Then marched me to a room and put me through an inquisition of questions. I had no passport with me and, if I had, should have had to pay $8 head tax which would be returned to me when I left the States. Then I had to be given a ticket permitting me to return onto Canadian soil stating that I was an "alien". So our little party returned to the Canadian side again and saw the sights there. We climbed a tower to overlook the Falls and took our revenge by touching our noses towards the USA. The folks here are great on picnics.

Yesterday - Rose, Lizzie and I went by boat to Toronto. I found Mrs Hearnden, who was very nice and gave us tea which is called "supper" here. Her husband got his car out and took us to Wychwood Avenue which was right across the city. It is huge with streets miles long. All round the docks and that part of the city the buildings are immense - 14 to 16 stories high. We found the Munt family and they were queerer than ever, but don't tell anybody I said so! They have not altered much - the least Lois and Janet, save that Lois looks worn. She was at death's door for several years and now has to take a daily dose of something or she would die. Poor Becky looks like one of the old girls in the Asylum [*Leavesden Asylum*]. A little pointed face, snow-white hair, talks and rambles incessantly - save when they shout at her. She cannot be trusted to do anything or look after herself. The old lady is 88 years old and is just like a child. She has to be washed, dressed and fed and Lois and Janet have to leave these two imbeciles alone during the day and look after them at night. I was glad I was Elizabeth Annie Kimpton. Jim [*Hawkins*] called for us and drove us home in the evening. It is a 75-mile run but only 35 miles or thereabouts across the lake. [*Lois Harris née Munt had been in Annie's Sunday school class, as recalled in* LETTER *20. In the 1891 census, Lois lived in Breakspear Road, Abbots Langley, with her father, John, and her mother, Emma, who was 41 years old then (ie, about 88 in 1937), and five brothers and sisters, Frank, Harry, Rebecca (probably Becky), Martha, and Jane (probably Janet). They would have emigrated to Canada in the early 1900's.*]

On Friday evening I went to a farewell meeting at the Westminster church of their minister, the Rev Frank Hendershott. There were about one hundred present and he was presented with a silver tea-service; his wife - with some lovely cups and saucers and a large bunch of roses; and his daughter - with a silver bangle and powder bowls. Then everyone had plates of ice-cream and cake. I don't like cake with ice-cream but everybody eats it. This morning was his last sermon and the choir came up the aisle, two and two, singing just like an Anglican service and retired in the same fashion singing, "God be with you". We all rise when the choir take their place and the parson comes in and sings, "Holy, holy, holy . . . . . ." in the morning and, "Praise God from whom . . . . . ." in the evening. The parson gives out the notices and says, "Let us worship God in our morning (or evening) offering". Then he comes down to receive the collection plates and we all rise and sing, "We give Thee back Thine own". We sing the Lord's Prayer to the same tune as at home and rise and repeat the psalm for the day - the parson one verse, the people the next. The new minister is to be inducted next Friday. When I went to church one Sunday evening the steward at the door said, "Goodnight".

I nearly laughed and said, afterwards, that the good man evidently thought we should go to sleep. I find that this is quite common. Most people say, "Goodnight," on meeting you in the evening. There are those who do not say, "Hello," whereas everyone says, "Goodbye". The tradesmen just walk right in your door and say, "Hello".

I mentioned to someone that I'd seen no oak-trees, so a number of women took me to a park and, most impressively, said:

"Don't say that we have no oak-trees. See, here is one."

"What," said I, "that spindly thing. I don't call that an oak." There is very little that I can score upon here! [*Annie was probably shown a Scarlet Oak which does not grow as tall or as broad as the English Oak.*]

What do you think of these rhymes? They were written up in a boot-repair shop kept by an Italian, Benevento Matti, who said to me: "I make them - I write them - I married - I family." He was highly pleased when I copied them out:

My friends did come and I did trust them,
I lost my friends, I lost my custom.
To lose my friends it grieves me sore,
So I resolved to trust no more.

*

Since man to man is so unjust,
I hardly knew which one to trust.
I trusted many to my sorrow, so
Pay today, I'll trust tomorrow.

We are eating bread made of soya beans and I've never seen so many kinds of bread. Manny's Bread says on the cart, "EVENTUALLY - WHY NOT NOW?" and on another, "YOU'VE TRIED THE REST NOW TRY THE BEST". There is Sally Ann Bread, Oliver Twist Bread, Cracked Wheat Bread, Whole Wheat Bread, All-Bran Bread, Dr Jackson's Bread, Buttermilk Bread, Carraway Seed Bread, Boston Brown Bread, Bond Bread and many, many, others. There's even Roman Bread which is supposed to cure everything, even deafness! Apparently it is forbidden to keep cows in the city precincts but many of the foreigners keep a cow and tether it on the waste land on the outskirts. One friend of Lizzie's went out to a piece of waste land to get some cow manure for her garden. The owner of the cow, a Polish woman, came to her and said vehemently:

"No, no laty, you no take. It my cow. It my shit." (!!!) She knew so much English and would not let her have any.

You ask about the cousins: Well, there is Jim Hawkins, who you remember; Lizzie Southam and her husband, Ted, who have a grown up son, Ben, living at Stratford, Ontario; Rose Cherry and her husband, Fred, with Fred Junior and Jimmy, a boy of 10; Betty Outram and her husband, Larry; May Love and her second husband, Frank, and two daughters, Esther and Jeanne Miles [*from her first marriage to William Miles*] and two little girls Pat and Elizabeth [*Love*]; and Ben Hawkins and his second wife, Alice, who live in Rochester, USA. These are the lot.

Auntie Lizzie is 57 years old, Marion, quite a number of years younger than me. Ben Hawkins and his wife, Alice, came yesterday from Rochester and took Esther Miles back with them for a week. They seem anxious for me to go and see them. I shall not go until my stay here is finished as my time in the USA will commence then. I have made myself a frock and am enclosing a pattern of it. I think the material, or "goods" as they call them, is of poor quality. I don't think I'll need my warm clothes and my frocks are dark compared to what folk wear here, so I don't know if they will be all right for San Francisco. I'm thinking of going to London (Ontario) to stay with Lizzie Hutchinson at the weekend but shall be back in a few days and must then think about going to Ottawa.

I wonder how the Abbots Langley Fête went off? Am very glad that you [*Fred and Muriel Kimpton*] are settled in Abbots Langley for I reckon that if I get on as well in Frisco as I do here, you will not see me until next summer. However, I don't think I'll like living in San Francisco. I'm afraid of the heat, although they tell me tales of the intense heat here. It has not started yet to my way of thinking.

I wish you would ask Teddy Beaumont to send me the *Sunday Pictorial*. I can send it to Joe, or perhaps it would be better to send it direct to him. The poor boy gets no English papers now. The address is 400 Duboce Avenue, San Francisco, California. Thank you, Fred, for sending *The Watford Observers*. I cannot think that I am so many miles from home when I read them. I am glad Bert is sending the cape, etc. He will have to hold me indebted until there is enough rent paid to cover it. Did you pay Teddy Beaumont for the small seeds for the garden, Fred? I only paid for potatoes and I guess he would never ask. [*Teddy (Edward) Beaumont, a family friend, was looking after the garden at 54 Adrian Road whilst Annie was away. Later, he would move there.*]

My dearest love to you all,

Your loving Mother.

PS. I forgot to mention George Threader [*Lizzie Southam's son from her first marriage to George Threader, Senior*] and his wife, Nellie, and their two children, Jackie and Barbara. However, they see very little of them as she [*Lizzie*] thinks Nellie sees herself above the Southams!

* * * * *

AT THE HUTCHINSON'S IN LONDON, ONTARIO

LONDON, Ontario, is set on the River Thames. The site was selected and the river and town named by Lieutenant-Colonel John Graves Simcoe in 1792 for the location of the capital of Upper Canada (later Ontario), but York (later Toronto) was chosen instead.

Annie travelled about 130 miles to London, Ontario, from St Catharines to visit Lizzie Hutchinson, by now a widow with a son, David. They were not related to Annie but were family friends who emigrated some years earlier from Abbots Langley:

[LETTER 15]

"She is quite sure we would talk all night . . . . . ."

125 Inkerman Street, London, Ontario, Canada
Saturday, 3 July 1937

MY DEARS,

I am staying here for a few days with Mrs Hutchinson and her son, David, having travelled by coach from St Catharines yesterday. I had to change coaches at Hamilton, and for the rest of the journey it rained in torrents. I've never seen blacker clouds. We passed Beamsville, Grimsby, Ingersoll (where dreadful flooding has taken place recently) and many little places but I could not catch their names. For miles and miles the roads were lined each side with cherry trees - but the cherries are not quite like the English ones, being redder and not so sweet. There are places where fruit is displayed by the roadside for sale. There are also huge vineyards and orchards but no fences - just a strand of wire. It strikes me as very strange to see cemeteries by the roadside (no wall or fence) all open to the road and they are immense graveyards. Hamilton is a large city with great factories and wide streets. I saw one huge building with HOLE-PROOF HOSE in great letters on the roof. It cost me $4.60 return to come here.

Mrs Hutchinson has not altered much over the years, save that her hair is white. She has a very nice home and is so glad to see me. Her son, David, who keeps her and the house, is the living image of his father as I knew him. But he is not as healthy looking. He is a mail carrier (postman) and is reckoned to have a good job as it is Government pay. There are more brick houses in Hamilton and London than in St Catharines, not frame-houses. This house is six-roomed with a large scullery sort of place outside and three bedrooms - one of which has been converted to a bathroom - all connected by doors and well furnished. David is a radio fan [*a radio ham or enthusiast*] and his room is partly papered with cards from all over the world telling him of reception, etc, and he has his own cards to send back to new people. They, like Lizzie [*Lizzie Southam*], have no cellar heating but huge stoves which warm the rooms in winter, and a handsome red, black and silver gas stove arrangement with big pipes going round. Lizzie Hutchinson has given me her bedroom and put up a folding bed for herself in her lounge. She is quite sure we would talk all night if we were together and, of course, I prefer it.

A lady friend called yesterday and took us for a ride round the city of London.

[LETTER 15 CONTINUED]
I saw the River Thames which looks like the Colne [*a small river in Hertfordshire*] but it must certainly have swollen to some extent for I was shown houses and garages on its banks which are still unoccupied as the floods reached up to the ceilings. They have Oxford Street, Piccadilly and Hyde Park. Last year, a very fine railway station was opened and our Lord Mayor of London and some of the Aldermen came over with all their regalia and robes and created a great impression as such things are never seen over here. There are immense buildings and hospitals and a very fine University and a large public park with picnic areas all around, each identified with a banner and name, etc. One I saw seemed interesting - LOGAN FAMILY REUNION - evidently a family party with grandparents, parents and hosts of children. There was a miniature railway for the children. We had an ice-cream and then came home for supper.

Everybody is most interested about my coming. They tell me it is because so many people go home for visits but very few come out here to visit them. I hear everywhere of the dreadful trade depression which is only just beginning to lift. It has lasted over five years with thousands brought to poverty and even now hundreds on relief. Only this week I read of garbage men on strike in Baltimore (which is, of course, in the States) as the city was unable to pay their wages - and of the dangerous state of their dustbins. I hear that it was very common for city corporations to be bankrupt.

I've got my pension all right: first three weeks', then four weeks' and shall have another due at the end of July. For the four weeks'- £2 in English money which gave me $9.87, so I'm in funds. [*Annie's Widow's Pension was payable to those over 55 years of age at 10 shillings a week - though Annie would only have got it since 1929 when it was first introduced; it was the same amount as the Old-Age Pension payable from age 70 in 1937.*]

* * *

Monday, 5 July 1937

I WENT to the United Methodist Church yesterday morning with Mrs Hutchinson and David - a very fine church. [*In 1925, the Canadian Methodist Church had joined with the Congregationalist Church and the Presbyterian Church to form the United Church of Canada.*] The choir struck me as strange: two rows of women in the front (all without hats) as if on a concert platform. The preacher was good and I could understand almost all he said but I find it difficult to grasp the Canadian accent with the queer "a" sound. He took as his text: I will lift up mine eyes unto the hills whence cometh my help; Sinai, the Law, Moriah, Prayer, Calvary and Redemption.

There is no service held in any of the principal churches during the summer months in the evenings, so we went round to Ethel's (Mrs Waite's) for supper. Her husband, who had been out here since he was 15, told me it was a real Canadian supper: lettuce, tomatoes, cabbage salad, pickles, cheese and bread - all cut up on separate dishes. Everyone helped themselves - even to the salad dressing. The tea is poured out and you sugar and milk it yourself. We had strawberries in glasses with two or three kinds of cake served with them. I like it better than meat and vegetables for supper but it seems a long time from 6 o'clock to half past eight the next morning. It is a hot day and hotter weather is predicted. We are going into the city after lunch.

It is thundering heavily and it seems likely that there will be a storm. As we came up the street a lady spoke to us and Mrs Hutchinson introduced us. "Come in and sit down and take a cup of tea," she said. We did so and had a look round her shop where she sells what she calls "antiques". I don't. She wanted my brooch. I've had several ask about it and it is thought wonderful. [*Annie's cameo brooch in a gold setting was returned to her daughter, Marion, after she died. Annie is shown wearing it in several of the photographs in the illustrated plates.*]

Have just returned from a tour over the KELLOGG factory which is an immense building (VISITORS WELCOME). White-garbed young men escort parties round. We saw the white corn. Then when it had been toasted quite brown, it was steeped for over nine hours in a salt and sugar solution to give it its characteristic flavour. It was then pressed between huge rollers into large shavings - then into more rollers to make into flakes. We saw girls perched up at the end of great machines putting the flat cartons in things that opened them up into boxes. Then we passed through rooms full of immense ovens (over 20 in a room) where the Kellogg flakes are heated for two minutes and come out as we know them [*Kellogg's Corn Flakes*]. The flakes were dropped into bags by other machines and a girl sat weighing them while others sealed them. Huge cardboard boxes were then filled with the cartons of flakes. To see the machine that closed the boxes and then gummed them was wonderful. It looked almost human. I am sending home the gift I received on leaving. I signed my name on a registration card and we came home.

I shall probably return to St Catharines on Friday and go to Ottawa next week. I'm hoping to have a letter from Joe and to have one from you waiting for me. I have already written to Uncle Joe [*Annie's brother*] and will write to Auntie Elsie [*the wife of Annie's other brother, Matthew*] next week. Give my love to Mrs Arthur Flint. I have to write to Miss Harris an account of my visit to Toronto [*Lois Harris née Munt in Toronto was the sister-in-law of Sarah Harris*] but by the time I've written my jumbled scrawl to you at home, I'm spun out. I was so glad to have Fred's letter. Did the remainder of the apples and pears go bad? Give my love to the Beaumonts.

* * *

8.30pm [*Monday, 5 July 1937*]

HAVE just had a car ride with a very nice man, Mr W Hutchinson (a nephew of Lizzie Hutchinson), who is in business near London and lives during the summer in a cottage by the lakeside. His business house was in the flooded area and he called to see me as his father knew mine [*Matthew Timberlake*]. We drove all round the city and saw where the River Thames (for the first time in knowledge) had risen and destroyed numbers of houses and gardens - rising up to the bedrooms and over the high bridges. We have had ice-cream blocks and now to bed. I see I've repeated myself as I saw the flooded area twice but you must excuse this as I write at odd times.

* * *

Tuesday evening, 6 July 1937

IT is very hot here, 90F in the shade and I feel it although I've got a cold somehow. My chest is tight and my voice very thick. I went down the street and got some ice-cream bricks. We sat outside on the veranda and ate them. I've bought myself a piece of material to make myself another thinner frock when I get back to Lizzie's. I shall need thinner vests, I fear. We went up to the city which is much bigger than St Catharines this afternoon. Mrs Hutchinson's little granddaughter is a rare one to drink at the bubblers. She asks for a drink of "waaater". Everybody is greatly exercised over the fate of Amelia Earhart, the flying lady. [*In 1928 Amelia Earhart was the first woman to fly the Atlantic Ocean; and in 1932 the second person to fly it solo after Charles Lindberg. Amelia Earhart left Oakland, California, with her navigator, Fred Noonan, on 21 May 1937, flying eastwards on a second attempt to fly round the world. She disappeared on 2 July 1937 while flying from Lae, New Guinea, to Howland Island in the Pacific Ocean. This was 2,561 miles with a flying time of 19 hours to reach a sand-bar only 2 miles long and 25ft high. Her last radio message was after 20.14 hours. Navigation was by celestial observations which Fred Noonan had used successfully as navigator in mapping out the PAN-AMERICAN AIRWAYS Clipper flying-boat routes across the Pacific to the Philippines (piloted by Captain Edwin Musick) in the early 1930's. A search was authorised by President Roosevelt involving 66 aeroplanes and 9 ships including an aircraft carrier, but no trace of them was found.*]

Will close and get to bed. It is very hot, not a breath of air indoors or out. My love to you all. Have thought of you all at Broadstairs and wondered what Roger thought of it.

Your loving Mum

PS. Did Mr Beaumont drown Topsy's kittens?

* * * * *

[LETTER 16]

"Drop the pegs into the bottle . . . . . ."

125 Inkerman Street, London, Ontario, Canada
Thursday, 8 July 1937

MY DEAR FRED, MURIEL, MARION AND BERT,

I am sitting on the veranda of Mrs Hutchinson's house and there is not a breath of air. I've never felt such heat, both night and day. You only sleep when you are too tired to keep your eyes open. Yet everyone goes about as usual here, simply lamenting the heat. I am going to a meeting this afternoon and am to recite for them. [*Annie was well known in Abbots Langley for her long recitations and solo songs.*]

I went on a Sunday school Bible Class picnic yesterday to Spring Bank Park. This is a mixed class of about 30 people who meet on Sunday afternoons - all elderly people. All look like grandparents, though white hair is very deceiving over here since many women in their early thirties have pure white hair. They tell me there are several such classes in connection with this church, all connected with Sunday school yet

Wesleyan Methodist Church.

Quarterly Ticket of Membership

DECEMBER, 1910

Beareth all things, believeth all things, hopeth all things, endureth all things.—
1 COR. xiii. 7.

I

Annie Angel

This particular Wesleyan Methodist Church Membership Ticket was for Annie Angel, a Class member at an unnamed chapel. It was found at a car-boot sale (with 19 others for the Class, each ticket named and initialled by the Minister) in the rear pocket of a Wesleyan Methodist Society Class-Book with records of membership 1906-1910.

each separate. I should think they take the place of the old Society Class. [*A system of Class-Meetings of about 12-20 members under a Class-Leader within each Wesleyan Methodist Society were established by John Wesley for the purpose of Christian instruction. The weekly attendance of Members and their contributions were recorded in the Class-Book which stated the Rules of the Society of the People called Methodists.*]

We were taken by a lady in her car, otherwise we would not have gone as the street-cars would have been too hot. I've never seen so much food provided: sandwiches of all kinds, salads, pies, tarts, pickles and ice-cream - all in a great leather container dragged from a car by one of the men. They had games after the meal. I was successful in two guessing competitions and received two prizes - one a little china bon-bon dish and a bag with powder puff, etc, in it. They had a game which I think would do for our Guild socials [*the Wesley Guild socials at the Abbots Langley Methodist church*]. An empty, quart milk bottle and half a dozen clothes pegs, "pins" they call them, is all that is required. Each one in turn tries to drop the pegs into the bottle keeping their arm up level with their waist, as people with long arms would have an advantage. Then the best competitors compete again and one or two little prizes are given. It is a quick game and quite fun.

I saw a black squirrel and folks shouted, "Where's our hats?"

"Why?" asked I.

They laughed and said, "Look out, he's looking for nuts!"

Your loving Mum

PS. I went to the Women's Meeting in London and recited *Beachy Head* and *On For Ever* and they just loved them. One lady said to me afterwards, "That first reading of yours" (by the way - they call them readings here) "was wonderful. It is the spirit of England." [*"Beachy Head" has been found, but not "On For Ever".*]

⋆

The following lines are by "Jim's Wife," on the saving of a boy's life by our late Signalman Coastguard Myles Mahoney (assisted by his Mates) on Beachy Head, August 1900. Mahoney (and his fellow Coastguards) before and since, have been the means of rescuing lives from a similar fate:

YOU KNOW the famous headland that watches Eastbourne town.
Have you ever climbed to the summit, and stood there, and looked down,
Down at the deep sea-water six hundred feet below?
If you have, I haven't. And wouldn't! If you paid me ever so.
I can't look down from a height: for everything seems to crawl,
And I go that dizzy and giddy, I feel I am going to fall.

And the day me and Jim and the children were up upon Beachy Head
Though 'twas really the finest outing we'd had since we were wed -
Though we'd sausage-rolls in a basket, and a mutton pie, and a tart -
And I'd trimmed up my old bonnet till it looked as smart as smart!

Though the sun was shining lovely - the thought of that fearful height,
And that deadly edge, and the children, and never a rail in sight
To save them from falling over! It so upset my mind,
"Jim," I says, "where's the pleasure? I wish that I'd stayed behind."

"Mother," he says, "don't worry. There's nothing on earth to fear!"
But I kept tight hold of Sally that *she* shouldn't go too near.
While the boys, little Dick and Harry, they shouted and ran and played -
Each with the spade we had bought him - not the very least bit afraid!

I tried my best to enjoy it, for the view was vast and wide,
We saw the great ships sailing, far out on the ocean tide.
We saw the Coastguard station, and the flag-mast on the grass.
I stood some minutes, watching, to see a sea-gull pass.

And a little longer, listening, to what the sky-larks said.
For oh! They did sing sweetly, up there on Beachy Head!
And when I turned . . . I can feel it . . . the horror that caught my breath.
Jim was running with Harry, their faces as pale as death.

And in a moment I guessed it . . . and the guessing turned me sick . . .
"Dickie!" I shrieked to them . . . "Dickie! Where is he? *Where is Dick?*"
And my husband caught me . . . "Annie! . . ." his very lips were stiff.
"Annie," he says, "we've lost him . . . he's fallen over the cliff!"

O Lord in Heaven! My youngest! My curly-headed son!
We ran to the Coastguard station for help. And there was one,
A splendid-looking Coastguard, a sitting at his tea.
Married, he was, and a father, 'twas afterwards told to me.
He jumped up straight - I can see him - "Mates! Bring a rope!" says he.

He ran to the verge of the headland, and laid himself flat on the turf
And searched for a sign of Dickie, down, down, to the sand and the surf.
But nothing showed, or fluttered, or cried with a human tongue.
"Quick!" he says. "lower me over!" And over the edge he was swung.

Over the terrible rampart, six hundred feet in height.
I couldn't watch him swinging . . . I hid my eyes from the sight.
But Jim, he watched with the others: and caught a shout of joy -
A shout that rang up to the summit - "He's alive! I can see the boy!"
Aye! He could see, but not reach him. Friends! Let me tell you, slow,
The facts of as brave a rescue as you will ever know.

The child had slid, and was standing, on a ledge six inches wide,
Clinging for life to the bare chalk, dumb, helpless, and terrified,
And sheer between him and rescue stretched two hundred feet, or more,
Of the vast, white cliff that rose upwards like a white wall from the shore.

If the Coastguard's nerve had failed him, we had lost our little son.
But the nerve of the man was iron! He saw what had to be done.
He must cross to the boy - though the crossing looked a task beyond human hope.
Without a thought of the peril he slipped himself OUT of the rope,

And quicker than I can tell it, he got off his boots and his socks,
And clinging naked-footed to the face of those treacherous rocks,
Striking his knife in the crannies and holding on to the hilt!
Sometimes scraping a foothold where the least little slip or tilt

Would have hurled him to destruction! Swarming, crawling, along,
From yard to yard of the distance, daring, and cool, and strong,
Like a fly on a wall he crawled over! And the watchers held their breath!
Knowing the man was playing, at touch and go with Death!

Crawled between earth and heaven, while the sea-birds screamed and fled
And the sea roared far below him - crawled across Beachy Head!
Got to the boy and caught him! . . . *at the very point to drop . . .*
And held him safe till the ropes came down and drew them both to the top!

Jim gave him his watch. 'Twas his father's. 'Twas all he had to give.
I stood there . . . holding Dickie . . . And the longest day I live
I can never tell my feelings. I shook like a shock of wheat.
"If I had the gold of the Indies, I would pour it at your feet.
You are married so they tell me . . . and home and child are sweet . . .

And we're working-folk! We're strangers. Mere strangers from London way . . .
And you've risked your life for my boy's life, that you never saw till this day! . . .
Man!" I says. "Who was your mother? May she be living to hear
That the son she bore is a Hero! . . ."; "She's livin'," he says, "never fear!

And a good mother too. But Lord love you! Don't call me a hero!" says he.
"Every Jack o' my mates here standin', would have done it as well as me,
And better maybe. Now young 'un," and he patted Dickie's head,
"No more of these *larks*!" As I'm living, that's what that Coastguard said!
And he handed the watch back to Jimmy, and says he, a flushing red,

"I'd as lief not keep it, Mister. Thank you kindly all the same."
And was turning off to leave us. Us, that didn't know his name!
And yet owed him a debt so mighty! So mighty! . . . I burst into tears.
"Oh wait . . . we could never repay you though we tried for a hundred years.

But as sure as the prayers of a mother can call down a blessing from Heaven,
As I kneel by this child you have rescued that blessing to you will be given."
He turned round as simple as nothing! "Now don't you take on," says he,
" 'Twas in the day's work, and a pleasure. And I'm off now *to finish my tea!*"

I don't know what Mullins was thinking, but he gave a cough and a sneeze.
And wiped his eyes for a wonder. And sat as mum as you please.
"It's well," I said, "with the country that can breed such men as these!"
Thank God! For the hero spirit that lives where the British tread.
Thank God! For the brave hearts beating in the Coastguards of Beachy Head.

[*This monologue "Beachy Head" was published in the early 1900s as a 4-page leaflet by Farncombe & Co Ltd, Printers, Eastbourne.*]

* * * * *

Annie Kimpton's cameo brooch

1. A studio photograph of Mary Ann Gates née Coleman, "Grandma Gates" - the maternal grandmother of Annie Kimpton née Timberlake, taken about 1880. Mary Ann and her husband James Gates lived in the hamlet of Astrope, by Puttenham, near Tring in Hertfordshire. She was also the maternal grandmother of the Hawkins family who emigrated from Abbots Langley to Canada in the early 1900's, whom Annie Kimpton visited in 1937.

Matthew Timberlake — *Annie (Elizabeth Annie) Timberlake* — *Mary Timberlake née Gates*

Matthew Timberlake, Junior — *Joseph Timberlake*

2. The Timberlake family taken about 1880 (before Fanny was born in 1881) showing Matthew and Mary Timberlake with their children. Matthew was a bricklayer from Nash Mills, near Abbots Langley.

Annie (Elizabeth Annie) Timberlake 1871-1938 — *Matthew Timberlake, Junior 1877-1934* — *Joseph Timberlake 1874-1942 (later of Hastoe Farm)*

Matthew Timberlake 1845-1933 — *Mary Timberlake née Gates 1846-1912* — *Fanny Dorrofield Timberlake 1881-1897*

3. A studio photograph of the Timberlake family taken about 1895 (before Annie married David Kimpton) showing Matthew and Mary Timberlake with their children. Fanny died two years later in 1897. This photograph and the other studio photographs were taken by William Coles *of 60 Queens Road, Watford.*

4. A photograph of Annie Kimpton née Timberlake, probably taken in 1897 about the time of her marriage to David Kimpton. She is wearing her favourite cameo brooch which is mentioned in her letters from Canada.

5. A studio photograph of David Kimpton, probably taken in 1897. David came from Leavesden near Abbots Langley, in Hertfordshire. He was a blacksmith at the St Pancras Industrial Schools and at the Leavesden Asylum.

David's family were recorded living at Leavesden Green, in the censuses of 1871, 1881 and 1891. Next door to them lived Phoebe Spencer. She was also living there in the 1861 census as a 30-year old. Phoebe was a dressmaker. In 1908, when she was crippled by rheumatism, she made Matthew Timberlake and David Kimpton her Trustees. Annie Kimpton née Timberlake was apprenticed to a dressmaker in Leavesden. It seems highly likely that she was apprenticed to Phoebe Spencer - and that was how Annie Timberlake met David Kimpton.

6. A studio photograph of Annie and David Kimpton's children, Joe aged 7 and Marion aged 2, taken about 1904 (before Fred was born in 1905).

7. A mounted photograph of Matthew Timberlake taken on his 60th birthday, 1 September 1905. Matthew founded the Wesleyan Methodist Society in Abbots Langley, Hertfordshire, in 1878.

Arthur (Reuben Arthur) Flint 1878-1962 — *George (Jeffrey George) Flint 1881-1965* — *Ethel Rose Flint (later Mrs Blades) 1887-1934* — *"Moss" (Maurice) Harry Flint 1865-1964* — *Margaret Flint (later Mrs Filby) 1883-1960*

Reuben Flint 1854-1925 — *Emily Flint née Dolamore 1856-1928* — *Florence Flint (later Mrs Lunnon) 1871-1952* — *Maud (Fanny Maud Flint) 1890-1934*

Hilda Flint (later Mrs Hulett) 1898-1974 — *Edie (Edith) Emily Flint 1895-1965* — *Len (Leonard) Flint 1892-1975*

8. The Flint family showing "Old" Reuben Flint, his wife Emily and their ten children taken on 21 June 1905 at the wedding of their son George (Jeffrey George) to Edith (Edie) Quebell. It was one of a series of wedding photographs probably taken at the Quebell's home in Abbots Langley, Hertfordshire. Arthur and George had established FLINT BROTHERS, builders and decorators, five years earlier in 1900. This photograph was taken by A J GIFFEN of St Albans.

9a & 9b. A FLINT BROTHERS' *manhole cover (above) in the drive of 75 Oakdene, Trowley Rise, the former home of Len, Amy and Ivy Flint and another (below) in the garden of 80 Abbots Road, Abbots Langley, Hertfordshire, the home of Reg Nice. Reg has pointed out that* FLINT BROTHERS' *houses can often be identified by the use of pebble-dash protection for the upper walls, above a projecting tile drip-course.*

Frederick David Kimpton 1905-1984

Joseph Matthew Kimpton 1897-1972

David Kimpton 1872-1913

Annie (Elizabeth Annie) Kimpton 1871-1938

Marion Timberlake Kimpton 1902-1982

10. A studio photograph of the Kimpton family taken about 1910 showing David and Annie Kimpton with their three children. David died of pernicious anaemia three years later in 1913, aged 41, when Annie was aged 42 and their children were aged 8, 11 and 16.

Matthew Timberlake, Annie's father

Jim Gates, Annie's cousin from Dover

Marion Kimpton, Annie's daughter

Annie Kimpton née Timberlake

Fred Kimpton, Annie's son

Carrie Gates née Plested, Jim's wife

11. Annie Kimpton's family with her cousin, Jim Gates, and his wife, Carrie, taken about 1917 in the garden at 54 Adrian Road, Abbots Langley, Hertfordshire. Annie's eldest son, Joe, was away in India with the army at this time during the First World War (1914-1918).

In 1931 Marion Kimpton married Bert Flint who was a carpenter with FLINT BROTHERS builders and decorators. Bert Flint took over FLINT BROTHERS at the time of his marriage to Marion and they moved into Conway, Marlin Square, next to the builders' yard. Bert's father, Arthur Flint, retired to his new house, Hempton, Greenways, Abbots Langley, which FLINT BROTHERS built.

12. Annie Kimpton in front of her home, 54 (on the right) & 56 (on the left) Adrian Road, Abbots Langley, Hertfordshire, taken about 1920. The covered way which was converted into a garage by her son, Fred Kimpton, is on the right. A magnifying glass discloses that the poster in the window says:

ABBOTS LANGLEY
WESLEYAN CHURCH
CHURCH
ANNIVERSARY
SERVICES
SUNDAY JULY 24

These houses were built by Annie's father, Matthew Timberlake, using the same kind of cream bricks that were used for the Wesleyan Methodist chapel and schoolroom (completed in 1881) and for the neighbouring Temple Villas (with the building date "1880" picked out in red bricks).

These cream facing bricks, known as "Suffolk Yellows" (from the Ipswich area), were used for the Leavesden Asylum and the St Pancras Industrial Schools (all completed in the 1870's). A few other houses in Abbots Langley were also built with these bricks: some in Adrian Road; two in the upper part of Abbots Road; one in Breakspeare Road; the earliest houses in Marlin Square along its southern side; and those on the approach to The Ring at Tanners Hill. Most likely a surplus quantity of these bricks was sold off after completion of the huge institutional buildings.

13. The Cadets of Temperance Festival at the Crystal Palace, Sydenham near Croydon, Surrey, on 20 May 1925. Mabel Botwright née Funnel recalled that she, Jack Botwright, Annie Kimpton's daughter Marion, and Ciss Smith attended as Cadets. Ciss Smith remembered that Annie made their special dresses. The Crystal Palace, a huge glass conservatory designed to house the Great Exhibition of 1851 in Hyde Park, London, was rebuilt at Sydenham and was later destroyed by fire on 30 November 1936.

In the July/August 1999 "Abbots Langley Methodist Church Newsletter", Ciss Smith wrote:

"My brother and I joined the Sons of Temperance - we called it the Band of Hope. Mr [Matthew] Timberlake was in charge, Mr Becket played the concertina for the singing and Mrs [Annie] Kimpton recited lovely long poems. We practised for a whole year the 12 songs which were to be sung at the Crystal Palace. There were five thousand children from all over the country singing their hearts out. We travelled in open-topped, double-decker buses with all the streamers flying. What an unforgettable day!"

Aubrey Cox — *Basil Funnell* — *Walter Cox* — *Bernard Funnell*

Harry Hamlin [Superintendant 1929-1937] — *Frank Flint* — *Aubrey Grey* — *Matthew Timberlake* — *Beattie Ellwood*

– West — *Dolly (Dorothy) Cox* — *May Miles* — *Emmy (Emily) Hart* — *Jack Botwright* — *Marion Kimpton*

Madge Cox — *– Wainwright* — *– Miles* — *Vera Miles* — *– Miles*

14 & 15. The Abbots Langley Wesleyan Methodist Sunday school outing in July 1925 to Sheethanger Common, Box Lane, Boxmoor, Hertfordshire. This is reproduced from Jack Botwright's copy of the photograph. The names were written later by Marion Flint née Kimpton on the back of her copy of the photograph. Three generations of Sunday school teachers were on this outing: Matthew Timberlake (Superintendent 1879-1929), his daughter Annie Kimpton, and her daughter Marion Kimpton aged 23 (a later Superintendent 1937-1970). Marion Kimpton is sitting next to Jack Botwright.

Arthur Grey — *Norman Flint* — *Levi Cox* — *Walter Flint* — *Roland Funnell*

Nellie Munt — *– Briars*

David Cox — *Dorothy Wainwright* — *Mrs George Flint* — *Annie Kimpton* — *Queenie East* — *Mrs David Cox*

Don Flint [in front of his mother] — *Nora Flint*

Gwen Tansley — *Kitty Tansley* — *Ivy Flint* — *Margaret Flint* — *Edna Flint* — *Hilda Cox*

In 1997 Jack Botwright's wife, Mabel, aged 91 handed copies of the 1937 Methodist Church Fête programme, the 1936-1937 Wesleyan Guild Syllabus, the 1936 Lord Mayor's Banquet Toast List, and this photograph to Mary Flint, Marion's daughter-in-law. She told Mary that Jack had been interested in Marion at the time.

Note: this photograph is divided into two parts with an overlap.

In Loving Memory of
FANNY DORROFIELD TIMBERLAKE,
WHO ENTERED INTO REST JULY 6TH 1897
IN HER 16TH YEAR.
ALSO OF MARION DOWSE,
OCT 20TH 1889 IN HER 4TH YEAR,
EDITH MARION,
DEC 31ST 1884, AGED 8 MONTHS,
MATTHEW HENRY,
MAY 11TH 1873, AGED 3 MONTHS
(WHOSE BODIES REST NEAR)
CHILDREN OF
MATTHEW & MARY TIMBERLAKE.
"BLESSED ARE THE PURE IN HEART FOR THEY SHALL SEE GOD."

IN
LOVING MEMORY OF
MARY TIMBERLAKE
SUDDENLY CALLED HOME,
JUNE 14TH 1914, AGED 68 YEARS.
ALSO OF MATTHEW,
BELOVED HUSBAND OF THE ABOVE,
WHO ENTERED INTO REST AUG 17TH 1933
IN HIS 88TH YEAR.
"OH HAPPY SAINTS ARE EVER BLEST
IN THAT DEAR HOME HOW SWEET THEIR REST."

16. The headstones and their inscriptions in the parish churchyard of the Church of St Lawrence, Abbots Langley, Hertfordshire, on the graves of Matthew and Mary Timberlake (on the right) and of their four children who died whilst young (on the left).

The cause of death given on the certificate for each of the children was: Fanny Dorrofield Timberlake - "Tubercular Peritonitis Exhaustion" (tuberculosis affecting the abdomen); Marion Dowse - "Croup Asphyxia" (an infection of the larynx preventing breathing); Edith Marion - "Bronchitis"; and Matthew Henry - "Astheneia and Convulsions" (weakness or debility, possibly from a fever).

RETURN TO 13 IDA STREET

FROM LONDON, Ontario, Annie Kimpton returned briefly to stay with Ted and Lizzie Southam in St Catharines before visiting relatives in Ottawa:

[LETTER 17]

"The flies and mosquitos are still selecting me for their prey. . . . . ."

13 Ida Street, St Catharines, Ontario, Canada
Saturday, 10 July 1937

MY DEARS,

Well, here I am again back at St Catharines and I'm not too sorry. I can keep cooler here. I came home here Friday evening by bus. It was crammed with folk going to Niagara. There was a cool breeze as we tore along but from the waist down it seemed like sitting in a hot greenhouse. I am enclosing a newspaper cutting telling of the weather. I get mosquito bites on my legs and arms and they serve me like wasp stings - great swellings and blisters. Lizzie [*Southam*] is alarmed as they fear infection here (we would call it septic). I found a letter from Joe, two from Marion and one from Bert's mother awaiting me. You can't imagine how glad I was and the snaps of the Broadstairs four are fine. I love them. My dear little boys - isn't it good of them all? That one of David alone is worth enlarging. I thought the Fête programme well put together. I reckon that neither the Anglicans nor the Catholics could equal that. [*There was little friendliness between the churches in Abbots Langley in 1937. A generation later, both the Anglican Vicar and the Roman Catholic priest attended Bert Flint's funeral in 1978 at the Methodist church, in recognition of his service to the village.*]

Lizzie has made arrangements for me to go to a garden party next week. It should have been a strawberry party but it was postponed because of the rain - so now it is a raspberry party. I bought two pieces of silky washed material in London for I shall die in my warm dark dresses. So I'm going to be busy. I am enclosing Alta's letter. She could not write in a more welcoming strain could she? [*This letter has not been kept.*] Am also enclosing a few snaps taken in front of Lizzie's house and another taken at the back and one of me with the lovely delphiniums, the tallest being 5ft tall.

* * *

Sunday morning, 11 July 1937

JUST home from church. As we left, a crash was heard and three cars were in collision. The first, an Oregon car, had stopped suddenly and the two following had crashed into it. The last one was the worst damaged - his bumpers were broken, his windscreen smashed and a little child badly cut. I heard the new minister this morning. He is a fine preacher, most imposing-looking in his gown and bands. He took as his text: Judge ye for yourselves. It seems strange to see fans being waved all over the church. I wonder how the Rev Albert Jones would cope with it if he cannot even stand the old clock ticking? [*The clock on the chapel wall by which the minister was expected to time his sermon.*] Here is an announcement given out in church today: "The Young Peoples' Association at Thorold invite the young people of Westminster church to a swimming gala and competition at No 15 Beach. Cars outside the church at 7 o'clock. All invited."

At home in England we think our petrol stations disfigure the landscape, but you should see the garish looking places over here: all glaring lights and signs for HOT DOGS, HAMBURGERS, FRIED CHICKEN, CHICKEN SANDWICHES, ICES, COCKTAILS, 44 BEER, COCO-COLA, ICED DRINKS, etc, etc. Then by the road (where the huts and camps are for tourists), there are signs such as, JOHN AND MARY . . . BATH AND BED . . . and GASOLENE AND GREASING. By the by, there is no paraffin oil or kerosene - it's called "coal oil" and petrol is "gasolene".

Jim [*Hawkins*] took Lizzie and me for a ride last night. We went to the Lakeside Road, all so green and cool, a lovely road with Niagara-on-the-Lake in sight and the USA on the opposite side. The green wooded heights were clearly visible and houses, jetties, boats, speedboats and lovely looking farms all along the American side. We went to Butler's Burial Ground, a place most beautifully kept up by the Government. It is the private burial place of General Butler and his family, a noted soldier who fought for Canada in 1700 when it was all bush along the Niagara River. He was one of the first British settlers. [*Colonel John Butler led the Loyalist Rangers and American-Indians against the rebels in 1778 during the American Revolutionary War.*] Jim tells me that the oldest dwellings in Canada are in this district. Jim is going to teach me to sing *O Canada!* so that I'll have a solo to sing for the Wesley Guild.

★

THE Canadian patriotic song "O Canada!" was composed by Calixa Lavallée in 1880 to French words by Sir Adolphe Basile Routhier and the English text was written by Robert Stanley Weir in 1908. The song was not officially adopted as the Canadian national anthem until 1980. These are the first two verses:

O CANADA! Terre de nos aieux,
Ton front est ceint de fleurons glorieux!
Car ton bras sait porter l'épée,
Il sait porter la croix! Ton histoire est une épopée,
Des plus brillants exploits. Et ta valeur, de foi trempée,
Protégera nos foyers et nos droits,
Protégera nos foyers et nos droits.

Sous l'oeil de Dieu, près du fleuve géant,
Le Canadien frandit en espérant.
Il est né d'une race fière,
Béni fut son berceau. Le ciel a marqué sa carrière
Dans ce monde nouveau. Toujours guidé par sa lumière,
Il gardera l'honeur de son drapeau,
Il gardera l'honeur de son drapeau.

O CANADA! Our home and native land!
True patriot love in all thy sons command.
With glowing hearts we see thee rise,
The True North strong and free; from far and wide,
O Canada, we stand on guard for thee.
God keep our land, Glorious and free!
O Canada! We stand on guard for thee.

O Canada! Where pines and maples grow,
Great prairies spread and lordly rivers flow,
How dear to us thy broad domain,
From East to Western sea! Thou land of hope
For all who toil! Thou True North strong and free!
God keep our land, Glorious and free!
O Canada! We stand on guard for thee.

★ ★ ★

Monday [*12 July 1937*]

I must close this letter. There has been a tremendous thunderstorm with hail during the night but the air is cooler. However, the flies and mosquitoes are still selecting me for their prey and my face and neck are getting like Miss Peckett's.

My dearest love to you all,

Your loving Mum

PS. Excuse the writing in pencil but I often write in my bedroom. What would you think of a shop (this was in St Catharines) double-fronted, which displayed a window full of Eno's Fruit Salts on one side and rolls of toilet paper on the other? And seen in Montréal, this advert across a shop window: "KING GEORGE PEAS IN TWO-QUART CANS".

You know that Americans call a sort of horse and cart - a "horse and buggy"? Well, this is what was asked:

"What is worse than a dog with fleas?"

"A horse with a buggy behind!"

* * * * *

[LETTER 18]

"I never saw such a mixture"

13 Ida Street, St Catharines, Ontario, Canada
Saturday, 17 July 1937

MY DEARS,

This is Saturday morning and I am in my room in my dressing-gown waiting until I hear Ted and Lizzie [*Southam*] move. Ted was working until 12pm last night so they do not rise quite so early on Saturdays. Usually he is away by 7am. The weather is still very hot. I do not enjoy it, perhaps because I'm not dressed for it. I cannot go around (as most do here) with no underclothes or in shorts. I shall be glad when it gets cooler and the flies and mosquitoes leave me alone. Otherwise I'm still having a good time. I'm thinking of going to Ottawa next week. I have been to the railway depot and to the bus station. The midday train leaves here at 1pm and gets to Ottawa at 10pm. The morning train is too early and the night train would mean staying all night in Toronto (where all trains change) and it would cost $16.89. The bus at night leaves here at 7pm and gets there next morning at 7am and costs $14 - so I'll go by coach.

I was glad to get all the letters from Muriel, Fred and Marion, and today I have received the *Methodist Recorders*, etc. After all, £70 was worth the effort made at the Fête. Who is the Mr Dock mentioned amongst those who died during the last quarter? Is it the Mr Dock from Kings Langley?

Jim took me for a ride round on Saturday evening. We went to Welland City, Port Erie (which is on the shore of Lake Erie), Stevensville, Chippawa, Ridgeway and Niagara where I said good-bye to the Falls. We came along by the Niagara River above the Falls and could see the city of Buffalo, USA, on the opposite side - and

[LETTER 18 CONTINUED]
then home. I sent for a block of ice-cream which makes a nice piece each when divided into four and we ate it before going to bed. We had supper at 6 o'clock: ham, potato salad, cheese, beet, tomatoes, tomato chutney, radishes, jelly, fresh raspberries and cake to follow. All these are on the table together and everyone has some of each of the first course on their plates at one and the same time. I never saw such a mixture.

On Sunday, I went to church twice and Jim [*Hawkins*] took me and Lizzie [*Southam*] for a ride again in the afternoon. The new parson is a good preacher. In the morning he took two texts, one: Christ standing in the midst, the door being shut when Jesus appeared after the Resurrection and: Behold I stand at the door and knock. I like his sermons. Our afternoon ride was to a fresh part by the Niagara River - to a place called Virgil. Then past queer little hamlets just like we read about in America - with a little wooden school and a little wooden church with a long open shed beside it where, in past years, the farmers put their horses and buggies but now use to park their cars. I am making myself a striped frock, blue with a fine black line in it. I hope it will turn out all right.

* * *

Monday night, 19 July 1937

I AM just going to bed. Ted, Lizzie and I have been to the pictures to see *Captains Courageous*. It was very good. I think Ted and Lizzie were disappointed because there was no *Micky Mouse* or something similar. We also saw Fred Perry in *Tennis Tactics* - some in slow motion, every movement of him very graceful. [*Fred J Perry won three consecutive Wimbledon Men's Singles Championships for Britain, 1934-1936. He then turned professional and also became an American citizen.*]

I'm sorry about my Fred's face. Do hope it's all right by now and that Roger is OK. Do you know, it comes over me how far you all are from me and I feel a fearful panic lest anything should happen to any of you. I feel I must come back at once and have almost to hold on to my chair and call myself a fool. I have written to Uncle Joe and Auntie Elsie, to Nellie Higginbotham and to Auntie Jennie [*Stanton*]. I will write to Miss Harris directly and reply to Mrs Arthur Flint [*Ethel Flint, Bert Flint's mother*].

I am enclosing two samples of chewing gum I had given to me in the street. I've got my return ticket to Ottawa - $14, as I said. Have had to have my shoes soled and heeled - cost $1.45. I'm getting quite expert with the money. On my way home this evening, I saw a large board on a fence saying: "CLEAN DIRT MAY BE PLACED HERE". It struck me as strange. The pieces of grass are very common here and the field looks all pinky-mauve where it grows. I've never seen any before. [*Annie probably enclosed some of the grass with her letter.*] The snaps are of places nearby and the girl's mother is Mrs Wenham. Lizzie's friend (the girl) and the young man are to be married in September. It is to be a church wedding which is quite remarkable as people over here get married in any old place. I got weighed the other day and weigh 142lbs.

* * *

Wednesday night, 21 July 1937

I'VE just returned from a Ladies Aid picnic at Niagara-on-the-Lake. A bus load of women and several full cars went from the church. It's a lovely place by the Lake [*Lake Ontario*] and there were games, competitions and a great supper comprising cold chicken and stuffing, ham, salads and pickles, pies, cake and ice-cream. Everyone brings something and tea is provided - all for 30 cents including the ride. Of course most of the grub is given. I had my first "popsickle" which is really sweet fruit-flavoured ice (not ice-cream but frozen water) on a small stick. There were two together in paper wrappers and you suck them or gnaw them as you prefer. There was lemon, orange or chocolate - so I chose the orange flavour. They had one competition which most of the ladies joined, the minister being umpire. They each kicked one of their shoes off as far as they could and the one that went the furthest won. Some kicked very high and some yards off.

One Sunday we passed a group of young fellows by the roadside and one of them appeared to be on the look out. "What are they at?" I asked Jim.

"Oh," said he, "they are playing Shoot and Crap." He laughed at my surprise, for crap suggested quite another thing to me. He said that it was no doubt where the word came from. It is an illegal gambling game and the police are always looking out for them, hence the suspicion of all cars that pass. [*"Craps" is the North American name for gambling with dice. Dice-throwing was introduced in New Orleans around 1809 by a French Creole who was known as "Johnny (Jean) Crapaud". Crapaud is toad in French - the nickname for a Frenchman derived from the heraldic device of the ancient Kings of France, three toads. Hence "Crapaud's game" and its forshortening. Crap was also a seventeenth century colloquialism for rubbish, which later came to mean excrement. Quite co-incidentally, Thomas Crapper was the name of the Victorian sanitary engineer who perfected the flush water-closet in 1875. His name was cast on the water cisterns and gave rise to a corresponding term which American First World War soldiers took back with them.*]

* * *

Thursday, 22 July 1937

SUCH a hot night and on such nights I sleep badly. Also, I was well-bitten at the picnic. I see by the records in the papers that Ottawa is hotter than St Catharines. That I will soon find out. When I told some ladies of our Fête and the £70 raised not being as much as hoped, they said: "Good gracious, money must flow in the Old Country. That is $350 and that sounds a lot." I'll close this disjointed epistle with my dear love to you all. Give my love to Marie and Jim and the youngsters. Has Robin had his tonsils operated upon yet? [*Robin was a son of Marie and Jim Kimpton. The Baptismal Register at the Abbots Langley Methodist church, with records from 1910 to the present day, shows he was christened Robert Thomas in 1931. Robin is a diminutive of Robert.*]

Your loving Mum

* * * * *

WITH THE STANTONS IN OTTAWA

OTTAWA, formerly Bytown, is the capital of Canada and is in eastern Ontario on the Ontario/Québec boundary at the confluence of the Ottawa, Gatineau and Rideau Rivers. Ottawa is a prominent cultural centre with three distinctive universities and the major employer is the Federal Government.

When Samuel de Champlain first visited the area in 1613, the rivers served as passageways for explorers and fur-traders. With the coming of the Napoleonic Wars, Britain needed timber and the Ottawa valley was an excellent source. Lieutenant-Colonel John By of the Royal Engineers constructed the Rideau Canal between 1826-1832 to make the Rideau River a safe route from the St Lawrence River to Lake Ontario, away from the USA border and bypassing the St Lawrence River rapids. He established his base at the site of Ottawa and this spurred the development of the city. In the 1850's, Queen Victoria chose Ottawa as the capital of Canada. In 1937, Canada's Prime Minister, William Lyon Mackenzie King, brought the architect Jacques Greber from France to redevelop the National Capital District.

Annie Kimpton arrived in Ottawa to visit her cousin Jennie (Edith Jane) and Jennie's husband Bob Stanton, who had emigrated to Canada in 1914. They had a son, Jack, and a daughter, Muriel. Jennie's mother, formerly Elizabeth Delafield née Timberlake, was Annie's aunt, one of Matthew Timberlake's sisters. Much earlier, Elizabeth Delafield had been widowed and had then married her brother-in-law, Joseph Dorrofield, when his wife, Fanny (née Timberlake) who was Matthew's other sister, died:

[LETTER 19]

"I felt I wished I could have told my dad . . . . . ."

Rivermead PO, Ottawa, Ontario, Canada
Thursday, 29 July 1937

MY DEARS,

This is Thursday and I arrived here last Saturday morning. My journey here was a bit tiring. I left St Catharines at a quarter to eight on Friday evening, having had to wait three quarters of an hour for the bus. He evidently meant to make up for lost time as we went hell-for-leather into Toronto where I had to change buses. We got there at half past ten and as it was a distance of 75 miles you can tell how fast we raced. The bus was a very large one and I had a pillow for 15 cents but, oh dear, what rough roads! We had two stops of ten minutes duration on the way, one at a place called Kingston and the name of the other I didn't catch. Then when we got to Prescott, the Ottawa passengers had to change again though by this time it was morning. The rest of the journey was over very nice roads [*a further 210 miles*] and I watched the sun rise. This part of the country seems more cultivated and orderly with not so many road-houses [*motels*] and glaring signs.

I was told that Ottawa was the place of the elite and I should think so. I got off at the bus terminus and (as it was only a quarter to six in the morning) I waited awhile then took a taxi (which cost $1.50) as it was such a long way from the city. I got here before my letter did, as they only go to the post office once a week to collect letters - either on a Friday or Saturday. Jennie Stanton made me welcome and soon got me something to eat. I should not have recognised Bob Stanton. He is a little man - a bit bent over, his hair and little tooth-brush moustache quite white, and he wears smoked glasses. He has a very responsible job as a golf-keeper [*a greenkeeper*].

The house (which is a two-storied white-painted wooden building - a typical Canadian house) has no carpets but has congoleum squares on all floors, with rugs and rockers. The ceilings are much higher than in Lizzie's house and the windows and rooms are larger. One queer feature is that there are no handles on the bedroom doors and every door is left wide open. I close mine up as far as possible and as they are very heavy, it stays put! I have Muriel's room and I can see that Jennie and Muriel have single beds in another room and Jack and his father are in another. Bob is a most polite little man, both to Jennie and to me. He has 15 men and boys under him and the golf club-house is to be seen in the distance. Their house stands alone with the golf-course, tees, greens and bunkers all around. During the summer no one is allowed to go outside while members are on the greens. Nor is any radio, loud speaking, singing, laughing or piano playing to be heard in case it puts any player off their stroke - because players and caddies pass close to the windows. A public road goes across the course and we take a 25-minute ride beside wooded slopes and pretty cottages with the Ottawa River running alongside. We can see the river from the house and it looks just like a vast lake. Then there is a 10-minute walk to the tram halt, a little shelter beside the rails. Parties of bathers, families and children board the tram at intervals and then we arrive at the city. Every notice and every shop has its name and goods duplicated in English and French. The French language is heard as much as English.

They took me into Ottawa on Saturday evening and we went to an immense place - a railway hotel - with huge stairways, vestibules and halls looking just like the House of Commons [*the Château Laurier*]. There are rooms where you can get meals at almost any price you wish to pay but we went to the cafeteria where the menu is given on huge silver-coloured cards. You take a tray with a napkin rolled with knife, fork and spoons inside and rest the tray upon chrome rails and slide it along as you select your meal. White-garbed chefs serve you and I've never seen such arrays of lovely-looking food before. It made you wish to try it all, with each thing in its own little dish. We had chicken cutlets, chip-potatoes, white sauce, roll and butter, with coffee served in individual silver coffee-pots. At the end of the rail a girl just casts her eye over your tray and gives you a slip stating the meal price. You then select a table and a girl in gold and brown uniform spreads your table for you and takes your tray and cash. We had ice-cream to follow. Apparently the place is always full of customers. Afterwards we went to a show and saw *The Singing Marine* which was quite good and then came back by tram.

When we got back, Jack (Jennie's son) was home. He is a tall dark handsome chap with black hair smoothed back and keen dark eyes. He has a big nose like Uncle Sam's and a big mouth with a lovely set of teeth. I think he is a book-keeper. His mother adores him. Muriel, her daughter, is tiny and wears glasses, has been very delicate and for five years has had eye trouble necessitating that she stays at home.

[LETTER 19 CONTINUED]
I think Jennie is a bit dominant and that Muriel has a bit of an inferiority complex. She is sensitive about her appearance, looks nice when dressed for church but at home would pass for only 18 - but tells me she is actually 29! Muriel has a slight cast or something in the left eye - at least the pupil turns slightly outwards.

It is quite cool and cloudy today and the water looks grey - reflecting the clouds. I've never seen such greensward - just like green velvet. Jennie's house is rent-free and she also has free ice from the big club-house. This is a great consideration in this land. The rooms are painted or distempered pale green or blue with white ceilings. They have no front veranda, only steps to the door as they would not be able to use it during the day as the golfers pass close to the windows. There is a pump nearby from a very deep artesian well for the convenience of club members and the water is ice-cold. They are very proud of it. There is no hot-water system and the water for washing and for the lavatory comes from the river and also no electricity - lamps and candles only. They have a nice radio which has to be muted during the day lest any noise should put the grandees of their stroke. In the winter they are so isolated that tradesmen cannot, or will not, come here and they have to fetch everything themselves from Ottawa. Some winters they bake their own bread as they can only go once or twice a week to the city.

I fear I would never go to church if I lived this far away. Jennie tells me that it costs her 4/6d [*Annie means the equivalent of 4 shillings and 6 pence*] per Sunday for the three of them - Bob, Jennie and Muriel - for the tram fare and their collection. Many of the churches here are closed during the summer until September, or several unite for a week or so. Jennie's church in Aylmer is closed, so we went on Sunday evening to the Methodist church in McCleod Street, Ottawa. It is the church where Uncle William was once minister and I saw the manse where they all lived and where Auntie Bessie from Watford stayed when she was engaged to Albert who paid for her to come out here. [*Matthew Timberlake recorded in his diary that his brother, William Timberlake, a carpenter who later became a Wesleyan Methodist minister, left England on 19 January 1871 - sailing from Liverpool to Canada on the* ALLEN LINES *SS "Peruvian". Jennie's sister, Bessie (Elizabeth Dowse) Timberlake née Delafield, daughter of Matthew's sister Elizabeth, married Albert Timberlake, a first cousin and the son of Joseph Timberlake, another of Matthew's brothers. Bessie would have come out to Canada to visit her sister, Jennie Stanton.*]

It is a large, square church and the great organ fills one corner of it - the pipes going up to the ceiling - and the seats in a semi-circle, sloping down slightly from the main door. There was no choir but a big man sat alongside the organist and sang a solo, *Just For Today*. The minister is an old man who took for his text: Because they have no knowledge, the people perish. A good sermon but I shouldn't think there were more than 60 people there and it was very, very hot. I felt I wished I could have told my dad that I'd been to one of Uncle Will's churches, but perhaps he knew. They have some magnificent buildings in Ottawa. The Houses of Parliament are very fine but, to me, not so imposing as ours at home. We hope to go sightseeing tomorrow. I shall get some views of Ottawa. It is queer to be so far from a shop and to have no post.

I have read one of John Buchan's books since I've been here, *The House of the Four Winds*. They have heaps of books and magazines here which suits me down to the ground. They also do a lot of crochet work, knitting, lace-making and reading as they are prevented from going out much in the winter, are restricted in the summer by the golfers, and are far from both neighbours and the city. I've never been in a quieter spot in my life. Everything here is beautifully clean, the paint spotless, the floors painted brown and with floorcloth squares. Bedrooms are the same, only a rug to stand on by the bed. In every room there is a hole where the stove pipes come through which are used in winter.

Jennie tells me that her Jack was very ill last winter with appendicitis ("appendiceetus" as they call it here). It happened when they were snowbound and Bob had to get a team of men to dig a path down to the tram and to carry him down to go to hospital. They were quite a while waiting before they could get a doctor here and he had to leave his car a long way away and struggle through snow above his knees. Jack had a narrow squeak for life as the abscess burst before he could get to hospital. It takes about an hour and a quarter by car to get to the hospital. I felt glad that England is so small!

I have sat by the window all the afternoon and have been writing and have seen no one pass down the road, save one car and a man with a roller. There is nothing but a flowerbed, clumps of trees, lovely undulating greensward and the mighty river in the distance - almost complete isolation. What must it be like in the winter? They tell me that when the snow is falling you can see nothing from the window but the snow falling an inch away or so. It is like a fine powdered sugar and (when on the ground) sparkles until your eyes ache and run from the glare. From these windows they often see people negotiating the slopes outside on their hands and knees. I'd rather hear about it than experience it. Old England for me any time. My bites are getting better and the huge freckles on my hands are fading with these two days of cooler weather. Two ladies have just come into view with their golf-clubs. They have white hats and skirts, blue jumpers, ankle socks and huge bare legs but they have no caddies. They are evidently going round the three-mile course on their own.

Jennie [*Stanton*] does not correspond with any of the Montréal cousins [*the Rev William Timberlake's children*] for they evidently think her far beneath them, or used to do so. I shall not go to see them for it will cost me quite a bit of money from here to Montréal and it is about a six-hour journey. As I do not really know them, except for Bowman [*one of the Rev William Timberlake's sons*], I don't mind if I never see them for I'm sure they think me very inferior. I shan't go. I will probably go back to St Catharines about August and will then write to Cousin Ben [*Hawkins*] about going to Rochester. He will find out roughly what it will cost for me to travel to Joe's and then I'll get the rest of my cash transferred to San Francisco. I told Joe that I'd probably come in August - so shall stay only about a week with Ben and Alice as my US travellers' visa will commence when I go to Rochester.

I had no letters from home last week. Do hope all is well. Shall have any that do come sent on to me - and will pick them up on Friday.

My dear love to each and all,
Your loving Mother

* * * * *

[LETTER 20]

"The black squirrels are very pretty"

Rivermead PO, Ottawa, Ontario, Canada
Saturday, 31 July 1937

MY DEARS,

I had a very enjoyable day yesterday. After a very light lunch Jennie, Muriel and I went into the city. Did I tell you it was a 25-minute tram ride and a 10-minute walk down a road to the tram halt? It seems strange to me to stand by this little shelter till the long tram comes along and the conductor opens a long barred door, the steps drop down and you enter. The conductor is also the driver, giving warning hoots, takes tickets and gives change, provides information, stops when warned by passengers pressing a button to stop at the next halt, opens and shuts the door and lets down the steps - all one man's job. In England there would be three men on it and not such long cars. It's odd to see the track alter from a single railway track into the city tram track.

We went to the Château Laurier which is a huge railway station and hotel with rest-rooms, stores and restaurants. There we paid $1 each and went for a two-hour motor car trip round the city with an accompanying guide who provides all the information. A very fine square tower has been built onto the Parliament buildings. On the ground floor of this is an altar of repose with a book with all the names of soldiers who have died. It is called the Peace Tower and has a carillon of 35 bells and is dedicated to the 60 thousand men who fell in the Great War [*First World War*].

I've got a book of the route we took. Ottawa is by far the finest city I've been in here - such wide streets, many with two islands where you cross. There are magnificent buildings and houses with large gardens and lawns. We passed one part where the guide said, "This is the residential part of the city occupied by the upper-middle class, mostly English-speaking people". I also saw Daly Avenue. This was the address given to me by Mrs Blakeman, the lady who shared my cabin on the SS *Manchester Regiment*. I saw the homes of all the great men of Canada: Sir Wilfred Laurier [*Canada's first French-Canadian Prime Minister, 1896-1911*], Sir Robert Borden [*a former Prime Minister, 1911-1920*], Mackenzie King [*William Lyon Mackenzie King, Prime Minister 1921-1930 and 1935-1948*] and the Papal Legate. I did not know before now that Lord Tweedmouth, the Governor-General, is John Buchan of the novels. [*Lord Tweedsmuir, formerly John Buchan, was knighted on his appointment as Governor-General of Canada in 1935. He is best remembered for his thriller "The Thirty-Nine Steps", published in1915.*]

We went again to the cafeteria and took our trays and had supper. I call it dinner: mackerel with anchovy sauce in a little oval dish, chip-potatoes, roll and butter, apple pie and coffee. I felt full-up which is more than I can say of my meals here generally. Then we walked and stared at the shops and then went to see *Spring Time* or *May Time* - I don't know which but a very nice film indeed with two of the most gorgeous voices I've ever heard. [*"Maytime" starred Jeanette MacDonald and Nelson Eddy; it was the biggest worldwide money-making film of 1937.*] Have either of you seen the picture? Then home by the queer tram which stops near the dark and drear road leading up past the large club-house (all lit up and full of gaiety) then up and up to this white-timbered house. By the way it costs 15 cents to go to the city by tram.

Jack [*Stanton*] had called at the post office so I have got your letter, Marion. I'm sorry about poor old Mr Hutchins. He once said to me, "I'm a great age, Mrs Kimpton, but there's no pleasure in them". I don't think Mrs Hutchins will live long without him - though he must have been a burden. I'm glad you're taking the raspberries and currants. The fruit here have not the sweet and beautiful flavour of home produce, nor have the vegetables - though I've yet to taste the much vaunted Indian corn. Most of the eats are overrated. I laughed over Roger and his clothes, bless him. He just wanted the beach.

It is a glorious day here. There was a thunderstorm before I got up but I didn't see it. I have never slept so much in all my life all at once, as I do here. I shall add five years to my life by my stay here! There is little else to do and the place is so peaceful with the immense river looking all blue and sparkling this morning. When I first saw them, I thought the huge rafts of logs were islands in the river but they are actually thousands of logs which have been floated down from the logging-camps on their way to the mills. Each log is marked and they float in the river awaiting the tugs to tow them in.

We wash in river-water which is pumped to the house and it is as soft as silk. In the winter this supply is shut off and they have to depend upon the water from the artesian well which is extremely hard. They have a huge tub indoors for general use and Jennie tells me that she also fills a dozen quart milk bottles with well-water for drinking purposes. I wouldn't live here in the winter shut off from civilisation for £1,000 a year. No tradesmen call, it's too far away. They have a radio using batteries which must not be on when members of the club are playing. Nor can we go outside the house, unless we slip across and go along the public road down to the tram track. I don't know whether this is just Jennie's idea (for she is very like her mother in many ways), but it seems any noise or movement may put the grandees off their stroke. This is an immense golf-ground, hills, dells, long stretches of green and many trees. The club has five men who do nothing but cut and roll the grass all the mornings and there are great whirling water-sprays going all night all over the place. Bob has a large area where he grows special turf to replace dead and damaged places on the course. His phone is often going with orders and messages from the club-house.

I've just been to the door to see a hummingbird hovering over the flower bed. The sun was too strong for me to see it very clearly but it was as big as a large butter-fly. I also saw some fireflies the other night, just like sparks among the trees. I would love to see a chipmunk, so everyone is on the look out for me as there are a number around here. The black squirrels are very pretty. Jim [*Hawkins*] went over a dead skunk in the road one evening and was in a rare state lest it had not been dead for some time, otherwise his car would have been tainted. Bob [*Stanton*] saw a mother skunk taking her three or four little ones across the road one day and was very careful to keep back until she had gone by or she might have squirted some of her lovely, scented secretion over him. If this happens it is necessary to burn your clothes to get rid of the odour. We had blueberry pie for supper yesterday - quite nice - a cross between blackcurrant and cherry in flavour. We have also had squash melons which are those small round ones with a rough grey-green skin. We eat them with sugar.

[LETTER 20 CONTINUED]

You ought to see the freckles on my hands and arms, great spots like large pinheads and some a quarter of an inch across. But I'm in plenty of company in Canada though most of the women and girls powder very thickly. Bob has just been telling me that this house is an old one - in fact one of the first log-houses. It was built by felling trees, splitting the logs and placing them one on another and plastering inbetween, where they are round, to fill the gaps. There are two lots of shingles on the roof - that is wooden tiles - and this, with the trees around, helps to keep the house and bedrooms so cool. In fact this is the first cool house I've struck since coming out here.

What do you think of this anecdote:

> A man's best friend and drinking companion has passed on. Several weeks after the cremation he met his friend's widow. "Please accept my sympathy," said he. "Your husband was such a good man and I know you will miss him."
>
> "Good man indeed," said she. "he never did an honest days work in his life. But at last I've got him working for me now."
>
> "What," exclaimed the friend, "surely you can't mean working? He's dead."
>
> "Yes I can," she said. "That's him over there in that hour-glass." (!!!)

You remember old Teddy Glenister gave me a letter for some friends of his in case I went near Orillia. [*Edwin Glenister was a builder in Abbots Langley whose yard was in Adrian Road, opposite Annie's house. Orillia is north of Toronto.*] Well I found that the place was umpteen miles away and would cost a heap to get there so I sent on the letter with a covering note from me. I had a very nice letter back from the old lady's daughter or daughter-in-law giving me a hearty invitation to visit them if possible. She said she had just lost her husband some two months past after a short illness.

I shall not see Sister Sebright, though I may have another day in Toronto. There is an exhibition there in August which Jim [*Hawkins*] is anxious for me to see. I shall stay here over the August holiday as young Ben Southam will be home and I know it grieves his mother for him to sleep on a camp-bed in the dining-room. So I'll go back next week and then write to Ben [*Hawkins*] in Rochester, wash and clean my togs and get on my way. Jennie tells me that Bessie [*Elizabeth Timberlake, sister of Jennie Stanton*] has given up her membership of the Watford [*Queens Road Methodist*] church and has gone back to Kings Langley [*Methodist church*]. I'm glad for I'm sure she will be happy with her friends there and her money will be a help to the church.

Please give my love to the Harrises. I have not forgotten that I owe them a letter telling them of my visit to Toronto. Whilst I was in London, Ontario, Mrs Perry (Nell Flint) and her husband came to see me. I missed her when in Toronto as she was out, so she and her husband motored all the way to St Catharines. Lizzie said Mrs Perry felt bad about not seeing me. She was in my Sunday school class years ago with Lois Munt and Rose Hawkins when I was a young girl. [*Nell Perry née Flint was almost certainly Helen, daughter of Harry (Henry) Flint. The 1891 census records the families of the three brothers, Harry, Reuben and William Flint living in Abbots Langley at that time: Reuben in Breakspear Road and the other two in Adrian Road. The change in place of birth of their children indicates that they had moved into the village between 1879 and 1881. It would seem likely that Harry and William and both their families emigrated to Canada in the early 1900's - for none of them were left in Abbots Langley by the 1930's.*]

I seem to have filled my letter with nothing this time, but time hangs heavy when you are all the time indoors. However, we may go to the city again tomorrow. When I read Marion's and Muriel's letters I'm at home with you all. I'm beginning to feel it's time I went to Joe. Will write again when I get back to Lizzie's. Not sure how far it is - must be two or three hundred miles. Remember me to all my friends, Marie and Jim, Mrs Brown, Bert's mother and Mrs George Flint. [*Mrs George Flint, Edie (Edith) Flint née Quebell, lived at Stonehaven, 24 Greenways. Her husband, George (Jeffrey George) Flint, was an amateur bee-keeper who handled the hives with only his cigarette smoke for protection. The illustrated plates include a photograph of the Flint family taken at George and Edie's wedding on 21 June 1905.*]

Poor old Jonesy, I thought North Watford was quite eager to keep him. [*The Harebreaks Methodist church of North Watford had declined to invite the Rev Albert Jones, whom they shared with the Abbots Langley Methodist church, for a further period of time. In the eighteenth century, the Rev John Wesley travelled 250 thousand miles preaching, often riding on horseback. He wished his ministers to be travellers too and initiated a pattern of a three years' stay in each ministry.*] I shan't go anywhere near Walkersville (the Rev Albert Jones's sister) and shall go to Joe from Rochester. How's the Women's Own progressing? I am so glad about the Wesley Guild. It's worth the trouble I'm sure.

My dearest love to you all,

Your loving Mother

PS. Here's a description of a baby:

"A baby begins life as an alimentary canal with a loud voice at one end and no responsibility at the other."

* * * * *

DOWSE'S

HYGIENIC FISHERY

(Opposite the Fete)

Hot Fish and Chips

Take a Supper Home with You!

An advert from the 1937 Methodist Church Fête programme. Arthur and Lillie Dowse, together with Eric Godman, ran the fish shop on the corner of the High Street and Langley Road. It had just moved there from Breakspear Road.

FINAL STAY AT 13 IDA STREET

ANNIE KIMPTON returned to St Catharines for her final stay with Ted and Lizzie Southam. During this time she received directions from Alta Kimpton for her trans-continental train journey to San Francisco. That letter is also included here:

[LETTER 21]

"It looks like Southend without the cockles, whelks and winkles"

13 Ida Street, St Catharines, Ontario, Canada
Monday, 9 August 1937

MY DEARS,

I am back again in St Catharines and had a very good journey back but it was very tiring. I left Ottawa at about 10.15am and did not get back here until nearly midnight. I am sending you the bus time-table of the route I took. The places we stopped at for a few minutes are marked in large type.

The day before I left Ottawa, I went with Jennie and Muriel [*Stanton*] for a tour of the Houses of Parliament and the Peace Tower. They are truly magnificent buildings and guides are continually taking visitors over them. The Senate Chamber, which corresponds to our House of Lords, is arranged much like our House of Commons but all is, of course, new. As you know, all the buildings were destroyed by fire a few years ago [*in 1916*]. The woodwork is made of golden oak and all the elaborate carvings are hand-done. Everything is very lovely, especially the marble floor in the great halls and corridors. The library floor is made of teak with ebony insets. It's no wonder they think so much of the Duke of Windsor here, for: "This was presented [*in 1916*] by the Prince of Wales, now Duke of Windsor," and, "This was given by . . . . . . " (etc, etc). It was a great blow to the people here when he had to skedaddle.

We went up the Peace Tower by lifts and saw the 35 bells and the clock with its transparent dials which show the lighted faces all over Ottawa and its immense pendulum in its glass case. The clock was made by a firm in Croydon, England [*Messrs Gillett and Johnson*]. However, the place I liked best of all was the lofty room with the altar of remembrance with floors made of black and white marble, and a stone altar with steps up to it in the centre. The white marble was given by France, the black by Belgium, and the altar a gift from England. All round the room are stone tablets telling the story of the war [*First World War*] and inset into the floor are the names of the various battlefields where the Canadians fought. All the carving and lettering was done by hand on the spot by carvers and stonemasons in the old way using hammer and chisel. On top of the altar is an area edged with gold - with four kneeling angels with outspread wings shading a glass top where the Book of Remembrance is to be kept when it is finished. Then each day a new page will be turned over.

They are more loyal over here than at home and keep up the remembrance of the men who died far more than we do. I went to an afternoon picture show with Shirley Temple in *Wee Willie Winkie* and they shewed some of the Coronation pictures as an extra. The children cheered at the sight of the Union Jack and the sight of the Queen reviewing the troops at Aldershot sent everybody frantic! They tell me that the schools make much of the Flag, etc, etc. [*Under the influence of American ideas, rebellion broke out in Toronto in 1837 led by William Lyon Mackenzie who was the grandfather of the 1935-1948 Canadian Prime Minister, William Lyon Mackenzie King. It was put down but it hastened the granting of self-government to the Provinces. The self-governing Dominion of Canada came into being on 1 July, 1867 with elected Provincial Governments, an elected Federal House of Commons and an appointed Senate. In the First World War, 1914 - 1918, Canada made huge efforts to support Britain. During the Second World War, the St Pancras Industrial Schools at Leavesden, near Abbots Langley, were used as a hospital for wounded Canadians after the Dieppe Raid in 1942. It was visited by King George VI and Queen Elizabeth. David and Roger Flint stood amongst a handful of citizens to watch them. Many years later in 1963, at a chance encounter in Montréal with one of these Canadians, David Flint was asked: "What was the name of that pub? We called it the Dirty Duck". It was The Swan in College Road, Leavesden, known earlier as The White Swan. In 1965, the red and white Maple-leaf flag was adopted by Canada instead of the Canadian Red Ensign. Britain's remaining legal links with Canada were severed in 1982 by the Canada Act, though the Queen of England still reigns as Queen of Canada.*]

We had tea in the Château Laurier, met Bob [*Stanton*] and went out to the Dominion Experimental Farms, some 8-12 acres of land growing and supporting everything: flowers, cereals, grasses, shrubs, trees, fruits of every kind; as well as various breeds of cows, pigs, horses, sheep, fowl and even bees - to find out what is best for Canada. What do you think of these names over a shop doorway in Ottawa: "I SOBCUFF" . . . and "T TWIRKTELL"! The police in Ottawa wear blue suits with a red line down the trouser leg and flat caps like our postmen. But those on duty at Parliament House, called Dominion Police, are in brown riding boots, blue riding knickers with a wide, yellow stripe at the side, red tunics with gold buttons and a white hat - most gorgeous [*the Royal Canadian Mounted Police, the "Mounties"*].

I went to the Dominion Church on Sunday evening. I have never seen finer buildings but very few people - apparently they get more in the winter. Ted says the collections [*the offertory*] suffer everywhere and there are always piles of big nickels which folk just put in the plate to pretend that they are giving quarters. [*Up to 1921, nickels or 5 cent coins were very small, but from 1922 onwards they were minted much larger in size and nearly the size of a quarter or 25 cent coin.*]. Everybody here thinks I've piles of cash to be travelling about so. Lizzie and Ted think I'm spending the savings of a lifetime in one grand slam and I don't contradict.

Yesterday afternoon, Jim [*Hawkins*] took me down to Port Weller where May [*Love*] and her children have a cottage for a week or so. They are the places that look like large bathing-huts. The place was packed with cars and people on the edge of the lake. It was most uncomfortable with it being hot and so many mosquitoes and flies. There are two rooms in these huts, each with windows and a small table in the corner with a few chairs and an electric grill. Each has two shelves made into bunks to take two people on each and everybody brings their own bedding and provisions. They all live in their bathing-suits and there are some wonderful sights to see, both men and

[LETTER 21 CONTINUED]
women. The fattest men have the smallest bathing-suits, dear oh dear, and some of the women are like elephants!! There are all nationalities here. I'd far rather stay at home but, of course, the children love the water. As it is fresh water I don't think it can be so good; and the sandy beach is filthy. I've had my first Indian corn this week and we can now pull it from the garden every day. I don't like eating it as they do here, picking it up and gnawing it. Also, I have artificial teeth so I cut it off to eat it. I like it very much. It is rightly called sweetcorn.

I walked up to the city the other morning and I've never before felt the sensation of drawing in hot air as I walked. It was suffocating. Then we had a violent thunderstorm and cooler weather followed. It is much cooler today and it is raining a little. Rose made us laugh by declaring that she went everywhere in her house and couldn't find a "spool cot" meaning of course a cool spot. She often talks backwards quite unconsciously. [*A spoonerism, the transposition of the initial consonants of a pair of words resulting in real but incorrect words and an amusing ambiguity - named after their exponent the Rev W A Spooner, 1844-1930.*]

This tale is appreciated out here where flies are so numerous:

A man begged a farmer to give him a shakedown (somewhere to sleep) for the night, anywhere would do.

"I've nowhere save an attic and no one would stay there because the flies are so terrible."

"I don't mind the flies," said the man.

In the morning the farmer said, "How did you manage to get any rest with all those flies about?"

"Oh," said the man, "they did not bother me. I bunched 'em."

"Bunched 'em - what do you mean? How did you bunch 'em?"

"Oh," said he, "I made a heap in one corner and slept in the other." (!!!)

We've been reading "BRITAIN SIZZLING" so I think you must be having hot weather. The papers said that it was 87F in England which is just a warm summer day in Canada. But in England they wear prickly tweeds and flannels for summer wear, live on stews, porridge and suet puddings and utterly refuse to budge from their insular prejudices and be like "us". It seems queer to see brown-haired children with a bit of a fairlock on their forehead where the sun has bleached it. Down at Port Dalhousie, where we went on Saturday night, many adults and children are literally copper-colour. There were crowds of people in all states of undress, roundabouts, flying machines, wiggle-wiggle, games of chance, hot dogs, hamburgers, ices, iced drinks and (on the lake) a helter-skelter and water-cycles. A man in a red bathing-costume (with LIFEGUARD across the front) parades along the beach and was sunburnt the colour of a Red Indian! It looks like Southend without the cockles, whelks and winkles. Of course, no houses nearby - just those glorified bathing-huts and cars everywhere.

I received two letters this morning from Marion and Muriel. I'm so glad to get them. I am glad the boys are better [*her grandchildren, David and Roger Flint*]. I wish I could have seen all the labourers at work. Fancy me with a light in the "lamantory".

[*Probably the way her youngest grandchild, Roger, pronounced the word "lavatory". Outside lavatories, which were attached to houses built since the Artisans Dwellings Act 1875, did not usually have electric lights in them*]. I shall not know myself when I get back home. I am so glad you are going to Dover. My love to them there and I'll write again soon. I'd forgotten about the Rev Gould coming to Abbots Langley. How I hope he'll come to our church. Surely our singing is not as dirge-like as the Baptists? So if they sample them - they won't get better music. [*Probably a retired minister coming to live in Abbots Langley and deciding whether to join with the Methodists or the Baptists.*]

I'm sorry Fred has indigestion so I'm enclosing a remedy which a man over here used with great benefit. He said it is not very nice but that he was a martyr to dyspepsia and dared not eat but now he can digest pork chops and pickle. So try it, my dear. [*Unfortunately the remedy is missing - probably Fred Kimpton kept it.*]

My dear love to you all,

Your loving Mother

* * * * *

[LETTER FROM ALTA KIMPTON TO ANNIE]

400 Duboce Avenue, San Francisco, California, USA
Tuesday, 10 August 1937

DEAR MOTHER,

We were very glad to get your letter. You had us worried for a while because we didn't hear from you. We are glad to know you are all right and having a good time. I'm not making this a long letter as I want to send it by Air Mail. Joe says it is too bad you didn't give us Ben's address in Rochester so we could have sent it direct there. As it is, we have sent it to St Catharines and hope they forward it to you in time. You undoubtedly will already have left Canada and completed your banking arrangements before this reaches you. [*Luckily, Annie was still at St Catharines when the letter arrived.*] You asked for the cost of the trip. There are different routes but the one we consider best is as follows:

Fare from Rochester to San Francisco	$56.16
Sleeper from Chicago to San Francisco	8.50
Meals about	5.00
Total cost	$69.66

Here is the way we have figured out is the best way for you to come: Take the NEW YORK CENTRAL RAILROAD from Rochester to Chicago and then the SANTA FE RAILROAD from Chicago to San Francisco. You make all the arrangements at Rochester since all the lines work together. You leave Rochester at 6.39am on a Thursday morning - arriving at Chicago at 6.55pm the same day. So, you see, you only need a day coach-ticket for the first part of the trip. *The Scout,* which is the name of the SANTA FE train for San Francisco, leaves at 8.45pm. This will give you time

[LETTER FROM ALTA KIMPTON TO ANNIE CONTINUED]
to have your dinner in the station. On the Chicago to San Francisco part of your trip you will take a tourist sleeper [*sleeping car*] ticket as you will have three nights on the train. After you have had dinner in Chicago, you can board *The Scout* train and go right to bed. Be sure and check with the porter or conductor on the train to see that you have the right sleeper section for San Francisco. From then on you have nothing to worry about as you do not have to change any more. You stay right on your own train until you arrive in San Francisco. [*The names of some other SANTA FE RAILROAD trains between Chicago and California indicated in the timetable were: "The Ranger", "The Chief", and "El Capitan" (this being a mountain in Yosemite National Park).*]

The reason for making sure that you are in the San Francisco section is that the train splits at Barstow, California, and the San Francisco sleeper stays in Barstow from 2.10am until 8.45am without being disturbed, thus giving you six and a half hours of quiet sleep. Then it is hooked onto the San Francisco train and you commence the last leg of your journey Sunday morning, bowling up the Imperial Valley to Oakland where you will arrive at 9.01pm Sunday night. [*The Imperial Valley runs south-eastwards, from Barstow - Alta meant the San Joaquin Valley which runs north-westwards to Oakland.*] You stay on the train until you get to Oakland Pier. The train does not go any farther, so you won't have to worry. We shall meet you there with the car and you will be home and indoors within half an hour. You may buy your ticket to San Francisco, not Oakland - it's the same price. You check your heavy luggage right thru' to us at 400 Duboce Avenue, Apartment 9. You do all the buying of tickets and checking of luggage in Rochester. Pack enough in your hand-grip to carry with you on the train, as your heavy luggage may not arrive for a couple of days after you do.

As you will notice - Monday, Thursday and Saturday from Chicago are the only days you can get a thru' train on *The Scout*. Therefore, as Sunday is the best day for us to meet you, you will have to leave on a Thursday morning. So early in the morning may seem awkward for you but it gives you a day-trip to Chicago and an easy connection there for your thru' train - also saving you about $10. Ben may be able to figure out a quicker, cheaper and more convenient way for you to come. He probably knows more about railroad travelling than we do as he has been out here some while. If he figures a better route, take it - but let us know the time of your arrival in Oakland. Air Mail the details if it is necessary, it only costs a few cents more. You can see on a map the states and towns you go thru' and we think that Texas, Arizona and Southern California are more scenic than Nebraska, Wyoming and Utah. You will change time as you come across, starting with Eastern Time at Rochester, [*there was also Central Time at Chicago*], Mountain Time at Clovis [*New Mexico*] and Pacific Time at Kingman [*Arizona*].

You have a hard trip ahead of you, Mother, but just take it as easy as you can and don't worry. You'll get here all right and can rest up then. I think I have covered everything, Mother, but you can get plenty more information from the railway office. Ben will help you. Let us know for sure when you're getting here.

Love, Alta

* * * * *

[LETTER 22]

"Up to the present I've seen no man for whom I'd give up England"

13 Ida Street, St Catharines, Ontario, Canada
Sunday, 15 August 1937

MY DEARS,

As you can see, I'm still in St Catharines and feel I'm just marking time. I've written to Ben Hawkins in Rochester to say I'm ready to come when he can arrange to fetch me but I believe he has visitors at the present time. I had a long letter from Alta giving me precise directions for my journey to them. When I answered the letter I told them I felt like the bit in the Bible which says that a wayfaring man, though a fool, might not err therein. [*Isaiah 35:8, refers to a traveller, though a fool, not straying from the highway of holiness.*] Joe says he thinks the cost of the journey, roughly speaking, will be $70 but folk here think it will be more. I've asked Ben to find out the exact cost as I don't want to draw more money than I need from the bank, so I can have the rest transferred to San Francisco. Then, the next day after the long letter from Alta, I had another come by Air Mail. I wondered what was up but it was to tell me that JWT had called them from a hotel in San Francisco where he and Marjorie had just arrived. So they went round. [*JWT, Joseph William Timberlake, another son of Matthew Timberlake's brother Joseph, worked for JOHN DICKINSON & CO, the paper-maker and stationery manufacturer, at their Croxley Mills near Watford. He went to Cape Town in South Africa in 1893 to set up a branch of JOHN DICKINSON & CO. He was married to Rose and had two children, Marjorie and Harold. Harold came to England for the First World War, was commissioned in the Inns of Court Regiment, and spent his leaves at Hastoe Farm, the home of Joseph Timberlake - the brother of Annie. In 1922 JWT helped to establish another branch in Australia.*]

Apparently Uncle Will was expecting me to be there already. So he quickly scribbled a note (which they enclosed with their letter) asking me to meet him in Chicago as I shall have a two-hour wait for my connection, and for me to write to him at the Stevens Hotel in Chicago where he will be for ten days. I wrote immediately telling him I was sorry to miss him and Marjorie, etc, etc (!!!!), but that I was still here, waiting to go to Ben's, so it was unlikely I would leave for San Francisco before 2 September. Joe thinks Thursday morning the best time to start as I shall then get there on Sunday night and he and Alta can meet me at Oakland Pier. I told Joe I should not see Will but that he would not weep, nor should I.

It's a lovely sunny morning and not too hot yet! Young Ben Southam came home last night for a fortnight. So I'm sleeping with Lizzie, and Ted has a make-up bed in the dining-room so that Ben can have his own room. Ben and his girl Marguerite are here and are a noisy young couple. I cannot get used to their way of talking. The girl says "staakuns" for stockings and "tickuts" for tickets. I've just come home from church. The minister, the Rev Millar, was good this morning. He took for his text: And Jesus came to John the Baptist. He divided his sermon into four parts: Men seek for Health, Happiness, Holiness and Heaven. Things which are not found by much seeking but come by observing the laws of health, unselfishness, Christ's laws, and

[LETTER 22 CONTINUED]
come to us as Jesus came to John.

This afternoon Jim [*Hawkins*] took Lizzie, little Elizabeth Love, and me for a car ride. We went to the Falls and viewed them from an entirely new aspect - a high point looking down on them from above the Horseshoe Falls. You could see the river beyond and in the distance the Peace Bridge between Buffalo, USA, and Port Erie in Canada. The sun produced an immense rainbow in the spray over the Falls, a wonderful sight. On the way back we had to wait in a long stream of cars for the great road-bridge over the [*Welland Ship*] Canal to close after a large boat had gone through. When the cars moved slowly on again, a car in front stopped suddenly, the next one ran into him, and the one behind us crashed into Jim's car and shoved us into the one in front. Fortunately we suffered only minor injuries and the car wasn't badly damaged. Jim's lights were damaged, his number-plate buckled and his bumper bent. Jim and I (who were in the front) will have stiff necks and I have a bruise on the back of my leg. Lizzie's knee and arm are bruised and one of her fingers was pushed back. Little Elizabeth was not even bumped. Poor old Lizzie is feeling very sorry for herself but I'm hoping she'll be all right in the morning.

I went on Friday evening to a shower party given by Betty [*Outram*] for her friend Renée Wenham. Everyone who accepts the invitation takes a gift. This was a miscellaneous shower - so all manner of things were acceptable. If it is a pantry shower - things for the larder store are given; a personal shower - means undies and general clothes-wear; a kitchen shower - means anything for the kitchen, etc, etc. About twenty people were asked but three were ill and three were on holiday - so they sent their gifts. The bride elect arrived and was invited to sit on a low seat under the centre arch between the two rooms. Over her was a white paper bell which showered confetti. Beside her was a large basket like a baby's bassinet, decked in white and filled with gifts of all sizes. She had to untie each parcel and read the accompanying words. Lizzie and I clubbed together and gave her a cake-plate in chintz-pattern china with a silver handle to clip on. I think it was the nicest of the gifts given. The bride-to-be is a nice girl and I like her mother, Mrs Wenham. She does an immense amount of fancy needlework and it was she who shewed me the bag-making.

I shall be quite ready to move on. I've been and seen quite a lot, made some journeys and also got through a bit of needlework. I have been to London, Ottawa, Toronto, Niagara Falls four times, Niagara-on-the-Lake, Niagara Gorge, Welland and umpteen other places. Six dresses and one blouse have been made since I came here, four for myself and three for Lizzie. I'm now making Ted two nightshirts.

* * *

Wednesday, 18 August 1937

I HAVE had a letter from Alice [*Hawkins*], Ben's wife, to say she will be coming to fetch me this week, probably Thursday. So I've packed my big trunk and got most of my things ready. Ben phoned to enquire the probable cost of the journey to San Francisco and they told him $103.66 which is a great increase on Joe's estimate. But

I'll let Ben read Joe's letter [*Alta wrote the letter*] when I get there and see what he says. I've been to the Imperial Bank here and drawn out the cash for my journey in American dollars and they will send the rest on to the bank in San Francisco. I've had another rambling epistle from JWT [*Joseph William Timberlake*] in answer to my letter. He says Joe is a very fine man and I'll be proud to see him. He would sure be proud to see me. As I said before, my stock and standing has risen among the relations!!!

I've just returned from the Tancock's farm where Ben, Lizzie and I have been to dinner and afternoon tea and to say good-bye to them. On the way back, we called at the water-treatment plant and collected Ted [*Southam*] and his bicycle and called and said good-bye to Mr and Mrs Webb who have a very nice house there. They have just had hardwood floors put in all over the house. Mrs Webb has arranged for a picnic later this week but I shall not be around.

Marion's letter and the letter from Bert were waiting for me on my return. Don't call your letters dull. I'm immediately at home when I read them. As for Bert's impudence, I shall just do as Grandma Kimpton [*Emma Kimpton, Annie's mother-in-law*] said: "Igner him". I don't think second-hand cars are cheaper here. Ben's car was second-hand, one with what they call a rumble seat (a dickey) and there is room for three in front. I reckon that he paid about £60 for it and it's the most awful rattle-boned thing I've ever ridden in. It goes fast and has a radio but, oh dear! He says licences are cheaper here and there are no small cars since so few roads are made up - only the King's Highway. You leap over the great ruts and go up on one wheel and up and down hills like switchbacks. Oh, by the way, no Bertram - up to the present I've seen no man for whom I'd give up England. Of course, I can't promise about the USA! Will tell you when I get there but a chance is a fine thing, you know. You mention, Marion, about your favourite grouse. I think my worst here are mosquitoes, BO [*body odour*] and olives. Also much of the cake made here to eat with ice-cream.

I shall write again from Rochester. I understand that Ben does not live in his house in the town during the summer but at a summer-cottage by a lake. To hear folks talk and see them dressed up you'd think they were wealthy, what with their cars, etc. But they have nothing behind them and (like Grandma Kimpton) think $100 or £20 a fortune. Ted Southam is something like Dad [*Matthew Timberlake*] in slaving for the church in the evenings, cutting grass, mending fences and trimming hedges. Uncle Fred Cherry rode up to see me and say good-bye last evening. I like him very much. Auntie Rose Cherry has a touch of quinsy [*tonsillitis*] and looks poorly. It's so hot and uncomfortable here to have colds and sore throats.

I went to a Ladies' Aid meeting on Monday night at a Mrs Wylie's home, a fat lady with a mighty laugh. There were 15 ladies and they each give 10 cents a week and are arranging for a Wiener and Corn Roast in the church grounds next Monday with pop [*lemonade*] and coffee. Each item - Wieners, corn or drink will cost 5 cents. There are three groups of ladies at the church who vie with each other to get money for the church. They are now working hard for an Autumn Sale. The minister came up with an idea for a wonderful radio performer and a group to give an outdoor performance at the back of the church. Said he: "I know Ross. He sure is some guy and can put it over swell. If all the Board of Managers (Trustees) and you ladies back me up and risk

$100 we'll stand to make $300 for he has been to Toronto, to Grimsby (etc, etc) and will go to St Kitts if we don't bag him first". So all thought it a fine idea. Ted says that church work over here is a money-getting business and neither minister nor people care one rap about spiritual growth - only money and numbers.

Fancy my David going to school [*Abbots Langley Infants' School where David Flint would start in September at the age of 5*]. You will miss him, Marion, but perhaps you will be like a tale Lizzie told me of an old woman she knew who, when consoled about the absence of her family, said: "Yes, I misses 'em and I wants 'em and I wants 'em and I misses 'em but I misses 'em more than I wants 'em!" I thought that rather good.

How does the Rev Benjamin Harris get on at the Baptist church? Does he make any difference to numbers? Does Mrs Harris still come to the Women's Own? [*Some ladies attended both the Methodist and the Baptist Women's Meetings. The Rev Benjamin Charles Harris lived at Westmead, Langley Road, opposite the Baptist chapel. It was built in 1895 and is now the Abbots Langley Parish Council office. A new Baptist church has been built at School Mead on the Hillside Estate.*] Did that lady come to speak from Watford? I have forgotten her name but Mrs Arthur Flint had it. What did Arthur Munt name his little daughter? [*She was named Hazel. Arthur Munt lived in Adrian Road and was related to Lois Harris née Munt in Toronto.*] Sorry this is a twaddly letter but I feel uneasy now that I'm on the move again and shall be glad when I see Joe.

My dearest love to you all and a warm kiss for David and Roger,

Your Mum

* * * * *

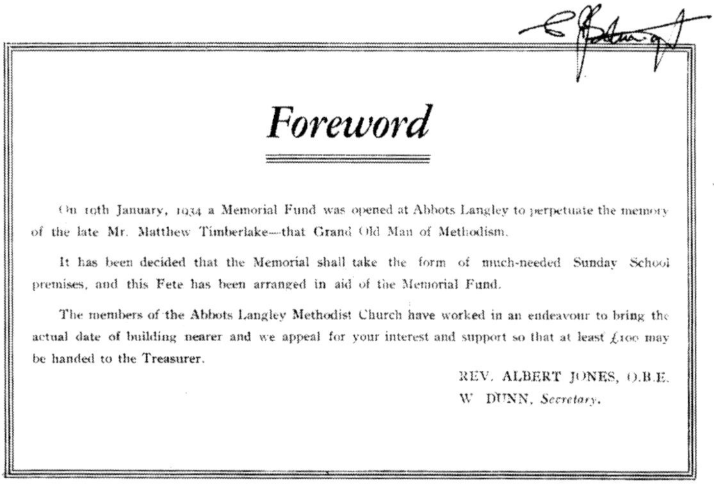

Foreword

On 10th January, 1934 a Memorial Fund was opened at Abbots Langley to perpetuate the memory of the late Mr. Matthew Timberlake—that Grand Old Man of Methodism.

It has been decided that the Memorial shall take the form of much-needed Sunday School premises, and this Fete has been arranged in aid of the Memorial Fund.

The members of the Abbots Langley Methodist Church have worked in an endeavour to bring the actual date of building nearer and we appeal for your interest and support so that at least £100 may be handed to the Treasurer.

REV. ALBERT JONES, O.B.E.
W. DUNN, *Secretary*.

The Foreword from the 1937 Abbots Langley Methodist Church Fête programme, with Jack Botwright's signature.

AT LONG POND, ROCHESTER, USA

TWO YANKEE TRADERS purchased two and a half million acres of land in 1788 from the Seneca Indians around the area where the Genesee River in New York State, USA, flows into Lake Ontario. Rochester, founded here on the lake's southern shore, was named after Colonel Nathaniel Rochester who in 1811, with the help of colleagues, built flour mills harnessing the power of the river to turn the water-wheels. Rochester became America's first boom town with a reputation as the "Flour City".

Three world-famous firms had their start in Rochester: In 1853, John Jacob Bausch and Henry Lomb opened a small optical shop; today, BAUSCH AND LOMB is an outstanding optical and health-care company. Then a young bank clerk named George Eastman started experimenting with dry plates and film; in 1888 he marketed the KODAK camera and launched a major new photographic industry. And in 1906 the HALOID COMPANY was formed, later to be renamed the XEROX CORPORATION; it was to develop the world's first automatic plain-paper copier.

By 1937, the city was known as "Kodak City". Some folk had summer-homes by Lake Ontario and the small lakes known as "ponds" that bordered the Great Lake. It was to one of these that Annie Kimpton came on her visit to her first cousin, Ben Hawkins, and his wife, Alice, at their summer-cottage by Long Pond before taking the train to San Francisco. Ben (Benjamin) Hawkins had emigrated to Canada with his brother Jim (James) in 1904. Later, Ben moved across the border into the United States. Alice was Ben's second wife and there were no children from either marriage:

[LETTER 23]

"I expect it was my nautical roll . . . . . ."

60 Grand View Heights, Long Pond, Rochester, New York State, USA
Monday, 23 August 1937

MY DEARS,

One more stage of my journey is over and I am at Rochester with Ben and Alice. Today is Monday and I left St Catharines on Saturday. Ben and Alice came to fetch me in their fine car, my big trunk beside me, and Ben in front - Alice driving! I felt a bit sad on leaving 13 Ida Street for they had been good to me but I've been eager to move on since I returned from Ottawa. I told you I had a letter from J W T [*Joseph William Timberlake*]. I wrote to him at Chicago and had another letter back saying how sorry he was to miss me, etc, etc.

When we got to Queenston Bridge, I had to get out and go into an inner room for questioning. The man in charge asked me umpteen questions but as I was going to Mr Hawkins' home and had been visiting Canada and had my return ticket from San Francisco, there was no problem. He also asked who I was going to see and how much money had I got?

I told him and where my cash was and said that I had plenty more back in England and was an independent lady with property of my own.

Had I ever been refused entry into the States?

No, for this is the first time I have travelled here. I'd only once gone with a party of 30 women for a picnic to the States but as I had no passport with me, they would not let me across the border even for one hour.

He had already been on the phone and when I said that he smiled and said, "Yes, it was on 5 June". So he had already got my description taped off. While he investigated, another man went outside and looked at the ship's labels on my trunk, came in and handed something to my questioner.

He asked where and when I landed, the name of my boat, where I got my passport and did I have any relatives at home, etc, etc? My passport was only visa'd for American entry - no time given. So how long was I staying?

I told him that I did not wish to return across the Atlantic in the winter weather.

"Why not?" said he.

"Well, I'm an old woman," said I.

"Oh no, no," said he. "Well, what do you say to nine months?"

"That's quite all right. Thank you very much."

"Well I'll put ten months and if you want an extension, I've no doubt you'll get it, Mrs Kimpton."

Ben was very glad all went so smoothly. They did not even open my trunk or bag. He says that it was because I am an independent woman ready to spend all my money. So all is OK.

This a very nice bungalow with a double-garage and the lawn goes down to the edge of Long Pond, which is really a lake about one mile across fed by a river or "creek" as they call them and running into Lake Ontario. Rochester is some 120 miles from Lewiston Bridge [*previously referred to by Annie as Queenston Bridge*] at Niagara. This place is 15 miles from the town itself. As Ben has one car to go to work and Alice has the other big 90 horsepower one for her own use, it is not quite isolated like Rivermead was at Ottawa. The houses here in Rochester look larger and finer than in St Catharines. More like those in Ottawa, though I expect there are poorer districts. This bungalow has the pond or really a lake in front of it and up the road (about 200yds) we cross a highway and there is Lake Ontario. On Sunday the waves were rolling in just like the sea, save that the water is not green but dull and muddy-looking in rough weather.

We passed miles and miles of apple trees laden with fruit and orchards of peaches on our way here last Saturday. Alice stopped by the wayside and bought a barrel of ripe peaches and some melons. We eat a lot of melon and bread and butter for breakfast and drink coffee. On Sunday for dinner we had chicken. They boil and cut it up into joints and we help ourselves - together with potatoes, marrow and peas. They eat tomatoes and cucumbers with their hot food. We eat lunch and dinner on the sun-porch and have breakfast in the kitchen. I have Alice's room as Ben thought I'd be more comfortable in a bedroom than on the sun-porch. So they are sleeping there. Mrs Wicks, Alice's mother, lives here - a very agreeable lady, a bit older than I am. She spoke of someone today and said they talked "broad English". The lady in the next bungalow told Alice today that she knew there was an English visitor, for I walked "English". I expect it was my "nautical roll" as Bert calls it.

Yesterday, some friends came to visit comprising father, mother, two sons and one daughter, the family name being Savage. I liked the man and woman (who originally came from Northampton) and they wanted to talk all about England with me but I don't like the young Americans or Canadians. We stayed home all day.

Today we have had a long ride and have been to the airport and watched the aeroplanes take-off, looking like great insects. You know, like one of those whose tail turns up when you touch it and of all colours: green, yellow, pink, red and blue. Then we went round a most wonderful park with two great reservoirs with fountains in them. We do not ride on the King's Highway now but on Route 16 or 18, etc, and the gasolene stations have SOCONY on them which, being interpreted, means STANDARD OIL COMPANY OF NEW YORK. Today is dull but I don't mind as I shall not get sunburnt. We are going round the town, shop-window looking. The battery of Ben's car has given out so Alice has to take him to work and fetch him home.

What do you think of this tale:

A young lady was on a streetcar and had no place to sit down. She looked indignantly at two young men who sat giggling.

"Haven't you a seat Miss?" they said.

"Yes, I have a seat but nowhere to put it," she replied.

"Well, why don't you hang it up? Haven't you got a hole in it? There's a hook," they said.

We called at the railway station yesterday and asked about fares, etc. If I had not had all the detailed information from Joe, I'd never have known about the tourist ticket nor of *The Scout* train. They part with no details about the Santa Fe Railway at these stations even though they have to fit in with them. I'll write again later this week. I feel in an inner ferment over my journey to Joe. Everything has worked like clockwork up to the present.

My dearest love to you all,

Your loving Mum

* * * * *

[LETTER 24]

"I wondered what Aparko Hots were . . . . . ."

60 Grand View Heights, Long Pond, Rochester, New York State, USA

Wednesday, 25 August 1937

MY DEARS,

This is a very lovely place and the lake this morning is just like glass in the sun and I'm sitting in the sun-porch. It's a long room across the whole width of the bungalow, wooden built of course and wide windows all round, a mesh door to keep out flies and mosquitoes, and a wide couch-bed where Ben and Alice are sleeping whilst I am

[LETTER 24 CONTINUED]
here. There is a big gramophone on a stand, a cabinet with flowers and plants on it, three rocking-chairs, nine high-backed dining-room chairs, a large round table and a settee couch-bed on the other side - yet still plenty of space. I've just helped Mrs Wicks wash up and make my bed. Alice has collected cucumbers and tomatoes from the garden and is at present going over the lawn with the mower. There are trees and grass down to the water's edge.

Yesterday, we went to Niagara Falls to see them from this side. It is certainly the finer view of the Falls from the other (Canadian) side but from this side you can get so close that you can almost touch them. There are lovely parks above the Falls but nothing so beautiful as on the Canadian side. We went down on the elevator to the beach and then as near as possible to the Falls (too close and the spray would soak you) and looked up at the immense cascade of foaming water, looking like green glass at the top. I saw the boats, including *The Maid of the Mist*, come and go out. We could only see them at a great distance on the other side. The boats are crowded every time and everyone on board has to don dark oilskin coats and hoods. They look like a boat load of the Ku Klux Klan.

We are here in Monroe County, in the district of Charlotte (pronounced "Shallott") in the town of Greece and 15 miles from Rochester city. Ben drives 25 miles to his job and we went 185 miles to Niagara and back yesterday. Alice, Mrs Wicks and Mrs Savage were in the car but oh, it was hot in Niagara city - but lovely when we were driving. I saw large bunches of red bananas for sale. We had our dinner in Niagara Park and another meal by the lakeside on the way back. We took a luncheon basket with potato salad, sandwiches of cheese, ham and tuna-fish, tomatoes, cucumbers, peaches, cake and a huge Thermos of coffee (as large as the old tea urns we used to have - only this one was in green and white enamel).

A motor boat with five people on board has just gone past and I can see many boats in the distance. A man has called to put on some door locks.

"It is going to be hot," I said.

"Yes," said he, "it's going to be good and warm." Mrs Wicks has been canning (bottling) peaches and making tomato juice. We had a bottle of olives with us yesterday. The others like them but I hate them.

Two friends of Ben and Alice, Mr and Mrs Llewellan of Hamilton, have just arrived. They are on a motor tour all round Lake Ontario and have (so far) done 500 miles. They will stay until the end of the week. Visitors make no difference to Alice. She has a number of studio-couches and simply makes up beds without any fuss. Mrs Llewellan suffers from rheumatoid arthritis and finds it difficult to get about. She tells me that she has had injections of gold to help her. Apparently doctors call it "the gold treatment" and in some cases it has worked miracles. She says that her doctor travelled to England to study the treatment. I told her that I had never heard of it. The husband is a lively little dark man - almost a midget for he is no taller than I am and he wears size four and a half shoes!

* * *

Friday evening, 27 August 1937

WE have been for a lovely outing - Alice driving, Mr Llewellan in the front seat and Mrs Llewellan, Mrs Wicks and me in the back. We went to Letchworth State Park and Letchworth Gorge about 75 miles south of here. They have good roads here but the hills are tremendous. You can see a road going into the distance for miles and miles - and then its up and down, up and down. And the road signs are profuse: WINDING ROAD . . . CURVE . . . BUMP . . . SCHOOL . . . DANGER . . . RAIL CROSSING . . . and the number of the road NY 63, etc, every half mile or so. This country is so immense I cannot grasp it. Field upon field with great woods and hills in the distance which they tell me are in Pennsylvania. Our way led up and up with signs saying STEEP HILL USE YOUR GEARS until we reached Letchworth. I cannot remember all the places we passed through: Wheatland, East Henrietta, Scottsville, Mumford, Caledonia, Mount Morris, Nunda and Perry were some of them.

There was a CCC (Civic Concentration Camp) party that we looked down upon when we got out. It's a for young men who are unemployed and they work on the roads, woods and parkland - like this place. We could see them assembling to go to dinner and there looked to be about one hundred of them. [*This was a CCC (Civilian Conservation Corps) Camp party. It was started in 1933 for unemployed youths, aged 18-25, who worked for one year and it employed over half a million. Their earnings, less keep, were paid to their families who had to be "on relief" ie, on unemployment pay. The camps were run by the War Department and some considered it a system of forced labour.*] The woodland trees here are fine specimens of red pines, oaks and maples in the main. There are picnic grounds here with strong wooden seats and round plinths of stone built up with a large slab of stone on top for a table. Fireplaces are also built of stone with gratings and plenty of wood to make fires to cook and to boil kettles in the shade. From these areas you can see the waterfalls through the trees.

There are three waterfalls - the Lower, Middle and Upper Falls of the Genesee River which runs through Rochester and eventually goes into Lake Ontario. They are not such large Falls as Niagara, of course, but we could get right down to the river's edge. The escarpment is all wooded and a continuance from that at the deep gorges of Niagara. The Falls run over rocks like stairs and the rocks are slate-like, not like our sea rocks. They are very pretty. I am sending you a postcard view of the Gorge as the Falls' pictures were on sale at another inn and we did not come back that way. [*The Letchworth Gorge was glacier carved and is part of the Finger Lake region.*]

We passed acres of Indian corn which is used for cattle and fowl feed, and also ground to make meal. Mrs Wicks is an American farmer's widow and knows everything about making cakes and pies, canning and farming. It is unusual to see notices over and over again advertising HONEY . . . TOMATOES . . . BERRIES . . . MELONS . . . PEACHES . . . and CORN, for sale. We passed immense churches, both Roman Catholic and Protestant. Mrs Wicks is hot against the Government as it makes for Catholic graft. All public offices appear to be given to them! I wonder what you would have said to see three elderly women in a car each sucking a large square of sweet on a stick (a "sucker"). I laughed inwardly as no one else did outwardly.

Each city I have been in so far has some great and mighty industry of which people speak with reverence: here, the great KODAK manufacturers are rampant and the name of George Eastman the millionaire is quoted (he is dead); at London, Ontario, it was KELLOGG'S Corn Flakes and Shredded Wheat; and in St Catharines it was the lightening fastener (ZIP) factories. All the street lamps here are painted with aluminium paint and are something like the shape of the sign of life in Rider Haggard's books with a bell-light hanging down. I saw many walls by the roads and fields - just like those around Bradford on Avon in England - flat pieces of stone, one on another. At Niagara the stones were rounded and large in size, here they are huge but flat. I wondered what Aparko Hots were and find they are a kind of hot dog. Then this advert struck me as queer - CHEW MABON TOBACCO AND TREAT YOURSELF TO THE BEST.

When we arrived home we had hot lamb chops and sweet potatoes which are cooked in plum sauce. I tried them - but never again. I don't like sugary and savoury things together but there were red onions, tomatoes, cucumbers and beet to eat with the meat; and apple sauce in little dishes to eat with cake for afters. I'm getting used to the scrappy sort of meals here. We never see a pudding - only a pie or a tart as I call 'em.

I think I shall leave here on 2 September. I am feeling a bit nervous about the train journey, especially the nights. But I won't say so and it will soon be over, won't it? So my letters from home might as well go at once to Joe's home. I'm very well but it's very hot and I've an ulcerated mouth which is uncomfortable. My mosquito bites are fading on my legs but I've had some sore places on them.

My dearest love to you all,

Your Mother

PS. Will Muriel send me the book with the knitted patterns for hats in it? I believe she made herself a green one and me a navy one.

* * * * *

[LETTER 25]

"Sure, your cousin is some wisecrack"

60 Grand View Heights, Long Pond, Rochester, New York State, USA
Sunday, 29 August 1937

MY DEARS,

My days go by so pleasantly here and the weather is good. I've been to church with Ben and Alice this morning. The church that they go to occasionally is in Charlotte. It is a small building not much larger than our schoolroom. It is Episcopal - Anglican we should call it, but very few attend. The service begins at 9.30am as the parson has another service to conduct at 11am at another village, Spencerville, some miles away. I get on fairly well with the prayer-book but it seems strange to me to pray for the President and the Governor of the state and no mention of George and Elizabeth and all the Royal Family.

This afternoon we read and rested and have just now come in from a call upon some neighbours of Ben, who farm nearby. It put me in mind of the tales we have read: the great big man chewing tobacco and spitting for yards; the little round woman totally unable to keep up with her brood of long-legged children; the great rambling wooden house with everything needing mending or repairing; half a dozen dogs; and Grandmother there as well. We sat on the porch which has screen doors and windows all round - all the seats and rocking-chairs all to pieces but most comfortable to sit upon; a great wooden pail of apples brought out for delectation - no apology for untidiness; the man just in from the fields with nothing on but his under-vest and trousers. He is so proud of his plump round wife and big plain boys and girls. He swore quite naturally in his talk. When his mother came in he said, "Say Ma, here's a little lady who has come all the way from England by herself and is going on to California. Isn't she damned plucky!" He told me the police were just bums but I was never to fear 'em, "Take no notice of the buggers". I think he has fallen foul of some. Ben says he is rough but straight as a die.

The home was the exact opposite to the one I went to on Saturday evening: a courtly old man and his wife (also farmers) dressed well, the wife with beautifully waved hair. They had three small daughters, one a widow. I think it is usual here if the daughter is left a widow, for her to go home to her father's house, children and all. If you remember, it is always so in American books. These three girls had just been on vacation (accent on the vay) and had driven over 2 thousand miles by car, crossing two states and touching five others - so they told me with pride.

By the way, the old lady at the farm told me her forbears were named Tennyson and were cousins to the poet. However, it made no impression upon anybody. She told me her mother was Scots and her grandparents came from England but she did not know which part. The people at the ramshackle farm were named Frisby and the aristocrats named Pyatt. I wonder if they are connected to the Mrs Pyatt we know? These people originally came from Lancashire. One man who was there was a bit of a braggart and went on to talk about men's superiority in most things. It takes men to do this and that. "Why," said he as if he was giving me some news, "God made woman out of one of Adams ribs".

"Yes, and God had to give him an anaesthetic and put him to sleep - or there would have been some yelling," I said. [*The Bible, Genesis 2:21, where God caused a deep sleep to fall upon Adam before taking out one of his ribs.*]

The man laughed until he cried and told Ben, "Sure, your cousin is some wise-crack". They are awfully queer folk. Just fancy heaping apple sauce over your potatoes and eating them and jam and cheese together!! I am being introduced to a number of folk as, "Ben's cousin - Mrs Kimpton - over from England - has been touring Canada - now going on to California to visit her son" (!!!) Great amazement - they seem to imagine me a millionaire and it makes me feel I'm here on false pretences having been all my life the poor relation - even with my dad.

One man said, "I came out here 30 years ago and have never saved up enough to go home on a trip. How did you do it?"

I told him: "We save the pennies in England".

[LETTER 25 CONTINUED]

"I believe you are right," said he. "We make money and spend it."

Then they tell me of the years of depression as though England had none. They also blame the war as if it happened here. People ask me: "Do they still do this in England? . . . Do they still do that? . . . Are there any fairs? . . . Can you still buy rock with words running through it? . . . What do you find different here?" . . . I tell them what they want to know to the best of my ability, but must say that people, food, houses and ways are all different. But you get used to things gradually. Tell me, Fred, what price is petrol a gallon at home? How much is car tax and what income tax do we pay in England? I don't know the answers to these questions and I'm often asked them. Also what make is your car and the make of Uncle Joe's? [*The standard rate of Income Tax in 1937 was 4/9d (4 shillings and 9 pence) in the pound.*]

I don't know if Miss Harris [*probably Sarah*] has ever read this poem. The explanation of the lines about the corncob in the winter was told to me. Apparently, in the far away farms they use the husks of the corn as lavatory paper and in many WC's a lot of them are tied to a piece of string. In the poem there was only one. They had to be like Job in the Bible and scrape themselves withal. [*Job 22:8, "took him a potsherd to scrape himself withal" to alleviate the irritation when he was afflicted with boils.*] I copied it from above a lavatory seat in a bathroom:

THE PASSING OF THE OLD BACKHOUSE SEAT

WHEN MEMORY keeps me company and moves to smiles or tears,
A weather-beaten object, looms through the mist of years.
Behind the house and barn it stood a half a mile or more,
And hurrying feet a path had made straight to its swinging door.

Its architecture was a type of simple classic art
But in the tragedy of life it played a leading part,
And oft the passing traveller drove slow and heaved a sigh
To see the modest hired-girl slip out with glances shy.

We had our posy garden that the women loved so well.
I loved it too, but better still, I loved the stronger smell
That filled the evening breezes so full of homely cheer
And told the night o'er taken tramp that human life was near.

On lazy August afternoons, it made a little bower
Delightful, where my grandsire sat and whiled away an hour,
For there on summer mornings its very cares entwined
And berry bushes reddened in the steaming soil behind.

All day fat spiders spun their webs to catch the buzzing flies
That flitted to and from the house where Ma was baking pies,
And once a swarm of hornets bold had built a palace there
And stung my unsuspecting aunt - I must not tell you where.

Then father took a flaming pole - that was a happy day,
He nearly burnt the building up when the hornets came to stay.
When summer bloom began to fade and winter to carouse,
We banked the little building with a heap of hemlock boughs.

But when the crust was on the snow and sullen skies were grey,
In sooth the building was no place where one would wish to stay.
We did our duties promptly, there one purpose swayed the mind,
We tarried not, nor lingered long on what we left behind.

The torture of that icy seat could make a Spartan sob,
The needs must scrape the gooseflesh with a lacerating cob
That from a frost encrusted nail was suspended by a string:
My father was a frugal man and wasted not a thing.

When Grandpa had "to go out back" and make his morning call,
We'd bundle up the dear old man with muffler and a shawl.
I knew the hole on which he sat, 'twas padded all around
And once I dared to sit there - 'twas all too wide I found.

My loins were all too little and I jack-knifed there to stay,
They had to come and get me out or I'd have passed away.
Then father said ambition was a thing that boys should shun
And I must use the children's hole till childhood days were done.

But still I marvel at the craft that cut those holes so true,
The baby hole, and the slender hole that fitted sister Sue.
That dear old country landmark, I've tramped around a bit
And in the lap of luxury my lot has been to sit.

But 'ere I die I'll eat the fruit of trees I robbed of yore,
Then seek the shanty where my name is carved upon the door.
I ween the old familiar smell will soothe my faded soul,
I'm now a man, but none the less, I'll try the children's hole.

James Whitcomb Riley

Copied at Long Pond, Rochester, USA
30 August 1937

[*The art and craft of privy building in the American outback - the average family 3-holer or even an exceptional 8-holer; the merits of furnishing with a mail-order catalogue or a box for corncobs; and the hazards of wasps' nests are similarly told in the humorous little book "The Specialist" by Charles Sale, first published by Putnam & Co in 1930 and reprinted over 600 thousand times.*]

* * *

Monday [*30 August 1937*]

ALICE has had a bilious attack this morning so is lying down. I've washed up, but don't know what else to do. As I said before, my stock has risen with the relations here as well as on the other side in Canada. Ben is proud to show me off. People are surprised that I am not staying more than a week with them with so much to see and so many people to visit. As it is most likely that I will never see Rochester again, I've decided to stay until Thursday, 9 September.

Much love to you all,
Your loving Mum

* * * * *

[LETTER 26]

"Ben eats his like a Christian - on a plate - and so do I . . . . . ."

60 Grand View Heights, Long Pond, Rochester, New York State, USA
Saturday, 4 September 1937

MY DEARS,

This is Saturday, 4 September and this morning we have had a severe thunderstorm and the air is somewhat cooler. It has been very hot and at 7.30am the other morning the thermometer showed 80F in the shade and it was near 90F later on. I've never been so hot and am glad I don't have to walk anywhere. This morning it was 47F in the shade at 8 o'clock whereas last Saturday it was 90F in the city!!!

I am sending you two Rochester newspapers so that you may see what kind of papers they have over here. Also a leaflet on the new, very large library in the city which I went over the other day. It's a lovely place. We went into the city to do a little shopping. We live some 15 miles from Rochester and 9 miles from Charlotte. We called on several of Alice's friends and they were all so interested in my travels. In fact one young woman prefaced almost every remark with, "For the land's sake". When I remarked upon it they said, "We never noticed it". [*Probably the lady really said, "For the Lord's sake," and Annie was confused by the American accent.*]

One word they use quite a lot is "ambition" and "ambitious" but they mean energy and energetic. Alice has been ailing these last four days and when I enquired how she was one morning said, "I'm better but have no ambition". A man today speaking of his boy said, "He's an ambitious little devil," meaning he's lively and energetic. I can understand the Americans mocking at the English way of dropping the H's for no one does here and it makes even the commonest talk sound superior. I've been told I must be careful not to say I feel "knocked up" as that means "in the family way", rather than tired - and makes folk laugh. I hate to hear one of their common phrases - if anything gets tangled or messed up, they will say: "It's all buggered up".

We went up a flight of stairs into a bank yesterday and at the top was a bubbler with the coldest ice-water I've ever tasted, like liquid ice. Nearly all the stores and business houses have them around. Have I told you about the Funeral Homes here and in Canada? It's customary, when a person dies, for the undertaker to come and take the body away and embalm it in some way. It is dressed in a coat, trousers, etc, if a man - and in their frocks, etc, if a woman - put in a casket (what we call a coffin) and it stays in the Funeral Home. Then everyone goes to see the body, whether you've known them or not. The service is held there, or if the body is brought home everybody assembles there and has a look. Sometimes the parson preaches in the house and sometimes in the Funeral Home. They are imposing gloomy-looking places and one I saw yesterday struck me as comical - it had black and white linoleum all down the steps right into the street.

I sent a wire to Joe to tell him that I am leaving on the 9th and shall see them on 12 September. To our great surprise, I got a tourist rate for the wire and it only cost me 35 cents. Alice has been trying to teach me how to tatt. It's far harder than it appears.

* * *

Sunday, 5 September 1937

HAVE just returned from church with Alice. Fancy driving nine miles to Charlotte. The service began at 9.30am and we got home at 11am. The parson expounded politics and mentioned names in a way quite foreign to English ears: telling us that John L Lewis, who will rave over the radio tomorrow as it is Labour Day and a general holiday, is worse than a gangster, etc, etc, etc. His text was: Come unto me all ye that LABOUR. [*John L Lewis was president of the United Mineworkers Trade Union and head of the CIO (the Committee for Industrial Organisation) who were in dispute with the steel manufacturers - with violent strikes and the shooting of 18 strikers dead by company police. In the Labour Day broadcast, John L Lewis berated President Roosevelt - who had responded to appeals by the CIO for Federal intervention by saying: "A plague on both your houses".*]

It is cool today so Alice lent me her grey coat because I've already got mine packed in my big case. I shall get my brown coat out tomorrow if it looks like being cool while I'm travelling to Frisco. Shall be so glad when the train journey is over.

We had hot dogs for supper last evening. The fireplace here is a big open chimney and they make a fire of charcoal and fix a frame with wires across it on the hearth and grill the hot dogs on it, over the glowing charcoal. They are like pork sausages and they eat them hot with bread rolls and butter. Usually the rolls are split and buttered, the sausage placed inside with a liberal supply of French mustard and then eaten. Ben eats his like a Christian - on a plate - and so do I, for I could never stretch my mouth far enough to eat them as others do. This is a popular meal out of doors. I prefer these hot dogs to Wieners. [*Annie tasted Wieners with the Southams - they were spicy German or Vienna sausages, akin to Frankfurters.*]

Someone told me that they had seen a paper from England and it had told of the death of Lord Rothschild at Tring. I wonder if that will make any difference to Uncle Joe? [*Joseph Timberlake, Annie's brother, once remarked that he had owned one of the first bicycles to be seen in Abbots Langley. He became the farm manager for the first Lord Rothschild, Baron Nathaniel, at Hastoe Farm which is over 750 feet above sea level in the Chiltern Hills, near Tring in Hertfordshire. He originally worked in the Estate Office at Tring and was asked to*

[LETTER 26 CONTINUED]
manage the farms (which totalled 5,000 acres) by the Agent, Richardson Carr, in about 1899. When roads were impassable during a severe cold spell, Joseph had skated to work from Abbots Langley along the Grand Union Canal which had frozen over and this may have impressed the Agent. Joseph became a tenant farmer of Hastoe Farm and three neighbouring farms in 1915. The Hastoe Farm herd of pedigree Dairy Shorthorn cows became almost world famous under his direction. Later Joseph took out a mortgage and bought the four farms. Annie and her children had often visited Hastoe Farm and the Tring Zoological Museum established by Sir Lionel, the second Lord Rothschild who died in 1937. Joseph Timberlake's younger son, Ken, took over Hastoe Farm when Joseph died in 1942. Further details about Joseph Timberlake's elder son, Robert, are given in Appendix I: "The Kimpton Family".]

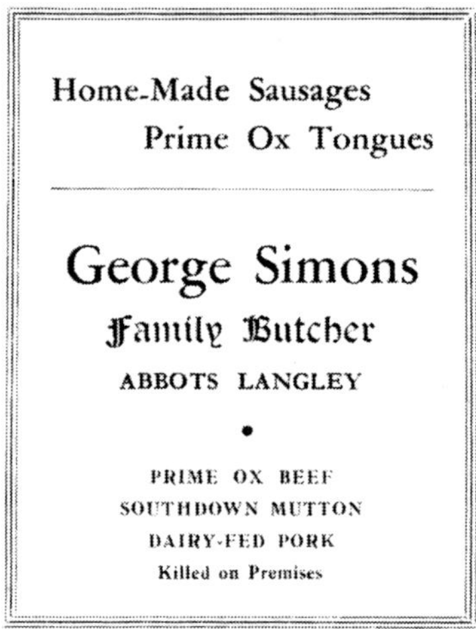

An advert from the 1937 Methodist Church Fête programme. George Simons' butcher's shop was at 17 High Street (opposite the Church of St Lawrence) and was one of the village's oldest businesses, having been established in 1832. George's sister, Katie, was the wife of Annie's brother, Joseph Timberlake of Hastoe Farm.

I wish you would send me a few of the new threepenny bits for this year as there are several boys who would love to have one. They would have to be sent to San Francisco. I've given one lad (Edward Savage) a sixpence, a penny and a ha'penny out of the few English coins I have with me and he was very excited over them.

We went on Sunday afternoon for the first walk I have taken here along the shore of Lake Ontario. It is all summer-houses, bathing-houses and garages, etc, and the waves lap the sands very like the sea, save that the breakers do not seem to start so far from the shore. All the houses have fantastic names: DUCKY WUCKY . . . JOHNNY JONES BOYS . . . DUNROMIN . . . I'M IN MA'S INN . . . WE'RE ALL INN . . . DEW DROP INN . . . and many more. Alice took a snap of me with the pond behind me. It's some pond, being about three quarters of a mile across and nearly two miles long. There are three such ponds close by but Long Pond is the largest. Ben took us across the pond in his boat the other evening.

Last night, Alice got her out her projector and shewed me a movie film. She used to work at KODAK and was able to get film there. I saw the Hawkins family and Auntie Esther [*Esther Hawkins née Gates, sister of Annie's mother*] come out of her house, down the steps and push one of May's babies in the pram (or buggy). Oh, I do wish I could have seen her in the flesh. She had grown very like Grandma Gates in her old age. The last scene of her was on the sidewalk (pavement) waving to them going off. [*Annie Kimpton's grandparents, James Gates and Mary Ann Gates née Coleman, lived at the hamlet of Astrope, by Puttenham, on the Hertfordshire border, near Tring. Annie's mother, Mary Ann Gates, was born there. Her place of birth was given as "Putnam" in the 1881 census and as Astrope for both her and her sister, Esther, in the 1891 census of the Timberlake and the Hawkins families in Adrian Road, Abbots Langley.*]

I've been to the city of Rochester this afternoon and got me a face towel for use on the train. My own is locked in my trunk which is to go off tomorrow night. I am leaving Rochester at 6.30am on Thursday. I will write to you as soon as I arrive.

Much love,

Mum

PS. A tale I was told by an old lady:

A man bought some pants at a men's store and returned to change them and was greatly embarrassed to find a young lady in charge. When she enquired the trouble he asked to be served by a man.

"Oh," said she, "he is on vacation. You need not mind telling me."

"Well," said he, "have you ever been in the Cathedral ballroom?"

"No," said she, "there is no ballroom in the Cathedral".

"No more is there in these pants," said he(!!!)

* * * * *

Britannia graced the tail-side of both the penny and halfpenny coins until 1937 when the "ship" halfpenny design was first minted showing Sir Francis Drake's "Golden Hind" in which he discovered California in 1579 and circumnavigated the world.

Train Journey To San Francisco

Between 1828 and 1850 the first phase of the railway system in the USA connected the large cities in the eastern states such as Boston, New York and Rochester. Further expansion westwards to Chicago and south to the Mississippi/Missouri region was completed between 1852 and 1859. Construction of a transcontinental railroad westwards from the southern states was delayed by the outbreak of the Civil War in 1862. However, California was little affected by the war and rapid advance of the railroad took place eastwards from there. The Central Pacific Railroad and the Union Pacific Railroad met at Promontory, Utah, on 10 May 1869. By 1885 the Santa Fe Railroad from Chicago had reached the Los Angeles basin. The last transcontinental line, the Western Pacific Railroad from Utah to Oakland, California, opened in 1910. The Santa Fe Railroad was one of the largest of the American railway systems (its full name being the Atchison, Topeka and Santa Fe Railroad).

The train journey taken by Annie Kimpton was by the New York Central Railroad from Rochester to Chicago, Illinois, and then by the Santa Fe Railroad from Chicago to Oakland, California. This journey was about 3,100 miles long and took over three days including three nights spent on the train:

[LETTER 27]

"A lady sits next to me with scarlet claws and lips"

Kansas City, Santa Fe Railroad, USA
Friday, 10 September 1937

My Dears,

Here I am on the last bit of my long journey and I think it is going to be the pleasantest. I left Rochester at 6.30am on Thursday morning. Ben and Alice drove me down to the station. Mrs Wicks, Alice's mother, was very sorry to say goodbye and wished me good luck. Alice packed me a box with food in it. We had taken my big trunk down the day before and got my train tickets. They are long strips, perforated at intervals, which are torn off at different stages of my journey. Rochester station is big but I shall be seeing bigger ones on the journey. I found the information that Joe sent me very useful and if I had not had it they would never have told me at the ticket-office. It saved me quite a few dollars - the difference between $104 and $69 or thereabouts.

I rode all day long to Chicago and my ticket allowed for a free bus ride at this station. On my long train-ride we passed deep railway cuttings all covered in yellow flowers [*Golden Rod*] just like those in our garden. Cleveland is a huge place with great factories many stories high. We tore past many smaller places on our way and only stopped at a few larger towns. I noticed that around Cleveland the dwellings were nearly all two-storied wooden houses - not bungalows. At Toledo, another great city, we saw huge towers and a young fellow said, "Ugh, ugh," just like a Red Indian. There had been no rain recently in this neighbourhood as the cars we could see on the roads had clouds of dust behind them. The railroad ran alongside the road for many miles and in places the houses on the other side of the road faced the track. All you needed to do if you wanted to commit suicide would be to walk across the road and fling yourself in front of a train! Toledo is the terminus for one of the Great Lakes' ports [*Lake Erie*]. As we went along, a white-coated attendant came and placed a sample of salted peanuts in our laps. It struck me as strange to see a big placard on the road saying, WELCOME TO OHIO. At each stopping place a man comes on board with ice and places it in a large ice-box at the end of each car (carriage). You can take a paper cup from a receptacle and get iced water from a little tap - everything for your convenience. I was thankful, though, to get out at Chicago.

★

WE got to Chicago at about 6.30pm and I transferred by bus [*from the NEW YORK CENTRAL RAILROAD station*] to the SANTA FE RAILROAD station and this train left at quarter to nine. As I had already booked my reservations at Rochester there was no trouble at all. I was in Car W, Lower Berth II. There is no one in the bunk above me and all the porters are coloured men in white raiment. The beds are much wider than ships' bunks and very comfortable. A man pulls down the shut-in roof at the side to form the upper bunk, comes and makes up your bed with two pillows and pulls down the blinds. There are two electric globe-lights in each berth, a hammock across the windows for small articles and two coat-hangers hang from the curtain rail (the curtains are made of the heaviest dark-green jean and button down the centre). Your suitcase goes underneath your bunk. There is a nice little dressing-room and several lavatories - "toilets" as they call them. Towels are provided and drinking-cups and ice-water. There is plenty of privacy and I undressed on the bed, slipped on my dressing-gown and went to the wash-room. There are two aluminium wash-basins with all the conveniences, a chair, and mirrors everywhere.

Santa Fe

Atchison, Topeka & Santa Fe Railway System

We have to go through cars and cars to get to the dining-car and for breakfast I had eggs, ham, hot rolls and tea for 26 cents, and I tipped the black man 10 cents. I am writing this letter in the lounge which is a car with long windows, easy chairs and writing-tables. A lady sits next to me with scarlet claws and lips. All the folk hereabouts look to have broad nostrils. You seldom see a pinched nose and the number of white-haired young folk is amazing. Great trains go past while we wait here for we do not depart [*from Kansas City*] until past 10 o'clock [*in the morning*]. The times are bewildering for there is Eastern Time, Central Time, Pacific Time . . . and I don't know if there are any more.

We are just pulling out of Kansas City and it's an awfully big place. Part of it seems to be built right up into a height. [*Kansas City, on the Missouri River, was the "crossroads" of the trails that led to the West.*] The black porter has just brought me a

[LETTER 27 CONTINUED]
pillow. I asked him if there was any charge?

"No," said he in his soft voice (by the way, all the porters seem to have gold fillings in their teeth - perhaps they think it looks effective against their dark faces), "all is included. But if you would like to give the porter something when you leave the train . . . . . ."

I'm told there are two Kansases - Kansas City in Kansas and Kansas City in Missouri [*the same conurbation but spread across the border between the two states*]. The fields around here are very bare and a lady told me that this part of the States is very hot and has little rain. The rocky gorges look like the rocks in Niagara. Each little farmhouse has a bunch of trees around it and you can see the "old backhouse" at a little distance away from the house.

I tried to get a pair of sun-glasses in Rochester but could only get dark ones. I wanted soft light-green ones so did not buy them. I now wish I had them for the sun reflecting from the houses, etc, makes one's eyes tired. We are running beside the road and I can see clouds of dust settling on all the hedges and trees. These cars are air-conditioned and have double windows - so no flies or dust. The conductor has just been along and asked me if I would like my berth for the next two nights reserved as a single, no one above me, both mattresses of the two beds on mine, more air and comfort, etc, etc, for an extra $1.50? I told him, "Yes". I would hate for a man to be above me. He asked me where I came from and was much interested that I came from England. He had always wanted to go there and hoped to one day. He has a conductor friend - an Englishman named Fletcher - who, "Sure is a nice fellow," and is always talking of England. He goes on this same route across the States to San Francisco.

The land we are now passing through is as flat as a table and I should think that they will never use all the corn that's planted. There are a few trees here and there in the distance and farms dotted about but it is very dry, flat and uninteresting. Some dry watercourses are to be seen with bridges over them. The railway cuttings look like whitish brown sandbanks and a long white highway can be seen running across the countryside with telegraph poles alongside. A black man in a wide straw hat stops his plough to stare at our train - which is a very long one. Now we come to a bit of green field. Do you know that the yellow flower we cultivate in our front garden (the yellow feathery one) is a noxious weed here and the farmers' enemy? [*Known in England as Golden Rod, it is rampant and invasive in the USA.*] The country now looks more fertile with more prosperous farms. A station with over 50 men standing on the platform. Have just passed Quenemo. Now lots of bush and scrub. The earth looks darker but only a small amount is cultivated.

A lady opposite me has just offered me a chocolate. She is going to San Francisco - lives there and has been visiting in Detroit. A girl at my table this morning had two rashers of streaky bacon and a pile of pancakes which she covered thickly with maple syrup. She ate them all together, with gusto. Alice's sandwiches were made with baked ham covered with pineapple juice, brown sugar and cloves. It certainly gave them a decided flavour. I faintly praise it but can't bring myself to eat the gooey syrup. We have just passed a station. I could catch the name - Peabody. They have evidently had

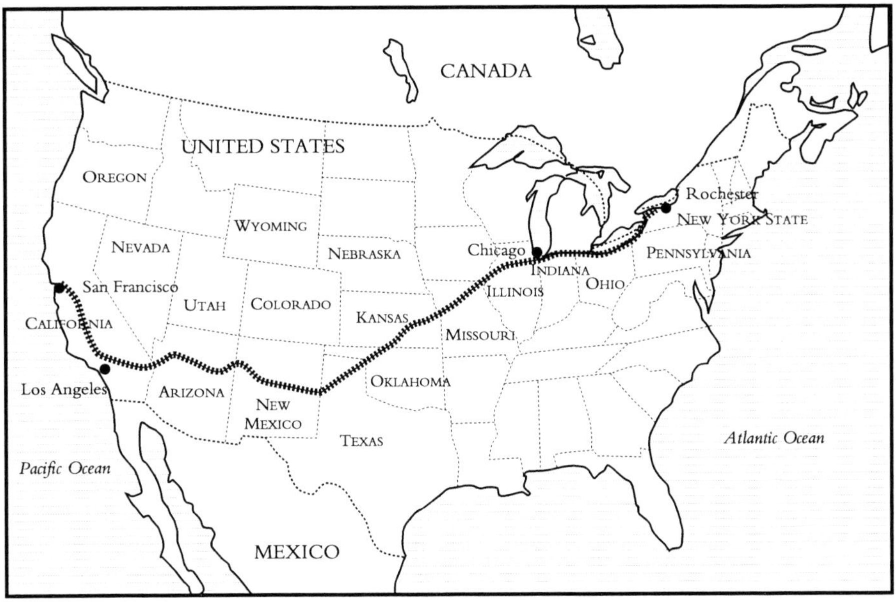

Annie Kimpton's railway journey across the United States in 1937.

floods here. The corn is growing in a swamp and long stretches of the land are under water. We pass many farms. A lady tells me they are called "ranches" and I saw a water-trough with about 20 mules kicking and jumping. All along the way, sometimes far and again near, one can see the main highway which follows the railway route south.

This train is wonderful. It rides easier than any bus. Have just left Newton with, WESTERN UNION [*the Telegraph Company*] above the station door and everything looking new. The sun is beating down and I have the blinds lowered, though I can still see the miles and miles of flat fields with just a few trees all in straight rows. A lady has just lent me her *Liberty* magazine to read. She says that there is a tale in it foretelling the downfall of America. A sort of spontaneous combustion, I imagine, to pay for its intense wickedness.

"What do you think of the Duke of Windsor?" said she.

I wonder how many times I've been asked that question? I told her that England doesn't think about him any more.

"Oh, he would have made such a good King. Look how he went into the poor peoples' homes."

I told this lady that his kind of goodness did not go very deep if he could so quickly forget his people and his promises.

"Ah," said a man, "he had no chance once in the clutches of a bad, American woman."

We have just passed through Wichita, an immense city which has outgrown its railway station [*the largest city in the state of Kansas*]. I hear that there are large oil wells here and saw the large tall drum-like containers for the oil. We passed Wellington

[LETTER 27 CONTINUED]
and stopped and were then shunted onto another line. I counted over 20 men doing this operation and none of them moved at all quickly. Some just sat on a low brick wall. The coloured men looked strange - some dressed in immaculate greys, some with lovely grey-blue shirts - their hands looking as if they had kid gloves on. So many American faces are of the Ben Busby type. [*Ben Busby lived in the High Street, Abbots Langley, with his sister, Mary. They were the village undertakers.*]

Have just been to dinner ("supper" time): roast turkey with dressing or stuffing, mashed potatoes, peas, tea and vanilla ice-cream - all beautifully served for 36 cents. I saw what the other ladies tipped the waiter, so I gave him the same - 10 cents. I've just seen the new moon through the carriage window. Now we have flat fields again. This is a dreary stretch of land - it has evidently been under water. Now we are in a deep cutting. Now we are back to the flat lands with great ponds and gullies full of water. The sun is just going to bed, everything pinks and golds. It is five minutes past eight and the porter is making up some of the beds.

* * *

Saturday morning, 11 September 1937

I HAD a very good night. The rocking and bumping noises do not disturb me and the beds are most comfortable. I think I'm a good traveller. We are now in New Mexico and passing through the most arid looking places, all sand and large dunes covered sparsely with what they tell me is sage. Then a mountain range of purple and reddish rock with the white highway visible here and there. We have passed several ranches surrounded by huts where the Mexicans live and by the side of the track a long line of men, darkies and Mexicans [*most probably Pueblo Indians and people of Spanish descent, not necessarily Mexicans*], who waved at the train. Then past a queer little station called Lucy. Now another looking quite Spanish in style with flat roofs, called Laguna. Next, we pass a siding filled with trucks laden with fir-tree trunks which must have come from a long distance for there is not a tree in sight for miles and miles.

Now I can see a New Mexican village in a valley with a few patches of corn here and there. Here are great ranges of sandy brown coloured hills, range upon range. One wonders how human beings can exist there. Then I see a flat-roofed house set right into the rocky hillside and all plastered over the same colour. Now we pass quite imposing flat-roofed houses built beneath great overhanging rocks and with many fields of Indian corn. The conductor tells me we enter Arizona at noon today and go right across the state of Arizona in nine hours and then into California. We are going past immense tracks of black stuff that looks like lava. Then a man on horseback driving a herd of cattle. All that can be seen for miles is just the railtrack and the highway with the occasional car or truck.

Now we are pulling in for Mt Taylor Camp. Now a station named Grants, with long lines of cabins and squalid looking buildings, lots of advertisements, petrol stations and a just few men. Once again we are passing through flat sandy plains with rock outcrops and great hills in the distance - then an isolated farm - what a life! Now there are patches of corn and greenery with little wooden houses with the washing hanging out. I'm told that the immense range of hills in the distance is part of the Rocky Range of mountains. [*Soon after Grants the railroad crosses the Continental Divide, the watershed of the Rocky Mountains which extend from Alaska in the North to New Mexico in the South.*] Then a little station called Blue Water with just two trees beside it and a village with the main highway running through it. Always the great hills in the background.

Every now and then a lady sits down in the other half of my two-seater and passes the time of day with me. They are most interested to know that I am writing down my experiences as we travel. "Just wait till you get to California. You will have something to write about then!" A man has just gone through the car with a basket of cheese crackers and vanilla wafers, but I don't need them nor the peanuts. Now, as we draw nearer to the hills, I can see that they are covered with small trees. As I mentioned, I paid $1.50 extra and have the berth to myself and it is very comfortable and airy. During the day I have two seats facing each other and a pillow, so I can put my feet up and doze if I like.

It is quite a journey to the dining-car, through four sleeping-cars and the lounge before you come to it. Between each car are very heavy doors and you step across the buffers of each car over rubber mats and on each door it says, WATCH YOUR STEP. Each car has lavatories at each end and ladies' and men's dressing-rooms. In the dressing-room are two long mirrors, a chair before a dressing-shelf with a mirror above, a spirit lamp to heat irons, two aluminium wash-bowls and a bubbler. There is also a shelf with face-towels all folded neatly and a receptacle with paper cups for use with the ice-water. Hot and cold water are available and then through a door is a little three-cornered lavatory with shelf, spittoon and paper roll - everything for your comfort. When you go for breakfast it seems strange to go through cars all curtained off with folk asleep behind them - and it smells like it too! A nurse is carried on these trains. She has a room at the end of this car and people with babies consult her and she prepares children's food. One elderly lady on this car has a hunch back and has her meals served here and the nurse sees that the lady has reading matter. The nurse is a pleasant-faced youngster in a grey-blue costume with a badge on her arm and she wears a square beret on her head.

Here the prairie is covered with delicate blue flowers and pretty green tufts but then for many miles there are no flowers - just sandy green tufts and red sandstone mountains. Now we are close to the highway again with patches of blue, white and yellow flowers. I've just seen a real local horserider in blue trousers, bright yellow shirt and wearing a wide hat. A solitary car with ladies in it has just crossed at a level crossing. I cannot imagine how anyone can live in such an arid looking wilderness but I'm told Arizona is much worse by far. We have passed the quite large town of Gallup and Indian squaws were selling pottery and Indian dolls to the passengers. [*Gallup is close to the New Mexico/Arizona state border.*] Now we are going across miles of prairie and we stopped at a station but I couldn't get the name. The heat outside is terrific. I just went outside onto the step and when you return to the carriage it's just like going into a refrigerator. We have just run by a little halt called Sunshine and rightly named. The sky is a deep blue overhead and pale blue in the distance with a few fleecy white

[LETTER 27 CONTINUED]
clouds. Now past a rough stone building marked, TRADING POST. It looks as if it is open to the sky as some are. Then another little railway halt with just two or three dwellings and one pretty wooden bungalow with a little stone wall round it. This is beside a deep dry gorge with great stones in it which looks as if a river should flow through it and named Canyon Diablo. [*The SANTA FE time-table indicates that the railroad crosses this on Canyon Diablo Viaduct. These apparently dry river-beds channel flash floods when rare thunderstorms occur; in just a short time these river-beds become raging torrents.*]

I can see great dark hills in the distance - miles and miles of empty countryside. Only the railway, the telegraph wires and a three-strand wire fence to show the presence of man. Now the shrubs are larger like stunted trees and I can see great mounds up to the sky looking like Fujiyama. [*The San Francisco Mountains, with Humphrey's Peak at 12,570 feet being the highest point in the state of Arizona, looking like Japan's Mount Fuji.*] The hills are now quite thickly wooded and I can see coloured flowers occasionally but the great rocks and boulders are awful. Now past some cultivated fields, corn, etc, and a halt named Cosnino. The slopes are now all thickly wooded with fir-trees. I should think there are millions of them. At the foot of the great hills are little ranches and homes with some cultivated ground and a few cattle and the inevitable backhouse. Now we are going past camps, hotels, advertisements, etc: A GREAT POWWOW 7,000 INDIANS . . . CALL AT PUEBLO INN . . . GREAT PLACES CALIFORNIAN OIL CO . . . and TEXAS OIL CO. We stop.

⋆

I GET out and walk for a few minutes at what I am told is a typical Western Town - Flagstaff, Arizona. Quite a big place but much of it garish to my eyes with many Indians and Spanish-looking people. Then the conductor shouts, "All aboard," and we get back on and off we go through more pine-woods. We have just passed a big hill which has had half of it removed by great mechanical shovels and men with machines with Caterpillar wheels filling wagons with red earth. Everything around is covered with red dust and it looks as if they are making a new highway.

I have just returned from the dining-car. The appointments are fine. We have a waiter to each table and a steward who sees you to your seat, gives you a menu, a serviette, and a card and pencil to write down your requirements. A glass of iced water is given to everyone before you start your meal. I had roast veal, mashed potatoes, sweetcorn, ice-cream and a pot of tea - all for 36 cents plus, of course, the tip for the waiter who brings your change on a silver plate and waits for the tip.

⋆ ⋆ ⋆

Sunday morning, 12 September 1937

LAST evening, several ladies in the car got together and wanted to know, yet again, what England thought of the Duke of Windsor?

I told them that England did not think of him any more. He was a back number and that we were quite satisfied with the exchange and that the majority thought it was for the best.

"Of course, people in England are shocked by divorce," they said.

"Not at all," said I, "but we bar a twice-divorcee, even if she was not proved to be the guilty party, from being the Queen of England."

"We felt so sorry for him poor fellow. In his last speech . . . . . ."

"Why?" said I. "When he said that stuff about the woman he loved and she was then another man's wife."

"Well yes," said one, "but we think he was so brave."

"Well," said I, "he has what he wanted. And England did not want and would not have her as Queen. So, as I tell you, England has no time for him or her and they are not now in the news and I don't expect she likes that."

They laughed and two separate ladies said afterwards, "We have a great respect for England and her Royal Family and are glad to know England is not stricken over the blow" (!!!)

Our train stopped at Barstow at 2am so we were stationary all night. [*This town is well into California.*] This morning we are waiting here till 8.45am and I've been out and around a beautiful hotel built here like a Spanish palace - arches, cupolas, a green shady courtyard, and flowering vines down all the pillars. I went into the reading room at the Barstow Hotel and saw an English *The Weekly Times* and among the illustrations was one of a flooded street in Willesden with an almost submerged lorry from the heavy rainfall on 13 August. I shall send postcards home for you to keep for me - they are the things I've seen. The porter told me that, last night, we passed a huge ravine called the "Bottomless Pit" as nothing has ever bottomed it! It is very hot here at 8 o'clock in the morning. I don't know what it will be like at noon but I'm well, couldn't feel better - a lazy life suits me admirably. I like having a spot of my own even if it is only two railway seats. It seems strange to see that this line runs to San Bernardino, Los Angeles - pronounced with a "g" as in San Diego. [*The line divides, going either to Los Angeles or to Oakland.*] Now we are off and they tell me we go through many tunnels. Fancy, I'm really in California and tonight I'll see my Joe.

*

AS FAR as the eye can see, on both sides of the train, there is nothing but great hills of sand covered with tufts of dry yellow growths - then a group of trees and a little wooden home. The highway looks like a black ribbon running across the desert. I've just seen the first birds since we left Chicago - two crows. Now a large white wooden building with two yellow buses in front of it - school buses. Evidently a school and a few children going to it on cycles. Now past a little station, Hinkley - a gasolene place. Past miles of desert and stop at a little place, Kramer, with about six bungalows nearby.

Have just bought a pair of sun-glasses. The sand is making my eyes ache. We are now passing a lot of isolated trees looking like cactus but which are called "Joshua Trees" and only grow in this sandy desert. [*Called "Joshua Trees" by the early Mormons either, as reputed, because they were likened to the Old Testament Joshua, who led the Jews to*

[LETTER 27 CONTINUED]
the promised land after Moses died or, perhaps, because they were likened to the trees on which Joshua hanged the five Amorite kings (the Bible, Joshua 10:26). The trees have trunks with a large girth and they grow 30-40ft with twisted, bent and tufted branches.]

The Mojave Desert (pronounced "Mohave") is really sandy here, not a vestige of anything living. Past an Indian settlement with all the folk dressed up and walking about - it being a Sunday. I wonder what you are doing? The time is different, I know. Now a station - Mojave: a little town, wooden bungalows, gasolene stations, a few stores, Indian kids running around - no one else seems to move. The post office is an old rail car called, SOUTHERN PACIFIC. Past great ranges of mountains, all grey and white. The conductor tells me that the mountains are the Tehachapi Mountains. Then past a huge place called, THE MONOLITH CEMENT PLANT and the air is full of white dust and everything is smothered. They tell me that in the spring these deserts blossom like the rose and I've bought a folder which describes them.

We are riding through the Tehachapi Mountains now and going through tunnels, 19 of them. It is an immense range of mountains with great ravines below. The train goes round in a letter S and down into a valley and then climbs up again for miles. It's a marvellous railway. Now down again between deep cuttings and through tunnels, round another S bend, a great place called Tehachapi Pass. [*The Tehachapi Mountains are the dividing line between southern and northern California.*]

⋆

I'VE SEEN oleander trees here in Bakersfield, where the train stopped for some time. It is a big town but one has to look for beautiful ponds and boulevards away from the railway, the ugliest side of the town. The oleanders look like rose bushes but they tell me there are seven different colours and they are often grown to shade the sidewalks. I also saw date-palms and bushes with red flowers which are pomegranates and I could see the fruits forming.

We are now quite a small train to what it was as the Los Angeles section has been detached. I've been down to lunch: braised veal, mashed potatoes, carrots, bread rolls, vanilla pudding (which was really rice pudding with custard) - all for 30 cents. At each meal we pay one cent tax but I don't know what for! We have just now passed an oil field. There are hundreds of structures looking like electric-light pylons [*oil derricks*]. The newer ones are made of metal but the older wooden ones were pointed out to us, each with a pump beneath pumping up the oil into great containers. The ground around was dark with oil. We passed fields of low-growing green bushes with a white blossom. I enquired and they tell me it is cotton. Rows and rows of palm-trees separate the cotton-fields, just like soldiers.

There are 40 or 50 telegraph lines running beside this railway and the inevitable highway. Nothing to be seen but sand. Now we stop at Corcoran where there are gigantic oil drums, all evidently new. Now we are stopping at Hanford where two passengers get off. The train gives a mournful hoot every time we go over a level crossing or pass near a tiny station. Then more cotton fields and a field of prickly looking plants which they tell me are pineapples. Next we whizz past a huge plant - COTTON OIL PRODUCTION CO. We pass orchards of fig-trees stretching as far as the eye can see on both sides of the train. Also where people were spreading figs to dry and fields where wheat has been reaped and huge granaries with sacks of wheat to the roof. Another station, Winton, with oleanders in all colours, palm-trees, fig-trees and vineyards.

A lady in this car says she has lost her platinum wrist-watch and everyone has had to give their address. The conductor has just been round and taken our tickets and asked me if I was for San Francisco - and gave me a ferry-boat ticket. A stout little lady with a six-foot husband has given me her address (with the accent on the "add") so that I can go with her one day to her husband's boat. He is a US [*National*] Guard. The stout little lady is an Irish Catholic and has kept a boarding house - 14 boarders and has worked hard. She now has a tall old fool for a husband and keeps her dollar bills in her stockings or he would want to drink it all if he thought she had a nickel! [*In the USA, as in Canada, a one cent piece is called a "penny", 5 cents is a "nickel", 10 cents is a "dime" and 25 cents is a "quarter".*] She has brought me some malted-milk biscuits, "To keep the worms from gnawing - waiting for supper".

★

THE FOLDER that Annie bought on her train journey was titled "Desert Scenes of California - The Land of Enchantment" and had a folding strip of 18 coloured pictures of the desert in bloom. Annie posted the folder to Mrs F Kimpton at 54 Adrian Road, Abbots Langley, with Greetings from "Mother to All". It included a poem "found written on the door of an old desert cabin". These are the first two and the last of its verses:

MORNIN' ON THE DESERT

MORNIN' on the desert, and the wind is blowin' free,
And it's ours, jest for the breathin', so let's fill up, you and me.
No more stuffy cities, where you have to pay to breathe,
Where the helpless human creatures move and throng and strive and seethe.

Mornin' on the desert, and the air is like a wine,
And it seems like all creation has been made for me and mine.
No house to stop my vision, save a neighbor's miles away,
And the little dobe shanty that belongs to me and May.

Lonesome? Well I guess not! I've been lonesome in a town,
But I sure do love the desert with its stretches wide and brown.
All day through the sagebrush here the wind is blowin' free,
An' it's ours jest for the breathin', so let's fill up you and me.

Western Publishing & Novelty Co, Los Angeles, California

★ ★ ★ ★ ★

SAN FRANCISCO AT LAST!

THE SPANISH COLONY of Upper or Alta California was initially a chain of 21 Missions built by Franciscan friars between 1769 and 1823 to convert the American-Indians. Settlers from the United States began to enter the territory and there were skirmishes with the Mexican authorities (the area had become Mexican territory in 1822 when Mexico declared independence from Spain). Upper California was declared independent of Mexico in 1846 and was then seized by the United States. The southern peninsular of Lower or Baja California remained part of Mexico. In 1848, gold-fever gripped California when it was discovered at Sutter's Mill near Sacramento. This led to an enormous influx of settlers and immigrants that made their way to San Francisco by land and sea.

San Francisco was set beside one of the largest land-locked harbours of the world. The area around it was very fertile, there were rich deposits of oil and natural gas, and the fishing was excellent. The city became a major financial, industrial and cultural centre with two of the country's most prestigious educational centres: the Berkeley campus of the University of California and Stanford University. In 1936 the San Francisco-Oakland Bay Bridge was opened connecting mainland California to the city and in 1937 the Golden Gate Bridge was completed connecting the city to northern California. The Bay area contained a vast cultural mix of Spanish, Mexican, Asian and European people. San Francisco was a truly cosmopolitain city when Annie Kimpton arrived there but it was still suffering from the effects of a decade of economic depression.

Why Joe Kimpton chose to "jump" the Canadian/American border and hitch-hike to San Francisco is not known. No doubt the climate and opportunities in California appeared attractive. He may have had English friends in the city or may have already known of English people such as the Carrs and the Curtises with local connections back home. Joe met Alta Farthing, his future wife, when she and her mother came to San Francisco from Portland, Oregon, and they happened to stay at the same boarding-house as Joe:

[LETTER 28]

"You do look a little pale - put a bit of rouge on"

400 Duboce Avenue, San Francisco, California, USA
Monday morning, 13 September 1937

MY DEARS,

I left off writing when darkness began to set in last night and packed my bag and sat and watched first one person in our car and then another, leave at one little station and another, until there were about half a dozen left who were either going to Oakland or to San Francisco. The conductor had already been through and given me a ferry ticket which I kept, just in case Joe didn't turn up. [*The ferry-boat connected Oakland Station with San Francisco across the Bay, but there was now a link over the newly built Bay Bridge and the ferry-boat was soon discontinued.*] The passengers near me had all made enquiries as to where, how and why, and all about me; and several ladies were greatly interested. As we neared Berkeley and then Oakland the lights shone all around looking so pretty. "Oh," said one lady, "how good to be back. There's no city like San Francisco," and all the others agreed heartily.

My tummy went over with the excitement and one girl near me said, "You do look pale - put a bit of rouge on".

Our car was almost at the rear and we waited while the baggage was taken off so I was the last off. Alta spotted me first and said, "There she is," and I saw my Joe coming along.

Dear boy, over and over he said - evidently not realising he was repeating himself - "You've come a long way, Mum," and held me tight. His face is so round and he has put on flesh but has not altered greatly. His hair is going back a lot and I can't think who he talks like - not particularly nasal or else I'm getting so used to the American sound. Some of his words sound like Jack Kimpton speaking [*John Kimpton, one of the brothers of Annie's late husband*] and then I hear Will Timberlake [*J W T*]. Alta is a dear little person. She looks like Nellie Dando but has a much prettier mouth and a rounder face. [*Nellie (Ellen) Dando was a friend of Marion Flint. Nellie was a nurse at Leavesden Asylum. She married Levi Cox in 1938, the brother of Walter Cox who was mentioned earlier in Annie's letters from Canada.*] She has evidently made up her mind to like me, for no one could be more welcoming.

I shall have to tell you about this apartment in my next letter, for I have not long been up and my head is going round and round. I think it's the train travel, though I did not feel it last night. Marion's [*Marion Flint's*] letter has just come in and three bundles of newspapers.

My dearest love to you all,

Your loving Mum

* * * * *

[LETTER 29]

"Joe was delighted with his caps . . . . . ."

400 Duboce Avenue, San Francisco, California, USA
Tuesday, 14 September 1937

MY DEARS,

I am writing this in the sitting room of Joe's apartment. This is an immense place. There are 80 sets of rooms here and it is four stories high. The front hall looks like the entrance to a cinema with a gilt rail up the centre steps, great pillars and a carpeted floor. My luggage arrived last night and I had packed my coats in my trunk, only reserving my grey woolly coat in case of need while travelling. It was so hot in Rochester that I was baked. Here it is cool and no one goes without a coat and hat. In Rochester everybody went hatless, save a few old ones like myself. We are on the ground floor of the block and I have not yet had the opportunity to get about and investigate, as I shall do before long. Joe and Alta are pleased to have me and there are a number of folk who want to see me. I am more of an object of interest here than I've been before. Mrs Carr [*Winifred Carr*] called up to know if she could come round yesterday

[LETTER 29 CONTINUED]
afternoon. She is a very pleasant woman in her fifties, grey haired and with good features. I was alone, of course, but she made herself known and was full of talk. Her husband [*Tom Carr*] came round with her this evening. He said he wanted to meet me seeing as it was 14 years since we last met.

Joe was delighted with his caps, etc, [*football team caps*] that I took out and Alta revelled in his boyhood and baby photos. He also proudly shewed to all the one of the football group with Dad in it. [*David Kimpton probably played for either the Abbots Langley Football Club or the Leavesden Asylum Football Club.*] Tonight we are going to Mrs Carr for dinner. Joe goes to work in his car which is fawn colour and roomy, a nice one. He comes home before Alta and then goes off to fetch her. I went with him last night and we called at a huge market filled with stalls and shops where Alta gets her supplies. We had lamb chops, potatoes, peas and peaches for dinner and coffee made in an electric glass coffee-maker. Joe goes to work half an hour before Alta and I get my own breakfast and my lunch.

I've been busy today unpacking and pressing and hanging up my apparel. I have a small chest of drawers for my use. This room is not like Fred's apartments - they were very lofty and square. This has two long windows almost to the ground and the little kitchenette leads out of it. The doors are wider (as is the hall-way) than in the London flats. [*Fred Kimpton, Annie's younger son, lived in London before occupying Annie's home whilst she was away. Fred worked for* CABLE & WIRELESS *as a wireless operator and was proficient in the Morse code which was in use in 1937. Muriel Kimpton was a teacher in Ealing, London. She and her mother, Mrs Turner, lived from 1926 onwards at Hazlegrove Cottages, next to Hazlegrove Farm, Abbots Langley.*]

The entrance hall to these apartments is a palatial looking place with corridors leading three ways, large pillars, soft carpets and staircases leading up. There is a glass case under which are the names and numbers of the tenants and a glass-fronted cupboard in the wall where letters are put for the mail. Our windows look out on another entrance in another street as this is a corner block. Mrs Noren, the daughter of Mr Curtis, rang up to know if I had arrived and wanted to know when they could come round. I had no luggage then - so they are to come on Wednesday evening.

* * *

Wednesday, 15 September 1937

JOE and Alta took me to the Carrs last night, to dinner. They have a grocery and provision store at the corner of a street and Joe says they are doing well, though they have had hard times. He is a pleasant man who tries hard to be funny. When we left, Joe took me for a little ride before going home. He was disappointed because it was not clear in the far distance but this city is vast. We went climbing up in an S shape to where we could look down on the city lights which I can compare to nothing but as if the sky, on a night when millions of stars are to be seen, had suddenly been turned upside down and you were looking down instead of up. Among them were hundreds of red ones - neon lights. The road put me in mind of a gigantic Tory of Bradford on Avon. [*Annie mentioned, in an article in the "Abbots Langley Wesley Guild Magazine 1931-1936", the terraces that the townspeople of Bradford on Avon called, "Going up Tory", derived from the word "tor" for hill.*]

I have not yet ventured out alone for fear I'd stray. [*Duboce Avenue is in Lower Haights, one of the central neighbourhoods of San Francisco.*] The houses look very imposing from the front but Joe says they are stucco in front and lath and plaster at the back. Joe garages his car across the street and we run up a steep wooden incline to a big place above, full of cars.

You remember his friend Bob Hotchkiss? He is married to an English girl or woman and made the match entirely by correspondence and it's a great success. She is a good sport and jolly but Joe says she drops her H's most dreadfully. He says all the English do more or less and confided to me that Alta is very glad I don't drop mine. I shall have to be very careful, shan't I? For I can so easily do it, that I know, and I mustn't disgrace my pretty little daughter.

A map of the San Francisco area.

This is a furnished flat, you know, and only a few things are their own but it is well furnished and looks pretty. There are plenty of maps and books and Joe tells me I can have up to eight books per week free from the library on their two tickets, if I wish. I went out yesterday to the great entrance hall to post some postcards and our door shut behind me and I could not get back in. So I went to the list on the wall, saw that the Manager was No 1 and rang the door bell and told him of my predicament. "Oh yes," said she, "I'll open it. You are Mr Kimpton's mother." So all was well. I have my own latchkey but, of course, had not got it with me.

Joe says the Curtis family are very wealthy folks but they appear to be very friendly from what I hear. [*Marion Flint recorded that the Curtises had connections with the village of Nash Mills, near Abbots Langley.*] But you know Joe's attitude: a little bluster and, "I'm no ass-creeper" (!!) "I tell 'em we work and can't keep up with their sort and ain't going to try," (etc, etc). "But they are keen to meet you, Mum. Winnie Noren [*née Curtis*] is planning that you and Alta and she go for a week to Los Angeles in October. But perhaps it will come to naught." Alta has a week's vacation then. He (Joe) is a fortunate man to have so nice a wife. Mrs Carr tells me everyone likes Alta and that she is always the same. Alta does not smoke. She seems to know how to manage Joe. He calls her "Bones" and when asked why said:

"Because she was nothing but a little bag of bones when I married her."

"I sometimes wish he wouldn't," said Alta.

So I told her he used to call Marion, "Bladder-Nose" and he roared with laughter. [*Joe, as a boy, was not very nice to his sister, Marion. She once recalled that he had deliberately melted the wax face of her doll by holding it in front of the open fire.*]

"I'd forgotten that. Mr Curtis's name is 'Dodie' and his son-in-law's is 'Cheesie' [*Chester Noren*]. Everyone calls them it."

"I shan't."

"What will you say?"

"Mr Curtis, of course."

"Oh well, we'll see."

This is a windy place and to see the fog out on the bay is weird. It looks like a white fleecy cloud or steam pouring in. Everybody is very proud of San Francisco and rightly too, for it is a wonderful place by all accounts. Joe is much as he used to be, does just as he likes and talks to callers if he likes - or reads and takes no notice and, "To hell with 'em". He is actually doing a clerk's job and doesn't mind the work but does wish he had a trade. They get the money.

"Your education has come in useful!" I said.

"Oh yes," said he, "but whatever you do, Mother, don't say "Grammar School" out here. That's the lowest form of education. It's High School or Collegiate which correspond to our Grammar Schools."

Joe and Alta were very bucked at Muriel's [*Muriel Kimpton's*] letter. Alta will answer it, for Joe is like Fred [*Kimpton*] and puts off writing till a more convenient season. I had two letters awaiting me and I'm back at home when reading them. Am so glad Topsy is all right. When I got here I couldn't find the snaps you sent of Broadstairs and I'm disappointed. I wanted to shew them. Where I put them, I cannot imagine - probably left them at St Catharines. I'm wondering how David [*Flint*] likes school? Don't let them forget me. I had a letter from Bessie Harris yesterday. I owe a great many letters. I am sending a little parcel to Fred. I hope he likes it.

I expect Fred has heard this tale. I heard it after I said that someone "bawled like a bull":

> An old lady met another old lady friend and said, "I haven't seen you at church lately".
>
> "Well," said she, "I'm growing so deaf I can hardly hear a word."
>
> "You must come and hear the new man. You'll hear him. He bawls like a bull."
>
> "Has he?" said the deaf old lady!

Have been washing out my stockings, etc, but don't know where to hang them out. Alta said up on the roof or in the basement but I forgot to get her to shew me. So I've rigged up a line across the kitchen with a bit of string and there you are.

My dear love to all,

Your loving Mum

* * * * *

[LETTER 30]

"I've not yet seen a San Francisco flea . . . . . ."

400 Duboce Avenue, San Francisco, California, USA
Wednesday, 22 September 1937

MY DEARS,

I meant to have continued my letters last week but the days just slip by. I am well and getting quite accustomed to life here. I've just come home from a lovely ride with Mr Curtis and Mrs Noren in their lovely car. Mrs Noren drives and they took me to San Mateo, Redwood City and Palo Alto by the road that leads to Los Angeles from San Francisco It has been warm today out at Redwood City - a cloudless blue sky and sandy paths. Many of the houses here are built in Spanish fashion.

We went to see Stanford University and went over the chapel. This is the most marvellous place of worship I've ever seen. There are a great number of buildings all among the grounds and they are devoted to chemistry, psychology, etc, etc, and this wonderful church. It has the most beautiful pictures and figures in fine mosaic. All with a background of gold, many stained glass windows and carved stone pillars. I hope to go again some day and will copy some of the fine inscriptions that are all around. This place was given in memory of the son of Leland Stanford who died in early manhood and the inscriptions are in memory of the father, mother and grandparents and this son, who was all they had. The place must have cost a mint of money. The mosaic and the carved stone were done by Italians. The pictures of the angels and Christ's life are most wonderful in the mosaic where no stone is more than a quarter of an inch across. [*Leyland Stanford Junior died of typhoid at the age of 15. Leyland Stanford Senior, a rail baron, made his fortune in the construction of the transcontinental CENTRAL PACIFIC RAILROAD.*]

On Sunday last, Joe and Alta took me to Golden Gate Park. This is a large place with the largest swimming and diving pool in the world, tennis courts, football grounds where nine matches can be played at the same time, great play areas and a zoo. The streetcars run there and all is so very spacious. We did not go down to the beach, leaving that for another day, but rode along a broad road and I had my first view of the Pacific Ocean. San Francisco is called the "City of Seven Hills" and I've never seen such streets and hills. All the city is built up, street above street. You can look down the long wide streets like switchbacks and at night, with all the lights and street signs, it looks like fairyland.

Last Saturday morning, I went shopping with Alta and I saw the most gorgeous flowers for sale at every corner of every street - dahlias as large as plates, roses, violets, lilies and all other kinds you can imagine. In one shop, English holly was for sale which is imported (it was thickly berried) and raspberries, strawberries and all kinds of fruit - and they tell me they get them all year round.

On Sunday Mrs Carr, Alta and I went for a walk to find a church to which I could go when possible and found a Methodist church close by, found the branch library and found my way to Mrs Carr's. [*This church would have belonged to the American Methodist Church, a completely different organisation to the Methodist Church in Britain and very much*

[LETTER 30 CONTINUED]

larger. After the Delcaration of Independence in 1776, the Church of England refused to administer to the "rebels" in North America, so the Rev John Wesley sent ordained ministers to the New England states. After his death (John Wesley remained within the Church of England throughout his life) Wesleyan Methodism spread rapidly until, by 1861, about one in three of American protestant church members was a Methodist.]

They took me down to Mission Street and I saw the old Roman Catholic church which was built by the Jesuits before the city of San Francisco was built. It's the oldest building in the city. [*Mission San Francisco de Asis - or St Francis of Assisi - more informally known as the Missions Dolores, was built in 1776 by Franciscan friars.*] The new church is built beside the old one and we went in and sat down. I looked at a prayer-book in the pew and I really must get one for you to see. All down the centre of the streets are great palm-trees making me feel as if I'm in a foreign land.

Our street is a windy street and the city is so vast that it has different climates in different parts but it is all very equable. I've not been out without my coat and once wore my fur. Not cold, not hot - and they tell me its often just the same or warmer at Christmas. The ocean breezes keep San Francisco cool while other places just inland are sweltering. There are no flies and no mosquitoes and I've not yet seen a San Francisco flea - and they tell me they are plentiful in places.

I've got me a new hat for everybody is in coloured garments. It's in green to match my coat and cost $2.50 and looks posh. I went shopping yesterday and also cooked the dinner. Joe goes at 7.30am and Alta at 8.00am. Then I get up and get my breakfast. Alta has breakfast at work. Joe drinks little tea so I make some for myself, wash up, make my bed and tidy round. I got steak, potatoes and cauliflower and made a toad-in-the-hole pudding [*using steak fingers, an alternative to the more usual sausages, baked in a Yorkshire batter-pudding mixture*] and apple pie. I think Joe liked it. At least he had two helpings and Alta liked not having to cook. She is the dearest little girl and she has a fine way with Joe, who is just the same as of old - save there is more of him. He is fat. He laughs in just the same way and acts the fool when in good humour, just as he always did. I think he likes me here as he gets a boost amongst his friends and acquaintances for my having come over here from England: "Plenty of the guys you meet have never been out of their own state and you have travelled through the states of New York, Ohio, Illinois, Kansas, Texas, New Mexico, Arizona and California besides travelling in Canada and crossing the Atlantic. So what do you think of that, Mum?" [*On the train journey, Annie also passed through Pennsylvania, Indiana, Missouri and Oklahoma.*] So, as I said afore, my stock has risen all round.

Joe sits reading and the radio is bawling a commentary on a baseball match between Sacramento and San Diego. Alta has gone round to her brother, Clifford [*Farthing*], whom I've yet to meet. They are both interested in stamp collecting. Alta wonders if it would still be possible to get a set of the new Edward VIII stamps? She would like them if possible.

Nobody seems to go to church here. They go to races, shows and ball-games on Sundays. We went to a little Italian restaurant for dinner on Sunday. Alta often does that as they work all week and it makes a rest for her. We had spaghetti with sauce and half a

These four postage stamps showing the Duke of Windsor as Edward VIII were issued in September 1936. The design was sent to the Post Office by Hubert Brown of Torquay and was added to the other invited designs. Edward VIII made the final choice; only then was it discovered that Hubert was a 17-year old boy.

chicken each with potatoes and spinach. There was a dish of all kinds of salads - radishes, tomato, cucumber, onions, olives, etc. Then we had strawberry water-ice and coffee. Joe says they are most reasonable in price and the food is good.

Mrs Noren took me to lunch and we sat in cushioned settees with high backs at oval tables. We had salad of chopped carrots and pineapple. Then we had filleted sole with sauce and mashed potatoes on a lettuce leaf with a small dish of hot diced beetroot. There is always a small dish of butter for every person and the rolls were sprinkled with poppy seed. Then we had pumpkin pie and a pot of tea. On the way back we called at a place thatched with large palm-leaves and had glasses of orange juice. As soon as ever a person sits at a table in any eating house, a glass of iced water is placed in front of them before they ask what you want or shew you a menu.

* * *

[*Thursday, 23 September 1937*]

MRS NOREN is calling for me to go downtown with her at one o'clock. I'd promised Joe an English stew for dinner, so have been out and got stewing steak, vegetables and have got it cooking. I must be ready for the lady and it must be part-cooked before I leave. Will turn the gas off while I'm out and get back to put it on again in time for Alta, who leaves at half past five. I've made some dumplings to put in it for Joe and I - for Alta is like most Americans and doesn't like puddings. It's all pie, pie, cake and salad. I cannot get a pudding basin anywhere. So when I make beefsteak pudding I'll borrow one from Mrs Carr who brought some here years ago.

In the shop most of the meat is cut up into steaks and chops. What they call roasts are all under large glass cases - they look lovely. The sheep carcasses, which are hung up, are decorated with paper frills round their necks and have buttonholes of flowers pinned on their backs. I laughed but oh, the shops are marvellous - like palaces - with lifts and escalators, a rest-room and chairs everywhere, and iced drinking bubblers. The highest building here is 32 stories high. They do not build like New York because of earthquake shocks and most houses are of wood for the same reason. [*San Francisco sits astride the San Andreas fault. This separates the North American tectonic plate of the earth's crust from the Pacific tectonic plate which is being forced northward causing periodic earthquakes. The*

[LETTER 30 CONTINUED]
massive earthquake that hit San Francisco on 18 April 1906 caused one of the worst disasters in the USA. Though the initial building damage was not very great, flames from ruptured gas mains burned for four days and destroyed most of the city. About 250,000 people, half of the population, were made homeless and had to camp out in Golden Gate Park.]

I went one evening with Joe and Alta to friends. Mr and Mrs Carr also went. Their names are Mr and Mrs Oldberg and they are Swedish. He is a musician and can play anything but is never in work regularly since the talkies came in. She goes out cooking. Another couple were there, Mr and Mrs . . . (Australians). We talked and sang and they all drank (save Alta and me) and all got very merry and good-humoured. Joe seems a favourite with many but he is just the same as ever to those he doesn't like. He sits and reads while they are here and leaves poor Alta to make conversation. She gets hot and bothered but seems to manage him very well. I shall get on quite well with her for she is very lovable. Must close and get my shoes on in readiness for Winnie Noren.

*

I GOT Marion's letter today and the *Methodist Recorders* and the *Watford Methodist Circuit Magazines.* My poor Roger [*Flint*] - to be stung by a wasp. I sympathise with him for they serve me cruelly. We have no wasps here. I couldn't help laughing over Elsie's ramblings. They shew what a disordered mind she has, poor thing. [*Elsie Timberlake, wife of Annie's brother, Matthew, of Treetops, Windsor Road, Church End, Finchley, Middlesex.*] Give my love to Bert's mum and Auntie Edie George [*Mrs George Flint, but called Edie George to distinguish her from Auntie Edie Flint, George Flint's sister*]. I don't forget anybody though I do not write to them all. I seem to be on the go all the time, either going out or preparing to go out. Have just got a letter from Elsie. Evidently she thinks I'm blowing my all in one grand bust on this trip - for she tells me to have a good time and hang the expense. St Peter won't let me take a bank book in (!!) I wonder how David [*Flint*] is liking school? It will be nice for you to have him come home at . . . . . . [*left unfinished when Winnie Noren arrived*].

* * *

Friday, 24 September 1937

YESTERDAY, Mrs Noren phoned me during the morning, saying she was coming to call for me to go to her house for lunch. As she is a small edition of Auntie Elsie, I hurried about and got ready and we drove to her apartment. It's a lovely place and she has and gets all money can buy; and the two men, her husband and father, adore her and obey her every behest. She has very fair golden hair, blue eyes and looks about 25. Indeed, when she called for me in her pretty pink-flowered frock, with no hat on her beautifully waved hair - her cheeks, lips and nails all matching the pink of her frock - she looked just like a doll and about 17.

I went downtown with Winnie Noren and she shopped. She is an indefatigable shopper (store after store) and I've never seen such service nor such wonders.

SELFRIDGES [*a major London store*] is a country shop to them. In some places, as you near the door - either to enter or leave - the door is invisibly opened by an electric eye and when you pass a certain spot the doors open, ghostlike. I bought a big stewpan to make my stew and also for when I cook beefsteak pudding. The saucepans were small and there were no pudding basins so I got a round red basin - one you put your flowers in. All they had were stewpans or Pyrex. Americans never make pudding crust - only pies. Mr Curtis is coming some time to dinner and I am to make a steak and kidney pudding. [*When Annie talks about pudding crust and puddings she was referring to suet pastry which was steamed, rather than shortcrust pastry which was baked.*] I never imagined there were so many kinds of fruits and vegetables in the world and they are all here.

They all like Joe. He was the first Englishman they had met and got to know and their circle of acquaintances seems large. Mr Curtis has told me that, twice. I came home alone from the Norens. Had to change streetcars but got home all right. I get a bit nervous when alone for the city is so vast and the traffic so rapid. Joe instructs me daily: "Watch where you cross. Look to the left. Go by the words, "STOP" and "GO" [*the words on the pedestrian crossing lights are now, "WALK" and, "DON'T WALK"*]. If you have to ask the way ask a streetcar driver, a newsboy, a taxi driver, at a gasolene station - but never ask a policeman." Everybody fights shy of them. I imagine there is no deed too dirty for a policeman here.

Alta and I are going to Los Angeles for a week in October to ride with Mrs Noren and Mr Curtis so the fare will be nil. All we'll do is share the cost of lodgings and food. With a gorgeous car - with I don't know how many dollars to take us about - we'll be all right. Joe will go round to Mrs Carr's for dinner at night.

I am sitting writing this by the sitting-room window facing a long courtyard and fence with a gate into the street. This is the side entrance to the great group of apartments and I can see the streetcars continually passing by. My cloth cap, that Elsie [*Timberlake*] gave me to wear on the boat, comes in fine here. For I'm one among many who wear them and I also wear her blue coat when going out in the morning. I've got to shorten my dresses for nobody wears any length here.

It's strange that, though I'm three thousand miles further away from you all, now I'm with Joe I feel nearer than in Canada - probably because he is my own. He is very much like scores of men you see here: big, fat, hair thin on top, a bad-tempered face - unless he smiles and then he's charming. As I said, he calls his wife, Alta, "Bones". It began when they were married. Now she is plump and he girds against her: "Disgusting, fat . . .", etc. I tell him to look in the shop window at himself. She sits all day at work and that tends to increase your "Rule, Britannia!" [*Annie's euphamism for "backside", probably derived from the "tails-side" of penny and halfpenny coins which showed Britannia.*] By the by, it does seem strange never to hear *God save the King* and to find Britain poked onto an obscure page in the paper and often sneered at.

My dear love to you all,
Mother

* * * * *

[LETTER 31]

"Prettiest, slim little Chinese girls standing outside who act as hostesses"

400 Duboce Avenue, San Francisco, California, USA
Monday, 27 September 1937

MY DEARS,

First of all, the enclosed sheet of writing belongs to my previous letter. I left off suddenly and then continued after returning home and must have mislaid it. [*This has been included in its rightful place in the previous letter.*]

I had Muriel's letter at the weekend. I am so glad that she and Fred are happy at Abbots Langley. If they had not been it would certainly have muddled things up. I am well and happy. I got up a bit earlier this morning as Alta was expecting the Filipino boys to come and clean. They come once a month to vacuum the carpets and rugs, polish round the floors, mop the kitchen and bathroom floors, etc. This is included in the service of the apartments. The last two or three days have been hot, very hot, but this morning it is just like a balmy English spring day - a soft breeze and bright sun. We really have two meals per day here - breakfast, and dinner at night with just a scrap for lunch midday. I prefer it to two meat-meals, though I miss the pleasant English tea-times. People drink coffee and seem to make and drink tea as a sort of concession.

Yesterday morning I went to the little Methodist church I found close by. It's a small place but I think I'll continue there as it's so close to home. It is mostly composed of Swedish, Norwegian and German members. The pastor comes from Norway. It is about the size of our chapel but not so high. Part of the roof is a sky-light and the electric lights are kept burning. There is a Sunday school in the basement and (above it) tiers of apartments - which is strange to me. The floor and front hall is covered with a thick grey carpet patterned in squares with a tinge of mauve flowers. The seats are comfortable armchairs, low and with a rounded back and with tip-up seats in polished dark wood - each with a rounded box on the back. Everybody is supplied with a tune-book as big as my tonic sol-fa tune-book. There was a good congregation and at once they spotted me as a visitor. When I told them I came from England they exclaimed and begged me to come again and also to their week-night prayer meetings. Joe approves. He has a good opinion of Swedish folks: "Good straight people". It was a very simple service and I've heard more powerful discourses. I'm not yet used to the personal note from the pulpit: "I'm glad to see Mr and Mrs . . . from San Diego visiting us again . . . " (etc, etc). One thing the parson said stuck in my memory: "It has been said that we can judge the popularity of a church by its morning congregations, the popularity of the minister by its evening congregations and the popularity of Christ by the attendance at its prayer meetings". He then urged all to attend. Joe plays golf with Tom Carr on Sunday mornings.

Last night, Joe took me and Alta for a wonderful walk. We went in his car to a distant part of the city, parked the car as soon as we could find a place by the side of the pavement (it is usually difficult as the streets are lined with cars), and we walked through Chinatown. [*This was the city's most densely populated area, formed by Chinese immigrants in the Gold Rush days of the 1850's and by Chinese workers on the trans-continental railway in the 1860's.*] I've never imagined such shops and sights. Everybody one met was Chinese, all dressed in European clothes but crowds of them - men, women and children. The shops are marvellous with wonderful silk goods, jewellery, ornaments, vases (pronounced "vayses" here), ivory and queer drug-stores with the proprietor in his horn-rimmed glasses making up his accounts - great long sheets all in Chinese writing. The eating shops - with pork fat, dried chicken, ducks, shark-fins - have the most awful looking objects looking like dried infants' limbs hanging up in rows. In the apothecaries' windows they have bottled rattlesnake and the most weird looking dried things to grind into a powder. The tall apartments look like pagodas. The dance halls have the prettiest, slim little Chinese girls standing outside who act as hostesses. There are places with windows level with the pavement where ducks, chickens, pigeons, rabbits and fish are kept alive in very close quarters, poor things. Joe tells me they are ready for patrons to choose for their meal alive - to be sure that you have it fresh. Some of the old folk look exactly like the old Bonzo figures [*Bonzo figurines, from the Japanese word for a Buddhist priest*] and there is this queer sing-song talk. The men are taller generally than the Japanese and I think popular feeling here is against the Japanese. Every Chinese store has a black-edged card displayed with this queerly worded message on it:

OBITUARY

> THOUSANDS OF OUR CHINESE ARE BEING MURDERED BY JAPANESE. CHINATOWN IS IN MOURNING. IF YOU ARE "HUMAN", PLEASE GO INTO A JAPANESE STORE AND "BUY" AND VERIFY THE "BLOODY" NEWS.

The word "BLOODY" is printed over a large blot of red, like a splash of blood. Joe says the wording is like them - queer. But it's evident what they want to convey and outside the Japanese shops (which are quite as beautiful as the Chinese) are small Chinese boys on picket. [*The Japanese invasion of China began in May 1937; this sector of the Second World War lasted until 1945.*] San Francisco's Chinatown (which is the largest in America) has sent thousands of dollars to China. Chicago sent stocks of anti-toxins, bandages, etc, and New York's Chinatown sent money. The Oriental babies are lovely and look just like those little wooden dollies we get with a little gown on and hair cut straight across the forehead. I've not yet seen a Negro baby but have often met families and parties of coloured people. "Dark Clouds" Joe calls them.

I'm going to make Alta a frock, wine-coloured, in readiness for our trip to Los Angeles. I don't think I'll get myself anything. Joe is anxious we should not discredit Mrs Noren. Tomorrow evening we are going to Mr and Mrs Hotchkiss for dinner. You remember the big man who once shared rooms with Joe? He has been married about two years. She came over from London to marry him after corresponding with him. She's pure Cockney and about his age - no girl, thin and dark - and they get on well. He says she keeps him short of money - just gives him 10 cents at a time and wants to know what he has done with it. Joe laughs at him. The folks here try to take a rise out of her because she drops her H's but she is as keen as a razor and answers back in fine style.

We listened in to a football [*American football*] match between the University of California and St Mary's University (which is a Roman Catholic one) and it was a big affair. I understand it is something like rugby football. Joe said, "I hope California lick [*defeat*] that Pope's bum-kissing bunch," and to his great delight they did - the first time for years. Joe has a wonderful ear and memory for music, recognizes the airs from operas, knows the good singers and movie stars that sing - and is amazed and a bit disgusted that I do not. He is very anxious that I read the newspapers to make myself better informed in matters of American politics, history and statesmen. I can't work up much enthusiasm for it and the newspapers are Dutch to me. Also, I don't love Americans in the bottom of my heart - only individually, not collectively - though being here, I disguise the fact. It's queer to hear England thought of as a mere speck in all things and America as the whole firmament.

There is to be a World Fair here in 1939 and it is to be on an island out in the Bay - adjoining the island where the join is in the big Bay Bridge, midway between here and Oakland. They dredged the harbour and made this island [*Treasure Island*] on purpose for the Fair buildings. It will be a stupendous affair and downtown in one of the Halls they have a large model under glass and people walk round an iron rail to view it. It is very realistic - every building, every hall, the gardens, the huge parking areas and thousands of miniature cars are all there. There was an immense visitors' book for people to sign their names. Alta and I looked back for pages and there was not one from England so I placed mine at the top of the page: "E A Kimpton, Abbots Langley, England". I couldn't get any more in and the group around (waiting to sign) nudged and stared and pointed to my name and Alta's. She got quite a kick out of it.

Would you believe that to get a place [*a job*] at a gasolene station a fellow has to have a college or university education? Every child must attend school till they are aged 18 and many stay till 21. People say that it is ruinous to parents as they must let the youngsters have cash and a car and they go their own way in all things - and that is why so many fight shy of being parents. No child may be chastised by parents here as boys may give evidence to any magistrate. Fathers have been sent to jail for trying to control their youngsters. They must be allowed to express their individuality!!!!

I sent a parcel of views, etc, and some socks for Fred. I hope they reached you safely and that Fred likes them. Please keep all the rubbish I send and I will sort it out when I come back.

* * *

Tuesday, 28 September 1937

AFTER dinner last night, who should come to visit me but the Rev Gustav Storaker (the pastor of the church I went to on Sunday morning) and his wife. I wondered how Joe and Alta would take it but Joe was quite the gentleman and talked most affably. They invited me to a house-warming of one of their members who is opening a new guest-house but I declined, being a stranger. They begged me to come to their Ladies' Meeting, held the first Thursday of each month - and would I talk to them of England? I would not promise that for I'm sure I wouldn't know what to tell them - though really grown-ups know very little of our land and the children nothing at all.

Did I ask you to send me some of the new threepenny bits? I don't know how they'd be sent. Perhaps in folds of soft paper, I should think, or in a little bit of material, or in a pair of thin stockings. But I would like some and wish I'd brought some with me. I wish I could come unexpectedly in and see you all and my house. I shall not know it again. Give my love to Mrs Brown and the Women's Own and a long kiss for my David and little Roger.

My dear love to you all,

Mother

The nickel-brass, twelve-sided coin - the threepenny "bit" - was first minted in 1937 and showed a clump of thrift or sea pink. This was originally proposed as an appropriate new design for the coin it gradually superceded: the very tiny, silver threepenny piece - the "Joey" - which was often saved in piggy-banks.

* * * * *

[LETTER 32]

"Joe had oyster fritters, Alta had rib steak and I had abalone . . . . . "

400 Duboce Avenue, San Francisco, California, USA
Sunday, 3 October 1937

MY DEARS,

This week has simply flown. I've had Muriel's letter but none from Marion. Probably it will come tomorrow. On Tuesday, I had a day at Alta's frock and on Wednesday, Mrs Carr and I went down to the city and went over the clothing factory where Alta works in the office. The works manager shewed us over and Alta brought all her friends in the office to speak to me. She tells me that I found favour. They make men's and boys' overalls, trousers, shirts and blouses. I never saw such machines nor women and girls work so fast - they do piecework. There was a man in the cutting department with long benches covered with material all marked out in sizes - and it looked as if the pattern was all scientifically marked out for hardly a bit of material was wasted. He had an electric cutter which cut 144 thicknesses of stout drill at once. These were then tied up in dozens of different sizes by other men and went to the stitchers. Machines with three or four needles were worked by women and girls at great speed and they turned seams and put on bands in one operation. Some did fronts and some did backs; then another did the fly-fronts. The button-hole machine went

[LETTER 32 CONTINUED]

along one side, reversed itself and cut out the centre at once. There were machines clamping on bachelor's buttons [*decorative, button-like flower motifs*] but the crowning one, to my eyes, was a button-sewing machine. The woman put a button on the needle and the machine made two or three stitches which went through the holes in the buttons, tied three knots under each button and cut off the ends. The manager told us they turned out five thousand garments each day. There had been another strike at the docks and they had only turned out three thousand five hundred garments for several days and many machines were idle. I have never seen people work at such speed. Bert would have been interested in the carpenters' overalls. [*Bert Flint, Annie's son-in-law, was a carpenter by trade with his business, FLINT BROTHERS, builders and decorators.*] They were white drill and had a number of pockets all over the front for nails - and had loops down the sides for hammers, etc, and the legs were kind of double about the knees and quilted. The man said that carpenters did not need tool bags any more but distributed their tools over their person like a Christmas tree!!

Then on Thursday, Mrs Noren and Mr Curtis and I went in their great car out to South San Francisco to lunch and then to see the great cemeteries and huge buildings where they keep the dead. The places are very lovely with marble corridors, glass roofs and stained-glass windows. The roofs have stained glass - like flowerbeds and trailing vines with the most lovely blues and reds. There are fountains, maidenhair ferns, basket-chairs, and the walls consist of numberless squares of marble which are the doors of compartments where they put the coffins and seal them up. Upon the door is the name of the deceased. There are the most lovely statues all about and I am enclosing some postcards so you can see the children's catacombs, as they are called. Then there are buildings for the reception of urns from cremations - these are smaller compartments and all copper. Outside are the graves of those who cannot afford to be placed in the catacombs and also the rich who have their own individual mausoleums. The grass is beautiful and a man told us there were trees of every kind from all over the world there. One of the great marble mausoleums with pillars of white marble and statues cost £40,000. He told us in dollars and we worked it out in pounds. The Roman Catholic Cemetery is called "Holy Cross"; the Protestant - "Cypress Lawn"; the Jewish - "Olivet"; and there is a Freemasons'; a Chinese; a Japanese; and many other burial grounds reaching for miles.

Then we went down to the great public library and got my card accepted. Mr Noren signed it for me as he is in the directory as an owner in the city. So I can get books if I want them - there are thousands. On Saturday morning, I went to see some shops in the city but I've not been by myself yet. The traffic is so great and fast and in some streets there are four rows of cars going along. There are so many different sections to the city and each seems to have different weather. We generally have wind around Duboce Avenue and there is fog in the Marina and so on.

I went to church this morning and the minister spoke well. It was a Sunday school rally. His text was: I have set the Lord always before me; and his sermon had five points: to put God in our daily walking, our talking, our reading, our thinking and our working. I thought what he said about reading was good: that we should treat our

An advert from the 1937 Methodist Church Fête programme. FLINT BROTHERS was started in 1900 by George Flint and Arthur (Reuben Arthur) Flint, called Arthur to distinguish him from his father, "Old" Reuben. The family lived then at The Gleanings in Marlin Square, Abbots Langley, probably the first house built by FLINT BROTHERS. Old Reuben Flint, was a stoker according to the 1891 census, probably at Leavesden Asylum, and had been a notorious drunkard. Once, when about to be thrown out of the Dog and Partridge at Hunton Bridge, he threatened to release the young rats he used for training ferrets which he kept tucked inside his shirt. Old Reuben was converted to teetotalism at a rally of the Sons of Temperance on Chapel Green.

You have bought this booklet to help others, now help yourselves.

Come to us with your difficulties when decorating or repairing your property. We have experienced men in all branches and personal attention is assured.

We have been in this village for 37 years, surely in itself a good recommendation.

Give us a trial.

FLINT BROS.

BUILDERS AND DECORATORS

Marlin Square,
Abbots Langley

'Phone: Kings Langley 7139.

Arthur Flint's first job was as a bell-boy in a London hotel. During the depression of the 1920's, FLINT BROTHERS built five houses on Hazlewood Lane to provide themselves with employment. Except for 1 Hazlewood Lane, these have since been demolished for the extension to Greenways. Arthur Flint became a Justice of the Peace; Abbots Langley parish councillor and its chairman in 1940; Watford Rural District councillor; and a director of the Watford and West Herts Permanent Benefit Building Society.

Arthur Flint handed FLINT BROTHERS over to his son, Bert, around 1931 when Arthur retired. Bert Flint (a carpenter) continued to employ his uncles, George Flint (a bricklayer), "Moss" (Maurice) Flint (a decorator) and Len Flint (a painter), together with Joe (a plumber) who was unrelated. House building stopped with the coming of the Second World War. During the war, Joe went to work in the DE HAVILLAND AIRCRAFT COMPANY factory at Leavesden Aerodrome and Bert taught himself plumbing. Bert Flint sold the house, Conway, and the adjacent builders' yard in 1964.

When Bert Flint died, technical drawings of the elevations and floor plans for four FLINT BROTHERS' houses were discovered, drawn by him in his youth at Watford Technical College. These drawings were given to the present-day owners of the houses: Stonehaven, 24 Greenways; 18 Greenways; Oakdene, 75 Trowley Rise; and Lakenham, Bedmond Road, Bedmond. The houses known to have been built by FLINT BROTHERS, though there are probably more, are:

Abbots Langley:
Conway & Lynton, Marlin Square;
The Gleanings, Marlin Square;
Hope Cottage, Marlin Square;
82 & 84 Marlin Square.

80 Abbots Road;
82 Abbots Road;
92 Abbots Road (much changed);
161 Abbots Road.

1 Hazlewood Lane.

16 Trowley Rise;
18 Trowley Rise;
20 Trowley Rise;
24 Trowley Rise;
35 Trowley Rise;
37 Trowley Rise;

Crosspaths, 39 Trowley Rise;
69 & 71 Trowley Rise;
71A Trowley Rise;
73 Trowley Rise;
Oakdene, 75 Trowley Rise;
Bledlow, 77 Trowley Rise;

Folly Four, 80 Trowley Rise.

Hempton, 8 Greenways;
Greenland, 18 Greenways;
20 Greenways;
Stonehaven, 24 Greenways.

Bedmond:
Lakenham, Bedmond Road;
Valley View, Bedmond Road;
Holcumbeech, Bell Lane;
Verulam Nursery, Harthall Lane;
Rosland, Harthall Lane.

[LETTER 32 CONTINUED]
minds as we do a Bank to store precious things, money, jewels, etc - not, as many do, as a garbage can in which everything worthless and filthy is placed.

This afternoon, Joe took us to the docks to see the fishing fleet. We went through the coloureds' quarters and saw numbers of "Dark Clouds", as Joe calls them. We could see the Golden Gate Bridge in the distance with its immense suspension cables - the longest in the world. The docks are very busy and Joe says the harbour is one of the largest in the world. We saw the boats getting ready to go fishing for sardines, the Coastguard boats, the speedboats; and across the bay we could see Oakland, Berkeley and Richmond cities and in the centre of the bay the island with the great gaol on it. They call it Devil's Island and it is where the gangsters are - Al Capone and all those. [*Alcatraz Island, meaning Pelican Island, was a Federal prison surrounded by cold water and currents too strong for even the best swimmers. It had opened in 1934.*]

On Fisherman's Wharf there are booths and cafés (where fish of all kinds are eaten) with huge coppers boiling large prawns and shrimps on the kerbs outside. I saw the largest shells for sale and cases of tiny turtles (with painted mottoes on their backs) also offered for sale - posted anywhere and guaranteed to arrive alive (but Joe said in America only). We went in one café and had shrimp cocktail: a glass of shelled shrimps with sauce of something (tomato juice, vinegar and oil) served with lemon and little biscuits. Joe had some red-hot stuff on his but I soon had enough and he finished mine for me! Then we went to a Greek place for dinner and Joe had oyster fritters, Alta had rib steak and I had abalone - with chip-potatoes for each of us, rolls and coffee. Abalone is a huge shellfish only found in California. Then, on the way home, we called for ice-cream and ate it at home. Joe bought a pound of the largest prawns I've ever seen and they are put in the refrigerator. No one thinks anything of buying on a Sunday here. [*In England shops never opened on a Sunday.*]

I hope to finish Alta's dress tomorrow morning. I have to go up to Haight Street to get some snap-fasteners. I have to get my shoes mended and a pin for my brooch. Mrs Carr is calling for me at one o'clock to go downtown with her as I want to get some cash from the bank as Alta and I are going on Saturday next to Los Angeles for a week with Mr Curtis and his daughter. This will be a 450 mile journey and we shall go to Long Beach and Hollywood (probably another 50 miles) so that by the time we return we shall have covered over one thousand miles!!! We will be staying for one night on our way at a tourist-camp cottage so that will be another experience - just to break the journey going and coming back. We are starting off at 6 o'clock in the morning on Saturday, 9 October and hope to go to Amy McPherson's Temple to hear her on Sunday evening next. So I'll have something to put in my next letter if all goes well on our journey. [*Aimee Semple McPherson, founder of the Angelus Temple in Los Angeles, was noted for her dramatic revivalist meetings.*]

On our way back home this evening (up and down the hilly streets where we seem to be at one time standing in the back seat and then the next with our knees higher than our heads) we passed the great factories where the DEL MONTE fruits are-canned. Yesterday I had some nectarines and Joe brought in some grapes (which are Valencia raisins when dried) and some plum-like fruits which are prunes.

"What do these taste like, Mum?" he asked.

"Something like prunes, only fresh," I said.

"Well," he said, "that is what they are."

Joe got weighed yesterday and he weighs 200lb!!! He has just the right wife. She never disputes with him and seems to understand his varying moods. She told me: "I understand Joe now and take no notice when he says dreadful things to me. For I know he doesn't really mean them - it's only his temper. I used to cry - but not now". She is such a pretty child, yet so practical. The radio is playing a waltz and Joe and Alta are dancing, he in his shirt sleeves and with his pipe in his mouth. Now the programme is changed and Alta has gone back to her weekly accounts. She keeps count of all expenditure and Joe audits.

What do you think of this tale?

A judge had three black men brought before him for some misdemeanour. They were all well known to him, so he addressed the first: "Well Pete, how are you feeling this morning?"

"Oh," said Pete, "I'm feeling poorly. Ahm feeling real sick."

"Well," said the Judge, "six months so that you will be fully recovered."

"Well Moses, how are you?"

"Ah'm feeling fine," said he taking warning by his friend's sentence. "Ah'm feeling like ah'm a young 'oss."

" Oh you are? Well nine months to curb your high spirits."

"And now Rastus, how about you?"

"Well Jedge, ah'm feelin' laak a bride."

"A bride?" said the judge, "How so?"

"Well Jedge, ah knows ah'm going to have sumpin'. Ah knows ah'm going to get sumpin'. But ah don't know how long it's goin' ter be." (!!)

I was glad to hear that Fred and Muriel had so happy a time in Dover. Do hope they (Jim and Carrie) will come to Abbots Langley. [*Muriel and Fred Kimpton had been to stay with Annie's cousins, Jim and Carrie Gates, who lived at 58 Nightingale Drive, Dover. Much earlier, Matthew Timberlake recorded in his diary that Joe Kimpton stayed with Jim and Carrie from 3 to 13 September 1914. Joe came home the next day and said that he was going to enlist in the army. Matthew Timberlake wrote in his diary for 14 September 1914: "Home / worried / young Joe enlisting / didn't go to work." On 17 September 1914, after Joe had enlisted, Matthew Timberlake wrote: "Home / taken up about Joe".*]

I expect my Topsy will have another lot of kittens before winter time. Has any more water seemed to come from that drain? Teddy Beaumont thought maybe it was not securely cemented at the joint or had been covered in too soon or something. He talked of uncovering it by the bricks at the back door. If it leaks the water may go under the house. I guess I'll not know my house next year.

My dear love to you all,

Mum

* * * * *

SOUTH TO LOS ANGELES

LOS ANGELES was founded by Spanish settlers in 1781 and was known as El Pueblo de la Reyna de Los Angeles (the Town of the Queen of the Angels). It became a United States city after the Mexican War of 1846:

[LETTER 33]

"I never saw such a farce in all my life"

San Fernando, California, USA
Saturday, 9 October 1937

MY DEARS,

This is a new address and a new situation for me. We left Duboce Avenue at 6 o'clock this morning. Joe saw us all off. He has several invitations to dinner while we are away. We are on our way to Los Angeles with Alta, Mr Curtis and his daughter, Mrs Noren. We have driven all day in their fine tan-coloured Buick car (425 miles in all) and we have put up for the night in two cottages in an auto-camp. Each cottage consists of a bedroom with a double-bed, a dressing-table, a mirror on the wall, two chairs, and has white spring-blinds, red curtains with bobble borders and is carpeted. The kitchen is painted cream all over, has a table, two seats, a sink with hot and cold water, a draining board, a gas grill with two burners, a cupboard with a drawer, a towel rack and tumbler, and a waste-can under the sink. There is a shower-bath with a curtain, a wash-basin and a lavatory - all in a small recess. The bed looks a comfortably sprung one and each room is fitted with electric light and kitchen utensils and crocks. Towels, soap and condiments are provided. Everything looks spotlessly clean and there is a garage next door for the car.

On the way down, we passed over the new Bay Bridge where every car has to pay a toll of 50 cents and then through Oakland, San Leandro, Tracy, Merced, Fresno, Tulare and Bakersfield - which is said to be the hottest place in California and it WAS hot. We have come by the valley route which runs inland and over the mountains [*by the San Joaquin Valley and over the Tehachapi Mountains*]. There is a continual stream of motor traffic and we passed fields and fields of cotton, corn, vineyards, olive groves, acres of water-melons spread over the fields, fig-trees and orange-trees in abundance, pampas grass, bamboos and thousands of palm-trees. We picnicked on the steps of the car on rolls and butter, ham, liverworst with apple sauce, and coffee from Thermos flasks.

Mr Curtis and Mrs Noren visited a friend in Tulare and Alta and I went round the shops in the brilliant sunshine. We bought lovely grapes (3lb for 10 cents) and we had three kinds: Tokay, Muscats and Fresno Beauties. Then we went into a hotel and asked to be shewn the ladies' room. A polite manager shewed us up the stairs to a room where wash-basins with hot and cold water, paper-towels, liquid soap (from a container over the basin) and lavatories were all to hand - and we spent not a penny. This is a feature of life out here and the service one gets is very wonderful. If you stop outside a shop or a filling station the proprietor comes running. In this hotel we saw a wonderful collection of birds, beasts and fishes of all kinds - heads, skins and stuffed.

I should think there were hundreds of birds. In one window was a fine stuffed lion - in another an antelope, otters, skunks, etc, etc.

By the way, last Wednesday Mrs Noren took me downtown to lunch. We had *enchiladas* (a Spanish dish), bell-peppers, noodles, Italian breadsticks and apple pie. In the afternoon a friend of Mrs Noren's joined us and we went around the shops and then into a bar for a drink. I had iced lemonade and they laughed at me as they had whisky and *hors-d'oeuvre* and said I was to tell folks (when I wrote to them) that they were luring me from the straight and narrow way into cocktail bars. I don't mind their jokes and laugh back.

I went on Thursday last week with Mrs Carr and a lady friend of hers (Mrs Mollering - a wealthy woman they tell me) to see Mrs Carr's son and his wife [*Leslie and Elinore*] in Oakland. Mrs Mollering drove us there over the Bay Bridge. They have a very nice and unusual bungalow on the side of a hill. We went up 20 steps to get to it. The wife is a typical American. Everything is "so cute", or "so darling", or "so perfect," that she has to repeat herself all the time. Tomorrow we go to Los Angeles.

* * *

Sunday night, 10 October 1937

HAVE had a queer Sunday. We got up early this morning and had breakfast all together and then left for Los Angeles. Mrs Noren knew of an apartment in the city and got it by mentioning the name of a wealthy friend of theirs. So we've got it for the week for $30. That divided by four is not so bad. It is a lovely place: a very large lounge (one side all windows), a large Chesterfield suite in fawn brocade, a bureau, two or three tables and half a dozen lamps. There is one great bedroom with two beds, a kitchen with an electric stove, a refrigerator, cupboards all in white, hot and cold water, two clothes-closets, a dressing-room with mirrors and a chest of drawers. The bathroom has a shower, a wash-basin and a lavatory or "toilet" as they call them here. Alta and I have beds put up in the lounge and Mr Curtis and Mrs Noren have the room with the twin beds.

We rode out to see Forest Lawn Memorial Park, the immense cemetery. Then we went to a restaurant for dinner - a very varied menu and I felt as if I'd eaten a ton. We then went to Aimee McPherson's Temple for the service. It was a large circular building like a theatre and it holds five thousand people and tonight it was packed. We could only find seats up in the gallery near the roof. Down at each side of the stage were about two or three hundred men and women forming a choir, the women all in white with red sashes across their chests. She is an attractive looking woman who wore a long pink-flowered gown and a white sun-bonnet which she took off when she warmed to her subject - which was a story or part-story of her life. She was then in a white dress with long flowing sleeves. They had children who sang choruses into a microphone about the Pearly Gates, a kind of Negro spiritual chorus. She kept starting parts of songs with choruses, with the choir keeping time by hand-clapping and then the congregation joined in and we all clapped hands. There was an orchestra, brass instruments, accordions, etc. There were queer songs and choruses and an exhibition

[LETTER 33 CONTINUED]
of drum-major stick twirling and catching to music. It was her birthday and she had great bouquets presented to her and read messages from many parts of the world. She had photos for folks who stood up when she asked for visitors to the Temple from different countries and states. I stood up when she called "England" and it was almost certainly the first country mentioned. There were visitors there from every state in America and Canada. I'm sending my picture home next week.

The crowning absurdity was when the curtains on the stage were drawn back: a miniature farm and buildings were displayed and a fine, black and white cow - which Aimee milked (whilst sitting on a stool) into a new can amid the plaudits of the multitude. She poured the milk out, had a drink herself and handed the rest to some of the orchestra. She made a rare begging speech asking all who did not intend to give, to hold up their hands. Whereupon we all forked out our nickels. Then she waved her hands and sang and shouted and folk stood and all who meant to change their lives were to follow her in prayer, aloud. Then crowds poured onto the platform and promptly knelt and Amee had more and more converts. Outside in the corridors were cases of sticks, crutches, splints, trusses and spectacles with letters from folk who have been healed - for she is a faith-healer. Mr Curtis says she is a millionaire but does a lot in the way of charity! I never saw such a farce in all my life.

After we came out, we four went out in an electric motorboat on a large lake and disturbed the ducks, swans and mud-hens [*Annie's term for a Moorhen but these were probably Common Gallinules*]. It looked so pretty with all the lights reflected in the water. Then we rode home at about 11 o'clock. Nearly all the shops were open and we were able to purchase stores. Sunday is nothing here. I saw baseball games being played, tennis and golf. We saw what is called the Rose Bowl of Los Angeles which is an immense stadium where football games are held and which can seat 80 to 100 thousand people. It has been very hot all day. Such clear air - one can see easily for 30 miles from a height. All around are dark mountains against the sky.

* * *

Monday night, 11 October 1937

I HAVE had another full day. The little dog, Patty, who travels with us (a little brown dog - an intelligent creature and most devoted to Mr Curtis and Mrs Noren) woke me up and we all had an early breakfast and were on our way to Long Beach. We soon came in sight of the ocean and it seemed strange to be riding on a highway for miles, with the Pacific on one side and immense oil derricks and containers on the other. They looked like a forest of trees. We passed by many of them working. Then past Seal Beach to Long Beach - and when we went to a point where the beach could be seen, it certainly is a long one. The sea is a most lovely blue and green with the breakers rolling in but there was no salt smell.

Mr Curtis and Mrs Noren have some friends at Laguna Beach but were not quite sure of the address as he was at a trailer camp. Eventually we found him and I had my first view of the interior of a trailer. They are really wonderful with every inch of space used. Each end had padded lounges which could be easily converted into beds, a slide being pushed across making it into two rooms to accommodate four persons. It had electric light, water, gas, cupboards all round, a wardrobe with a long mirror, a locker which concealed a bath, and another - a night commode. Everything has to be kept scrupulously clean and tidy but the gay curtains and cushions with an awning outside that forms a tent (where there were chairs and benches) made it look very attractive. The owners, Mr and Mrs Cox, were leaving for their house in Los Angeles at the weekend so we were fortunate to see them.

I also saw another trailer next door (a Mr Haddock) which was even more full of gadgets. These men are ardent fishermen and fish for all kinds and have good catches. I think the nomadic life appeals to them. You would have laughed at Mr Haddock's fisherman's hat - a broad-brimmed felt one with diamond-shaped holes all over the crown and the brim cut into a fringe. He had a conger eel hung up outside and showed us its teeth and said they were "b . g g . r s". I heard that Mr Haddock retired from the movies about six months ago and that his was the first invention of sound in the talkies - and he made $100 per week. Apparently he made $500 per day during the war, working for the government. Now that is money, isn't it?

Mr Cox and his sister came out with us in their car to lunch where I tasted clam chowder for the first time. After lunch, we drove to Dana Point to see the lovely view. You cannot imagine the scenery - the great rolling mountains, the rows of immense palms, the blue sea and the white houses within the trees. Very few were tall buildings - mostly bungalows or two-storied of every shape and description - no two alike but very Spanish-looking. Above all, it was very clear with bright sunshine. These are the names of some of the places: San Pedro, Sepulada, Boulevard, Alhambra, Santa Ana and many more. We passed large places where rabbits and chickens are and advertisements saying, FRYING RABBITS AND CHICKENS - the poor things just waiting to be killed. I saw signs, SIT AND GOBBLE SANDWICHES . . . and, DON'T BE LEG-SHY WEAR MISSION HOSIERY . . . and, CABINS FOR BUDDY AND SADIE. A sign on a gas service station said, IF YOU CAN'T STOP SMILE AS YOU PASS BY. We came home by miles and miles of orange groves and got out and stole one or two oranges. At Laguna Beach, Mr Cox got permission to visit a gentleman's garden nearby. A very genial old chap picked us a bunch of lovely flowers. He had orange-trees, grapefruit-trees, banana-trees and alligator-pear trees [*another name for avocado trees*] and a remarkable tree called a humming-bird tree whose flowers, when pressed, looked like little birds. He gave us each a little branch. It is 60-odd miles out to these beaches, so we made it a full day and when we reached home we had tea/dinner. There is a fine bath and shower in these apartments and (last night) I had my first shower-bath and liked it and shall have another tonight before I go to bed.

I have got a grey hat to go with my grey coat and skirt and wore my light frock with the grey coat and hat today. I had my hair waved once again, the first time since I left home. But the breeze blows the short hair all over my eyes and it's a curse. I was so glad to get the Dover snaps and also Marion's letter. I've had another from J W T [*Joseph William Timberlake*]. He has forgotten that he wrote to me from Montréal. I must answer him, I suppose. I've never had so much correspondence from him before.

[LETTER 33 CONTINUED]
I have to write to both Ben Hawkins and to Bowman Timberlake [*in Montréal*]. I'll get some postcards when I go to Hollywood and send from there. Swank.

I forgot to mention that when we started out today we went down Western Avenue for 12 miles before we turned and we could still see as much in the distance then and did not know how far the street extended in the other direction before we entered it. Our address is 634 South Gramercy Street, Los Angeles.

* * *

Tuesday, 12 October 1937

HAVE had another very full day. We started out in good time and even then the sun was hot. To me it seemed a peculiar, clear sunlight. We drove to see a lion farm, the only one in the world. They now have 250 lions there of all ages and sizes, magnificent animals. We saw the trainers display the animals (eight or nine fully grown lions) walking along a row of wooden posts and then array themselves on boxes arranged in tiers. We saw umpteen of them fed and heard many details about them. They are trained for circuses and the movies. The trainer wrestled with a great lion and it rubbed its head against him and licked his hair like a great cat. The trainer also bottle-fed a five-week old lioness cub. It was most interesting and there was also an ostrich farm and an alligator farm, which we did not visit.

After lunch, which we had at an open-fronted place where you sit on a high stool at a counter, we went down Olvera Street - which is the oldest street in Los Angeles [*closed to wheeled traffic but built in the 1920's for tourists*]. It is purely Mexican and the postcard I'm sending you gives but a faint impression of it and it is not a bit too highly coloured. We went through a very old house which is preserved much as it was a hundred years ago, including the furnishings. There was Josefs - the greatest candlemaker where hundreds of candles of all sizes, colours and patterns are sold. This man still makes home-made candles for sale. I've never seen so many swarthy black-haired people, both young and old, in all my life - crowds of them. The dolls were either Spanish senoritas or Indian squaws. Great Mexican hats, slippers made by hand from strips of coloured leather, all kinds of pottery, tiny ornaments, striped silks, trays of Mexican jewellery and the queerest coloured sweetmeats all made a picture that could not be seen elsewhere. You can imagine how Eastern it looks to see rows of tall palm-trees lining the road like soldiers. I thought the markets in San Francisco were large and varied but those here are very large and as long as half the length of Adrian Road [*the street where Annie lived*] with fruit and vegetables of every description displayed.

We came back to the apartment for dinner tonight and Alta and Winnie (Noren) got dressed to go downtown. Suddenly, Alta came running back to get me to put my hat and coat on and run with them to a big church on the corner of the block where a grand wedding was in progress. Fancy, a wedding at 8pm! There were 20 giant candles tied to the pews at intervals with wide pink ribbon with pink dahlias. I was in time to see the bride walk out in white with three bridesmaids - each with a man in evening-dress attending. It must have been a society wedding for some of the fur wraps, etc, were most gorgeous. Since then, we have been up onto the roof garden. A very fine one with a grass lawn, flowerbeds, rockers and tables, etc. A place to write, sun-bathe or take tea. There was a fine view of the city lights and I sat on one of those hammock swings and swung and rocked. Perhaps I may go there in daylight. Mr Curtis has been down to one of the newest barbers' shops where he had a face massage - cream and all. The newest service where (he says), "They would go to hell for a nickel and the round trip for a dime".

An advert from the 1937 Methodist Church Fête programme. Arthur Dobson was helped at this time by his wife, Ellen, and his eldest son, Archie. Small boys were sat upon a wooden box placed on the barbers' chair to have their hair cut.

* * *

Wednesday morning, 13 October 1937

WE set out quite early in the car and first of all went to visit a friend of Mrs Noren's, a Mrs Abey, who has a new home in Beverly Hills - which is where a lot of the film stars live - a sort of annex of Hollywood. This home is really one of the most modern kind of homes I've ever entered. Everything for comfort and easy working. She has a Negro maid who was slowly ironing and who gave us a broad smile shewing her white teeth with gold fillings. I'd love you to see the bedroom and shower cupboard with glass doors so that no shadow falls; and the beautiful lavatory seat covered with white plushette with black figures - so there's no cold seat to sit on while you dry your feet. The double-sink and drainer are all pure white and peach, the cupboards for china have lattice doors and the door-bell chimes - no heart-scaring electric bell.

Mrs Abey went with us to Hollywood. We went to the famous Hollywood Bowl which is really a natural stadium - all seats in tiers set into the hills. You will see a view of this in one of the pictures I am sending to you. We stood on the front of the stage and had a snap taken but, of course, it cannot shew the immensity or beauty of it. They have plays, operas and concerts here; and the acoustics are so perfect that a person sitting up in the highest tier of the hillside seats can hear perfectly well.

Then we went through the crowded streets of Hollywood with its wide pavements. We saw the queer CHINESE THEATRE which has outside it the hand and foot prints of many famous stars set in the sidewalk. Their autographs and often a

[LETTER 33 CONTINUED]
message are there as well, such as the one from Eddie Cantor which has two round eyes drawn at the top and, "Here's looking at you, kid!". We also saw those of Shirley Temple, the Marx Brothers, Joe Brown, Norma Shearer, and many more - but could see none of the dead and past stars. [*The tradition only began in 1927 when film actress Norma Talmadge accidentally stepped into wet cement at the opening of Grauman's Chinese Theatre.*] But as I'm no film fan they did not convey much to me except to admire the lovely grounds and homes. They are like English mansions in size but have the peculiar Spanish, Mexican or American air that these Californian cities have, to me. No two houses are alike. Even the streets where the working class live - all differ.

Mr Curtis took us to lunch at a café in Hollywood. I had bacon rashers, corn fritters, diced carrots, peas, chocolate pudding and a pot of tea. I bought some postcards and the saleslady said: "Are you visiting? I knew you were English. I am also. I came over from Newcastle. Everybody knows a John Bull!" [*The national nickname for an Englishman from the name of the farmer in "The History of John Bull" by John Arbuthnot, 1712.*]

The shops and markets are very beautiful and also the jewellery and antique shops. I saw a replica of the crystal drop I wear around my neck and the saleslady told me it was topaz. Hers was damaged and valued at $7. The flowers there were gorgeous and the weather like midsummer. How I love the trees, the palms, the pepper-trees, the great canyons and the white houses perched so precariously up on the sides of the hills.

Alta and I came home by ourselves on a streetcar and made tea, had a meal and then started out on an adventure of our own. Alta has an uncle and aunt living in Los Angeles whom she has never seen and had been unable to contact over the phone. After searching the town for a telephone directory we found one in an hotel and phoned her uncle's place of business. There happened to be a man there who knew his locality but not the number of his house - only that it was so many blocks from so and so. Nor did he know whether it was on the east side or west side of the street. We had to take two streetcars and one bus and then walk down a long street. Alta went to a house and asked for information and the man said we had better try further along at the new houses. We did and happened to enquire at the house next door but one to Mr Farthing [*Alta's maiden name was Farthing*]. They were very nice people and glad to make Alta's acquaintance. It is another beautiful American house and they have two fine cars because her aunt is a school nurse for three schools and takes classes now and then, probably hygiene. She has a woman who runs her house for her each day because she makes good money. We are to go there for dinner on Friday. On our way there we saw a great number of coloured people (mostly women) who looked as if they were going home from work - and it was almost 9 o'clock. I saw these signs over a store: ORANGE JUICE IT'S A DEVILISH FINE DRINK . . . and, ORANGES AT 25 CENTS FOR FOUR DOZEN. Also there was a figure of a gigantic dog with bulging eyes like lamps urging you to, EAT AT THE DOG; and a restaurant built in the shape of a hat with a smaller hat above it called, THE BROWN DERBY [*a brown bowler hat*]. Mr Farthing drove us back in his car and we did not get to bed until nearly one o'clock in the morning.

* * *

Friday midnight, 15 October 1937

I FORGOT to write of my visit to what they call the Exposition Park [*site of the Olympic Games in 1932*] with its very beautiful grounds and lakes with lilies growing in them - red, pink, yellow, mauve and white - and numerous fish. There are rooms full of specimens of Californian fruits, vegetables, birds, beasts, fishes, minerals and manufactured goods - very like the great Exhibitions we have had at home. There were rooms filled with pottery and Mexican work, wonderful leather goods and relics of ages past that have been unearthed.

One evening, two friends of Alta and Joe called to see Alta at the apartment - Captain and Mrs Isabel Davis who live at Long Beach. She is a sweet-faced young lady and the man (who is called "Cap") is a big jolly man full of talk and jokes. "Do you still have tea-cosies in the Old Country?" he said.

"Yes," said I. He laughed uproariously.

"I never saw or heard of such things until I saw Mrs Carr's. When I come to San Francisco, I won't forget to take a rise out of you two Englishwomen. Fancy," he said, "coming to California where you can cook eggs on the sidewalk - and wrapping your teapots up in a bloody blanket!" I'm just beginning to get used to the expletives people use here. They shocked me at first, but Joe tells me it's very usual and only a habit of speech. I dislike it intensely though - like the people who do it.

We shall have a few snaps to send if they come out all right. At Santa Ana, there was a café in the shape of an Indian wigwam [*or teepee*] and, outside, a smaller one with, MEN'S TEE PEE over it. We had our pictures taken outside and thought the letter should have been altered - though it was quite evident what it meant.

Did not get up quite so early this morning but had a look around the stores in our immediate neighbourhood before going to lunch with Mr and Mrs Cox. They have a bungalow in Los Angeles but are only there three months of every year, the rest being spent going from place to place in their trailer. They have an interesting place full of curios that they have picked up in their travels. He retired years ago when he was making good money. When people expressed surprise at his giving up so much, he said he was going to learn how to play! He has bungalows all around him let to Japanese tenants whom he says are the best in the world, never owing him a penny. He is a travelling friend of Mr Curtis but I think Winnie would soon tire of them. Alta and I had a job to get away. He had shells, rocks, agates, petrified wood, etc, etc, to shew us. He does the most marvellous fretwork and had a model of Nelson's Column in white sycamore - hundreds of pieces with lions, flags, plaques and Nelson on top, some four and a half feet high. Mrs Cox knits and weaves rugs and he fishes and collects geological specimens. We had a lovely dinner: lamb, peas, potatoes, mint sauce and rounds of pineapple with cream cheese and a cherry on top served on a lettuce leaf. All individual salads are served on a lettuce leaf and this is eaten with the meat course. We had cake, strawberry ice, whipped cream and tea.

Then Alta and I went off to her uncle's where we had another blow-out. Again the pineapple salad with braised beefsteaks, beans, potatoes, cherry pie and tea. Then we went with them to their church, a Seventh Day Adventist - a new experience. It was a young peoples' service and it was surprising to see the young fellows - there were quite

[LETTER 33 CONTINUED]
as many men as women. Then they drove us in their car out past where her three schools are situated in quite another part of the city. One is in the Mexican quarter. It is called Pio Pico and she has 400 pupils in the one school.

Alta and I have just got in from going to dinner with Mr and Mrs Farthing and their little girl, Gloria Mae. Mrs Farthing does so wish she could get some English farthings. She has never seen one and as her name is Farthing is most interested. I told her I'd get you to send me some out. I don't know if I got rid of the quantity I used to have in the kitchen cupboard in that coloured sugar-basin. But send me out a dozen will you? Wrap them in tissue paper. Do hope you won't forget the threepenny bits. Must now get to bed. I get mixed up with my news when I leave writing for a night.

The 1937 farthing was the first to show the "Jenny" wren, commonly regarded then as Britain's smallest bird. Together with the halfpenny and the threepenny bit, these were new designs originally proposed for Edward VIII's coinage.

* * *

Saturday evening, 16 October 1937

HERE I am in another auto-camp where we have put up for the night. This is a nicer one than before: two large bedrooms, a large kitchen which is well furnished, two clothes-cupboards, and a toilet and shower bath enclosed by a glass door. It is all well carpeted with good beds, electric lights everywhere, a lock-up garage which is entered from the cottage, all utensils, etc, and everything is spotless. There are pictures on the walls and silk runners on the dressing-tables. We have made good progress having come some 300 miles since leaving Los Angeles. We came by the coastal route which is the loveliest drive you could imagine. For the greater part of the way you follow the ocean which was a shimmering blue-green in the sun. I am sending you the route we took, so you can trace it [*included next*].

We had breakfast in the open air at Santa Barbara under large umbrellas. Then we visited the old Mission [*Mission Santa Barbara built 1786, rebuilt 1820*] and the Civic Hall. I am sending you the folder with the descriptions of these places for they are past my words. I wish I could have stayed longer to examine all the wonder and beauties. I hear that the Duke and Duchess of Windsor may come to stay at Santa Barbara as it is said to be a favourite spot of the Duke's. I don't wonder for it is very, very lovely and a great many wealthy people live there. The Brother who conducted us around the Mission was in brown habit, white knotted girdle, his rosary and cross on one side and flat black sandals on his bare feet. The old fellow who led us round the wonderful Civic Hall asked all where they came from and we all had to sign his register. Just above my name was someone from China and also someone from Bournemouth. The names of the places we passed by fascinate me: Ventura, Conchita, Montecito, Santa Ynez, Santa Maria, Santa Ana, Godova, Lompoc, Zoca Creek. If I had money, I would like to live at Santa Barbara for a long time.

* * *

Saturday evening [*16 October 1937*]

I AM sending you a map of California and I'd like you to follow our journey down to Los Angeles and back:

> The inland route down [*by the San Joaquin Valley*]: San Francisco, Oakland, Tracy, Modesto, Merced, Fresno, Bakersfield, San Fernando, Burbank, Los Angeles.
>
> Then the return by the coastal route: Los Angeles, Santa Monica, Ventura, Santa Barbara, Santa Maria, San Luis Obispo, Paso Robles, King City, Salinas, San Jose, Santa Clara, Palo Alto, Redwood City, San Francisco. Also see where I went to Long Beach, Balboa, Laguna Beach and to Dana Point.

Do you know they teach children to pronounce Z [*zed*] as "zee" over here: "x, y, zee"? I want you to read the Californian Mission Trail. You will recognise many of the names I've mentioned in previous letters. We stayed at Pismo Beach and had bowls of clam chowder [*stew*] with bread or crackers and butter. I'm enclosing a menu which was pinched - you can see the folks here know what to eat.

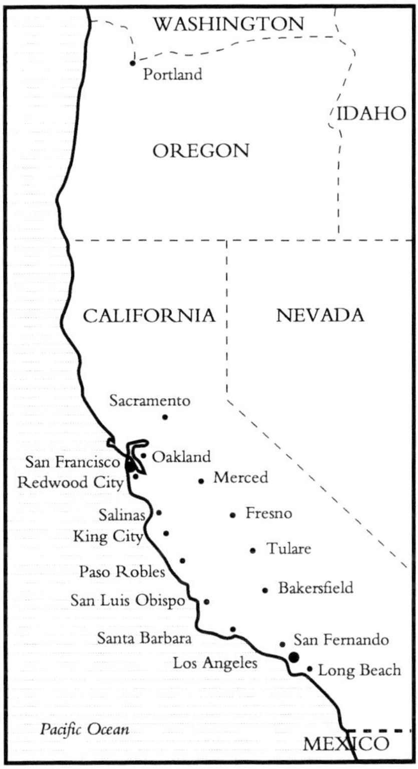

Another map of California.

*

SIGNS I saw on the road:

DON'T MAKE YOUR WIFE COOK - WE SERVE BREAKFAST FROM 6.30AM.

IF YOUR WIFE CAN'T COOK DON'T DIVORCE HER - KEEP HER FOR A PET AND EAT HERE.

EAT AT HASKEL'S AND ENJOY OUR PARLOUR - WE DO YOUR KITCHEN WORK. (With a little parlour depicted - complete - like a dolls' house.)

All along the highway at about 200 yard intervals you can see words [*advertising a shaving soap*] that, when put together, make a sign thus:

EVERY SHEBA - WANTS A SHEIK - STRONG OF MUSCLE - SMOOTH OF CHEEK - BURMASHAVE.

STOMACHACHE - DOCTOR - TOOTHACHE - DENTIST - WHISKERS - BURMASHAVE.

This is placed on a large board at the entrance to some American cities:

WELCOME TO . . .
DRIVE SLOWLY AND SEE OUR CITY
DRIVE FAST AND SEE OUR GAOL!

And you can see this, it looks so peremptory: THIS IS PRIVATE KEEP OUT.

* * *

[*Around midnight on Sunday, 17 October 1937*]

WE were up betimes this morning (Sunday) and pulled out of the auto-camp at 7.30am. We drove home this trip by the Roosevelt Highway and you will see the front of the Stanford University Chapel at Palo Alto that I visited. These pictures are not in the least bit exaggerated. If only I could describe the colours of the flowers, the butterflies, the mountains and the beautiful mosaics in the buildings!! It makes me ache to have you here, Marion, to see the colourings and decorations. Even the table colours are gay and in keeping with the clear atmosphere. Passing through as a traveller, of course, one does not see the poverty, etc, but I'm sure it is not so bad to be poor in a warm and colourful country as in a grey cold one. We saw people picking raspberries and tomatoes, garden peas in bloom and fields of roses - and this in October. I saw a place called, DOLLS HOSPITAL QUIET and a hospital for dogs - quite a large building. I have told you of our journey home in the previous pages and we got here at 11.30pm. There was a letter from Marion awaiting me and some papers. I love David's drawings, bless their little hearts [*her grandsons, David and Roger Flint*]. Am so glad they remember me well. Remember me to all my friends and tell the Rev Albert Jones about Aimee McPherson. Sunday is the only day Joe gets at home and I'm glad to be with him. This morning when we started it was chilly and very misty but tonight the weather is beautiful.

Holidays are fine and Winnie and Dodie (as we all call Mrs Noren and Mr Curtis) were the kindest of people to us - going out of their way to make it interesting for us. They would accept nothing for gasolene and it must have cost something covering 1200 miles and often going at 70 miles per hour. Will write again next week.

My dear love to you all,

Your loving Mum

* * * * *

Christmas In San Francisco

THANKSGIVING was followed by an American Christmas which were both enjoyed by Annie Kimpton. Her Christmas present for Mr Curtis and Winnie Noren arrived just in time:

[LETTER 34]

"I had my picture done on Olvera Street . . . . . ."

400 Duboce Avenue, San Francisco, California, USA
Wednesday, 20 October 1937

MY DEARS,

With this I am sending a pencil written account of my trip to Los Angeles and a whole lot of souvenirs and pictures. I've put them in order as much as possible as my journey went. I'm afraid the pencil writing is rather faint but I hope you will be able to decipher it. [*This is the previous letter.*] I had my picture done on Olvera Street, Los Angeles, by a young Italian or Mexican; Alta had hers done also - pencil sketches. I wonder if you will think them good? I think Alta's is - though she looks a little stern. [*The drawing of Annie is included in the illustrated plates; Alta's has not survived.*]

I've not done much these past two or three days but feel more rested today. I've asked you in my long letter to send some farthings - a dozen; and also threepenny pieces (the new coinage) - at least eight of them. Then I want one of you to get me a small etching of St Albans Abbey. [*The Abbot and monks of St Albans were given Abbots Langley in Saxon times; the Norman Abbey was five miles from Annie's home.*] I must give Mr Curtis and Mrs Noren a little gift for Christmas in recognition of their kindness to Alta and me. The journey would have cost us a considerable sum - to say nothing of the jaunts out every day and all day. They have a lovely home and want for nothing and it's difficult to think of anything suitable. It would have to be a good one - say up to 10s [*ten shillings*]. I don't suppose there is any cash to be spent as the rates and what I owe Bert are due. But if you can send these out, the settlement must wait till I return. If the coins are wrapped in tissue paper, I think they'll be all right.

Joe has just the same queer temperament but Alta passes by all his bitter speeches with, "Oh, he don't mean it. He'll get over it in a little while." He loves her but tries to hurt her - just as he always did to those he loved. He cannot find fault with her ability, for her manager (when she introduced me to him on my visit to the factory) told me: "We all think highly of your daughter and her work is eminently satisfactory" (!!!) Alta was pleased. Fancy, she was brought up at a Seventh Day Adventist college and graduated from there. She shewed me her diplomas with the names of all her teachers and professors attached; and she has six or more little badges or medals for speed and efficiency in shorthand and typing. Before she left Portland, Oregon, she went regularly to church but does not go in San Francisco. Mrs Carr told me no one had ever seen Alta in a temper. She was always the same happy, lovable and even-tempered little thing. Joe is the luckiest fellow to have her.

Wish Margaret Flint many happy returns from me. [*One of the daughters of Bert*

Flint's uncle, "Moss" (Maurice) and Nell Flint. They lived at Crosspaths, 39 Trowley Rise, Abbots Langley. Moss suffered from the effects of gas on the Western Front in the First World War.] I was the first to see her in the world. Tell Mrs Kate Buckoke how sorry I am about poor old Bill [*Bill Buckoke, a builder, lived at 91 Breakspear Road, Abbots Langley*] and I'm sorry for Phyllis Bull. Let's hope she will soon have a home of her own. Joe grinned over New York being coupled with San Francisco in Auntie Edie's geography. [*Edie Flint, sister of Bert Flint's father, who from 1928 - initially with her sister, Maud, and later by herself - kept the small general store and confectionery corner shop at 25 Marlin Square, Abbots Langley. The entrance to the shop was then on the corner of the alley which cuts diagonally across Marlin Square, but it has since been bricked up.*]

Where has Fred dumped all my rubbish? In the attic? I've been trying to picture what my rooms look like but . . . . . .

My dearest love,
Mother

* * * * *

[LETTER 35]

"I'm sure Englishmen would rebel"

400 Duboce Street, San Francisco, California, USA
Thursday, 28 October 1937

MY DEARS,

This has been quite a busy week for me. I went one day with Mrs Carr to a friend of hers (a Mrs Mollering) for lunch and to meet some other ladies. Mrs Mollering has a fine car and came and fetched Mrs Carr and me. She has a very beautiful home and plenty of money. Mrs Carr said, "Bring a bit of work with you". So I started on some crochet but did none of it after lunch. We had creamed crab, asparagus, a salad, tiny hot rolls, ice-cream and cake with tea because three of us were Englishwomen. Afterwards we sat in the drawing-room and told dirty stories and laughed.

One evening, Joe took Alta and I to a Chinese restaurant for dinner. I've sent you one of the menus and marked what we ate. We sat in a recess with a curtain over the door and drank green-tea (which I did not like) out of little handleless cups. It is impossible to pick out exactly what you are eating, save that I could make out shreds of chicken and pork; and there are piles of it. I came across something that tasted like cooked Brazil nuts and Joe said it was water-chestnut. There were bean shoots, bamboo shoots and many other things all piled up in a dish. Joe ordered one portion which was quite enough for the three of us - so you can see the amount of food they provide. Every worker there is Chinese, of course, with their polite smile and lisp. The place was spotlessly clean. Joe tells the story of the "laundly" man: "Please fetchee laundly tomollow - shittee on shirt 5 cents extla". There was a most magnificent electric-light chandelier, all bronze with green pendants. But I shall not choose to dine at a Chinese restaurant again. In San Francisco just now, there is a sort of boycott of Japanese stores because of the Chinese war. But Joe will take me to a Japanese eating house one day.

Another evening Joe, Alta and I, Mr and Mrs Noren, and Mr Curtis went for dinner to a Spanish place. It was like a Spanish patio - a large courtyard with wells and booths and what looked like dwellings all around. There were vines and cacti around the lattice work and a stage at one end. On the dance floor in front of it, men in red, green or blue blouses with Spanish hats played cello, guitar, castanets and gourd rattles. On the bare tables were candles on mounds of wax drippings. There were coloured glass lanterns and girls in fancy Spanish dress and men in silk boleros with black braiding to wait upon you - all very attractive. I liked the soup and coffee but can't say I liked the rest. I've marked on the menu what we had to eat. At 10 o'clock they put on a sort of concert: dancers and singers - singly and in couples. One man was in black with red satin lapels, red tie and sash, and red godets in his trousers - all outlined with gold braid. They certainly could dance! When the band played the customers danced: Joe with Alta . . . Chester with Winnie . . . all with the crowd. And Mr Curtis and I sat, watched and talked. I get on very well with him.

The weather here at present is cooler but sunny during the day. It is very strange to see the fog coming from the sea. It looks like a cloud of smoke and those who live in the part of the city near the Bay often get fog while other districts are clear and bright. When I send a snap of the city I'll put an X where we live. You would have laughed to see us on Monday evening coming back from the library. I have a ticket now and can have four books per week - so back we came with twelve (four each). It is a fine library and has a great number of books.

Mr Noren went fishing yesterday and came back with 240lb of striped bass. He brought round a large one for us weighing 15lb. Alta cut off a large piece for her sister and I cooked the rest with tomato sauce today. It was very good indeed and there is a lot left for tomorrow. I made a lemon pie and it also went. I don't go about the city alone much for the traffic is so fast and great and I'm nervous. One thing I notice is that none of the boys here, big or little, look as smart as English children do. All of them wear long trousers, open-neck shirts and sweaters of all descriptions. Usually they go to school or high school in a pair of shabby overalls or flannels, and the woolly thing they wear is evidently much shrunken. Even tiny tots wear the same. Men go about in overall suits which have the firms' names for whom they work plastered across the back in large letters. I'm sure Englishmen would rebel.

Last Saturday we had Mr and Mrs Hotchkiss round for dinner and I made steak and kidney pie - so I'm keeping my hand in at cooking. I'm relining a coat this week - so I'm also keeping my hand in with needlework. We are going to Bob Hotchkiss's for dinner this Saturday evening. It's their wedding anniversary - one year. I went walking one day around the junk shops with his wife. She is a real Cockney; and to the delight and dismay of folks here never sounds one H and talks of, "Taking 'ome 'alf a 'am". However she has turned out well. I think she is over 40, thin, dark, false teeth but pretty eyes and full of fun and never ceases talking. Bob worships her.

I got a letter from Muriel and Marion last week but have received none this week as yet. I've never been to Northampton and was much interested. [*Muriel and Fred Kimpton had been to visit Fred and Ivy Followell. Fred Followell's mother was the sister of*

Carrie Gates (who lived at Dover) whose husband, Jim, was a first cousin of Annie Kimpton. In 1998, Ralph Followell (Fred and Ivy's son) recalled playing as a child (on a return visit) in the long grass at the Methodist Church tennis courts in Greenways.]

I hope you get the packet of papers and pictures of Los Angeles. It will take me some time to sort them out when I return. I am sending Mr Adkins' magazine back as you sent me my own and his by mistake. [*Mr and Mrs Alan Adkins and their son Kay lived at 48 Adrian Road, Abbots Langley. They were Methodist chapelgoers.*] Don't forget to try and send me the coins I asked for and I'd be glad if I could have an etching or pencil drawing of the Abbey (St Albans) for Winnie Noren. I shall give the coins to some of my young friends at Christmas. Will write again early next week.

My dearest love to you all and my precious boys,

Your Mum

* * * * *

[LETTER 36]

"Had never seen or tasted Yorkshire Pudding . . . . . ."

400 Duboce Avenue, San Francisco, California, USA
Monday, 8 November 1937

MY DEARS,

Marion's letter of 25 October came this morning. You cannot imagine how I love to get them. I'm at home while I'm reading them. I've laughed to myself all day over Roger's escapades and I know Joe will do the same when he gets home. Roger is something like my Fred for mischief but I always had mother next door - so he had two women on the watch for him. [*In 1998 Flora Botwright, then aged 94, recalled that there was a connecting door between 54 and 56 Adrian Road when Flora first moved into 56 in 1930 which she and Fred Botwright rented from Annie.*]

I did not go sightseeing much last week but took several walks by myself during the day. The streets are miles long and go up and down like giant switchbacks. We had Mr and Mrs Balzar to dinner on Saturday evening and I cooked beef and batter pudding, peas, string-beans and potatoes. Folk have a queer way of serving glasses of fruit salad as the first course - then, for desert, ice-cream and raspberries. This couple, Billie and Wally, had never seen or tasted Yorkshire Pudding and Joe feared they wouldn't like it but they did and had two helpings. They are a nice couple. He is of German extraction and she is an American. I believe he was born in California.

Did I tell you that the great streetcars pass this house both ways as we are on a corner [*the intersection of Duboce Avenue and Fillmore Street*] and they run all day and almost all night? It is surprising what one can get used to. I sleep calmly through the din as our rooms are set back along a courtyard. We are not close to the street. Today is dull but it is still warm. I've only seen one shower of rain since I've been out here and it's never felt chilly. Yesterday, I went to church in the morning. I cannot go but once in the day as Joe is only home on Sunday - so I try to fit in with their plans. This morning,

Winnie Noren called asking me to go to her house for lunch tomorrow. I take a streetcar outside this house and go up Fillmore Street as far as it goes, then transfer to what they call the "dinky car" to Union Street, cross the street and go on to Franklin Street. I've only been once alone. [*The "dinky car" was a cable car. The cable car system was invented in 1873 by Andrew Hallidie, an English-born mining engineer, to tackle the problem of transporting people up and down the city's steep hills in the days of horse-drawn vehicles. The system is unique to San Francisco.*]

Alta and I went to Golden Gate Park yesterday (while Joe played golf) and saw the Aquarium and the tropical fish - some very lovely and some very horrible ones. Then in the evening we went to Mrs Carr's. I'd relined a coat for her during the week so I took it over. I like her. She is a most friendly woman but I've soon had enough of her husband. He tells me what a great man he used to be and is always trying to be funny and play practical jokes. But they tell me he is most subdued in my company. Joe says he's afraid of me but I think it's because I'm elderly and English.

I was most interested to hear of the Banquet and Len Flint. If I had been at home I'd be worried over that. Did Ivy go to the party? Has she given up Sunday school? Has Mrs Len Flint given up Women's Own? [*The "Lord Mayor's Banquet" was an annual event that took place at the Methodist church in Abbots Langley. Further details are given in Appendix III : "The Wesley Guild". It would appear that Len Flint was upset over something that took place or was said, hence the reference to his daughter, Ivy, and his wife, Amy. Len Flint was Bert Flint's uncle and he lived at Oakdene, 75 Trowley Rise, Abbots Langley. Len served on the Western Front in the First World War.*]

Give my love and good wishes to Sue. I do hope all is well with her. [*Sue Simons née Collins, wife of George Simons the butcher in Abbots Langley.*] I shall have a multitude of letters to write before Christmas. Tell Arthur Dowse how sorry I am about Lillie and to give her my love. Also tell Walter Cox to remember me kindly to his mother. So Elsie [*Timberlake*] is going to Chipperfield for a time? It is a long time since she first thought of it - but she usually gets there in the end, whatever she plans.

Did Fred get the parcel with the socks in it? How about the coins? A lady here tells me that her friends in the Old Country (as all call it) send flat things inside the newspapers (right inside) and they always arrive safely. I got the one threepenny bit quite all right and it excites great interest. Very few people have seen any English money and the copper coins cause great amusement as there is only one here - the cent (the size of our farthing) which is called a "penny". I happened to keep a few pence and sixpences and one shilling in my bag. I wish I'd kept a florin and a half crown also but it doesn't matter. I've several boys who would like a new threepenny bit for Christmas. [*In pre-decimal coinage a farthing was one quarter of a penny and two farthings made one halfpenny (pronounced ha'penny); a sixpenny piece was known as a "Tanner"; there were twelve pennies to a shilling or a "Bob"; a florin was a two-shilling piece or a "Two-Bob bit"; half a crown was two shillings and sixpence or "Two and Six"; a crown was five shillings (but these were not in general circulation); there were twenty shillings to a pound or a "Quid"; and a guinea was one pound one shilling.*]

I'm still all right for cash having drawn very little since the big lot for my journey here. I don't pay Joe anything but try to help all I can with cooking and mending. I shan't send gifts to folk at home at Christmas, for you may have to pay duty and I don't want you to send me anything either. I shall wait until I return to bring some keepsakes. Alta talks already of my getting an extension of stay here but of course it's early days yet.

I've been up to Haight Street today to get some carrots, etc, to make a thick stew of the remains of the beef joint. Joe loves stew and Alta loves thick gravy so I can please both. I got 2lb of fine Tokay grapes for 10 cents. Last week we had strawberries for desert. I get through a large number of books in a week. Tonight we get another dozen. I am making crochet lace for Alta for a dressing-chest runner. She needs a new one.

What is said in England about the Duke of Windsor and the giving up of the American trip? [*In October 1937, the Duke and Duchess of Windsor naively visited Germany to see new housing developments and were used as pawns by the Nazis; they met the leading Nazis and finally met Adolf Hitler at Berchtesgaden. The Duke had planned a visit to the USA to study labour conditions, but the anger in Britain and the USA following his German visit led to its cancellation.*] I made some of the women stare when I suggested that perhaps the Duchess did not want to come. Why? Well, he has a roving eye, you know; and she knows her country's women - who better? It stands to reason that she was stolen fruit before and now nothing fresh. In fact, he knows just how far he got when she was Mrs Simpson. Also he knows and must recall the other two men, etc, etc. It was quite a new point of view. One American paper stated that the Queen, the Duchess of Kent and the Duchess of Windsor were all in an interesting condition(!) I'd like the Queen to have a son, for if it should come to pass that Mrs Simpson had one, it might complicate matters for George VI and his family later on.

Give my love to Fred and Jack, Flora and Mabel and Mrs Charlie Bot. [*The brothers,*

An advert from the 1937 Methodist Church Fête programme. Fred Botwright was Agent for Brentnall & Cleland at their wooden office, perched on stilts on the side of the railway embankment next to Kings Langley and Abbots Langley Railway station.

Fred and Jack Botwright, and their mother, Mrs Charlie (Ellen) Botwright née Gates, were all nicknamed "Bot". Fred was married to Flora (née Blake) and Jack was married to Mabel (née Funnell). Mr and Mrs Charlie Botwright lived at 83a Breakspear Road, Abbots Langley. Charlie came from Dagnall in Buckinghamshire, near Tring. Ellen was the daughter of Ephraim Gates of Watford and they were married in 1900 at Queens Road Wesleyan Church. (Ellen was probably not related to Annies mothers' family - the Gates from Astrope.) Charlie Botwright had been a baker in Aldbury in Hertfordshire, near Tring.]

Marion's birthday will be close-to when this letter arrives. [*Her birthday was on 23 November and she would have been 35 years old.*] Many happy returns to you, dear child. I've never had to pay any excess on the letters and I believe a penny-ha'penny is enough on an ordinary letter. Alta was pleased with the stamps and hopes you will try for an Edward VIII tuppenny-ha'penny one [*two and a half pence*] though I fear they cannot be got now. How is my Topsy? A kiss for my David and little scamp Roger. How I wish you had one of the fine washing machines here, Marion.

My dearest love to you all,

Your Mum

* * * * *

[LETTER 37]

"Almost everybody here has been married twice"

400 Duboce Avenue, San Francisco, California, USA
Wednesday, 17 November 1937

MY DEARS,

I fear I am late with this letter. Was so glad to have two letters, one from Fred and one from Marion. Of course Muriel can cast out the old chair if it is too worm-eaten. The one in the back bedroom is, I fear, also touched with worm. As for the old mangle, I don't know if it would be any good for Mrs Martindale [*who lived in Marlin Square*]. If it would, ask Marie to tell her to get it - otherwise I don't know what to do with it. There's nothing wrong with it save that the roller is worn. Since mother died I have used hers in the scullery. I'd be glad if Bert would repair the front bay-window. I made arrangements with Fred that if repairs were costing a great deal, he would pay and I'd settle with Fred on my return. I'm afraid a new front fence would mean a big outlay but perhaps Bert would patch it up? I was sorry Fred did not like the socks and that you had to pay [*import duty*]. I shall keep all the stuff that I get until I come back and pack it in my trunk. Was so sorry to hear of Mrs Cox's death. Give my sympathy to Walter and his sisters. [*Mrs Cox's late husband, David Cox, had been Matthew Timberlake's right-hand man in the Abbots Langley Wesleyan Methodist church. David Cox lived at 12 Adrian Road. Dolly Brownsell née Cox (mentioned in the Introduction) was David's daughter; and Levi and Walter Cox (mentioned previously) were his nephews.*] How is old Mr Buckoke? I've heard nothing of Marie and Jim [*Kimpton*] lately. Is all well?

It does not seem possible that it is November. We have had one wet day here and

[LETTER 37 CONTINUED]
the night it started I felt ever so hot in bed. Joe tells me it is always so when rain is about to fall. Apparently it usually rains in the night and in the morning the roads are beautifully dry. We have such bright warm days. The sun is clear and bright but not hot. This city is so white - roads and houses. None are dark, probably because so many are wooden. No bungalows but great massive-looking apartment houses. I am enclosing the little magazine of the church I attend. You will see that they have included a bit about me. You can see they are all Scandinavians by their names, can't you? I went to the Ladies' Aid meeting last Wednesday. They hold them each month. There were a lot there and the women are so alike - big, plain and fair.

Alta and I went again to the Golden Gate Park on Saturday and had a look round some of the great exhibitions there. There is an immense aquarium with the most wonderful coloured tropical fish [*the Steinhart Aquarium*]. Then there are rooms displaying stones of all kinds [*the Natural History Museum*]. I'd never imagined that there could be so many kinds, let alone in one country. I saw a section through one of the great redwood trees. It was marked out in the sections with the year and this one was a sapling when the Romans entered Britain. There was a display about the oldest tree that had been felled and it shewed that it started to grow when the Israelites left Egypt. There were rooms of birds and beasts of California. We had no time to go to the Fine Arts rooms as they closed at 5 o'clock, so we came home.

We called on Alta's mother who is a little, dark woman. She is most energetic but never very well as she is a diabetic and has to have injections of insulin each day. She lives alone in an apartment and (that evening) we all three went to the pictures. I've been twice in a week, the first time since I came here. We saw *The Awful Truth* and laughed a lot. [*This was a comedy starring Irene Dunne and Cary Grant.*]

We often go round to Mrs Carr's. They are Joe's oldest friends and Joe goes almost when he likes. I can understand now why the telephones are here. They ring their friends up before they start out to call on them, so saving a fairly long car journey for nothing. Then, after you have been out for an evening with light refreshments you call your friends the next morning with kind enquiries and thanks, etc. [*Telephones were still relatively new and not widespread in Abbots Langley in 1937; for instance Bert Flint had a telephone for the FLINT BROTHERS builders' business, but neither Arthur Flint, George Flint, Len Flint nor Moss Flint had telephones in their homes at that time.*]

I've been busy today. I went up to Haight Street and bought meat, etc, and made steak and kidney pudding, with potatoes and savoy cabbage and made an apple pie. It all went well and Joe and Alta liked it. I saw boxes of strawberries labelled, ALL FRESH TODAY. Fancy, all kinds of flowers and fruits in November. But as an old man, John "the Bootmaker", said to me, "It is only in California that it is always warm. In some places in this country it is doggone cold."

I met a young lady who is married to her second husband and then came in contact again with her first - a very nice man. I was told that she lived with her first husband for 11 years. "What was the trouble?" I said - and was told, "Oh, no trouble," she just got tired of living with the same man and the other fellow - who is also a very fine man - met her and was attracted! They agreed to separate, had a big party with friends and announced what they were doing. Then got separate apartments but lived together with her new man a week after having told their friends. She got a divorce by mail in Mexico for incompatibility of temperament. Then flew to Reno and was married to the new man two days after the decree was made absolute. She then parted the furniture with her former husband and arranged his new apartment for him. Mr and Mrs Noren went to the lady's apartment for their last meal together and Winnie stayed afterwards (with her) while Chester escorted him to his apartment. They both wept a bit and there you are. She married at once and he has waited two years and is now walking out with another girl. Joe says almost everybody here has been married twice and some three times. You never know where you are and you have to be more than careful when speaking. This week a woman got a divorce because her husband insisted on wearing shorts and she disapproved!!

I'm getting used to the money here and to the traffic. I got two little coloured caps for my little boys. Just like the ones the little boys wear here. They wear them perched on top of their heads. They call them "beanies" and are the same shape as the ones sailors wear here - only theirs are white. I went down to see the parade on Armistice Day, or "peerade" as they call it here: soldiers, sailors, Boy Scouts, girls' and women's clubs all decked out in fancy uniform, the Salvation Army, and I don't know what else - as well as bands and guns. I liked the sailors but not the others much. Our soldiers are much smarter. People here think there is no army but theirs because, of course, England is so tiny. Joe tells me never to argue any point as they don't know and it's no use telling 'em. The newspapers also seem bitter against England. Why didn't England pay their war debts? Everything is blamed on that. [*The Allies borrowed $10 billion from the USA between 1914 and 1918. America refused to waive the debt when the Allies suggested it was a contribution to the common cause. In 1922, Britain agreed to repay 80% of her loan to restore her financial prestige; 52% of the French and 75% of the Italian debts were cancelled. However, all three countries relied on meeting their payments out of reparations from Germany. Britain was paying interest on her part of the loan.*]

You ought to have heard the Rev Gustav Storaker on Sunday morning, Temperance Sunday. Talk about rave over the repeal of Prohibition [*in 1933*] and about boys and girls drinking, etc. I was thinking it did not fit our staid congregation when suddenly a man got up, took his hat, and marched out. I'm sure the cap was fitting when he talked about Christian parents having the stuff [*alcohol*] in the home, etc, etc. The parsons here talk a great deal plainer than at home.

I don't think I told you about the luncheon I had at Mrs Noren's the other week: a salad first - a mound of grated carrot with pineapple, syrup and creamed mayonnaise on a lettuce leaf - then salmon with a white sauce with parsley stirred in (this was very good), peas, cucumber in vinegar, hot rolls and butter, and pumpkin pie with whipped cream. We had Lime Rickey to drink before lunch and coffee afterwards. To me it seems an awful waste of time and money especially as they dine again at half past six in the evening and it is "ditto repeato" with the addition of a soup course and meat joint and vegetables, etc.

On Monday morning, I met Mrs Hotchkiss (Kitty) and we walked and shopped. I like her. I have no need to talk, only acknowledge by a laugh, a grunt or an exclamation. She talks continually and knows everything and is English, double-dyed.

There are two great Colleges here, Stanford and California. A wealthy man, who had had very little education, interviewed Stanford College with a view to his son taking his college course there. The boy's pals and his girl friend were all going to the other College and the boy was in a fearful stew since he knew it was of no use to argue the point with his father as that only made him more stubborn. So the boy went to his father's attorney almost weeping over the problem.

"Never mind, I'll talk to your father and I'll see it is all right," said he.

Calling upon the wealthy man soon after he was told of this decision, the attorney said, "Stanford, eh . . . . . . ?", hesitatingly.

"Yes, what's the matter with Stanford?"

"Oh, nothing at all but . . . . . ."

"If you've got anything to say, say it."

"Well, do you know that both boys and girls use the same curriculum there?"

"Good heavens, cannot they afford two?"

"And do you know they shew one another their theses?"

"You - you - don't mean it?"

"I sure do. And I know positively they matriculate together."

"What in the world is this generation coming to. Say no more. My son will go to California College. No Stanford for him." I thought that a rather good tale.

I have received a coloured postcard of the High Street from Mrs Hince [*wife of Freddy Hince, parish councillor and chairman 1932-1933, who lived at 30 Marlin Square*]. Are there any others showing different parts of the village? So George Dunn won't be speechifying this year. I fear more that Mr Pratt may remember my speech!! How I'd like to see the Rev WG Baldwin again. I shall be glad to hear of him and the Banquet. [*George Dunn was very verbose; he married Nora Flint, daughter of George and Edie Flint, and they lived at 20 Trowley Rise; he worked for* JOHN DICKINSON & CO *at Apsley and served with the Royal Signals in North Africa and India during the Second World War. Stan Pratt was a rousing piano-player for the village Boy Scout Gang Shows and also served in the Second World War; he lived at 73 Trowley Rise with his wife, Win, and daughter, Dawn; and he worked for the* BANK OF AUSTRALIA *in London.*]

Joe tells me we get radio programmes from New York here but I cannot tell which ones you may get as you are eight hours ahead of our time. People here seem to think that we in England have very little radio, music or otherwise as we have no advertising. We hear some good music here but that is, of course, Bach and the rest. To my mind the programmes here are piffle and the jokes - well, I can't see 'em. I'm too dense. I've got *Anthony Adverse* to read, so have quite a lot to get through [*a historical romance by Hervey Allen*]. Do hope my David's cold is better. Does Fred wear a hat? This letter is only gossip. I shall have to start a daily diary again.

My dear love to you all,

Your Mum

* * * * *

[LETTER 38]

"Folks there are called Webfoots because they have so much rain"

400 Duboce Avenue, San Francisco, California, USA
Friday, 26 November 1937

MY DEARS,

Thanks for the letter and Banquet programme. I should never have recognised the names without an explanation. [*At the Wesley Guild Banquet, members proposing toasts were given pseudonyms. In 1937 they were in the form of anagrams: for instance, "Lady Nita L Fornim" was Marion Flint.*] We read, or rather I read and Joe and Alta listen to letters from home with great interest. Poor Mr Creasy, what an awful bit of bad luck for him. [*Charlie Creasy was the village baker and his bakehouse, now The Old Bakehouse in Marlin Square, was accidentally burned down one night in November 1937. This fire was the first call-out for the village's "new" Volunteer Fire Brigade that had been set up in 1936. They had a fire engine with extending ladders and the one-time fives court of Langley House in The Crescent had been converted into a Fire Station. The original fire brigade of untrained volunteers, set up around 1905, used to keep its equipment in a handcart at the smithy which was behind the old King's Head in the High Street. Matthew Timberlake had been chairman of the Parish Council fire committee which managed the Volunteer Fire Brigade.*]

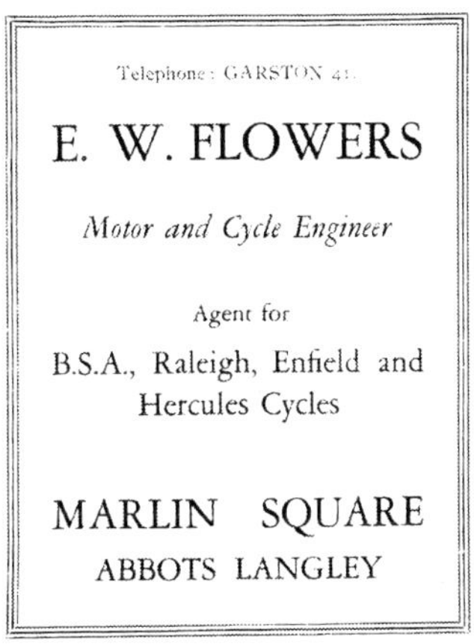

An advert from the 1937 Fête programme. Ern (Ernest) Flowers was a member of the Abbots Langley Volunteer Fire Brigade.

We are having such lovely sunny days. Like our own summer save that the sun is not hot - it is just bright and clear. I've had a pleasant week. Last Monday, I met Kitty Hotchkiss and we went downtown looking at shops, etc. Then on Tuesday I went to lunch with Mrs Noren and Mr Curtis and then down Market Street with her. I see both kinds of stores with these two women: with Kitty, I go to the Jewish and Japanese and 5 cent stores; and with Winnie Noren, I go to the grandest emporiums

[LETTER 38 CONTINUED]
you can possibly imagine; one being the wife of a working man and the other with plenty of money.

Mrs Carr, Alta and I went to the AMATEUR BROADCASTING COMPANY on Tuesday evening. About 16 people played and sang individually and everyone then voted for them. The contest is repeated and a selection made. Those voted highest go to the Golden Gate Park Theatre to perform for three weeks. It is so different to our programmes. This one was for an hour given by the HOMESTEAD BREAD COMPANY and an advertisement for this company is given several times during the hour. All big firms give these programmes and pay great sums to their artistes to perform and broadcast their goods. No one here can believe that we have good music and singing at home without advertising as these businesses pay enormous sums to advertise. Then on Wednesday, I made a cake and pie and did some shopping. They cut meat very differently to English butchers and I am only just getting used to the strange joints and the money here.

Thursday was Thanksgiving Day and people make as much fuss as at Christmas. Enormous numbers of turkeys are eaten with cranberry sauce and pumpkin pie. We had Alta's mother here to dine and we had a nice chicken, beans, potatoes, sweet potatoes (which I don't care for), cranberry sauce which is cranberry jelly, celery, apple pie and vanilla pudding (they have no custard powder here) and coffee. Mrs Farthing said it was a very nice dinner. [*Thanksgiving is a harvest festival held on the fourth Thursday in November commemorating the meal held by the Pilgrim Fathers in 1621 at Plymouth, Massachusetts, to give thanks for their first harvest.*] After dinner, Joe read a book and Alta and her mother worked out her Family Tree. Alta has 72 first cousins living but knows very few of them. They come from Portland, Oregon, and folks there are called "Webfoots" because they have so much rain. When the football players come from that state they bring their mascot, a duck, and call themselves the "Oregon Ducks". [*Alta's unusual first name was possibly inspired by the Spanish name "Alta California" for Upper California, which included Oregon where she was born.*]

On Thanksgiving morning I went to see my first football game here. It was between two high schools (Lowell and Polytechnic) and the students are young men and women. It was in the Golden Gate Park Stadium - a great green oval marked out with white lines; an immense place seating thousands of people. I thought it was something like rugby football but Joe says not. Each side has a band [*of musical instruments*], one in red and black and the other in red tunics and white trousers. There is a great clock at one end ticking off the time and they play a quarter of an hour at a time and it is tremendously hard. They run with the ball in their hands and can pull and roll each other down as they please. I laughed to see them kneeling or squatting in front of the ball. They wear padded helmets and shoulder guards, etc, under their jerseys and look immense. We sat high up in the stadium in the clear bright sun. I wore my little close brown velvet hat and often had to shade my eyes with my hand.

At the street corners there are masses of flowers for sale - roses, sweet peas, carnations, violets, lilies of the valley and English holly. Even though the colours are marvellous the scent is very poor and the fruit has not the fine flavour of our English fruits, save of course for grapes, figs and pomegranates. They have seedless oranges and lemons and gorgeous vegetable markets and many sorts of vegetable I cannot name at all. All the shops are being decorated for Christmas now and they have great fir-trees decorated with electric lights and with streamers right up into the domes. In THE EMPORIUM in Market Street they have escalators and lifts on each floor and a roof garden and every floor is decorated. In the huge ground floor (which goes up to a dome and has a gallery around it where people sit) there are immense wide red ribbons coming from three red bells. There, in an alcove, is Father Christmas seated in a kind of sleigh with four reins in his hand made of silver ribbon. Each strand is many yards long and harnesses four white prancing reindeer with huge antlers amongst the icicled fir-trees with the ground all silver. I have never seen so much preparation everywhere for Christmas, nor so many fancy boxes and decorations for the outside of parcels. They tell me that the city goes mad on decorations. Everyone has a tree, not necessarily for presents but for lights, candles, coloured balls, chains, etc. People hang wreaths tied with red ribbon in every window and in the Golden Gate Park a kind of outdoor play is performed with shepherds and sheep, etc.

Joe says: "You'll soon see the Hay-rabs and the shepherds serenading old Marvill's sheep and everybody saying, 'How sweet, how lovely'. The poor old sheep who are there all the year can't make it out at all. Americans are easily pleased." He says the queerest things just as he always did. Today is pay-day for him and Alta. "Yes," says he, "the American Eagle squawks today and shites a little bit for both of us!" [*The "American" Eagle, a bald eagle - so called because of its white-feathered head, was pictured on dollar notes in 1937. It was adopted as a national emblem in 1782 because of its fierce demeanor though it is really a somewhat timid carrion-eater.*] To see him sometimes at night dancing to the radio, solo, is very funny. I laugh but he is easily the other way. As Mother used to say, "All honey or all TD". [*What TD stood for is not known.*]

I'm glad you liked the pencil sketches. I think the length of my nose surprised me. Alta's chin is small and square and has a little cleft in it and her mouth is firm. Joe says she is not brilliant, only painstaking and plodding - and you know he was never that. He soon gives up. She says: "You know, Mother, Joe's inclined to be lazy," and: "It's no use waiting for jobs without work," all this in her definite little way. She loves Joe devotedly and never argues with him but seems to manage him quite well and he thinks a lot of her. But, as you know, he was never demonstrative. I think he is lucky to have her. Thanks for the farthings and the threepenny pieces. I've got enough now, I think. I don't think I'll send presents home in case you have to pay duty but bring things with me when I return.

* * *

Tuesday, 30 November 1937

I'VE just come in from shopping. The sun is so bright and warm with a slight soft breeze, just like spring in England. It begins to get dark at about half past five and we have no twilight. I'm going to sit down near the open window and sew. The sun does not shine straight in our window and that is a good thing in the summer. I've not seen a mosquito since I've been here and only one or two flies. Now and again we see a flea and all unite to hunt for it, for they are a lively sort.

Has JWT been to Abbots yet? [*Joseph William Timberlake from South Africa, uncle of Annie.*] Have you seen Uncle Joe lately? [*Annie's brother, Joseph Timberlake.*] I must get my Christmas correspondence forward, for when I began to make a list of people I wanted to remember - it was a formidable one. I'm so glad that Fred and Muriel are happy at 54 [*54 Adrian Road - Annie's home*] in case I don't come home when my ten months are up next June. I may try for an extension, though of course it's early days yet to think of it. When I read of the fog and the cold in your letters it is so hard to realize it. This Californian winter is like our summer and we have only had one wet day since I've been here - and then not cold rain but really quite muggy. I've not used the vests I brought and shall bring them home again unused; and my silk nighties are heavy - though I wear them. This is a letter of gossip, I fear, but is the best I can do this time. 54 Adrian Road never had so many guests - the old house must feel astonished. [*Jim and Carrie Gates from Dover were probably visiting Fred and Muriel Kimpton.*] Kiss my boys for me - my big boy, David, and little mischief, Roger. Give my love to Flora [*Botwright*], Violet [*Flint*] and to Lillie Dowse.

My dear love to you, all four,

Your loving Mother

PS. What do you think of the Yankee newspapers? Alta doesn't like me sending them but I'm most interested in the papers' view of England.

* * * * *

[LETTER 39]

"If I wasn't TT I'd have an uproarious time . . . . . ."

400 Duboce Avenue, San Francisco, California, USA
Wednesday, 8 December,1937

MY DEARS,

It seems so strange to be wishing folks a Merry Christmas so early in the month and to be walking about during the day in the brilliant sunshine. I wrote to Jim Gates this mail and recalled how, last year, I was preparing to go to Dover - and now I'm thousands of miles away. But, my dears, I hope you will each have a very happy time this Christmas and the best New Year you've ever had.

Today I've been to lunch with Winnie Noren. Then her friend, Mrs Abey from Los Angeles, came and we went out riding in her car around the city and down the beach road where we sat and ate hot dogs. I don't love them but I do as everybody else does. They are hot toasted rolls with a long sausage in them smeared with French mustard and covered with dill pickles. The rolls are split, the sausage, etc, inserted, a paper doyley twisted around, and we sit and eat them. I tell you we have to open our mouths wide! Then on a little further and we went into a café for drinks. If I wasn't TT [*Teetotal*] I'd have an uproarious time but I drink lemonade or Lime Rickey, etc, etc. [*The more usual American cocktails are called Scotch, Brandy, or*

Gin Rickey; these are the juice and rind of half a lime, with an ice cube and a measure of Scotch whisky, brandy or gin topped up with seltzer water in a tall glass; Annie would have had extra lime juice in hers instead of the alcoholic liquor.] Then they drove me home and I cooked sausages, potatoes, chard, and made pancakes.

Last Saturday Alta, Mrs Balzar (Billie) and I walked around the Presidio which is really the army headquarters with very nice officers' houses. The lovely lawns and gardens with arum lilies, carnations, roses and nasturtiums were all in bloom. Then we walked over the Golden Gate Bridge. It's an immense one with six lines of motor traffic and two sidewalks and is the longest suspension bridge in the world [*It was 1.2 miles long between anchorages, the main span being 4,200ft.*] Until I came here, I did not realize that there were two new bridges in San Francisco. This city has certainly something to be proud of since these were built during the depression and made work for so many. The Bay Bridge is only for motor traffic and underneath there is a road for lorries and heavy vehicles. [*Completed in 1936, the San Francisco-Oakland Bay Bridge was a two-level road and rail bridge some 4.5 miles from shore to shore.*]

Joe took us to the cinema last week and I had a good time. We saw an English film *The Lives of a Bengal Lancer* [*starring Gary Cooper*] and *Ruggles of Red Gap*. Charles Laughton as an English manservant was good. [*One of the great comedies: the manservant, Ruggles, is mistaken for an aristocrat when in the Wild West.*]

I went to church last Sunday morning and the Rev Gustav Storaker preached on the miracle of healing the blind man. He made one point that I'd never noticed: that when the man was cast out of the Temple, excommunicated poor fellow - a dire thing for a Jew - Jesus found him and He must have looked for him. The Rev Storaker then said: "If there is a poor soul in trouble, Jesus will look for you and find you whether on 14th, 24th, Belcher Street or anywhere in San Francisco or even in the whole world, if only you are willing to meet Him". [*Belcher Street was a short street, only one block long, off Duboce Avenue opposite Joe and Alta's apartment. The church on the corner of Belcher and 14th Street was probably the one Annie attended.*]

I wonder what you will do at Christmas time? Also if Jim and Carrie [*Gates*] have been to Abbots Langley? I've sent a number of cards. I don't think I've missed anybody and I had a lot more acquaintances to remember as well, in Canada. There seems little to tell you this week. You would be surprised to see the fuss they make here over Christmas. Already the street lamps have been hung with figures of Father Christmas halfway down on both sides, or with figures of carol singers, cello players, etc, to vary the pictures. They appear to be made of wood or thick cardboard. Then down Fillmore Street, at the end of each block are fancy lamps which are normally fitted with plain electric-light bulbs with a large one in the centre. Now they are coloured green, yellow and red alternating down the streets for miles. They look very effective and each lamppost has a wooden Christmas tree painted green with rings, stars, etc, all over them in various colours. I am sending you a postcard of the lower part of Fillmore Street. The cable cars commence a long way back up another hill and are then met by the streetcars which keep on and on till they pass our side entrance.

Last Monday one of the Filipino boys (employed by the apartment manager to clean) came in to vacuum our carpet, polish the hardwood floor and clean the windows. He is a yellow-skinned man with long straight black hair and a long flat face with a huge flat nose and narrow black eyes. I have difficulty in distinguishing Filipinos from the Chinese and Japanese. He was quite talkative and in his queer English asked me if it was far to England and if there were apartment houses and hotels there and if there were Filipino boys there and if it cost many dollars to get there? "Your King Edward. He fine man," said he.

"A silly one," said I.

"No, no, you can't stop love," he said. "King good, throne no good if he cannot have love. He very fine man." (I laughed.) "Your Balwon, he not know love. Balwon should go, not Edward." [*"Balwon" was Stanley Baldwin, the Prime Minister, who was instrumental in the abdication of King Edward VIII.*]

Well my dears, I'll dry up for I want to catch the post. We have just returned from the library with 12 books!! Four for each of us. I forgot if I addressed my last letter to Marion or Fred but don't you mind, the letter is to all four of you.

My dear love to you all,
Your loving Mother

* * * * *

[LETTER 40]

"They take the streetcar for just two or three blocks!"

400 Duboce Avenue, San Francisco, California, USA
Monday, 13 December 1937

MY DEARS,

This is Monday afternoon and I am waiting for Joe to come in and then put in the meat and get on with the dinner. He leaves work at half past four or five o'clock and waits here until half past five and then fetches Alta. I have been to Mrs Noren's this afternoon. She phoned to say they had been out hunting yesterday and (while Mr Noren went off with his gun) she and Mr Curtis had picked mushrooms. If I liked, we could have some for fetching as she did not have time to bring them to our house. So off I went and now have a large bagful. Joe and I love them. I took the streetcar outside our house first, then changed on to the dinky car (as they call the cable car) and then walked along Union Street till I came to No 2635 [*near the Franklin Street crossing, said Annie in LETTER 36*]. I pressed the button opposite Manager, as the whole house belongs to Mr Curtis. One then hears a buzzing sound and you can then open the door, pass along the carpeted hall, up the stairs for two floors and press the bell for the Noren's apartment. I walked quite a long way on my return. I astonish people by walking about. They take the streetcar for just two or three blocks!

Mrs Noren took me last Friday to the Opera House to hear the first of the season's Symphony Concerts. I walked down to meet her quite early and we had a look in the City Hall. It is comparatively new and a very fine building all floored with white and grey marble and with bronze and gold railings with ornamental work round the huge galleries and down the great staircases. The entrance hall has great marble pillars and the stairs spread in a great circle. There are a number of courts there where civil cases are heard with the name of each judge on the door. We peeped into several. This is where all the licences are procured - dog, car and marriage. No criminal cases are tried here. [*The Opera House, City Hall and Main Library were part of the Civic Centre complex completed in 1915 in time for the Panama-Pacific International Exposition which was held to mark the opening of the Panama Canal and San Francisco's revival after the 1906 earthquake.*] Then we went to the Opera House and sat in the vestibule on satin-covered lounges and watched the elite of San Francisco come to the concert. Some were very fine ladies in wonderful fur coats, the policemen nearly falling over to help them out of their cars. I saw the press photographers take their photos for the papers and then we went upstairs to the balcony where our numbered seats were. I am sending the programme.

On Saturday, Alta and I went down Market Street and did some shopping. The streets are full of Christmas trees of all sizes for sale and we went in a large yard and saw men spraying the poor things with a kind of whitewash to make them look like silver-white trees. They certainly looked very effective though I like green ones best. Hundreds of different things are sold for table decorations: Santa Clauses and reindeer, the manger and child, the shepherds, the wise men, stars, sacks (miniature ones) for presents, and I don't know what. Everybody gives gifts to everybody and ties them up in the most elaborate boxes with huge sheets of beautiful paper tied with ribbon. I have never seen such waste though, of course, it's good for trade. At last I've seen some rain. We had two days of showers and a thunderstorm during the night - a most unusual thing. They get rain but not thunderstorms. Some places nearby have been flooded but San Francisco has the best weather of any place in California, I'm told.

Joe took us on Sunday afternoon to a part of the city that I'd never seen - down towards the ocean. It is the road past the city abattoir and (when the tide is out) the smell of the mud and the slaughterhouse beats anything I've ever smelt. When we got past we went to where the fresh-boiled shrimps are sold. We bought some (2lb for 25 cents) from a wooden booth kept by a spotlessly clean old Chinaman - Qung Hing Ling - and a large parcel of oranges (25 for 10 cents) from an Italian fruit truck. We got a lovely view of the Pacific and the mountains on the opposite shore with Berkeley and Oakland in Marin County [*really in Alameda County*] in the foreground with the two bridges, the sunny blue sea, white boats and houses. Just like a picture postcard.

When I read your letter, Marion, which arrived this morning I thought how I'd like to be in all the activities of the church. That is one thing I miss here but we cannot have Abbots Langley in San Francisco. Alta wishes me to ask Fred if he or any of his office friends get foreign stamps, will he please get her some? Did I tell you she is an ardent stamp collector? I'm sorry you are having trouble in getting an etching of the Abbey. I'd have thought there were quantities about. Of course I don't mind my letters going round as long as you censor them! If some of my friends perused some of my epistles, my reputation as a decent woman would be shot!

A very happy New Year to you all, my dear ones

* * *

[*Tuesday, 14 December 1937*]

I AM starting another page as Alta forgot to take my letter to post this morning. So I'll include something Joe wants to know. Will Fred get Jim Kimpton to give him the actual dimensions and measurements of each ring in a regulation-size dartboard? Joe and Tom Carr are about making themselves a new board and they would like to know by Christmas. Send a piece of paper with just a section of one on it and mark the width of each ring. Fred will know what to do. I believe there is a first, second and triple line or something. I know Jim plays darts matches sometimes.

Here's a tale I heard told: A certain couple had been married for 20 years and had no family when, to their great joy, a little daughter was born. The man was beside himself with excitement and went about telling everybody and decided to put the great news into the local paper.

He was interviewed by a polite reporter who said to him, "Certainly sir, certainly. How many insertions?"

"Well," said the man, "er - I'm sure I don't know. Each night for 20 years - figure it out for yourself." (!!!)

Joe is going with Mr Curtis tonight to see the finals of the Amateur Prize-Fighting and Alta and I are going to her brother Clifford Farthing, his wife Marie, and their little girl Beverly. He and Alta are eager stamp collectors. I'm making a thick stew for dinner with apple and cranberry tart to follow. Joe likes stew. I am sending you a *San Francisco Examiner*. I've taken out the "funnies" as they call them as Joe lets a friend have them. You can see the bitter tone towards England and France. No wonder Americans dislike England. No day passes without a sneer or jibe.

A little boy here had been used to riding with his father in the motor car on Sundays. One day he went out with his mother on a week-day and, after a while, said: "Where are all the sons of bitches and bastards that Daddy and I see on Sundays?" (!!) To call one a "son of a bitch" is the worst and most insulting thing you can call him. To call him a "b.gg.r" is nothing at all. Alta made me laugh the other day. I was feeling a bit tired and she said to Joe: "Mother looks all pooped out," a common expression for "washed out," or "tired out." It sounds most queer doesn't it?

Your loving Mother

PS. Have you seen JWT? [*Joseph William Timberlake*]

* * * * *

[LETTER 41]

"Do English people keep Christmas?"

400 Duboce Avenue, San Francisco, California, USA
Friday, 24 December 1937

HAPPY NEW YEAR MY DEARS,

I waited before starting my letter until now as I was hoping the picture [*of St Albans*

A 19th-century engraving of St Albans Abbey from Verulamium, which was the site of the Roman town.

Abbey] would arrive. It came last night just as we had almost given up. We think it very nice indeed and had only just got it tied up with pretty paper and ribbon, etc (as everybody does here) when Mr and Mrs Noren and Mr Curtis came by to fetch Alta and I to see the illuminations all around the streets. Every other house had Christmas trees of all sizes, shapes and colours in the windows and some of the great apartment houses twinkled with them away up in the top rooms. Many houses had the palm-trees in the streets and small shrubs in their gardens all lit up with coloured lights; and some had huge rhododendron bushes with each flower backed by a reflector making them look like giant roses. I should think that millions of electric light bulbs are used and innumerable stars, crosses, wreaths and candles. Many Santa Clauses are life-size. One house had Santa on the chimney and his gnomes climbing all over the roof. Another had a white Christmas tree in the window and snow falling continually in the moonlight - most effective. Prizes are given for the best decorated house. All the huge Banks have Christmas trees in their doorways and wreaths tied with red ribbon in each window. Every lamppost has coloured lights, Santa Clauses, trees, flags and mottoes in electric lights, and flags across the streets, etc.

We drove out to Golden Gate Park where, in a field on a sloping hillside, a flock of sheep were feeding and three men stood in Arab costume with crooks; and a huge white illuminated star hung on a tall tree at the far side. These were all floodlit and hundreds of cars stop and the folks get out to gaze. The poor old sheep, who are there all year round, can't make it out. We did not stay to hear the shepherds sing! A streetcar has just passed the window all decked with red and green stars, great letters saying MERRY XMAS, huge speakers playing "Holy Night" [*"Stille Nacht"*] and, when the streetcar stops, a voice wishes everybody "Merry Christmas" (etc, etc). Everybody here goes slightly mad. I think Americans do so on the slightest provocation.

They ask: "Do English people keep Christmas?"

I tell them: "Yes indeed, but not the outward extravagance as here. Shops are beautifully decorated and our homes. But our house decorations and Christmas trees are in our homes, never in the windows. It's a family festival, not a street one."

They do not understand that. For if a birthday party is held they advertise it in the paper; and if they eat in a restaurant, it's a public proceeding. I'm sure they are more ignorant generally than we are about matters concerning other countries. But England - her ways, her armies and her politics are known less here than in any other country. There is only one country, America; there is only one state, California; and to thousands there is only one city, San Francisco. The last two are excusable for there is no place like them in the world. I am enclosing a Church bulletin. Note the Cantata spelt "Cantatta" to which I went on Sunday night. I got Alta to go with me and we heard some good singing. Note the names in the choir!!

We were asked to a party at Mr and Mrs Balzar's (Wally and Billie's) last Saturday evening. There were nine of us: three Kimptons, three Balzars and three friends from Oakland. Each three provided six gifts not costing more than 10 cents each and Joe was Santa Claus. We had a crab dinner: table-cloth, serviettes, plates, mats in red and green, red candles, red bon-bons [*Christmas crackers*], red and white salad on green lettuce, great bowls of crab and dishes of prawns, French bread with butter, wine, Coca-Cola, pumpkin pie and cream with coffee to finish. They had made a fine mock fireplace across one corner of the lounge with boxes and red-brick paper, with charred logs and an electric lamp. The Christmas tree was on the mantelshelf, nine stockings hung along the shelf and a little pile of presents was on each side of the hearth - all tied with gay paper and cellophane ribbons. Joe put a pillow under a dressing gown and wore a mask and beard, and we had as much fun and laughter as if we were kids.

Mrs Balzar, Senior, has asked us over to Oakland for Christmas Day and we shall go in Wally's car which can take all six of us. Joe will drive over to his house in the morning with me and Alta and leave his own car at Wally's place. So I shall go across the Bay Bridge again. I've gone shares in the gifts that Alta and Joe have given to their friends and we sent them from the Kimpton family: Mr and Mrs Carr had a cap and a tapestry table-cover; Mr and Mrs Hotchkiss - cigarettes and table-runners of ecru lace; Mr and Mrs Balzar - socks and bath cubes; Mr Curtis - a year's subscription to *Reader's Digest*; Mr and Mrs Noren - the etching of the Abbey; and Mrs Balzar Senior - a pair of salt and pepper castors in chrome with heavy black bases.

Mrs Farthing always gets money from Joe. I feel sorry for her since she lives alone in an apartment and until lately has been working for the city. She has been in a coma which results occasionally from diabetes - Marie's mother used to have them, I remember - and has been off work some weeks. Joe says that she'll not have her job again as they are only too glad for an excuse to put women off and then she will have to go on relief, for she has no income. I feel how lucky I am.

The papers here give nothing of English news whatsoever and if it were not for the English papers and letters I receive, the land and all that goes on would be dead to me - as it is to hundreds here. Joe talks and thinks American but underneath (as it is with every English person who had any good time whatever in England) it is home. Once Joe said: "I hope to die at home, Mother. If I had money enough, I'd come home. I'd love a little business of my own and a bit of money to back me." But I don't know how he'd stand the weather now after all these years.

I have just been up to Haight Street to get some lamb chops for dinner tonight as we shall be out tomorrow. I hear we are to have goose which I've never yet tasted. Saw a big man walking along with a red umbrella up. He looked funny but no one notices here. Now the shower is over girls go by bare headed, wearing ankle socks. When it rains here, the streets run like rivers as they are so hilly and the cars going up part the water in great waves. One can easily understand how it floods in many areas. Joe has just come home. It was up to his ankles and he has had to take off his boots, socks and trousers just in coming from his car across the street. He got soaked in the stream coming down the hill. Tonight we hope to go to hear carol singing, etc, at the Civic Centre. The Norens are calling for us.

I had a letter from Auntie Lizzie [*Southam*] in Canada. They have had severe snow for two days and two nights. She said that when she had dug a path to feed her chickens, it was up to her waist. I'm glad I'm here, though today it's raining. I had a letter from Alice Hawkins in Rochester, USA. She tells me that the huge lake or pond is completely frozen over and is a wonderful skating rink. It froze while it was still, so making a smooth surface otherwise, Joe says, it freezes in ripples or waves. I had very nice letters from Bert's mum and Beattie Ellwood and a note from Auntie Elsie [*Timberlake*]. I'll answer all after Christmas. I wonder what you are doing today and what my little boys will get for Christmas. Give them a big kiss from Grandma Kimpton. I am sending a newspaper so you will see how the little boys here look. I have just got your cable, Fred and Muriel. Thank you. I love to be remembered. An hour seldom passes when I do not remember you all.

Your loving Mother

* * * * *

[LETTER 42]

"The best mother-in-law in the world . . . . . ."

400 Duboce Avenue, San Francisco, California, USA
Thursday, 30 December 1937

MY DEARS,

I must begin my letter or I'll not get it off this week. First, thank you very much for the pound note but you should not have done it. I am not short of cash yet and hope not to send home yet awhile. Also for the lovely cards and the snaps of my lovely boys. They are good. Joe has a bad cold and I have one - the first since I came here. It does not interfere with my appetite or sleep, nor have I a cough like Joe. So it's nothing to moan about. I was glad to hear about the sale of work - £20 is worth working for. Tell Bert's mother I'll write to her very soon.

I must tell you about Christmas. On Christmas Eve, Mr Curtis and Mrs Noren called for Alta and I and we went to the Auditorium [*which is also in the Civic Centre*

[LETTER 42 CONTINUED]
municipal complex] for the annual carolling . It's an immense building where prize fights, concerts and broadcasts, etc, are held. We went into the gallery but the MC [*Master of Ceremonies*] asked everyone to come into the great hall so as to make a better effect. He very cleverly got people there early so that he could coach them before they went on air. We sang parts of the carols and (in the middle of them) we had to say: "We wish you all a very merry Christmas". The Mayor [*Angelo Rossi*] - a little bald-headed man, a Dago [*a nickname for a Spaniard*], Joe says - read his speech and everybody enjoyed themselves, remembering that their voices were going far and wide. Do you ever hear anything from this side? Then we got in the car and went for a ride through the decorated streets, across the Golden Gate Bridge to Sausalito on the other side; and made a round through the town, which is very pretty by night with its lighted houses far up on the hillside. It has more homes and not so many great apartment houses as in the city and is, of course, a small place compared to San Francisco.

On Christmas morning Joe, Alta and I rode round to friends and left the little gifts we had for them. The Norens brought their gifts on Christmas Eve and took their gifts from us back with them. We called at Alta's brother's, at her sister's, her mother's, at Mrs Carr's, then on to the Noren's and saw their Christmas tree by daylight. Alta and I went over during the previous week and Alta trimmed the tree and I looked on. It was a very nice one and underneath were boxes and boxes of gifts in all colours and tied with coloured ribbons as everybody does here. I had a pair of pillow cases, some tea-towels and some coat-hangers. Winnie embroiders her gifts which makes them much more valuable. I've never had so many Christmas gifts in all my life and I felt quite embarrassed: cards, hankies and I don't know what. Whilst at the Noren's on Christmas morning, everyone had to drink everybody's health. They all wished me a very happy time during the coming year and Alta drank to, "The best mother-in-law in the world," which was as fine a compliment as I've ever heard - bless her.

Then we left and went on to the Balzars. We left our car there and went with them, in theirs, across the Bay Bridge (the toll being 50 cents each way, one car and five persons) to Mrs Balzar, Senior (who has the prettiest and nicest cottage in Oakland), for Christmas dinner. She is a little German lady and most hospitable, with two sons. One, Wally, is Joe's friend and a younger one, Cort, lives with his mother. They have an elderly man, Al Jones, who has boarded with them for umpteen years and is one of themselves. We had a large goose for dinner fairly bursting with stuffing or "dressing" as it is called here, mashed potatoes, peas, great basins of cranberry sauce and gravy, and a German vegetable which is called "sweet sour" which is red cabbage cut up fine, boiled with apples and with vinegar on it. It is rather nice but, to me, very unusual. There was white bread and pumpernickel bread, which is brown bread [*rye-bread*] with caraway seeds in it. Then we had coffee and huge cakes which are called coffee-cake and which you are allowed to "dunk" (so I was told) and that means dip in your coffee. Folks here do not seem to make so much of plum pudding [*made with suet, flour and dried fruit, and then steamed for several hours*] and mince pies. They are only found among the English residents. Wally took two flash-light pictures of us at the table but I've not yet seen them [*one is shown in the illustrated plates*]. We laughed and talked, listened to the radio, looked all over the house - inside and out, ate sweets (candies) and now and then had what our hostess called "a little trink". Wally acted as Father Christmas, for we all had gifts from everybody. Then we had supper which was almost a "ditto repeato" of dinner - then home.

I went to church Sunday morning and with Alta in the evening to hear the children recite, etc. It was very nice, especially the infants. Joe has been home for two days this week and took me out on one of the days for a lovely ride. We covered over one hundred miles to Inspiration Point by Half Moon Bay beach. A fine road winds up and up to one thousand feet above sea level and (at the top) there is a parking place for cars and a wall on one side over which one can view the landscape. We passed an immense chain of lakes [*which follow the San Andreas fault-line*] between the mountains from where the city gets its water and they were lovely to see. I saw my first giant redwood tree. [*The tallest trees on earth are redwoods.*] There were a great number of smaller trees but this was a giant and a notice by the road pointed down a ravine to where it stood, a little way from the road. As you will see from the pieces I'm sending you, they are a kind of pine-tree and the feathery stuff is called Spanish moss and hangs in great festoons from the branches of some oak-trees. I don't like the look of it on the trees - it looks like some sort of fungus.

We stopped on our return journey in San Gregorio and we had a Coca-Cola at the village store. It was just like those you read about in American stories and it sold everything from dustbins and horse-collars to ice-cream, cakes, vegetables and groceries. It is also a post office and I can't think of anything necessary for living that they didn't stock - even underclothes, mackintoshes and wading boots!! It is asparagus growing country all around and one sees fields of it on the hillsides. Then we would pass great mountains, bare and bleak. Joe tells me that nothing will grow on them. However, the farmers in their numberless little ranches know the fertile ground. As we neared home we went along a new highway running in sight of the Pacific which was a beautiful blue. Every time I go and see these beautiful views I wish so much you could be here. I don't know what you'd say, Marion. I wish I could take pictures of it all. I saw a man turning over the earth on a great hill with four horses and four ploughshares and the horses had to pull hard too!

The next day Joe took me down to a great building called the Legion of Honour in Golden Gate Park [*the "California Palace of the Legion of Honor", in Lincoln Park really*]. There were wonderful collections of pictures, statues in marble and bronze, tapestries, furniture, old Egyptian and Indian things, pottery, precious stones - all arranged most beautifully. Each room had skylights and the most fine hardwood floors, marble corridors and courts with statues, flowers and little fountains set in beautiful, blue mosaic flooring. Many of the curios and treasures are lent by notable people and each item is given plenty of room. There is no overcrowding. There is enough to interest you for a twelvemonth. You would like the art rooms, Marion - pictures in oils, watercolours and pencil drawings in black and white. We only had time to just walk through a few rooms. [*Many years later, when she was in her late fifties, Marion Flint took up oil painting and sold many pictures to raise funds for the Abbots Langley Methodist church.*]

Last night we went to the Norens for dinner with Mr and Mrs Carr. So we were a bunch of English folk - apart from Chester Noren who is a Swede and Alta who is an American. We had a good meal. Fruit cocktail was first which is just fruit salad, diced and served in fruit-cups. Then we had salad of celery, olives and radishes cut like flowers, baked ham, mashed potatoes, mashed turnips, peas, apple sauce and little hot cakes served with butter. Then there was plum pudding - all flaming with brandy and served with what is called a hard sauce which tastes like butter, eggs, sugar and brandy [*brandy butter*]. We all ate to repletion and got home at half past twelve.

Bye the bye, I got up on Christmas morning at 7 o'clock and listened to King George VI's speech. We are that bit before or behind you, I don't know which! [*Pacific Time was eight hours behind Greenwich Mean Time in winter.*] Joe and Alta gave me a very nice black silk petticoat which was what I wanted most. Mrs Noren was delighted with the etching and is getting it framed to match her own pictures. She also had a beautiful buttonhole or "corsage" as they call 'em. Mrs Carr had roses, Alta had lilies of the valley and mine were little narcissi with maidenhair fern. Can you beat that for a kind thought? I am going downtown tomorrow evening to see the town go mad on New Year's Eve. I think Alta and I will go, for Joe says you cannot take a car as the streets are impassable. Americans go mad (I think) at the least provocation.

I gave Alta a nice piece of material and I shall run her up a frock and make Joe a new belt - he does not wear braces. If he had not lost some of his hair he would look very young - his skin is beautifully clear and fair. He plays golf every Sunday morning with Tom Carr and goes to a course 15 miles out of town - there are numerous golf links outside the city. Now my dears, I'll close. I'm afraid this is a wearying letter but I'll not remember all the happenings on my return unless I put them down. A very happy New Year to you all and God bless you.

Your loving Mother

* * *

Monday, 3 January 1938

THIS letter is still awaiting to be posted. I did not go to see the "makin' whoopee" on New Year's Eve as I've a bad cold. One of my old sort, a sort of flu and I stayed indoors. I stopped in bed each morning till nearly midday and now feel better this morning - so am going out in the sun. I think I caught Joe's cold. He is very scared at the thought of my being ill - so I'm glad my cold is lessening. Will write again during the week. I feel glad that I'm away from the snow. Oh dear, it does sound awful to read about it.

Love, Mother

* * * * *

NEW YEAR : NEW BABY

ANNIE KIMPTON applied for an extension to her US visa so that she could visit the Golden Gate International Exposition in San Francisco in February 1939, though she was torn in two by the thought of a new grandchild back home:

[LETTER 43]

"Voices here are so hard and strident"

400 Duboce Avenue, San Francisco, California, USA
Thursday, 6 January 1938

MY DEARS,

Here we are in 1938 and I've started the year with a cold. It is getting better but I've stayed indoors most of the week. I did not go to church on Sunday morning but stayed in bed. Joe is alarmed lest I am ill out here but I think it will go away. We went to Mrs Hotchkiss's for New Year's Eve and probably I should have stayed at home. We had a good time and a good dinner of turkey and all the accessories, plum pudding and mince pies. She is an Englishwoman who came out to marry Bob just over a year ago, having never seen him. She was only here a few days before they were married and she told me her heart came into her mouth when she first saw great big Bob come on board to meet her!! He says: "I had my courting to do after marriage," and he still does it - flowers and candies every pay-day out of his own pocket-money. Everyone says it has been the making of him. Winnie Noren sent for me to take tea with her on Tuesday but I couldn't go. I think she had some American lady there for me to meet - so may think I meant to dodge her, but I didn't.

I was so glad to get Marion's letter. I wonder if Roger has swallowed one of the marbles, poor little boy? [*Marion Flint had to retrieve a marble from her 3-year old son's throat by up-ending him and thumping his back.*] I read and hear of your wintry weather and of it also in Canada. I'm glad to miss that. Here we have sunny days and cold evenings and sometimes fog from off the sea. I wonder sometimes when folks talk here of cold evenings what they would think of ours at home in England? I am glad to hear the garage is a success. Marion hoped to get a snap of it to show me. [*This was the garage at 54 Adrian Road, Abbots Langley. The house was partly built over a covered way leading to the backyard, probably to suit Matthew Timberlake's bricklaying business. This had now been converted by Fred Kimpton into a closed-in garage.*] Has Muriel finished teaching yet? How is the money-bag coming on Fred? Have you been able to put any money by? I don't want you to spend money on the houses, Fred [*referring to 54 and 56 Adrian Road*]. I do want you to add to your nest-egg towards your own place some day. Bert has not said whether the rent coming in is keeping up with expenses? I fear not. I got $4.97 for the pound you sent me - so that was not bad was it? We never get English news on the radio here and nothing about England in the papers either. When we turned the radio on for the King's speech at 7 o'clock Christmas morning it gave me quite a shock to hear the English announcer. It is so long since I heard an educated English voice, so soft and clear. Voices here are so hard and strident.

As I sit I can see a continual stream of streetcars pass. Two lines pass just outside the house and they are the noisiest streetcars anywhere (I should think) as we have Duboce Avenue on one side and Fillmore Street on the other. So we have a double share of the row but it's surprising how soon one gets accustomed to it. Alta is getting her hair permed tonight so I shall go with her if I feel well enough. I've never seen the process, save having seen women sitting with a huge metal contraption over their heads as I passed the barbers' shop windows. So my Topsy is keeping well and happy. I feed the two tiny goldfish and the one tinier minnow that we have in a little tank on the mantelshelf with green weeds, sand and tiny stones with an electric light behind. It looks very pretty. As soon as I put my face near they all three come staring at me, thinking I've got food for them.

Did I mention that Joe talks of my applying for an extension of my pass here? He wants me to go to see the British Consul before long and find out what steps to take. What do you at home think? Would it make any difference to your plans, Fred? You'd better let me know. Give my love to Flora and Fred [*Botwright*] and the two bairns [*Ken (Kenneth) aged 5 and Alan aged 2*]. Tell Marie to write a line to me when she can and tell me news. I am sending some *Cosmopolitans* and American magazines this week. Let Miss Harris have them when you have all finished with them. Give my love to them down at Rosebank. [*The name of the Harris's house.*] I am so sorry to hear that Mr Harris is not quite so well. I remember that last winter he kept warmer in bed so perhaps that is why he is not doing so well now. I am not quite so heavy as when I left home or when I left Canada. Not a lot lighter but I am thankful for small mercies. I weigh 135lb which I make 9 stone 9lb. Is that correct? Joe weighs 200lb and Alta 128lb. She is quite plump. Joe calls her "Big B . . " and makes fun of her legs but she has little hands and feet. When she married Joe she weighed under 100lb - so married life must agree with both of them. Well, my dears, this is an empty letter but I've not seen or done much this week having spent a good many hours in bed, being the best place for a cold. A kiss for my David and Roger from Grandma Kimpton.

My dearest love to you all,
Your loving Mother

* * * * *

[LETTER 44]

"Perhaps my ideas of heaven are simple and foolish . . . . . ."

400 Duboce Avenue, San Francisco, California, USA
Wednesday, 19 January 1938

MY DEARS,

This letter is late but I've been waiting for one from home. I got Muriel's on Monday and one from Marion this morning to my great pleasure and relief. I'm so glad David has mumps so slightly. Perhaps Roger may not get them, though it would be a wonder if he didn't. As for the boudoir pillow, it was not my choice. Alta brought it home for me to send to you and Muriel - something more than just a card; and I thought the flimsy hankie would be of no use at all to Marion. So I decided to post the pillow to Marion. I remembered that Muriel wears an arm ring [*bracelet*].

I did feel so grieved to hear about Mr Harris. Somehow I always thought of him being there when I returned. Abbots Langley won't be the same to me without his friendly face. I will write a line to Bessie and Sarah. I was only a girl when he came to Abbots Langley. Such a handsome fellow and it was of great interest to us younger fry to see how the elder girls set their caps at him - but, alas, he was engaged to the girl at Bedford. I feel like Mrs D Cox. Won't my dad be glad to see him? Perhaps my ideas of heaven are simple and foolish but the fact that so many whom I've known and liked have gone, takes a lot of the fear of death from me and I used to dread it so. [*Frederick Harris came from Bedford and was Chief Engineer at the St Pancras Industrial Schools at Leavesden. His brother, Charles Harris, married Lois Munt of Abbots Langley who Annie went to see in Toronto. Frederick's wife, Peggy, died in 1918 and his elder sister, Bessie, came to keep house. When Bessie became crippled with rheumatoid arthritis, his younger sister, Sarah, came to look after them both. He retired in 1937 to Rosebank (now 106) Abbots Road, Abbots Langley. Frederick's son, Leslie Harris, became a Circuit Steward in the Watford Circuit of Methodist churches. This information was given by Leslie's wife, Freda, aged 96 in 1998. As a former Circuit Steward and because of his father's connections with the chapel, Leslie Harris was invited to perform the stone-laying ceremony for the new hall at the Abbots Langley Methodist church in 1962.*]

As you know, I caught a very bad cold from Joe just before Christmas and though I joined in the visiting, etc, I had to give in afterwards and cosset myself and it is now better. My chest is clear and I can breathe easily and the cough is gone, so I'm going out again. Today, Mrs Carr is calling for me at about half past one and we are to go to Mrs Noren's. I would like to come back fairly early so that I'm home for Joe. I've been up to Haight Street and bought some liver to put in the oven with potatoes and onions to cook slowly. I shall have to turn off the gas while I'm away but hope to return in time to cook a bread-and-butter pudding.

We had a wet day yesterday but today is sunny and warm with a blue sky. Joe took me down to the beach one warm Sunday. It was the first time I'd been on the sands. San Francisco has no lovely sands. They are untidy and dirty - all drift wood. There are no shells, no sea weed - so there is no salt smell. Behind the beach there is a gorgeous esplanade. On our way there we went up "the crookedest street in the world" (according to Ripley) a one-way street that can only be climbed by cars as it is too steep to go down and is composed only of S turns, but one gets the most beautiful view from the top. [*Robert L Ripley wrote the "Believe it or Not!" book in which this single block of Lombard Street is featured.*] We also went to Telegraph Hill where a huge tower has been erected. Some think it an eyesore but it was a bequest from some rich woman and was her design and plan. [*Coit Tower, a memorial to volunteer firemen, was built in 1933 with funds left to the city by Lillie Hitchcock Coit, an eccentric who chased fire engines, but she did not design it.*] You can see the city lying spread all around and the two bridges, Golden Gate Bridge and Bay Bridge. San Francisco lies on a peninsula with the Pacific Ocean on one side and the Bay on the other.

We went to Mrs Carr's for dinner on Sunday night and there we met Joe's friend, Alec Milne, and his wife, Florinnine. He is a Scottish chap, little and alert; and she is a Southern-born girl from Alabama and "raised" (as they say) in Connecticut. I'd been told of the Southern drawl and now I've heard it. She talks so slowly and Joe tells me all Southerners do. They live in Redwood City and we have an invitation to go there. She has been in bed with whooping cough, hence the late introduction. By the way, Arkansas is pronounced "Arkansaw" and in the word Connecticut they do not pronounce the middle c.

Just round the block from our home is the New Mint, only built last year and built right down into the solid rock. It is an immense building and folks here are very proud of it. [*The Old Mint south of Market Street, built in 1874, produced its last coins in 1937 and was turned into a museum; this granite building was one of the few to survive the 1906 earthquake and fire.*] Now they are clearing away a huge slice of the rock on the other side of the road to put up another gasolene station. It is very unnecessary because there will be four stations in the square.

I went one evening to the largest picture theatre here - THE FOX THEATRE. It holds eight thousand people. Its entrance halls and vestibules, rest rooms, etc, are all crimson and gilt in French style with great chairs to sit on in the vestibules like gilt thrones, and large oil paintings with massive gilt frames. The seats at the dressing-tables and the wash-basins are like huge gilt sea shells; and the rooms are lit all round by electric lights in the shape of old gilt candlesticks. There are long gilt-framed mirrors everywhere - yet all is so beautiful that it did not look gaudy. You felt as if you were in a Louis XIV palace. It seems strange to sit here and listen to the radio and know it is the real voices of film stars and singers: Eddie Cantor, Nelson Eddy, Jeanette MacDonald, Grace Moore and many more on the Hollywood programmes. We are so close to them.

I told you that Joe wants me to ask for an extension of my visitor's visa, didn't I? If it will make no difference to Fred and Muriel, I might stay now that I'm here for it's not very likely that I'll come again, though folks tell me I'll have a great urge to return. I'm anxious to hear what you think? Does Bert get enough cash to pay my expenses? He didn't forget to pay up Dr Britten - the club I mean? [*Some patients could pay regular contributions into sickness "clubs" run by doctors.*] So sorry to hear that Ethel is ill with the flu. Give her my love and tell her to get better. [*Ethel was Bert Flint's mother, Mrs Arthur Flint née Gomme. In the 1891 census Ethel was living at Temple Villas, Abbots Langley, with her father, Arthur Gomme, her mother, Mary, and her younger brother Rupe (Rupert). Arthur had been born in Longwick, Buckinghampshire, near Bledlow. Rupe was born at Bledlow, served in the First World War, and was a carpenter at Leavesden Asylum. In 1938 Rupe lived with his wife, Emily, and daughter, Betty, at Bledlow, 77 Trowley Rise, Abbots Langley. In 2000 Betty Hoare née Gomme recalled that Arthur Flint used to take her as a child with him when he paid the workmen building the FLINT BROTHERS' houses in Trowley Rise in the late 1920's.*

When I hear of my friends being ill it makes me feel goosey [*get goose pimples*]. I'm so far away. It is almost as if they wouldn't be ill if I were there which is, I know, quite ridiculous. How is Sue? [*Sue Simons.*] Is she home again and Lillie Dowse? I'd like to give Winnie Miller something for the Service League but don't know if there is any cash? I guess not, so I think I'll send a couple of dollar bills and get her to change them. There won't be much lost in the exchange. How does my Topsy get on with no one there? I reckon she is lonely. Fancy my little Roger remembering me so well. I am very glad. Give them both a kiss from Grandma. I want to post this letter as I'm going downtown with Mrs Carr this afternoon, window-gazing.

My dearest love to you all,
Mother

* * * * *

[LETTER 45]

"I've never felt so full in all my life"

400 Duboce Avenue, San Francisco, California, USA
Thursday, 27 January 1938

MY DEARS,

Have just returned from posting two rolls of magazines for you. I went to the sub-post office on Market Street as the old gent at the one close to us, on Fillmore Street, is an insolent old man to English folk. He just hates them and Joe said, "Don't go there again". Then I went round to the shops to get meat, etc, for dinner. The sun is gorgeous, like an English spring morning. San Francisco is never very, very hot or very cold. In some parts of California just now there is deep snow and ski-ing and in other parts hot sun, flowers, etc. Here we are between the two.

I went with Alta on Saturday to see the British Consul and they told me to go to the American Immigration Office and said I'd have no trouble. At the American place, a very polite man looked at my visa and said I was to come in May and was quite sure there would be no objection to my staying longer because I already had ten months - so why not more? So I'm waiting to hear what you have to say about it? Then we went in the elevator to the top floor of one of the tallest buildings here (some 30 stories) and looked from the windows. They do not allow people up on the roof without a pass. I think someone committed suicide there a little while ago. Then we did our Saturday shopping in the huge CRYSTAL PALACE and changed our books.

On Sunday I went to church in the morning and then went to San Mateo with Joe in the afternoon to watch the golfers. It was a beautiful drive up in the hills and along the coast road where you can see the beach and sea on one side and the city spread out like a panoramic picture on the other. Large new sections of the city are being built and we passed Miraloma Park and Laguna Honda Park. Don't the names sound pretty? It was so clear that we could see islands 30 miles out in the Pacific Ocean; and on the other side we could see the Bay and Berkeley and Oakland across it. At half past five Joe took us to LUCCA'S for dinner. It is a famous Italian restaurant near Fisherman's Wharf and I am enclosing the menu. Here you can eat as much as you like [*for a fixed price*] and I got Alta to note down the things we had - for I could not remember them all. The place is always full and the food is excellent but I prefer English places with plenty of light. Each table is lit by tall candles in holders covered with innumerable layers of coloured wax-droppings as the candles are of different colours. I've never felt so full in all my life.

On Monday I went down to the City Hall with Winnie Noren to the Memorial Service for the airmen who died when the *China Clipper* went down. The Captain's widow, Mrs Musick, lives in this city as well as several of the others. It was a great shock for everybody. There were a large number of people there: some big pots from the army, navy and air force; the Mayor; a band of drummers who gave a muffled drum roll; a string orchestra; a lady with a wonderful voice who sang during the service; heaps of Star and Stripes; and I spotted a Union Jack. Winnie thought I was mistaken but, upon enquiry, we found it was the Canadian Legion and it was the Union Jack. [*Captain Edwin Musick with Fred Noonan, his navigator, had flown the "China Clipper" flying-boat which mapped out and inaugurated the Trans-Pacific service from San Francisco to Manilla in the Philippine Islands with stops off Honolulu, Midway, Wake Island and Guam for PAN AMERICAN AIRWAYS in 1935. The service was later extended to Hong Kong. It was the "Hong Kong Clipper" which went down with Captain Musick and six crew on 11 January 1938. This was on the return flight from New Zealand of the San Francisco to Auckland service, island hopping via Hawaii, Kingman Reef and Samoa, which the "Hong Kong Clipper" had inaugurated on 23 December 1937.*]

How is my dear little David? I'm afraid Roger will follow suit with the mumps. I had a letter from Auntie Rose at Worcester and one from Mrs Roberts. She tells me that Mr May is dead. That is Mrs Woodward's brother-in-law isn't it? I also had a nice letter from Flora [*Botwright*]. I love to get letters. I suppose everybody knows I'm away from home? Did any Christmas cards come for me? I think I'll write to Auntie Addie this week. She will tell me about Auntie Polly Eaton. I never saw her after Dad's death. [*Addie (Adelaide) and Polly (Mary) were sisters of Annie's late husband, David Kimpton.*] She was very fond of him and thought I helped his death and I resented it. She came to Grandma [*Emma*] Kimpton's funeral.

I sometimes look at Joe and think I can see his Grandfather [*Alfred*] Kimpton, save that Joe is so fat. He is a strange mixture - so well informed in so many subjects. He seems an authority upon geography; there are very few countries that he cannot discourse upon. Music he loves; and he can put his finger upon the weak spots in his friends and acquaintances in an uncanny way. Equally, he is very undemonstrative. I don't think he has kissed me since I went to Los Angeles but he is always afraid lest I should be bored, or lonely, or work, or have a cold - and is scared for me to cross the thoroughfares. He is just as he always was - silent or very communicative. "All honey or all TD," as my mother used to say. But I know he likes me to be here and he has the one girl in the world who will put up with his oddities and thinks him wonderful. How is Topsy? Must close to catch the post.

My love to you all,
Mother

* * * * *

[LETTER 46]

"It is a chance I shall not get again . . . . . ."

400 Duboce Avenue, San Francisco, California, USA
Friday, 4 February 1938

My Dears,

I had a letter from Marion on Monday morning and then had one from Fred [*Kimpton*] with his great news. I WAS surprised but very pleased and if you had kept it from me any longer should have felt hurt. Joe and Alta laughed over the news and Alta said, "It's a pity you did not send that card after all". For it's a funny thing but I bought this card in Los Angeles on purpose for Fred. Then, when we returned I thought maybe he and Muriel would think it a bit too personal. So I did not send it - but send it now for future use. [*Muriel Kimpton was expecting her first child; this becomes clear later in the letter.*] I mentioned in my last letter about staying on here but did not say for how long as I wanted to know what you all thought. I don't want Fred and Muriel to feel that they are obliged to stay on in Abbots Langley just because I am here, but if I get an extension - it will probably be for another year. I should not return till 1939 - so that I can see the wonderful Fair to be held here and opening in February next, if possible. Now what do you say? Joe and Alta want me to stay and (though I'm torn in two at the thought of a new baby) it is a chance I shall not get again. And he or she will be there when I come back.

We have had two or three wet days here and when it rains it certainly does! This morning the sun is shining and the sky is blue but the wind comes round the corners. We went down to the library to get another batch of books last night and I remarked on the absence of stars. Joe said: "It's the rainy month and will soon clear off and then no more rain for nine months, save maybe a thunderstorm". Before we get rain it seems like a heat-wave and in the night you have to cast off the bed clothes as if it were midsummer in England. The girls and boys go bare-headed and bare legged all the time. The ladies don transparent mackintoshes and carry transparent umbrellas - for as soon as a shower stops the pavements are dry and white again. I am enclosing a booklet on the public library here. You can see what a fine place it is. It is not very far away but we ride down. In fact, streetcars are used here just to go a block.

I've just been to the butcher's and got some steak and kidney and put it into a casserole with vegetables for dinner tonight. Mrs Noren is calling for me at one o'clock and we are going to a lady friend of hers for afternoon tea. I've met her once and she asked Winnie to bring me today. I think she is the lady who told me she was raised in Alaska. Alta's mother was raised in South Carolina. They pronounce the word raised as "raaysed". I've just finished a little flowered red rayon frock for Alta. She looks nice in it and everyone compliments her on it. Folks say, "You sure are a good sewer". They don't know how many hundreds of garments I've made, do they?

On Wednesday I went riding with Winnie Noren in her car out to South San Francisco, Daly City and Nervale. The roads there are lined with eucalyptus trees and they look so miserable since they shed their bark in the autumn and stand tall and bare-looking and the leaves seem to hold water and look as if they are weeping. Winnie took flowers to a hospital where one of her friends is very ill. The Curtises [*ie, Mr Curtis, his daughter Winnie, and her husband Chester Noren*] live in what is called the Marina District and we stopped before we got there and had tea - toasted English muffins and baked apple. Then she brought me home in time for me to cook vegetables, etc. She is something like Elsie [*Timberlake*] - younger of course - but does love to manage and arrange. Her husband, Chester Noren, and her father, Dodie - Mr Curtis, obey her every look as the husbands do here. She is more than kind to me but I sometimes have an engagement when she phones me up. It is unfortunate - but, alas, - "Oh well, it's a pity but do come tomorrow or the next day," and there you are . . . . . .

We went to the cinema on Monday night, a small one close by. They were typical American films - college days and football (American style) but very amusing. I can't follow the rapid high-pitched talking yet - and people say we English talk so fast. In several cinemas the ladies have a piece of ovenware or china given to them every Monday. So Alta and I got two red pottery plates and on another occasion (at another cinema) two dinner-plates decorated with coloured flowers on a cream ground with a silver band round the edge - very pretty. Some people go regularly and get a complete set in time.

I shall send you a *San Francisco Examiner* to see. Joe takes it each day. The paper is owned by a man called Hurst [*William Randolph Hearst*] who hates both England and France. Alta says: "Don't take any notice of the papers," but I tell her the papers guide the people. I notice that he has calmed down a little lately and his cry is now: "Buy American", as the crafty English have said: "Buy English", and that is how we in England are prospering. That and not paying our debts. They are to increase their navy here only for self-defence: NOBODY, NOBODY, NOBODY shall induce America to go to war again, etc, etc.

I had a very nice letter from Jim Gates this week. Carrie [*Jim's wife*] says she will be pleased to hear when I'm home again. Jim says that - as I've got a ten-month visa granted me which is now getting on - they want me at Dover next Christmas or before (!!) Yes, Fred, pack up the interesting cards and letters and let me see 'em. Am so glad Muriel is well but don't go putting up curtains or pictures. As for Fred feeling queer, I think it's an old wives' tale. Though I remember Mother saying that before she had Matthew, Dad had morning sickness for a time - greatly to the amusement of his labourer, old Harry Brown. But Fred has had tummy trouble and indigestion before. Lizzie Southam sent me a paper telling of her church's success. I'm enclosing it and a picture of a cottage for Bert to look at. I shall be sending him a couple of magazines directly and I think Jack Botwright would like to read them. [*Jack Botwright was the Hospital Engineer at Shrodell's Hospital, Watford. Jack and Mabel Botwright and their son, Roy, lived at 59 Trowley Rise, one of the few council houses in Abbots Langley.*]

Tell me all your plans and what you do my dears. Don't shut me out because I'm over here. I love to get your letters, Marion. I'm at home while I read them and I feel so excited over this new grandchild. You can't imagine.

Your loving Mum

* * * * *

[LETTER 47]

"For there is only one country, America . . . . . ."

400 Duboce Avenue, San Francisco, California, USA
Tuesday, 15 February 1938

MY DEARS,

I was so glad to receive my batch of letters and papers. No, Muriel, I shan't ever think you are crazy to be thinking and planning continually for the baby. I'm glad and feel ever so excited myself. I said to Joe: "Fancy, my Fred a father," but after the first thought it seems quite right. What does early summer mean with regard to the baby coming - May or June? I missed writing last week for it was a most uneventful one. We have had rain here for 17 days - some days continuously, now and again great cloud bursts. Today it is clear and bright and the papers say that, probably, the rainy season is over for another nine months. They say that the rainfall itself was not extraordinary but was so long drawn out that many places nearby were flooded and rivers were overflowing. Joe says that when the snow melts in the Sierra Nevada Mountains they will overflow again. However, it is never what I call cold but the winds are so strong that they nearly take you off your feet.

Last night we went to the movies to see Eddie Cantor in *Ali Baba comes to Town*, and *Indictment of Portia,* plus *Popeye* and *The News* as extras. Muriel spoke of items you were listening to on your radio. We hear nothing, nothing at all of any English programmes or English news. The little bits that are in the daily papers have to be dug out with a toothpick from under the American news. Many here think of England as it looks on the map [*ie, small*]. At first it seems impossible to an English woman who has always known England to be head and shoulders above all lands. It's certainly salutary and educating to have to sit quiet and listen to God's own people in God's own country, talking. For there is only one country, America; only one state, California; and only one city, San Francisco; and if I lived here long enough I should think the same. At any rate it's no good telling them of England for they just look blank and pitying at you. Many firmly believe that we live in mackintoshes and under umbrellas and rarely see the sky for fog!!

Mrs Carr asked me if I would make her three sets of men's pyjamas. I don't mind, though Joe said it was a confounded cheek on her part. She is to knit a little peach-coloured jumper for me in return. So what could I say? Though I look a sight in a jumper. The men wear coloured cotton pyjamas so they are easily made.

We had Mr and Mrs Wally Balzar and her brother, Mr Marten, here to dinner on Saturday evening. Joe wanted an English dinner - so we had roast beef, Yorkshire Pudding, peas, potatoes; and I made one of Gladys Grave's trifles - and they had never seen or eaten one before and it was greatly enjoyed. As they always serve salads, we had little individual dishes with lettuce, tomato slices and asparagus tips, with mayonnaise and paprika. It looked very pretty but I can always dispense with it. Joe mixes little glasses of whisky sour (which is whisky with lemon juice and seltzer water) for his guests before dinner but all our friends know that I drink no alcohol and get me Coca-Cola instead. [*Annie belonged to the "Band of Hope". The Order of the Sons of Temperance, Lodge No 1205, the Langley's Hope Division, was founded by Matthew Timberlake and met in the Abbots Langley Methodist church schoolroom. The secretary in the 1930's was Teddy Beaumont. Annie had "signed the Pledge"; this was printed on the membership certificates: "I do hereby agree (the Lord helping me) to abstain from all intoxicating liquors, as beverages, and to discourage the use of them by others".*]

We went to the Noren's one evening, played cards and talked. Winnie served a large dish with scrambled egg in the centre, tiny cocktail sausages in strings all around and sprinkled all over with tiny segments of tangerine, with hot toast and coffee - queer but very good. Another evening, we went to the Balzar's and Mrs Balzar served what she called a "light dinner". There was a great dish of three kinds of salami (which I call breakfast sausage or German sausage but one kind had garlic in it), bowls of brown chilli beans, macaroni cheese, salad, coffee and banana cake. It is surprising what one gets used to. The beans were hot but the rest cold. I like most things, or rather, I eat them - except olives and I loathe them.

We all laughed at Roger's recognition of Grandma Kimpton among the bell-ringers. It certainly had the look of me with that close-fitting brown hat. Fancy Elsie [*Timberlake*] thinking of Cromer? If she moves there she will be just a nice distance and I'll be able to visit her for a week when I get back. How are Sue Simons, Lillie Dowse and old Bill Buckoke? I hear very little of the Dunns. Does Mrs Dunn come to chapel? Does the flourishing Baptist place make any difference to ours? [*Billy and Rosie Dunn were the parents of George and Tom. Billy was the organist at the Methodist church, Abbots Langley. They lived in Hazelbury Avenue and Billy worked for the LMS Railway at Euston, London.*]

I'm sorry to close as I have to go out to the store to get vegetables for dinner and then I can post this. Alta says that, far from my being an expense to them, I save them money and they have a more varied menu. But I think she says that because she likes me here and she certainly is sincere in that. My dear love to you all and a loving kiss for my David and Roger.

Tell me everything when you write please,
Your loving Mum

* * * * *

[LETTER 48]

"No one ever takes things to the police . . . . . ."

400 Duboce Avenue, San Francisco, California, USA
Friday, 18 February 1938

MY DEARS,

The rain seems to have gone. At any rate they tell me it will probably only rain a little during the nights. The days since Sunday have been bright and sunny and I've been out each day. I've sent some magazines and newspapers so that you can see the type of papers we get here and you will see the account of the cloud-burst on Sunday.

I've never seen so much water come down at once. The streets were rivers. It is so hilly and the drains are not built for such torrential rain.

Yesterday I went over to Mrs Noren's for lunch and for a ride around with her in the afternoon. They are very kind to me and I should not see so much were it not for them. We went to the oldest burial ground in the city at Laurel Hill. It is not used now as burials are forbidden in the city precincts and continual arguments arise over this place. It's the only one left now and it extends over so much valuable ground and they want to build over it. [*It was later converted into a playground*]. I've seen where other places are now avenues and streets and saw huge shovels digging out graves and tombstones and bones from another derelict graveyard. Folk seem indifferent here over such things. One thing I noticed made me realize how young this city is. I was prepared for very, very ancient things as we have in England and saw a small engraved stone which said:

> TO THE MEMORY OF THE FIRST INHABITANT OF THIS
> SILENT CITY, JOHN ORR, WHO DIED AUGUST 1850.

When I exclaimed, "Why that's not old," it was remarked: "Indeed it is for San Francisco. He was one of the old Forty-Niners in the time of the Gold Rush" [*in 1849*]. Then we went riding around the Presidio, which is the military section where all the soldiers live. Long streets of officers' homes, guardrooms, barracks, drill grounds, a hospital and a YMCA theatre all cover a very large area with views over the Bay. Then we went to the Marina Beach which is the finest part of the Bay and saw the fishing boats chug-chugging home. Then round Fisherman's Wharf and saw the boats unloading their catch of great live crabs. There is no large assortment of fish as we have but immense quantities of crab, lobster, prawns, shrimps and abalone. English people here bewail the lack of different varieties of fish. I did not realize until I was in Canada what it was like to only get fish from the lakes there. And here there only seem to be giant fish such as great striped bass and tuna but no haddock, herring, etc, or very little and that coming from far away.

I took my parcel of *Methodist Recorders* and *Watford Methodist Circuit Magazines* round to the Rev Gustav Storaker this morning. Mrs Storaker says they greatly appreciate them, never having any English papers or periodicals. She thinks the magazines lovely and they are greatly interested in my village church. They want me to give a talk about England to the Ladies' Aid Meeting. I told her I'd answer any questions to the best of my ability but didn't know how to give a talk upon England as there was so much to say. [*Annie was the Abbots Langley correspondent for the quarterly "Watford Methodist Circuit Magazine" as indicated by cuttings kept of the wedding of Bert Flint and Marion Kimpton in 1931. These show that Fred Botwright, friend of the groom, was best man at their wedding; the bride was given away by her brother, Fred Kimpton; Gladys Baldwin, a friend of the bride's from Furzedown College days, was bridesmaid (books given by Gladys to Marion at Christmas were all inscribed to "Kim"); Sue Simons played the organ; the Rev W G Baldwin (no relation to Gladys) was the minister; and the reception was in the Abbots Langley Methodist church schoolroom. Among the presents received was one from the Abbots Langley Ladies' Hockey*

[LETTER 48 CONTINUED]
Club for which Marion Kimpton played. Shortly before their marriage, Marion and Bert had been lying on their backs in the fields near East Lane. A poacher, George Barnes the village sexton, mistook their white upturned shoes for the ears of rabbits and shot at them. Fortunately they were only hit in the legs and feet. George Barnes paid Dr G W Alment to remove the pellets, though some would surface years later. Marion's pupils' letters of sympathy, dated 10 July 1931 when she was away from school, also mentioned her "secret" - that she would be leaving to get married at the end of term - and how sorry they were.]

The Abbots Langley Wesleyan Methodist chapel and Temple Villas in the early 1900's - drawn by Matt Flint, one of Annie's great grandsons, based on an old postcard in Fred Dobson's collection. The schoolroom is behind the chapel and the wall abutting Langley Road was part of Joseph Chalk's builders' shed. On 17 August 1914, men of the 1st Battalion of the Princess Alexandra's Post Office Rifles were billeted in the schoolroom. Matthew Timberlake recorded in his diary that he sent a letter on 10 October 1914 to the Captain in charge about damage done to it. Matthew Timberlake and Annie Kimpton had five soldiers billeted with them, and Arthur and Ethel Flint had two soldiers billeted at Conway, Marlin Square. In the 1950s, the British Legion held a re-union for the First World War survivors. Bert Flint could remember the names of the two soldiers billeted with his family (when he was 12 years old) and met one of them again at the re-union.

I was greatly interested in the little sketch of the proposed new schoolroom you sent me but why tear down the old one? I should think it would be very useful to hold meetings in and save wear and tear of the new one. And what is the idea of extending the arch in the chapel? Surely the place is too big now for the size of the present congregation? We all sit like "birds in the wilderness" at most services. Will the same heating apparatus and the old stoke-hole be used? Will the hot water be extended to the schoolroom and the classroom? Will the children go in at the side? [*In 1934, The Matthew Timberlake Memorial Fund was set up for a new Sunday school building, Matthew Timberlake having been Sunday school Superintendent for 50 years. However, due to the intervention of the Second World War these plans were not implemented. In 1962 the chapel was renovated and a new hall was built at a cost of £17,000. Some of this money was raised by the local church and some provided from other sources including the J Arthur Rank Foundation. The new pulpit and altar were placed at what had been the old front entrance end. This entrance was blocked up and the cream bricks were rendered over outside. The new premises were officially opened in 1963 by Matthew Timberlake's granddaughter, Marion Flint, the Sunday school Superintendent. During the renovation of the chapel the old wooden pews were removed. Joe Kimpton, Fred Kimpton and Bert Flint had each carved their names on one of them when boys. Bert Flint cut out the relevant pieces and sent them to Joe and Fred, much to their delight.*]

I'm anxious to know what you all think of my staying till 1939 (if I can do so) and whether Fred and Muriel will approve of stopping in Abbots Langley? Let me know what you think yourself, Fred. This Exposition is to be a wonderful affair. They have in some way drained the water out of the Bay by the side of the great bridge and built up an immense artificial island. Buildings, towers, car parks and grounds are being erected out in the Bay. Down in Golden Gate Park various trees have been marked to be taken for the site. Several people have also donated huge palm-trees from their gardens. I saw two being dug out by the roots when I went to see Mrs Hotchkiss. They dig around the tree about 10ft deep and make a scaffolding to support the tree.

* * *

Sunday, 20 February 1938

IT is a lovely sunny day. Alta and I have been downtown. We went to have breakfast at MANNINGS, a place renowned for food and coffee. There we sat in a little cubby-house and ate French toast (which is a slice of bread dipped in egg mixed with a little milk and toasted on both sides under a grill) and drank most beautiful coffee which they grind themselves. There is a continual crowd there. Alta goes there every morning for breakfast. She has maple syrup poured over her toast but I don't care for it, especially for breakfast. I bought myself a brown hat to take the place of my old velvet toque [*a small round brimless hat*] which now looks disreputable. It's a fine brown straw hat which comes down behind, something like a straw tammy [*a Tam-o'-Shanter Scottish cap*] cocked over one eye and a bit with a ribbon bow perched up high. I can wear it with my brown coat. My shoes look like boats now so I'll have to get some smarter looking ones. Everybody here has very smart shoes but the very high heels are for the young ones.

I went with Mrs Carr to lunch with a Mrs Mollering last week. She is a wealthy woman and has a lovely home. She is having it redecorated afresh and the hardwood floor of the drawing room burned off and stained a lighter colour. It will cost $800 which sounds a huge sum but when calculated in pounds is not so great. Alta picked up a diamond ring the other morning at the streetcar track. It had, "TO KAY FROM JACK" engraved inside and the jeweller's name. It was white gold with one large and ten smaller stones. An advertisement appeared this morning and Alta called on the telephone. A reward was offered and Joe said they ought to give at least $5. A girl came to our apartment but Joe had gone golfing and I was at church when she came.

She was a working girl and had only done two days work last week, so she gave Alta one dollar and said she would remember her later. She had had the ring six months and there was still $50 owing on it. That is how everything is done here. No one ever takes things to the police and Alta just stared at me when I said she should (when she came home with it). Joe said to her: "I told you Mum would say so. Any English person would."

> A story was told the other evening which went over with great acclaim but which to people at home would not mean so much:
>
> A young father was planning what to name his first baby boy and decided on a plain name - John. But when asked in church - "Name this child," said - "Franklin Delano" to the surprise of all. When questioned he said, "Well, when I was carrying him to church I changed my mind. For there is only one man in the land who can crap on you, piss on you, and smile at you at one and the same time - and that is Roosevelt. So I changed the name at once."(!) [*Franklin Delano Roosevelt was first elected President in 1933. At the time, the national income had reduced to half what it was in 1930 and 1 in 4 were unemployed. He initiated the "New Deal" to reduce unemployment and improve working conditions - but he also extended Federal regulation. He was re-elected in 1937 and again in 1941; he died in office in 1945.*]

I went with Alta last night to visit the home of one of the girls [*Lorretta Bohmann*] who works in her office and to meet her married sister, Mrs Cahill, who went on a trip with the American Legionnaires because her husband was in the war. [*The American Legion, founded in 1918, was the equivalent of the British Legion*]. They went to France, Switzerland and Italy and had a fine time and she brought her pictures to shew me. The next European trip is to include England. Her mother and father came from Switzerland and she went to her father's birthplace and met people who knew her family. The old lady talks very halting English but, of course, the girls are American. Their name was Bohmann. I had some very nice pie and they told me the recipe:

> Take the white of three eggs, beaten until stiff. Add three quarters of a cup of castor sugar a spoonful at a time and beat into the stiffened egg white with a teaspoonful of vinegar and a teaspoonful of vanilla essence. Then spread the mixture into a buttered Pyrex pie-plate and bake in a very slow oven. When cool, fill with sweetened whipped cream flavoured with vanilla and sprinkle chopped nuts on top.

Everybody puts their pies into the ice-box and they set fine and I can tell you this is a really fine pie [*called a Pavlova*]. Alta has gone over to see her mother who is not very strong. She has diabetes and has to inject insulin into herself every day. I've made rhubarb pie for tomorrow's dinner and some sausage rolls for us tonight. Joe is on the settee finishing his library book; and we go tonight to get a fresh lot of books.

Next Tuesday is a holiday, Lincoln's birthday, and (if fine) Joe, Alta and I may go to San Mateo for a ride. [*Abraham Lincoln's birthday had already passed on 12 February; he was born in 1809. The next Tuesday would be George Washington's birthday; he was born on 22 February 1732.*] Business is very bad in the city and Joe is fearing that his job may end. They are starting to make engine parts by a kind of standard so they can be bought anywhere and if that comes off his firm, THE ENTERPRISE FOUNDRY, will be pushed out of business. Each week men are being laid off and the relief queues grow longer and longer. Everything matches this country in being so vast.

I weighed myself this morning and weighed 136lb or 9 stone 10lb without shoes. So I am a bit lighter than when I left home but a lot too heavy for my height. But that cannot be helped. What can't be cured must be endured. I am so glad Muriel is so well and so happy about the baby. If she drinks all that milk the baby will be as plump as the photo of herself as a baby. I remember seeing it once. Will close with my dearest love to you all. Kiss my pretty boys for me.

Goodbye and God bless you,

Your loving Mum

* * * * *

[LETTER 49]

"The wind flutters your skirts"

400 Duboce Avenue, San Francisco, California, USA
Friday, 25 February 1938

MY DEARS,

Was so glad to get Fred's letter this morning and to know all is well with you and I was glad to get the cards. I must write to Cousin Polly Aldridge and to Nellie Higginbotham [*of Ashton under Lyne, Lancashire*] some time but there seems to be so many to whom I ought to write and by the time I've finished my letter home, I'm at a loss. I wonder what you would say about the weather here today? It seems unbelievable to me that it is only February but it's like summer-time in England.

I've had a full week. On Monday, Mrs Noren came over to take me for a ride. She and Mr Curtis were going to look over new homes. He talks of selling his apartment house and going in for something smaller. I've never seen such beautifully furnished places. Every house here is different - there are no two alike in the city. Where this new building estate was situated (a year or so ago) was just sand-dunes and no one had ever thought of utilizing the area. Now there are streets and avenues everywhere. The bathrooms are most beautiful with their pale pink, green and mauve tiles and shower-bath with cellophane curtains [*most likely some other semi-transparent material*], painted walls with seascapes, landscapes and flowers, and immense built-in cupboards or "closets" as they call 'em, all fitted with rods, hangers and lights and lined to the ceiling with cedar-wood. The kitchens are all-electric, fitted with cupboards galore and every gadget possible. In the basements are garages for two or three cars and the houses always have a fun-room having a separate entrance where there is a liquor bar, lounges, etc, and a separate WC and washing accommodation. Here, youngsters can play billiards and entertain friends without, "Getting your drawing-room all messed up by a lot of kids all lit up," as Winnie says.

Tuesday was a holiday, Washington's birthday and Joe took Alta and I out for a

[LETTER 49 CONTINUED]
ride. We intended starting quite early but as it was foggy we waited until half past nine and then set off. There are three routes out of San Francisco: the main highway; the coastline; and the Skyline Boulevard. We rode on the Skyline Boulevard and it is rightly named. You go up, up and up, round and round for some time. It was foggy. It was very strange when we reached Inspiration Point to look over the valleys and canyons as they were filled with white clouds looking like masses of soap-suds. We stood in brilliant sunshine and across on the opposite skyline we could just see the top of Mount Diablo peeping above the clouds.

We passed Redwood City and came to Santa Cruz and I should think we passed about 20 signs along the road saying, DANGEROUS BUT PASSABLE - which indicated that a slide of rock and earth had fallen down on the highway owing to the heavy rain, which makes landslides very frequent in these mountain areas. Sometimes a little section of fencing or wall appeared on one side and at first I wondered why - until I saw that wherever these were placed was a steep gorge. We stopped at a place called Boulder Creek where a river runs through a picturesque forest of pines and redwood trees. People have bungalows and chalets built all among them and use them for week-end and summer-cottages. At the entrance to one of the roads leading in is a strange house built like a miniature castle, all towers and turreted with a big gate like a castle entrance and all faced with abalone shells.

During the day we had brilliant sunshine and I think that induced Joe to keep on to Monterey where we again got out and looked around the beach and saw where the amusements and shops were, in season. It's a lovely place and Joe says it is swarming with people then. [*Monterey was the first capital of California, 1775-1848, when it was Spanish.*] The sea was a beautiful blue and one could see the contour of the shore for a very long way. We stayed to look out at some large rocks in the sea which were covered with birds and seals. Although my sight is not very good, I could readily make out the cormorants and pelicans on top of the rocks with the shiny black seals covering the base. There were also a number of seals floating around between the shore and the rocks. The piece of green plant with red berries I am sending is a from a plant that spreads all over the sand-dunes and looks lovely. The leaves appear very shiny as if they are always wet and contrast with the very pretty red berries. I ate my first hamburger at a place called Soquel. They are quite appetizing and satisfying when one is hungry but I wouldn't choose them as dainties, as so many do here. They are minced or ground steak with onion, placed between a big fat toasted soft bun with French mustard and dill pickle, forming a very thick sandwich.

Then we took a route which is called Seventeen-Mile Drive; and it is certainly a very lovely one. A toll of 50 cents has to be paid for every car upon entering it and the gatekeeper (a woman in semi-Mexican dress) said, "Keep to your right, always keep to the right," and indeed there were so many winding roads it was as well to know. I was told that the beautiful houses, mansions and estates we passed are occupied only by very rich people. They are quite secluded as the drive passes through immense woods all the way. At the end of the road we again passed through gates and came to Carmel [*Carmel-by-the-Sea*]. This is a lovely seaside resort and (although the season had not commenced) there were a number of people bathing and lying around almost nude, sun-bathing. At first sight the sands and cliffs look like the Chiltern Hills - all chalk but the sand is white and very lovely. I'm putting a little in an envelope for you to see. [*Annie sent home an envelope of very fine silver sand inscribed, "White sand from Carmel beach, Tuesday 22 February 1938, Washington's Birthday". The Chiltern Hills are about 10 miles north-west of Abbots Langley, near Bledlow.*]

Joe says we must go again some time when we can have time to look round the town and see the old Mission. I forgot to say that at about the middle of Seventeen-Mile Drive, we broke the journey to see the Lone Tree Rock [*the Lone Cypress Tree*]. There are some very ancient yew-trees here and, by the look of the gnarled and twisted roots which sometimes grow down over the rocks like great brown and grey snakes, they appear to be prehistoric. They are known to be many hundreds of years old and there are a considerable number of them. There is a slab of rock rising high up and out to sea at one place and right at the top grows an ancient yew-tree. We climbed up the rock and stood upon the point by the tree having to step under and over strong cables placed around the tree and rocks to hold it securely as it is quite a landmark now. [*These are Monterey cypress trees which are found nowhere else and grow within a short distance of the seashore; they are asymmetrical, each one having a unique beauty.*]

We came home by a different route and went by places which had recently been flooded in the storms just passed. There were miles of asparagus fields and other crops looking just like bogs. The streets were clear but great heaps of mud were banked by the sides of the roads and we could see where the water had been in many houses. We stopped to dine at Redwood City and had fruit cocktail, soup, salad, a New York steak with vegetables, little hot muffins and butter, ice-cream and coffee. As we had waited until 7 o'clock for dinner, we did it justice and arrived home about 9.30pm, having travelled 280 miles in 12 hours.

Then on Wednesday afternoon Mrs Carr and I went to Mrs Noren's for tea. We went up on the roof where they go to sun-bathe and, oh, the sun was hot, my face was scorched and I had to shade my eyes all the time. From up there we could see the Bay and the Bay Bridge and the boats coming in and out of the harbour.

Saturday morning Alta and I went down to California Street to the FURNESS WITHY offices. They tell me that if I stay here longer than one year, I'll have to pay the difference I got for getting a cheap return ticket. They advised me to go down later on and get it settled because they are booked up now for months ahead and expect to be overwhelmed with people returning from the Fair. It may cost me perhaps $23 more and that won't break me. [*This was an additional charge for Annie's return journey home by a FURNESS WITHY & CO ship which sailed between West Coast (North America) and Manchester via the Panama Canal.*]

We went by cable car down Sacramento Street. I had not been on that one before and there is an inside car and seats also on the outside with the big genial man working the brake-cable in the middle of the car, behind your back [*the gripman who controls the hold on the moving cable*]. This car swings round corners and outside passengers hold tight to the iron supports and the wind flutters your skirts.

We had Bob and Kitty Hotchkiss to dine with us last night and we gave them meat pie, peas, potatoes, trifle and coffee. They played rummy and they went home and said they had a good time.

* * *

Sunday evening, 27 February 1938

DID not go to church this morning. I slept late for we did not go to bed till very late last night. This afternoon, Alta and I have been out in Golden Gate Park to listen to the city band which plays there every Sunday in the year. I'm enclosing the programme. It's a very large place where the audience sit. A sunken garden with immense plane-trees that are clipped and trained to grow quite flat on the tops and (when in leaf) look from the terrace like a smooth green surface - almost as if one could walk upon it [*called the Music Concourse*]. Hundreds of people sat upon seats in the sun and listened. I was impressed to see the numbers of men there; they almost outnumbered the ladies. We then had a walk round the Japanese Tea Garden where the cherry-trees were just coming into blossom; saw the seals outside the Aquarium being fed; watched teams playing baseball in one of the parks; and then came home to dine. We shall probably go to Mrs Carr's later in the evening.

We have just listened to what is called the *Ford Sunday Evening Hour*. It comes over the radio on Sunday from Detroit and is the only programme given over the air without advertisements and costs Henry Ford hundreds of dollars every time. He chooses the closing hymn himself; and there is very fine symphony music and usually some famous singer. There is a chorus of Negroes from the old-fashioned revival hour in Los Angeles on the radio. They have been singing, "Guide me, O thou great Jehovah" and, "The chariot's a-coming and nobody's going to leave me behind".

We shall probably go to the pictures at the CASTRO THEATRE [*a beautiful Art-Deco cinema*] tomorrow evening. As I've mentioned before, several picture-theatres in the city give a piece of china to every lady in the audience once a week. So if it happens that we go that evening, we get two plates or dishes for our home. But Joe always fears that it will be what he calls a "bum" programme on china evenings.

A travelling photographer snapped Alta and I walking in Market Street one Saturday morning and we had one photo sent to you. It's not particularly good but you can see the tall buildings behind us. Did you have to pay anything on the letter, etc, that was kept back by the authorities? A lady I know tells me she sends little gifts to her folk at home enclosed in newspapers and they have always got them safely without any duty. I think I'll try it some day. We all appreciated your joke, Fred, about the tall girl.

Is it true that the League of Nations is completely bust? What do you all think about Mr Eden's resignation? We see quite a lot of loud talk about it in the papers. Isn't Lord Halifax a bigoted Catholic? I don't trust any of 'em. [*Anthony Eden resigned as Foreign Secretary because the Prime Minister, Neville Chamberlain, was ready to recognise the conquest of Abyssinia in 1935-1936 by Italy under Benito Mussolini. Lord Halifax was the new Foreign Secretary and was in agreement with Neville Chamberlain's policy of appeasement. The Emperor of Abyssinia, Haille Selassie, lived for a time in some secrecy at Hazelwood House, Abbots Langley, after his exile in 1936.*]

You should have seen the great flags at each side of the big buildings at the bandstand this afternoon. On one side was a great Stars and Stripes and on the other side a corresponding one - white with a deep red band at the bottom, a red star in one corner, a huge black bear on the white, and the letters CALIFORNIA REPUBLIC. Every man bares his head when he sees the Stars and Stripes. I understand it is compulsory. [*The first, homespun version of the Californian state flag was flown in 1846, when independance was declared from Mexico during the "Bear Flag" revolt in Sonoma.*]

I received the *Watford Methodist Circuit Magazines* and the *Parade* yesterday. I think the piece about Mr Harris was lovely, it seemed just HIM. I was ever so fortunate last week with letters from Fred, Marion, Nellie Higginbotham, Polly, Marie, Colleen Drake and also two magazines. How's that for mail? [*Colleen Drake was the wife of Tom Drake, a near neighbour at 64 Adrian Road. He had a motor car for hire in 1937, according to the Kelly's Directory; many years later he gave driving lessons to David Flint*].

I have had a *Sunday Examiner* sent home to you so that you can see what sort of Sunday paper we get here. Isn't it colossal? Alta is very pleased with the stamps Fred enclosed. She had neither the Sarawak nor the Venezuelan ones. We laughed over Topsy and the old cats, poor little wretch. Tell Muriel not to be caught out as I was once, going up the road with four tom-cats following me and one of them even followed me through the chapel door! I suppose they could smell Topsy. I felt so embarrassed.

My dear love to all four of you and my dear little boys,

Your loving Mum

* * * * *

[LETTER 50]

"Folks tell me I don't look my age . . . . . ."

400 Duboce Avenue, San Francisco,California, USA
Friday, 11 March 1938

MY DEARS,

To my great joy a letter came from Marion this morning and I also had one on Tuesday. I went for nearly a fortnight without any mail and now two together. This morning is a wet one so I shall stay inside. I have the windows open and can see the folk and the streetcars going up and down from where I sit and write. I'm very happy and contented here, provided I can get all the good news from home. But if I did not hear much or had not my return ticket and the knowledge that I can come home when I like, I should quite understand homesickness. Fancy, Renée Lowe is to have a baby and I thought they were above such things. So our baby is to come next month? I have not heard any date yet.

I'm sorry to hear about Mr Annear. He thought a lot of Grandad [*Matthew Timberlake*] and he (Grandad) thought a lot of Dicky Annear, as he called him behind his back. [*Richard Annear had been the boys' headmaster since 1900 at the St Pancras Industrial Schools, Leavesden, and was on the staff before then. He had been on the Vestry from*

1892 and on its successor, the Parish Council, 1901-1931; and was its chairman in 1909. He lived in Langley Road in 1938.] It makes me feel sad that all that generation will soon be gone and makes one realize more clearly how we are stepping into their places. Folks tell me I don't look my age - for I make no secret of it - but I think I'm looking older and my hair is getting greyer. Thanks for the *Radio Times*. Joe made no comment upon it but I realize how much more dignified and seriously minded our tastes are. Here, it is little more than shrieks of laughter, queer noises and (to my mind) second-rate jokes and jazz. Even the very few Sunday moments only give a few Sankey hymns and the speakers carefully avoid any sermon. This is said in confidence for we are very sensitive to criticism here and I avoid it, of course.

I went downtown yesterday and met Mr Curtis and Mrs Noren. They asked me to lunch and then we went shop-looking [*window-shopping*] to the tailors and to the bookshop. For Winnie has to pass her opinion on her men's attire and she is a shrewd shopper and has the cheek of the old boy. I've never seen such wonderful gadgets as there are for housekeepers [*housewives*]. How I would love to get you girls a washing machine, etc. How does that Newlyn gas heater in the scullery answer [*"do the job"*] and the new gas stove? We have constant hot water here in the bathroom and sink; and the rooms are steam-heated. I've not seen a fire since I've been here. The flowers down Market Street are more than wonderful, of every kind and colour. I got four grapefruit for 10 cents, each one measuring 13 inches around. I like them for breakfast.

I'm sending a little folder about the Exposition. The island out in the Bay was artificially made and (after the Fair is over) two or three of the buildings will be used as hangars because the island is to be used as an airport and these buildings have been made to last. [*Treasure Island was used by PAN AMERICAN AIRWAYS for the China Clipper flying-boats until the Second World War; then it became a naval base.*] If it is fine on Sunday, Joe will take Alta and I up to Sacramento. We shall need to start very early in the morning because it is a long journey for one day. But if it's wet we shall not go. They tell me that later in the year it is terribly hot there and you are baked alive but now it is quite cool. Did you see any reports of the floods in Los Angeles and district? They are said to have been very serious in places but everybody says that the papers exaggerate. In this city we have no extremes.

I had a very nice letter from Mrs Miller last week and will write to her very shortly. Have you heard any news of Auntie Bessie? Is she quite well again? I do hope Topsy's family will arrive before the house is empty [*Fred and Muriel were going to Dover*] or else she will be in Muriel's cupboard or bed if possible. Do let me know all about everything. I am so glad Muriel is keeping so fit and happy. Marion said something about a snapshot of the house with garage doors. I'd like to see what it looks like. Do you have the alley open for tradesmen? Those flower seeds that were in the Christmas card are supposed to be planted when the warmer weather comes. I don't know what they are but have been told they will grow all right. I'm glad that David has gone up at school. It is only fair because it was mumps that kept him away. Tell him he must write a letter to Grandma or draw me a picture. I'd love to have one. Does Ivy Flint still take the Primary class in Sunday school and does her mother come to Women's Own? [*Ivy Flint was the daughter of Len and Amy Flint.*] What makes poor

Mr Hamlin so unusually busy just now? I've not communicated with the Sons of Temperance. Shall wait until I know for certain about my stay here. Then I think I'll write to Mr Miller or whoever is WP [*Woman's President*] and formally resign my offices as WP and RS [*Roll Secretary*] if I have not been turned out for being absent.

This letter is full of nothing but I have not been far these past few days - only out to the stores for meat, etc. The streetcars go by loaded with people all standing up and hanging on outside to get home out of the rain. Mrs Carr has been in hospital for two days to have her tonsils out. We called to see her last night and she is getting on well and will soon be serving in the shop again. She is a nice woman but (like most folks here) she does like to know your business and I cannot get used to that.

My dear love to you each and all,
Your loving Mother

* * * * *

[LETTER 51]

"People don't economise on the cents as we do on the pennies . . . . . ."

400 Duboce Avenue, San Francisco, California, USA
Tuesday, 22 March 1938

MY DEARS,

I am late writing but waited till your letter arrived. What a shocking thing about little Hilda Miles. I am so sorry. A nice little girl - she was a Cadet and so bright [*in the Cadet Section of The Sons of Temperance*]. Her poor mother and father and family, uncles, aunts and cousins. They are very united and will all grieve. I'd like to send my deepest sympathy. Perhaps you will see Will or Ethel. [*Hilda Miles was run-over on her way home from school when she darted across the High Street in Abbots Langley at the sharp bend by the old Kings Head. She was the daughter of Maurice Miles, Captain of the new Volunteer Fire Brigade. Keith Miles (who was not related and who lived at 84 Marlin Square) saw it happen as he walked from school. In 1998 he recalled that the vehicle was a blue FYFFE'S banana lorry. Bert Flint, who was passing by, used the travelling rug in his car to cover her body.*]

No, the floods have not touched San Francisco. In this city we are free from any extremes of weather. Of course it has rained and rained and everyone says it's most unusual to keep on for so many weeks. The rainfall is far ahead of last year but there are very few wholly wet days. The sun soon comes out and the streets are dry in no time and I can go out. The fire engines have just gone screaming by to a fire somewhere in the city. Fires are numerous, for so many of these great buildings are wood-shingled. The engines go by with the siren going continually and cars rush to the side of the road and stop for them to go by. It is the same for an ambulance.

Joe took us for a very nice ride one Sunday - down the Peninsular. We went by the Skyline Boulevard route as far as Mountain View and Emerald Lake and returned by San Mateo to South San Francisco. I am sending a piece of newspaper which has the route on it and the description of the hills and flowers. It is true to life though, of course, we did not go to Niles. Trade and business are very bad in the city and Joe fears that THE ENTERPRISE FOUNDRY may have to close for lack of orders. I hope not while I am here, for I don't want to be any burden to them. We are going to the Noren's for dinner tonight so I have no food to prepare. I am making up Alta's piece of green material into a dress and I've got myself a piece of blue pin-spot stuff to make up later on. I have not yet got new shoes to go with the brown hat and coat, but will wait for dry weather. I see the rain has started again and the streetcars are scuttling by crammed with people.

I'm enclosing two little books I had given "for my little grandsons" so give them one each. I hope they liked the picture books I sent last week. Tell David the train is like the one Grandma went on - with the dining car and the black porter.

I'm so interested in hearing about the proposed new schoolroom. If the fact that Abbots Langley has never appealed for help during the past will be an argument for aid now, then this is largely due to my dad's independence and his work on the upkeep of the chapel property and it's time the Circuit did something to help. I should hate to see the old schoolroom pulled down. It was my Sunday home for so many years. Just as I'd hate to see old Nash Mills chapel destroyed where Grandpa [*Joseph*] and Grandma [*Elizabeth*] Timberlake worshipped. But, of course, time marches on and takes us with it. So what matters at all really? [*Annie and her brother, Joseph, were the first children to attend the new Sunday school in 1879 with their teacher, Mr Collins. The schoolroom was not pulled down until 1962 when a new hall was built adjoining the refurbished chapel. The Nash Mills Methodist chapel, founded in 1842, is now a Community Centre and a new Methodist church has been built beside it.*]

I am so glad that Muriel and Fred are happy at Abbots Langley. I was afraid they would get fed up with the village. I must wait until May before I apply for my extension to my visa. But the time flies and if I don't get it I'll be home again in no time. However, Joe hopes I can get it. It is half past four and Joe will soon be home so I'll continue this tomorrow. Do you keep the letters I send addressed to 54 Adrian Road, Marion? How is Uncle Joe and how is Sue Simons?

* * *

Friday, 25 March 1938

I'M making another start with this letter. We had our dinner at the Noren's. We had clear soup, a salad, oysters rolled in tiny rashers of bacon, little hot biscuits and butter, roast turkey with stuffing, potatoes, peas, mashed rudebakers (which are like swedes or turnips), tea-cakes and ice-cream - a gorgeous spread. There were two Americans at the dinner but I have forgotten their names for they address everybody by their Christian names. The man gave me three very nice pictures to take to England so I'll send them home when I can get a piece of cardboard. We then all played rummy and we did not get home until midnight.

Joe had a bit of bad news. His job is to terminate on 5 April and he seems very pessimistic about getting another. Indeed, when one goes past the public buildings and sees the crowds of men sitting on the seats outside, reading and talking, or in the library, all out of work (some have been out for two or three years) - it's enough to make one fear to be out of work. I feel worried for him because he is not a boy any more and knows the years are against him. We heard on the radio that the United States is seriously considering deporting those who have been in the country under ten years and who are not citizens and compelling all others to become naturalised - so as to make more work for people. I wish it were possible for Joe to take out his papers but of course he has no right-of-entry and would get into trouble. He'd like to to come home if he could get work there but, of course, Alta's family are here. Her mother is diabetic and injects herself with insulin twice a day. She is a pleasant woman. Joe says she has a one-track mind and can only think of one thing at a time and he wouldn't live with her for anything. So many folk here who have a car and act as if they were millionaires have nothing at all behind them. They live from hand to mouth and $1,000 is spoken of with bated breath, yet it is only £200. I begin to understand why they think I must be made of money. In England, we don't think the same about money as here. Over here, people don't economise on the cents as we do on the pennies and that is why England and the English are better off. The common people I mean. We think it dreadful not to have a penny behind us.

Tonight we are out to dinner again to Bob and Kitty Hotchkiss. I like her (though she does drop all her H's) and I sometimes go down to her house and we go out together and look at shops. I ought to say go up, not down. Alta says, "Don't you take the streetcar, Mother? You never walked all that way!" I tell them I can't get enough walking and certainly won't spend 5 cents to go that bit of a journey. Joe laughs - but they won't walk anywhere. Well dears, this epistle is full of nothing. As soon as the weather settles I'll be able to go further afield and see more sights and have more to tell. I've got a big book from the library, an A E W Mason omnibus book with three stories: *At the Villa Rose*, *House of the Arrow* and *The Prisoner in the Opal*. It's fine. Bert would like these detective yarns. Tell Bert's mum [*Ethel Flint*] that I believe it is her turn to write but I'll be writing to her very shortly.

My dearest love to you all,

Your loving Mum

PS. I think the enclosed photos of the two bridges are very good. See the eucalyptus trees in picture four, all bare and barkless?

* * * * *

[LETTER 52]

"I can't make head or tail of the news"

400 Duboce Avenue, San Francisco, California, USA
Friday, 1 April 1938

MY DEARS,

I was so glad to get a letter from Muriel last night and to know she is so well and happy and able to walk to Bedmond [*a village about a mile from Abbots Langley*]. By the

[LETTER 52 CONTINUED]
time this reaches you I guess you will all be tiptoe with expectation. I am. Yes, I'd like the baby to have hair like Fred's and Muriel's and a nice-shaped nose. I don't care if it is a boy or girl as long as it is perfect and doesn't cause too much trouble to come. But it is sure to be beautiful isn't it?

We are now having the most glorious weather. Last Sunday, Alta and I went with Joe to the golf-course and walked round to the tenth hole and then sat in the car and read until they finished. Mr Carr then went home and we went for a ride. This golf-course is 25 miles from San Francisco and is beautiful - great hills at the back and the ocean on the other side, all ups and downs, trees and pools, a fine clubhouse, seats and drinking fountains all around the course. There were scores of pairs and foursomes playing, men and women. There are a number of golf-courses about and 20 or 30 miles is no distance to travel to play. We had hamburgers for lunch with apple pie to follow and coffee.

Joe was planning to take us for a long ride but, unfortunately, when we were on the Skyline Boulevard, with thousands of cars tearing by so closely, one of the tyres punctured and the ride was off. After bumping along until we reached a bit of spare grass, Joe changed the wheel after much strenuous exertion for the ground was soft and sandy and the jack sank about 4in into the soil. Joe was so mad and dirty that we went back home and cooked dinner and went round to the Carr's after 7 o'clock. Almost all the stores keep open all day Sunday - at least, all that sell things to eat. One couple who keep a grocery and provision store at the end of the next block from here are open always until 12pm at night, weekdays and Sundays. Alta has never seen the place closed.

On Wednesday I went with Mrs Noren and Mr Curtis in their car across the bay into Marin County [*the region north of the Golden Gate Bridge*]. They were looking at houses and vacant acreage as they are thinking of building a summer-cottage or week-end house with the intention of adding to it in a few years time when Chester Noren retires. I saw San Quentin prison which is a Federal one and has thousands of convicts. I believe it's the biggest prison here. I'd love you to have seen the view on this ride. The great rolling green hills and mountains with highways winding around them and through them. They cut great wedges out of the mountains just like a piece of cheese and make roads and tunnel through great rocks. Then we rode along the bay shore, Tomales Bay, and went up side roads that looked like English fields save that the poppies were all orange - and a prettier sight you can't imagine than these flowers against the green grass.

The piece of land that they are thinking of buying is a plateau where a house could be built with huge trees around and a high hill covered with forest nearby - perfectly virgin land. We climbed up by the side of a little creek rushing down in a series of waterfalls. There were wild deer and quail running across the paths. A man has been paying the owner of these acres to take out the ferns from a part of it and has made lots of money. Mrs Noren says she'll see that no one has any of them if they buy it! I laughed for there are millions of them but it's a lovely place with no one near, looking out across the Bay to Mount Tamalpais [*at 2,586ft, the highest peak in the Bay area*]. Joe says they don't realize what it will cost to cart lumber there to build and the long drive that will need to be gravelled to the house, etc, etc. However, I reckon they know what they are doing for they are willing to pay $10,000 just for the ground - I don't know how many acres. A stream comes from the mountains and is the most beautiful clean water and will supply their needs, always.

What do you think of these names? They are places we drove through on the way and when we went on to Yolando: Fairfax, Butterfly Valley, Morningside, Sleepy Hollow, Woodacre, Forest Knolls, Jewell, Lagunitas, San Geronimo and San Anselmo. All these are pretty little townships with San Anselmo being the largest. This would be the shopping place for the Norens if they decide to build, being the nearest. We also passed places with Indian names such as Tokaloma and Olema. No one could get from place to place without a car or some other vehicle because they are so far apart and there are no buses, etc. We looked over houses in Inverness and Ross, both great places and small places. They stand fully-furnished in the hands of estate agents, their owners having crashed in the dreadful depression and the banks have taken over the mortgages. I never saw such bargains but Winnie doesn't want other peoples designs or furniture and I don't blame her if one can afford to choose - and they evidently can!

I told you last week that Joe's job had petered out. Everywhere men are being laid off. If business should pick up, Joe could go back. But that is a forlorn hope, Joe says. I'm sorry for him for he gets very depressed.

I can't make head or tail of the news. We read of war here and there and threatened everywhere. Is England scared or is it like before 1914 when all the public were blinded until it was upon us? Is it true that all are to have gas-masks and the children instructed in school about the use of them? Who is England to fight or who is going to fight her? How I wish you would send me a couple of *News Chronicles* just to show people our newspapers. I often see the *Daily Express* quoted over here.

Thanks, Muriel, for the crossword puzzles. The ones from the *Evening News* are the nicest I've found and I'd almost forgotten what they were like. I shall enjoy them and have already done one. Also, I'd like a Weldon's fashion book - one with a nice pattern in it of a plain summer-coat and dress for me. I got one in Canada and Alice Hawkins begged it. I can't get any English books here at all. I'm a little smaller than I was - 45in instead of 48in hips and 36in instead of 38in bust measurement, but fear I'll never be slim again. I'm ever so interested about the rockery - I think that will be an improvement. Sow those Californian seeds, Fred, in a sunny place. I hope they'll grow and have seeds to resow. I am getting a camera and film so that we can photograph this house (or as much as we can) to show you what it is like outside. I must dry up as I have to go up to Fillmore Street this morning to get some buttons for Alta's dress and its a good walk and very hilly. I must take my time when climbing hills. The enclosed came in the monthly statement from my bank here, WELLS FARGO. You should see the place now. I don't know if the film *Wells Fargo* came to England [*it was about the bank and stage-coach company*]. I expect not as it is pure Californian, but it was good.

My dearest love to you all and a kiss for my David and Roger,

Best love, Mum

* * * * *

[LETTER 53]

"Busy giving the angels a new blue shining . . . . . ."

400 Duboce Avenue, San Francisco, California, USA
Saturday, 9 April 1938

MY DEARS,

I got Marion's letter on Wednesday and was more than pleased with my David's letter. It is a lovely one and written beautifully. Which dwarf is he in Snow White? [*The dwarf "Happy" in a Sunday school play.*] So Mr Annear has passed on - another of Grandad's old friends. I'm always sorry for women who are left in old age. It must be so much harder than when young because they have so much time to sit and think and miss them. I'm beginning to count the days till I hear Fred and Muriel's news.

I've had quite a lot of good times just lately. As mentioned in a previous letter, I went one day with Winnie Noren and her father, Mr Curtis, over the Golden Gate Bridge into Marin County where they are thinking of buying a great piece of land which stretches from the road right up through the forest for miles. Mr Noren is a great hunter and fisherman and goes each weekend whenever possible. It seems strange to me to realize that, here, anybody can carry a gun and there are no game reserves and a man can shoot and fish, what and where he likes.

Then on another day I went with them to take Patty (Winnie's little brown dog) to be looked over by a vet at the dog and cat hospital. It's a lovely place, with a large hall and counters where your name and business is noted by an efficient young woman. Then you are passed on to the surgery where a doctor meets you. The dog was stood on a steel table, the man examined her all over, asked questions and said that she was in good condition - and took a dollar and a half for so doing. At this place there are dogs and cats for sale and many who have been picked up as strays. Many were beautiful. One cat I saw (sat sulking in his cage) was a lovely mole-coloured tom. He had a plate of untouched fish by him and when I spoke to him, gave a loud miaow and came to me. I talked to him and told him how lovely he was and he rubbed his head on my fingers and commenced to eat his dinner at once. You could see he had been a pet. It seems a pity that they should have to be put to sleep if they are not claimed because (I guess) some one has lost them.

I am enclosing a programme of a Revue I went to at the War Veterans' Auditorium. You will see what a long programme it was! Mrs Carr, Alta and I went and the place was full of fathers, mothers, uncles and aunts - for it was put on by a dancing class of 200 pupils. Alta's little niece, Beverly Farthing, is a pupil and you will find her name among the performers. She appeared in eight items. It was a remarkably fine show and the tiny tots who danced, both girls and boys (many of them were only between three and five years old), were beautiful. The colourful costumes and lighting effects were very fine. Then there were big girls and big boys (young women and men really) who danced, sang and gave acrobatic displays. We liked it all but it kept on far too long. I heard that when the excessive length of the show was mentioned the teacher said, "If I did not include all who wished to perform, the mothers would kill me!" Dancing, etc, is thought of very highly here. I expect this is because we are so close to Hollywood. Joe says all the women see future Hollywood stars in their "brats". Then on another evening, I went to a play put on by the WPA [*Work Progress Administration*] people. These are unemployed folk who do relief work for the city. It was well acted and I enjoyed it.

Joe's work finished on Tuesday so on Wednesday he took me for a drive out. We went through South San Francisco and on past golf-courses and up mountain roads which wind round and round in S bends and then down through Redwood City to the Santa Clara Valley to see the blossoms. Fancy going through places like Cupertino and Chinatika and to Los Gatos or "Place of the Cats". In this place there are gates guarded by giant-size stone cats. Then on up the mountain road with great gorges by the roadside. In some places you can look down upon the tops of the telegraph poles on the road below which you have just come from. In the valley, for miles and miles, as far as the eye can see there are plum, apple and cherry-trees in blossom. They are all in straight rows, each about the same size and pruned to shape - not huge and straggly as often we grow our fruit trees. This is the prune producing district and last Sunday was the Blossom Fiesta in Santa Cruz and about 60 thousand people went there from all around to see the blossoms. Then Joe took me to see Holy City [*about 56 miles south of San Francisco*]. I've heard a great deal of the mad sects and religions started and carried on by so many people here but never came across any until I saw this place. I am sending an article taken from a Sunday paper on this very place and it describes it much better than I can. Also, I am enclosing a couple of postcards of this place which I bought at a little souvenir shop. I sat in the car and just laughed at the inumerable inscriptions all over the place. Even rows of giant Santa Clauses with lettering across their tummies. Do read the article, it's all perfectly true. I saw 'em all but I didn't see Father Riker. This Father evidently does not like coloured people by what he says in his inscription propaganda. A man was on the flat, tiled roof that you can see in the picture. "Busy giving the angels a new blue shining," Joe said.

We returned by a different route through more trees in blossom. On the way we passed Bay Meadows Race Course and the races were on. We drove past hundreds of cars parked outside, stopped and climbed up a steep bank where we could look over a low fence right on to the course itself. Far away, we could see the stands crowded with people. We saw the jockeys riding the horses along in a preliminary canter, then saw them return and go into their starting stalls. Then we saw them start the race, go round the great course and come flying past us to the winning-post with the jockeys yelling and slapping the horses with their sticks. Before they started, Joe said he fancied one with the jockey in green and white and said (if he had been inside) he would have placed a bet on it. Much to his delight, we saw the horse in the lead and (although we could not see if it came first at the finish) we heard on the radio that night its name announced as the winner. We could hear the names of the horses from where we stood. It was very exciting to watch these lovely creatures.

We went last Sunday afternoon to Fisherman's Wharf. I've never seen so many crabs and lobsters. Tell David I saw some pelicans with their long bills and pouches (such cunning looking fellows) flying around and settling on the fishing boats in the harbour.

I went to church on Sunday morning. They are such friendly people. The Rev Gustav Storaker thanked me for the *Methodist Recorders* and said he enjoyed them very much. It is Lent and the services are upon the subject. On Sunday it was: The silence of Jesus. I like to go and hear the good man. There are a great many Roman Catholic churches here. Joe says the city is full of Irish and Italian Catholics. He warned me to be very careful what I say in any company on religion or divorce because so many whom you would never suspect have been divorced - sometimes twice - and many are Roman Catholics.

I'd like you to give the little envelope with the stamps to Jimmy Beaumont. I don't know if he is still collecting them. There are two Chinese ones among them. Don't you love the picture of the little chap with the football? I thought it so good. Roger will like the one showing the little ducks having a waterchute down the old toucan's bill. [*Jimmy Beaumont was Teddy (Edward) and Jane Beaumont's son. They lived at 75 Breakspear Road in 1938. Their daughter, Molly, was "Akela" of the Abbots Langley Wolf Cub Pack and later married Frank Hoadley ("Skip"), the Scoutmaster of the 44th South West Herts Scout Troop. Arthur Flint loaned the money to the Scout Troop in 1930 to purchase the plot of land in Langley Road on which the old Scout Hut was built in 1933.*]

I don't see much of English politics or news but I think we see more of war-scare news here than at home. Sometimes I feel afraid, remembering how very little we common people knew of what was coming before the Great War [*the First World War*]. We were very much in the dark and other nations are often so much more in the know than we ourselves.

Remember me to Mrs Lea and tell her I have a free library of thousands of books and can have four per week so, because we are three in the family, we can get twelve each week. I get through a good number, I can tell you. Also remember me to Mrs Norman [*who lived at Hope Cottage in Marlin Square*]. Tell her I'm seeing so many strange things that I wish I'd plenty of money and a long life before me to see more things. I am so glad Muriel is so fit and do pray all will be well with her and the dear baby. I shall be so glad when it's here now.

I'm keeping very well and if it's fine tomorrow (Sunday) Joe, Alta and I with Bob and Kitty Hotchkiss hope to go to Sacramento. I don't know how far it is but know

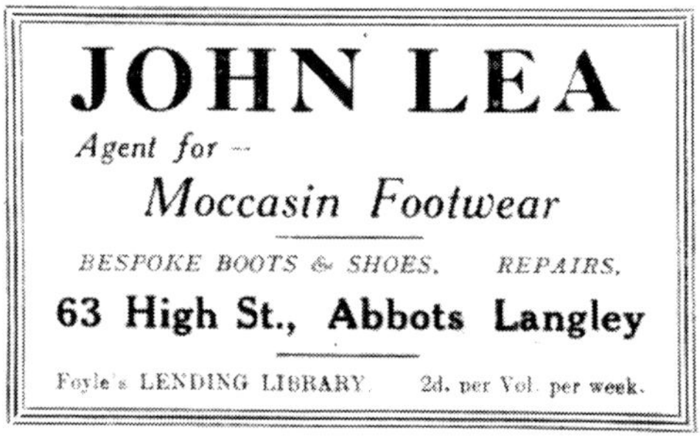

An advert from the 1937 Methodist Church Fête programme. Mrs Lea ran a Foyle's lending library in her shoe shop, adjacent to her husband's cobblers' workshop.

it's over 100 miles. We start at half past seven in the morning and will take lunch with us. We hope the old car will behave well. Joe is a fine driver and I always enjoy going with him. So if all's well I'll have more to describe in my next letter.

My dearest love to you all,

Ever your loving Mother

* * * * *

[LETTER 54]

"The children's toys and dollies were very touching"

400 Duboce Avenue, San Francisco, California, USA
Wednesday, 20 April 1938

MY DEARS,

I am late with this letter for though I meant to write last week, one thing and another prevented me from sitting down to do it. Joe took Alta, Bob and Kitty Hotchkiss and me to Sacramento last Sunday week and we had a fine day. We started early at 7.30am and went over and called for Bob and Kitty. Then we went over the Golden Gate Bridge into Marin County. It was very lovely there and the great green hills were shaded with orange and blue - poppies and wild lupins. The very names of the places we passed seemed romantic: San Rafael, Ignacio, Petaluma Creek, Sears Point and then into Sonoma County or the "Valley of the Moon". [*This was the title of an autobiographical novel by Jack London, published in 1913, which idealised life in the Californian countryside. He farmed here at the Beauty Ranch, Glen Ellen (near Boyes Hot Springs) where he died in 1916.*] This is one of the loveliest and most fertile valleys in California.

We stopped in Sonoma city to look at the old Mission [*Mission San Francisco Solano, 1832*] built by the Spanish Fathers [*Franciscans*] many years ago. It is the farthest north of the Missions and was erected by Father José. We could still see the huge redwood beams fastened with rawhide - just as they were before there were any iron nails to be used. On the opposite side of the road is an original gambling house - just as it was when used by the cowboys and ranchers when they came into town, like you read in American stories. We passed through Joachim, Murietta and then into Imola in Napa County and through Suisun, Fairfield and Vacaville. The Sacramento Valley is flat and they have had many floods lately. We could still see fields and fields of water and bog. It is an asparagus growing county and also a great fruit-growing region. We passed areas of housing and bungalows with strange looking people who (Joe said) were Mexicans. They are not at all beautiful (to me).

We got to Sacramento and it was hot but not enough to spoil our sight-seeing. We saw Sutter's Fort which is the original fort built by Sutter in the early days of California. It is a walled place and the old guns are still pointing through the walls. The gate has a very large wisteria growing over it. It is now used as a museum of old Californian objects: thousands of curiosities, clothes, furniture, weapons, the original coaches that brought the pioneers across the vast deserts, rudely made pots and pans, hand-made chairs, tables and Indian goods. There were many relics of people who had perished and (for me) the children's toys and dollies were very touching when one thought how many miles all these things were brought by ox-wagons across deserts, rivers and prairies. They were wonderful people and mostly English.

Sacramento is the capital of California and the Congress meets there. We went over the beautiful Congress buildings and sat in some of the Members' seats, looked at the marble pillars with gold eagles and all around at the great banners each side of the Speaker's chair. We saw the Stars and Stripes and the Californian Bear flag, the beautiful windows; and then went through the halls of curios with the most beautiful Indian work. There were hundreds of the finest woven baskets and beaded work, cases of flint arrow heads, Indian chiefs' feathers and regalia, and beads and stones of great beauty. We saw a skeleton in a sitting position of an Indian taken from his tomb and another of a medicine-man who was executed by the Indians and we could see the arrow heads still sticking through his bones. There were canoes hollowed from tree-trunks and so much more that days and days would be needed to see them all. We then climbed up to the dome of the Capitol building and looked over the city and valley for many miles to the Sierra Nevada Mountains in the far distance. [*John (Johann) Sutter, a Swiss, built a fort at Sacramento in 1839 to protect his huge Mexican land grant. He also took over Fort Ross from Russian fur hunters and bought all their livestock. But on the declaration of independence by California in 1848, his land claims were declared invalid. When gold was found at John Sutter's mill 40 miles east of Sacramento in 1848, it triggered the 1849 Californian Gold Rush. Prospectors overran and pillaged his property; he became deeply in debt and was ruined. His son laid out the present city.*]

Afterwards we went into the park where there was a summer-house made from the trunk of a redwood tree and another section for a table, some 10ft across with seats around it for picnicking [*a photograph taken there is included in the illustrated plates*]. All the wood was over a thousand years old. There were many of these features around as well as baseball grounds and tennis courts. All the park was very well kept and had lovely flowerbeds with stocks, roses, lilies and pansies - all in full bloom. Sacramento is at its best now, for in the summer the temperature can reach 120F and Alta says it just gets you down! We stayed until late afternoon and came home by the road which follows the Sacramento River. The only untoward incident during the whole day was a puncture in one of the car's tyres. It was dark before we reached home - about 250 miles for the round trip.

I find I can walk and climb better than most women here. I think they use the motor and streetcars too much. Joe took me out to see the Japanese Tea Garden in Golden Gate Park because the cherry-trees are in bloom and the magnolias are coming out. It is so pretty with all its little trees, bridges, steps and waterfalls and with a typical Japanese house with sliding panels and statues of gods outside the doors. There was a huge stone Buddha and a place where you can take green-tea in tiny cups served with Japanese cakes. [*The Japanese Tea Garden was created and managed by Makota Hagiwara, an American landscape architect of Japanese ancestry, for the Exposition of 1894. It was added to by the transfer to it of a ceremonial gate and pagoda constructed for the Panama-Pacific International Exposition of 1915.*] I saw a cardinal bird the other day, black with scarlet shoulders and scarlet under his wings - a fine fellow [*the Northern Cardinal*].

Alta thanks you very much for the stamps which were given to you by your friend. She was able to use all but two in her collection. She will be sending some American ones, though fears they will not be of big denominations but hopes they may be useful. If you can get any more stamps she would be glad. I got Muriel's letter yesterday and was so interested in the plans for the garden and the account of the preparation for the baby. I suppose you wouldn't look at the old cradle in the attic? Quite a number of people would go into raptures over it if I had it here - an old cradle with rockers!!! They pay fabulous prices here for old glass and for cut glass. If I ever come out here again I'll know what to bring. I'm thinking and wondering what is happening at home all the time and shall be glad when the month is over and the darling is here. I want to know about everything.

Your loving Mother

PS. I will address this to Marion today but you know my letters are to each and all. My Topsy has been good for a long time, hasn't she? I see no cats here save a few scrawny creatures and sometimes a dead one in the street. Everybody keeps dogs - petted animals. A woman I know had her dog run over last week. She was prostrated with grief and so was her husband. They both wept and wept and are having it cremated and are getting a tiny urn for its ashes. The whole affair is to cost $300!!!!

Here is a tale for you Fred [*Kimpton*]:

Three men met in the smoking room of a hotel and found they were all on their honeymoon. Marriage was discussed and one said, "Well, I married for love and I am certainly getting what I married for".

The next man said, "Well, I'll say quite candidly that I married for money and, I'll tell you, she has plenty of it".

The third one said briefly, "I married for honour".

"Well," said the other two as he paused, "did you get honour?"

"I sure did," was his reply.

* * * * *

[LETTER 55]

"I've not had a rasher worth eating since I left home!!"

400 Duboce Avenue, San Francisco, California, USA
Monday, 25 April 1938

MY DEARS,

This letter will be late again. First of all, Marion, when did you get that rude letter from Bessie? I left home last May and did not know anything of young Bessie till Fred told me in his last letter, and till Fanny told me the little she knew. I've never written to Bessie and am glad I haven't. I certainly will not now - bust 'em. Who is she to say what you are to say and what not? She is jealous of more than just my travelling.

[LETTER 55 CONTINUED]

My children's married lives are certainly different from young Bessie's and my children are better brought up, though I shouldn't say it!! [*Bessie (Elizabeth) Timberlake née Delafield was a sister of Jennie Stanton of Ottawa and she was married to Albert Timberlake, both of them being Annie's first cousins. They had three children one of whom was Bessie Emily who was born in 1903. She was of a comparable age to Annie's daughter, Marion Flint. Fanny Delafield was also a sister of Jennie Stanton.*]

I am continually wondering what is happening at home. I do hope you are all well and all is right with Muriel. Am anxious about her and I'm so far away. We are all well here but Joe is still out of a job, poor boy. Alta is very glad I'm here. She says that when he was unemployed last time he was so depressed and miserable that he was dreadful to live with. But I'm here to keep him company. It's dreadful for a man to be in an apartment all day and in a city.

I went to four churches on Good Friday with Winnie Noren. People go in for a short time during the three-hour services and leave in batches during the singing. We went to two Presbyterian, one Roman Catholic and one Episcopalian - this is like the Anglican Church. In the Presbyterian church a man sang that song, "The pilgrims throng thro' the city gates" [*the first line of the hymn "Calvary," to music by Henry Vaughan, words by Paul Rodney*]. In the Episcopalian church a choir of boys sang; and in the Roman Catholic church an unseen choir sang - most beautifully - parts of Stainer's *The Crucifixion*. The large statues in these churches are all covered with purple silk on this day. Men went around with shallow oblong baskets on the end of long sticks to take the collection and this they do frequently so as to catch all the worshippers. It seemed strange to kneel beside women telling their beads [*reciting the rosary*]. They worship and laud the Virgin Mary far before Christ; and to hear a great big priest pray: "Holy Mary, Mother of God, Empress of Heaven, Queen of Heaven, Lover of Sinners, Queen of Virgins, who bearest in Thy white hands the souls of penitents, intercede with Thy Son for us . . ." (etc, etc) seems most strange.

On Easter Sunday Joe drove Alta and I over the Golden Gate Ferry to Point Reyes to the property Mr Noren has bought. It is a piece of land 20 acres in extent, all virgin land, hilly and partly covered with forest. The men dug trenches and planted privet hedges. Then some friends of the Norens came and they made a barbecue and we ate out of doors the most lovely beefsteaks I've ever tasted with salad, tomatoes, fruit, cheese and coffee. [*The land bought by the Norens was probably just north of Point Reyes Station looking across Tomales Bay and close to the eastern boundary of the Point Reyes National Seashore region. Tomales Bay is a long, narrow inlet running north-south from the Pacific Ocean and it follows the San Andreas fault-line.*]

We came home a different way to the others and went to the top of Mount Tamalpais. A really terrifying ride but with the most gorgeous scenery, the road winding up with innumerable S bends. Often the wheels of the car were only inches away from the edge when going round the sharp turns and you could not see the bottom of the gorges. It was wonderful and grand but my tummy felt more settled when we got down to the little town of Fairfax and then on to Sausalito to the ferry. We had to wait half an hour for the ferry-boat. The one we missed carried 75 cars and the one we went on carried over 100 on the bottom deck. It's an interesting sight to see four lines of cars being driven on to the great deck. We got out and walked up on to the top deck to see the lights of the Golden Gate Bridge and of the city houses on the mountain sides.

We went out to dinner last week to Mr and Mrs Balzar's. She told us she was going to give us something unusual and she certainly did. There was a huge round platter with boiled rice heaped upon it and bananas cut in halves placed around. We all helped ourselves to rice and bananas and then flattened the little heap down a bit on our plates. Then a number of little coloured pots with various things in them were handed round: first we took a portion of grated cheese and put it on the rice; then chopped hard-boiled eggs, chopped nuts, followed by onion chopped up in vinegar; then shredded pineapple, shredded coconut and sliced tomatoes; the bananas were sliced on top and (to crown it all) curried meat in a thick brown gravy was poured over. It was veal in this instance but beef is often used. It is a Malay dish and we all ate it and it was very filling. The Balzars and Alta had a good second-helping but Joe and I had only the rice and the curry. We finished with ice-cream and coffee.

On Sunday we went to Mrs Carr's for dinner. It was her wedding anniversary - 30 years. Her son, Leslie, and his wife, Elinore, were there and we had a nice evening. We had baked Virginia ham. The ham is boiled first and then baked with cloves stuck in it and with pineapple rings and syrup all around and basted with the syrup. I didn't like the sweet gooey stuff but the ham was good. With it we had peas, asparagus, new potatoes and chocolate cake as dessert. Wherever I go, I have queer things to eat. I often manage to eat everything but I often wonder what in the world my dad would have done. I've learned to like olives, asparagus and coffee very well indeed. Their tea-making is poor and the bacon is only streaky stuff. I've not had a rasher worth eating since I left home!!

I'm writing this letter in relays; in pencil now as I'm in bed and cannot use ink. We've been over to the Noren's this evening just to call and I'm going with them for a ride to Burlingham tomorrow morning. They are going to interview an architect about the proposed new house. They are certainly very kind to me.

I've never heard such queer expressions as people use here. I heard one lady say (talking of her husband) that Henry always knows as soon as he enters the house how she's feeling. Yesterday he said:

"Mamma, you are feeling depressed?"

"Yes, Henry," she said, "I'm feeling right down. I'm sure sitting on a cigarette-paper swinging my legs." How's that for feeling in low spirits?

A man remarked to Joe one evening, talking of riding in a car with a nervous man: "You know, Joe. He's a jitterbug".

Alta would be very glad if you would send her a set of the new stamps: ha'penny, penny, penny ha'penny, tuppence and tuppence ha'penny [*the new George VI postage stamps*]. How does the money coming in compare with expenses? Are they covered? I don't want you to spend money on sending papers, stamps, etc, if there is enough cash to cover them in next-door's rent. Let me know. I suppose there is no record sent of any dividends that the Keystone Trust pay into Lloyds Bank for me?

I have a piece of navy silky material with white spots on to make up for myself.

Annie asked for these stamps to be sent to her; they were the only values of George VI postage stamps issued by then.

Up to now, every woman wears her coat - for though the sun is bright and warm, the wind is very strong. Here in Duboce we are sheltered, but round the streets and hills the wind comes from the ocean and (I can tell you) it does blow! This is a very meagre letter but I send you all my dear love. A loving kiss for my David and Roger. I'm hoping for good news.

Goodnight and God bless you all,

Your loving Mum

* * * * *

[LETTER 56]

"Mum, have you fed the denizens of the deep?"

400 Duboce Avenue, San Francisco, California, USA
[*Monday, 9 May 1938*]

MY DEARS,

I did not write last week for I was all on thorns waiting for a cable. It arrived on Saturday morning at 9 o'clock. We were in bed because Alta likes to stay a bit longer on Saturdays and Sundays which are her free days. Joe opened the envelope in case of any untoward occurrence and said, "Good news, Mum". I was so glad to get it. I am now possessing my soul in patience until I get a letter. I'm wondering if he is like Fred. Fred's curls did not come thickly till he was some months old. [*Fred and Muriel Kimpton's son, Anthony David, was born on Friday, 6 May 1938.*]

Joe took us for a little ride around on Sunday down to the yacht harbour. It's a pretty sight to see the motor boats and sailing yachts. We took one or two snaps of us against the lighthouse. The sea was fairly calm and beautiful. We were near the Golden Gate Bridge and could see Alcatraz Island (Devil's Island of California) very plainly. This is where all the dangerous gangsters and murderers are imprisoned. Al Capone is there. [*The real Devil's Island was the notorious French penal colony, Ile du Diable, off the coast of French Guiana, South America. Transportation to it was abolished in 1938 but the last prisoners did not leave until 1953.*]

You cannot imagine how windy a city this is. Here in Duboce it may be quite still but as soon as you reach the top of the first hilly street the wind blows you all around. It seems to rise without any warning or reason and they tell me it is like this all summer until autumn - bright warm sun and high winds. People say, "Oh the cold wind," but I've not been cold since I've been here - only chilly now and then in the evening wind.

Joe took me down to Cliff House one afternoon last week. This is an hotel with rooms full of curios for sale. There are the most lovely redwood articles: bowls, platters, trays, lamps, etc. I've never seen such a lovely polish as this wood takes but the things are very dear. I'm enclosing postcard views of these two places. You can see the seals quite plainly on the postcard. Also, I'm sending a book of views of San Francisco. They are very good and clear though, of course, they only show sections of the city. I've seen all the places pictured save Oakland City Hall and the Redwood Highway.

Alta and I went downtown on Saturday morning. We met Mrs Noren outside THE EMPORIUM which is a very large store selling everything - something like SELFRIDGES. The streetcars stop at the door and there is a continual stream of ladies going in and out. They have escalators to every floor. We did a bit of shopping and a deal of looking and then went to SOLARIS to have a drink. Winnie paid for us and (in this place) if you buy a drink they give the eats free. They bought us a large dish with hot potato-crisps in a napkin, a dish of *hors d'oeuvre* - triangles of toast with all manner of sauces and cheeses in fancy form and hard-boiled eggs in halves with fancy fillings; then a plate of Spanish *enchiladas* and there were plenty of bread sticks. I had lemonade which came with a cherry, a slice of orange and ice. The others had a couple of gin fizzes, I think.

Kitty and Bob Hotchkiss came on Saturday evening and we played rummy and fan-tan which is the old sevens-down. We talked about a trip to Yosemite [*a Californian State National Park*]. They would join us but it's a long trip - some 200 miles there and we should have to stay in an auto-camp for two nights, probably. If they went it would help with expenses because they would pay half. Joe says the horse power of cars here is different to that in England and his car would be about 30 horsepower there.

By the way, I've been listening to a music-hall programme relayed via New York from England. It comes on Saturday mornings here and is, of course, broadcast on Saturday evenings at home. It was most enjoyable to hear the familiar accents and voices. Yesterday was Mothers' Day (Sunday). I went to church in the evening as we were late rising in the morning and so missed getting a bouquet of flowers which was given to every mother in the morning congregation. Everybody goes mad here over these special days. Joe says they are just an advertising stunt to sell more goods.

Joe has a little job to help a man fix a car which may take an hour or so this week but there seems no sign yet of a permanent job for him. I wish there were. I went to Kitty Hotchkiss today and went with her down Fillmore Street and bought me a new hat to wear with my navy rig-out, when I get it done. We are invited to the Calvary Presbyterian church for a wedding on Saturday night at 8 o'clock. It seems a queer custom but I must tell you about it next week. Joe is a queer man. He has fits of moodiness and fits of gaiety when he keeps us aching with laughter (just as he always did) and says the most queer things. Yesterday, as we looked across the Bay we could see Oakland and the great hills beyond. "Look," he said, "at our beautiful Marin Hills - looking as bare as a baboon's behind." I'd been down to the Golden Gate Park Zoo a short time ago with him and seen the cages of baboons and the simile seemed very apt. We have two tiny goldfish in a little aquarium on the mantelshelf and I usually feed them in the mornings. This morning he said, "Mum, have you fed the denizens of the deep?"

I'm enclosing a programme of a play I saw at the Alcazar Theatre given by the WPA people. This is the Workers Public Assistance and the city employs such folk to make roads and parks, sew clothes for the poor, etc - a kind of poor relief. [*Really the "Work Progress Administration" which was set up in 1935 to provide funds for relief work. This included the employment of writers, artists, musicians and actors as well as the carrying out of extensive public works; by 1938 it employed over 2 million jobless including 8 thousand musicians.*]

I'm sending home two cards I got. One is a novelty "speaking card". I sent one to Muriel. I thought they were so "cute" as we all say here. The roll of papers, which I hope you'll receive, contains two beanies for David and Roger [*Flint*]. I should not be surprised if they refuse to wear them, though out here all the boys, big and little, wear them when they wear anything on their heads at all. They stick them on the back of their heads and keep their hair back with them. They must be stretchable as there is only one size sold. The snaps I'm sending are of us at Sacramento. Alta is disgusted because she looks so fat and I look so miserable with my mouth drawn down. But photos can't lie, can they? So there we are. The little pictures were given to me for Roger and David and the other picture is of a little boy eating his spinnach with his eye on a chocolate cooky. "Isn't he cute?" says Mrs Balzar.

I go on the 21st to apply for an extension to my visa. If I get it, I'll be here for some time. If not, I shall be home in July. There will be no need for Fred and Muriel to turn out because of my return. I shall be only too glad for them to stay for years if they like. Joe thinks I'll be sure to get it but you never know with these mad Yanks. I shall write to all my friends and neighbours when I know for certain about staying. Alta has a week's vacation at the end of the month so we plan to go for a day or two up to the Russian River area with Wally and Billie Balzar. They camp in a kind of cabin, I believe.

So my Topsy has had another family. She will be on the razzle again before Muriel gets home. I do hope everything will go well with them both (baby and Muriel, not Topsy). There will be no need for Elsie's [*Elsie Timberlake's*] "Chloe" - a "nigger name," says Joe. [*The New Testament name Chloe had been in use in the English-speaking world since the seventeenth century but it was popularised amongst American black people by Harriet Beecher Stowe's book "Uncle Tom's Cabin" in which Aunt Chloe was Uncle Tom's wife.*] Why not Richard or Roderick? Anthony is a nice name but John Ashby has his baby boy named Anthony John. Not that that matters one bit. They will never know him. I'm filling my letter with trifles this week but I seem to be waiting to know what my new grandson is like, etc. What do the boys say about it?

My love to you all and a kiss for both my dear little boys,

Your loving Mum

* * * * *

RUSSIAN RIVER

UPPER CALIFORNIA or Alta California, comprising California and Oregon was part of "New Spain" in the late eighteenth century. Russian interest in California was in the large schools of sea-otters whose pelts brought a high price in their trade with China. The skins could be exchanged for quicksilver (mercury) which was the essential element for extracting gold and silver from Russian ores. The Russians settled along the Californian coast when the sea-otters in Alaska had been hunted to extinction. In 1812 the Russians built Fort Ross (a corruption of "Rossia", the Russian name) on the coast near Russian River but it was abandoned in 1842 when the sea-otters in California had been reduced by hunting to near extinction.

Joe, Alta, Annie Kimpton and the Balzars came for a few days break to the banks of the Russian River where it entered the Pacific Ocean north of San Francisco. The river's name and the nearby settlements of Moscow and Sebastopol bore testament to the presence of the Russians on these shores nearly 150 years earlier:

[LETTER 57]

"Yesterday we walked to Moscow . . . . . ."

Greenwood, Villa Grande, Russian River, California, USA
Sunday, 29 May 1938

MY DEARS,

As you will see by the above address, we are now spending a long weekend at the mouth of the Russian River, just where it enters the sea. I am writing this whilst sitting on the beach in the shade of a huge rock with towering cliffs and rocks all around. It is a little inlet and the tide will be in before long and cover where I'm sitting. The cliffs above and the slope we climbed down are all covered with grass and flowers of all colours and description. I've never seen so many and such lovely sorts. I want to pick them all. Our party consists of Wally and Billie Balzar, Joe and Alta, and me. We have a four-roomed cottage about ten miles away by the side of the river. It is furnished and we cook and wait on ourselves. We came on Friday night in two automobiles bringing some food, some bedding and Billie's pots, pans and cutlery because (although there are some here) she likes to have her own. We are a merry party and just now the two girls are beachcombing and the two boys have guns and are shooting at targets on the rocks. The sea is all dotted about with huge rocks, some like small mountains. Just beyond where we came down, we looked upon rocks covered with thousands of mussels but they were quite inaccessible. The nearest place to our cottage (which, by the way, is one of many more all hidden among the trees - either up high on the heights or low down in the gorge itself) is Monte Rio where there are a few stores and houses. I think we are about 60 miles from San Francisco.

This area was occupied many years ago by a Russian colony and we came through Sebastopol and yesterday we walked to Moscow - which is just a farm at the end of a road. This was once a tram track and Moscow was the terminus. There are thousands of redwood trees all around us and everything is built of redwood. They grow in

[LETTER 57 CONTINUED]
groups and are tall straight trees. Some have been cut down and the huge stumps left hollow to make monstrous fireplaces for barbecues. We walked to Moscow yesterday and I gathered a huge bunch of flowers of every colour from the sides of the road which go up several hundred feet. These included wild pink roses, yellow lupins, yellow poppies, wild sweet-peas and scores of others I'd never seen before. People plant a rose here and there and it soon climbs up trees as high as a house and is a mass of colour. The young people are very good to me and make me one of themselves.

One day last week, Billie took Alta and me to Redwood City to her sister's house. Her mother, Mrs Marten (a very lovely lady), and a lady friend whose name I forget also came. We went for lunch to see the wedding presents of Miss Luela Swett (to be Mrs Grant Jones) who is Billie's niece. She is a popular young lady and has many friends and so had heaps of presents. I've never seen such an array. The drawing-room of the bungalow looked like the showroom of a store. A large crocheted cloth in lace pattern made of fine fishermen's twine covering the large dining-table was (to my mind) the most unique because it was made by Mrs Marten (her grandmother) and will certainly be an heirloom. There were lamps, china and pottery, silverware, blankets, eiderdowns, five electric clocks, toasters, coffee percolators, everything one can think of for kitchen use in red and white - even curtains, cloths and a garbage can, a bedroom suite and what not. More than I can remember. We ate lunch out of doors in the lovely garden under a pergola covered with climbing roses with huge pine-cone-shaped hanging lanterns and flower baskets decorating it. There were fig-trees in fruit and apricot-trees to shade us for it was really hot. Redwood City has the most charming houses and bungalows.

Joe, Alta and I went to the church to see the young couple married. I am enclosing our invitation card. It seems queer to me to have the wedding at night but certainly everything looks colourful by lamplight. Here, the bridesmaids walk first (singly about a couple of yards apart) with very slow measured pace one after the other and then the bride on the arm of her father. There were four bridesmaids or maids of honour, each dressed in powder-blue lace with Victorian posy-bouquets of pink roses. The bride's dress was white with square neck and long sleeves and buttons down the bodice-back and with a long train made of tiers of lace frills all billowing around her. Her pendant was her mother's betrothal gift from her father; and her bracelet was one her mother-in-law had as a wedding or betrothal gift. The church was full of people and few of those going on to the reception (some 200) wore hats and many were in evening gowns - which is different to our ways. They have no prayers nor an address nor do the couple kneel for the benediction. A friend of the couple (who sings over the radio) sang from the choir gallery twice while we waited: *I Hear You Calling Me* and *Because.* Then after the ceremony he sang *Sweetheart, Sweetheart* from the show *Maytime.* This is different to our procedures, isn't it?

I am enclosing a programme of a mountain play that took place on Mount Tamalpais. I thought it was too great a hike for me to undertake so Alta went with some girls from her office. Joe and I got up early and went over to Mrs Noren's and then went with them to their newly acquired land at Point Reyes. Joe and Chester and another young fellow dug out foundations. Winnie and June Furzoni (the young fellow's girl) and I dug out thistles and giant stinging nettles and planted marigolds, cooked hamburgers on the camp stove, made lunch, drank coffee, and washed-up in the running brook. A strange Sunday, but if I had not gone nor would Joe and we enjoyed it all immensely.

This week is Alta's vacation so we two went to the pictures on Monday and saw *A Yank at Oxford* [*in which a brash American is entertainingly taught some real values, starring Robert Taylor, Maureen O'Sullivan and Vivien Leigh*]. On Tuesday we went to Redwood City to lunch; on Wednesday to afternoon tea at Winnie Noren's; and on Thursday to the show at the GOLDEN GATE THEATRE - a picture show and then vaudeville which was good. Then on Friday we packed and in the evening came here. It seems strange to think I'm sitting here on the sands in the shadow of a great rock with the great Pacific Ocean booming in behind me. The other two have guns and have been target shooting and have now gone to get a starfish. I've just killed two ants - each nearly one inch long - awful looking things. One sees the weirdest looking insects or "bugs" as they are termed here.

There seems no prospect of Joe getting a job yet. He had a day or so and a few hours helping a friend but business is bad out here. He is the same as ever - in high spirits or very depressed. He makes me laugh at the things he says sometimes. Driving along Webster Street the other evening, we passed what he calls the "Niggers' Heaven" or where they live. "They ought to be made to have reflectors in their a . . . -holes for I'm hanged if you can see 'em," says Joe - and you really cannot at night.

Here is a child's tale:

> A teacher was explaining the meaning of the word frugal (to save) and told the class to write something including the word. One boy wrote: A young lady was walking in a wood and met a young man. She said, "Frugal me, frugal me," so he frugalled her and they lived happily ever after.

We have just come back from the beach at the mouth of the river and when we came near to the beaches at Monte Rio they were full of people and scores of children, boating and bathing. Joe says they have come in today and from now on the place will be filled with visitors; and as everybody has a car you can imagine what a lot of cars there are. We ride miles and miles along roads and highways and never see a pedestrian - nothing but a constant stream of cars. Many roads have no place for walkers, only a single track for cars with a white line up the middle.

The girls are preparing dinner and a programme from New York advertising SANBOURNE COFFEE is on the radio with a beautiful operatic singer for us to listen to. I listened to President Roosevelt the other day. He has a fine voice and delivery. We shall soon have Mr Bergen, the ventriloquist, with his Charlie McCarthy [*his dummy*], you know; and at 7 o'clock Mr Ford's programme - the only programme in America without advertisements. Tonight Miss Helen Jefson, an opera singer, is the guest of the evening. This is another queer Sunday but I have to fall in with the others. The Rev Gustav Storaker will think I've either gone home or to another church.

I saw in the WO [*The Watford Observer*] that Grandad Windmill had died. He was a good age. I'm ever so interested in the Grand Fleet Scheme. Do hope a lot of folks will take them (the boats). At the church here they have barrels and they are opened every now and then. Lizzie Southam [*of St Catharines in Canada*] has a box and collects cents in it. She kept it one year and lots of friends dropped the odd cent in it. She sent me word that she had collected $2, that is 200 cents. [*The Grand Fleet Scheme was to raise money for the Matthew Timberlake Memorial Fund at the Abbots Langley Methodist church. Each collection box represented one of the ships at the Silver Jubilee Review of the Fleet by King George V in the Royal Yacht "Victoria and Albert" at Spithead, between Portsmouth and the Isle of Wight, on 16 July 1935. It was popularly remembered because the BBC radio commentator had been imbibing and could only repeat: "The Fleet's all lit up".*]

So you are going to Worthing. I've never been there but remember that when Rose Slaughter, Amy Bayford, Lillie Simmon and I went to Brighton we could see the lights of Worthing pier from where we sat on the parade. That year Worthing had an epidemic of typhoid [*the summer of 1892*] and no guests were there and it was said that the grass grew in the streets. It cost Worthing Corporation a lot [*for a new drainage system in 1894*] as, I believe, it was traced to the water - but it is so long ago, I forget. Lillie Dowse [*neé Simmon*] remembers our gay time there.

Give my love to Vi. I am so sorry she is ill. It's a pity Harold couldn't feel hurt in his body, sneaking little wretch. Grandad always said he was a cruel little boy and would make a cruel man and time proves it. [*Vi (Violet) and Harold Flint and their children, Colin and Jean, lived at Lynton in Marlin Square, Abbots Langley. Vi had been a nurse at the Leavesden Residential Schools. Harold was George and Edie Flint's son. They had been the original occupants of Lynton and named it after their honeymoon destination.*]

I cannot imagine our houses with anything but red-brown paint work but expect they look pretty. Did the fence get painted? I'll have a new one before I cover the trellis over. One thing is sure - there is none other like mine, is there? [*Adrian Road had open ditches until a combined drainage and sewage system was laid in 1884. And like many houses in Abbots Langley at that time, 54 Adrian Road had a hand-pump in the backyard because a piped water supply was not laid in the village until 1886. The medical officer to the Watford Rural District Council had reported that Abbots Langley was the least healthy parish with the highest death rate per annum in the whole District because of pollution of the wells. These wells were shallow and tapped the water in the gravel cap overlying the clay upon the hilltop of Abbots Langley. The well in the backyard of 54 Adrian Road was still there in 1938, covered by a wooden lid. Matthew Timberlake's Will, dated 4 December 1925, left 54 Adrian Road to Annie together with the first option of acquiring 56 Adrian Road on payment of £100 each to her two brothers, an option she took. It also stated that Annie, on her death, was to leave 54 Adrian Road to her daughter, Marion - an unenforceable request but one that Annie kept. A copy of the Will was included in the Deeds of 54 Adrian Road, loaned by Ray Greeves whose mother, Daisy, lived there until she died in 1999.*]

I wonder what the boys will say about the new baby?

My dearest love to you all,

Your loving Mum

* * * * *

[LETTER 58]

"I've only half a one for this baby . . . . . ."

Greenwood, Villa Grande, Russian River, California, USA
Sunday, 29 May 1938

MY DEARS,

I've written a letter to you all and addressed it to Conway but felt I must answer Muriel's letter. [*Conway was the name of the house where Annie's daughter, Marion Flint, lived in Marlin Square. It was named by Ethel and Arthur Flint, Bert Flint's parents who were its original occupants, who followed the tradition of naming it after their honeymoon destination. Conway adjoined FLINT BROTHERS builders' yard and provided a telephone for the business and mugs of tea for the workmen. The Council road sweeper always left his wheelbarrow overnight in the builders' yard. Once, the Council billed Arthur Flint for sand that his men had taken from an unmade road in Bedmond. Arthur Flint billed them in return for leaving the wheelbarrow overnight. Nothing more was heard.*]

I am so glad to hear of her and the dear baby. I'm not surprised at his hair being fair. Fred's was quite golden-brown as a baby and folks said he would be red-haired. But you see - he will have brown eyes. I think Anthony David is a lovely name but call him "Anthony". Don't let folks say "Tony". I cannot remember whether I gave Marion my golden half-sovereign to keep safely for me. I used to keep it in a wooden box in the bottom of the medicine cupboard. But wherever it is, I want the baby to have it. David and Roger have sovereigns but I've only half a one for this baby, bless him. Take a snap of him as soon as you can. I'm eager to see his picture if I cannot see him. Fred weighed about 8lb and 2-3oz when he was born.

I went last Saturday to apply for my extension but don't know how long they will make me wait for an answer - but will let you know as soon as possible. As I've said before, my going or staying need make no difference to you. I'd love you to stay as long as you want to.

My dearest love to you both and the precious infant,

Your loving Mother

* * * * *

David and Roger Flint found the sovereigns that Annie gave them - in their father's coin collection after their mother died. Gold sovereigns of value one pound went out of general circulation in 1917.

Point Reyes

Summer in San Francisco for Annie Kimpton included many vists to Point Reyes where Chester and Winnie Noren were building their new house in virgin country. Annie helped and enjoyed the out-door life - except for the mosquitoes:

[LETTER 59]

"Fancy him having reddish hair . . . . . . a throw-back to my colour"

400 Duboce Avenue, San Francisco, California, USA
Tuesday, 7 June 1938

My Dears,

I was so glad to get Marion's letter but so sorry to hear about Mrs Riddoch. If it had been him, I should not have been surprised. Poor old dear, it seems a shame he should have such sorrow. It seems so much worse for an old man to be left. I shouldn't wonder if the long strain of his illness had undermined her constitution so that she had no strength to stand an operation. If you see him, give him my sincere sympathy. Abbots [*the Methodist church*] will miss their monetary help as well as their interest.

Now, about that dear baby. Fancy him having reddish hair - probably it will change to brown like Fred's but he may be a throw-back to my colour. Uncle Matt was a lovely red-haired baby. [*Uncle Matt was Matthew Timberlake, one of Annie's brothers. Fred and Muriel Kimpton's son, Anthony (later called "Tony") kept his reddish hair.*]

I had a very interesting trip this week. Winnie Noren called up to see if I'd like to ride with her and Mr Curtis to Boyes Hot Springs where he was going for a week's rest and for the mineral baths and waters. Of course I said, "Yes please," and took the streetcar and changed on to the dinky car or cable car and then waited on the Marina till they came along and picked me up. This place, Boyes Hot Springs, is about 60 miles over the Golden Gate Bridge (50 cents toll each way). It is a lovely ride into Sonoma County along a flat valley with hay fields, the haycocks ready to cart and the green grass already knee-high again. They have three crops each year here and the grass is burned on the roadsides and waste-lands to prevent forest fires. On each side of the valley there are prosperous looking farms with great herds of cattle. Petaluma is a great chicken rearing and egg district. I've never seen so many fowls. The season has hardly started at these health resorts. It really gets going this weekend when all the schools close for the summer and people leave the cities and take their children to run wild in the country. It was fearfully hot last Tuesday but they tell me it is unbearable at Boyes Hot Springs later on. I saw in the paper last week that San Francisco was 79F, Sacramento and Stockton were 96F and Fresno was 100F. Boyes Hot Springs is on the way to Sacramento or at least in that direction. [*Sacramento, Stockton and Fresno are all Californian towns in the Central Valley or San Joaquin Valley between the Coast Ranges and the Sierra Nevada Mountains.*]

Mr Curtis is staying at the Verdis Resort and there are separate apartments around shady patios. There are chairs, drinking fountains, a communal dining-room, a dance hall, swimming baths, a play-room, radios, bicycles and cars for hire, and also beautifully cooked and served food. Literally everything you might need. But I should get bitten to death by the mosquitoes in the evening, I know. Mr Curtis treated me to lunch and we rode into town and looked at the baths. I saw several invalids being helped out of their chairs to take to the baths. Winnie and I drove home in the late afternoon and had dinner at San Rafael. Then on again to San Francisco where she dropped me at Union Street and I came home by streetcar at about half-past seven.

Joe has not found a job yet. I wish he could do so. I had a man here the other morning about my visa extension. He came to check up again upon my statements and I had again to hold up my hand and swear that any information I gave was true, etc, etc. He said that extensions for one year or more are settled in Washington but for less they can be settled at Lewiston where I entered the States. I said that as long as I stayed for the Fair I was not particular to within a month, so he put down ten months. I asked how long I'd have to wait before a decision and he said about a month, so I shall not know just yet. At any rate, I shall not be home till the end of July if they decide to kick me out.

I've had rather queer Sundays for the last two weeks. Have been up to Point Reyes to the Noren's property where the men dig the foundations for the new home and we cook over a camp stove and eat out of doors. It is a lovely unspoilt spot, quite virgin land. They have plans for a country house and intend doing a lot themselves at weekends. There is enough wood to be gathered up and trees to be sawn to last them all their lives and clear running water from the mountains which will never run dry. The plot is on two large plateaux with hundreds of trees of all kinds, ferns and flowers, blackberries, thimbleberries, wild gooseberries, heaps of mint, and a soil that will grow anything and everything.

I'd like you to see men building houses here. Grandad [*Matthew Timberlake, a bricklayer*] would have despised such building - a great wooden frame covered with chicken wire, tar-paper and plaster. No need to bother about cold, frost and rain here. The roofs are tiled or asbestos-shingled in many colours - no two houses alike, mostly white walls with colour-tiled paths and steps. Many are built in the Spanish fashion with flat roofs and cloister-like openings and doors. I wish you could see these sea views with bridges and islands, the great docks and boats with the rolling hills in the background. I shall always see them for the rest of my life.

I must take my last batch of *Methodist Recorders* round to the Rev Gustav Storaker. He will wonder what has become of me because I've not been to church lately. Has Bert read Francis Beeding's books? If he hasn't, get Mrs Lea to get them for you. Bert would love them. Of course take what you like in the way of money of mine toward the family "boat" [*for the Grand Fleet Scheme*]. My money here is still lasting out. If I need more before I come back I shall write to Fred or Bert to lend me some until I return. Joe laughed when I read of the little-bedroom clearance: "You'll have to stay yet awhile, Mum, for you'd have nowhere to lay your head".

I think Joe would like to come back to England if he could get a job. I wonder if he could? What do you think? Not necessarily in Abbots Langley or Watford, of course. I am sending the Russian River snaps [*one is included in the illustrated plates*] and some postcards. Did you ever get a newspaper with two little beanie caps in it? Also I'm sending a few *Life* and American magazines. [*"Life" magazine was relaunched in its new photo-illustrated form in 1936.*] When you open the packet of American magazines you will find some Morning Glory seed. Plant them at the end of your lattice, Marion, where they will get the sun. They are such pretty flowers. I shall get some of the giant sort which are prettier still.

* * *

Friday morning, 10 June 1938

I AM just finishing this letter and shall go out to post it. I have to go a short distance to a sub-post office and this means crossing a wide junction where four roads meet and I don't like it. We have an office just up this street (Fillmore) but I hate the old fellow there. He is very nasty to English people, hates them and shews it. Joe says not to go near the old devil.

I wish you could see the berries as they call them, such a profusion in all the stores: raspberries, strawberries, loganberries, thimbleberries and great cherries. All very cheap but to my mind they haven't the flavour of our fruit. I bought beans yesterday. They call them string-beans (Kentucky Wonders). One can hardly imagine the long distance between places here - 600 miles into the next county, etc. I never get over my amazement. [*Annie confused the distance between states and counties.*]

Give my love to the Harris girls and to the Beaumonts. I'll write to them because I'm sure I'm staying on. A kiss from Grandma to my dear little boys, all three of them.

My dear love to you all,

Your loving Mum

* * * * *

[LETTER 60]

"There were two dragons cavorting around . . . . . ."

400 Duboce Avenue, San Francisco, California, USA
Thursday, 23 June 1938

MY DEARS,

You will be waiting to hear from me. I delayed writing in the hope that I might have heard about my extension and so have something definite to tell you. I'm still waiting to hear and my ten months was up on the 21st. Alta and I went last night to see Anna Neagle in *Victoria the Great* and it was very fine. I enjoyed it more than any picture I've seen since I've been out here. It was a bit of England and home. Perhaps you have seen it? If not you must do so. The picture shown with it was *Mad about Music* with Deanna Durbin. She is a beautiful singer and looks just like a child but oh, what a voice.

Last week, there was a great Chinese Festival in Chinatown and a procession

[LETTER 64]

"I get sunburnt and the mosquitoes poison me . . . . . ."

400 Duboce Avenue, San Francisco, California, USA
Monday, 18 July 1938

MY DEARS,

First of all, thanks very much for the snaps of the baby and yourselves at Dover. Isn't he lovely? What a lot of hair he has, with that pretty crest of hair and his beautiful chubby arms and legs. I felt very envious of his other Grandma. That photo of Mrs T [*Mrs Turner, Muriel Kimpton's mother*] and the baby is very good. I laughed over Fred and the pram and cannot quite appreciate that he (the baby) is Fred's son. Jim Gates looks just as usual but Auntie Carrie's [*Carrie Gate's*] face is in shadow. I must write to them again. I am so glad the holiday was a success. Marion and Bert are preparing for theirs now.

I've had a busy week. Last Monday I had a call to see if I would go over and sit for a while with Mrs Helin who has had a heart attack and whose husband has had to leave her alone while he tried to get a practical nurse (as they call them here) to stay with her because his business calls him away all the week from Monday to Friday. Of course I went round. He came home at midday and could not get anyone so we took her into hospital to be cared for until Friday. It costs $6 a day for room only, everything else extra. I have never seen such exorbitant rates of payment as here and also for doctors and nurses. People are afraid to be ill!

Then on Tuesday I went over to Winnie Noren's to lunch. A lady, Mrs Waite, was there and we went out for a car ride to Golden Gate Park in the afternoon. On Thursday, Joe and I went downtown to see the President [*Franklin Delano Roosevelt*]. I am sending a paper which includes an account of the visit. I had a very good view of him and he is just like his picture. To moneyed people his name is anathema but workers say he has done more for the poor people than anybody before. We had to wait quite a time for the President's coming. I'm told they had an awful job to find an open car for him to ride in through the city and when they finally got one it had a flat tyre before they had gone any way.

I laughed inwardly as I stood in this American crowd. For next to me was a tiny Chinese lady with her straight black hair combed back with a black comb stuck in it, wearing a black gown and a kimono-shaped little jacket. Then in front of me was a great tall Negro lady with her fuzzy hair combed and fastened down with numbers of bobby-pins. Many of these coloured ladies dress well. This one had a brown plaid costume and wore hornrimmed glasses. On the other side of me were white American men and women. There was no procession as we understand them and the cortège went by in a moment: the state cops in navy-blue on motorcycles riding first; one or two cars with Mayor Angelo Rossi and others; then the President's carriage with him smiling and waving his hat; and behind a contingent of Federal cops in khaki on motor cycles, all with their sirens blaring at full blast. Then we came home and listened to his speech from the banquet.

[LETTER 64 CONTINUED]

In the afternoon Joe and I rode part of the way up Twin Peaks to see the fleet of warships in the Bay, a most impressive and beautiful sight. I counted 47 ships but the papers say there were 67. We saw the President's boat, the *USS Houston*, move slowly round as he inspected the fleet. We sat in the car because there was such a strong wind - almost enough to blow one off the edge of the mountain. San Francisco has a lot of wind and fog. It is sea-fog and is generally high up. The city, lying between the Pacific Ocean and the Bay, gets both wind and fog which tempers the sun's heat. So San Francisco never has the extreme heat of towns just inland.

Thursday night we went to see *Snow White and the Seven Dwarfs*. It was wonderfully clever. [*It was Walt Disney's first full-length animated cartoon film in Technicolor.*] I think if I had been a small child, the face in the magic mirror and the wicked Queen would have scared me more than the Witch. I've seen old gals very much like her!

Friday evening we had Billie and Wally Balzar over and Clifford (Alta's brother) and Marie Farthing and their little girl, Beverly, came in unexpectedly as well. So they all stayed and we played rummy. We had toasted cheese-sandwiches, ice-cream with raspberries, coffee for refreshments, and Coca-Cola to drink while the game was on. We laughed a lot and Billie and Wally are such a noisy couple. The company left at midnight and the manageress complained that she couldn't sleep for the noisy party. Joe said, "Oh, heck to her".

Joe had a few hours job on Saturday. In the evening we went by ferry to Sausalito and up to the Noren's new ranch where they are building. We stayed in the tents all night. Everybody worked all day Sunday and then we pulled out Sunday night over the long roads, down the mountain side through Olema, San Geronimo, Forest Knolls, Sleepy Hollow, Fairfax, San Anselmo and into Sausalito, and then over the ferry and home. It's a strange Sunday for me but, of course, I join in with the others and it's an outing from the city for Joe and Alta.

I wish Bert could see this new house-building. They have concrete foundations, wooden-frame walls, and tar-paper nailed all round outside. Alta painted the door and window frames with the first coat, primer I think it's called. Joe, Chester [*Noren*] and the carpenter erected the wall-frames and then started nailing on the tar-paper which is thick black stuff, and silver-coloured the other side. Winnie and I cooked and washed up and then planted foxgloves up in the woods. The leaf mould was 6in-10in deep before we got to the earth when making holes for the plants. I love the woods and the trees and to be out of doors. I get sunburnt and the mosquitoes poison me - so though it's a pleasant change, I'm glad to get home again. Tell David and Roger that I saw a pretty mother-deer with two fawns, a long snake, some queer efts [*newts*] in a rotten tree-stump, a chipmunk, some quail, a pair of herons fly over (with their long legs sticking straight out), some big brown, red and gold butterflies as wide as Roger's hand and lots of tiny bright blue ones, and some green frogs.

Mr Curtis (Dodie) could not come with us as one of his sets of apartments is empty and Sunday is a good day for people to view them. So someone must be there and, of course, as the apartments are his he stops at home. He has six sets of four unfurnished apartments in the block, each one with bathroom, stoves, Frigidaire, umpteen cupboards and closets. Each is rented at $50 per month. He lives with Chester and Winnie in one suite and (he told me) they live rent-free and he boards with them and so cries quits. All the halls and stairs are heavily carpeted and all the place is heated by steam and a janitor comes in each day. Usually an owner living-in would see to this himself but Dodie is an independent man and does not work. He says he is sick to death of the apartments and will soon sell them. His tenants have all been there between six and eight years and this is his first experience of having any empty rooms and he hates it. I guess he doesn't want to be tied to these apartments.

Joe has gone down to the city and outside it is bright and sunny with a strong wind. No one goes out without a coat and many still have on their fur collars. Only the kiddies run around with little on. They don't seem to mind the wind. People tell me that June and July are the windy months here and the really lovely weather comes late August until Christmas. I've never been cold in San Francisco. I only wish I did not need to hold on to my hat as soon as we cross the threshold.

I've just got Marion's letter. Of course I'm sorry about the Hamlins as it makes so much more work for those who think more of the church than themselves but it's the best thing that could happen. Let them go and good riddance. It will blow over so speedily and will prove who really love the place. They have been a thorn in the flesh for years. I remember how he served Father years ago. I hate to work with folks whom you fear to offend all the time. Her bitter tongue (Mrs Hamlin's) will always estrange people. What do Lily Coles and Margaret Flint base their offence upon? Probably Lily is tired of the job and Margaret also because it means sticking to it to be a Sunday school teacher. Certainly it can't be offended love for Mr and Mrs Hamlin. [*Harry Hamlin was an upholsterer who lived in 1938 at 86 Marlin Square, Abbots Langley. He was Sunday school Superintendent and resigned over some trifle; many felt his wife was behind it. Lily Coles lived with her parents, Mr and Mrs Edward Coles, at 52 Marlin Square. Margaret Flint was the daughter of "Moss" (Maurice) and Nell Flint. Annie's daughter, Marion Flint, became Sunday school Superintendent instead and served for more than 30 years.*]

I've seen the church live through umpteen storms with offended members. Sometimes I used to wonder what was going to happen to the place when I was young. But I remember Father sailing through all. He was a champion sticker. Is Harry Hamlin giving up the Matthew Timberlake Memorial Fund secretaryship? Will the Millers quit? They seem to be the only dear friends of Harry Hamlin. Is Nellie Munt returning or will she still keep on the fence? The funds will miss his regular quarterly payments but not his presence in the church. The Rev W G Baldwin [*the previous minister*] would smile wouldn't he? As I'm going to stay another year, I wonder if I'd better formally resign my position in the Sons of Temperance or if they've automatically gone on as if my absence is permanent? You might sound out Mr Miller . . . . . . I sometimes wish I was home to take part in the fray but I can't be in both places.

Joe and Alta talk of me coming again in a few years but I tell them they forget how old I am. Alta tells me no one would take me for more than 50-odd years but I know better. Twelve months from now, if all goes well, I shall be nearly home again. I'm sorry for Bert with his teeth. That is one thing where anticipation is no better than realization. The dread of going to Mr Hodges is worse than being there. My teeth [*Annies false teeth - see LETTER 21*] give me no bother whatsoever. They are really fine. I cannot bite an apple or pick a bone with my front ones but there are not many who can. Otherwise, I can eat like anyone else. [*Bert Flint suffered with pyorrhoea and had all his teeth removed by William J Hodges, the dentist, whose practice was at 12 Marlin Square. Mr Hodges attended on Monday and Thursday, 11am to 7pm, but his dentists' chair sat permanently in the front room and could be seen from the street.*]

Didn't I hear something about a little piece of Anthony's hair to shew me the colour? I'd love it. Have you heard anything of Annie Henden's health? In Lizzie's letter from London, Ontario, she said Annie was very ill and had to have a nurse in twice a day. I'm getting all behind with my correspondence and owe a dozen letters. I am glad my Topsy is all right. Have you got new neighbours in Adrian Road? Who is Harold Flint roundsman for? He is unstable as water and he will never excel.

My dearest love to you all and a kiss for my three grandsons, bless 'em,

Your loving Mum

* * * * *

[LETTER 65]

"So tight - like a little girl's knickers"

400 Duboce Avenue, San Francisco, California, USA
Tuesday, 26 July 1938

MY DEARS,

I've just had your two letters put under the door and I've been revelling in the home news. First of all, I'm very glad the Hamlins did not attend that meeting. When nothing is said there is nothing to answer or continue. What in the world is Margaret Flint so greatly exercised over on Hamlin's behalf? And who is Mrs Lawrence? Surely not the lady who is so friendly with Bert's mother? [*Mrs Lawrence lived at 5 The Crescent, Abbots Langley, and her husband "Larry" worked at the Timber Merchants at Cassio Bridge Wharf, Watford.*] As for Marie Kimpton, she is not dependable. Who interfered with Hamlin over Sunday school finance? Marion, I'm glad you are taking over the Sunday school though it will be a tie. You'll make a success of it if any one can. I can imagine how Grandad [*Matthew Timberlake*] would smile and glow over this. When I read of the doings, I feel I wish I was home. But my tongue can't do any harm out here.

I laughed over Fred's description of "miserable Hamlin's sexless streak". Years and years ago your dad nearly died with laughter because I said, when told that men who couldn't get children "had no ink in their pen", that I knew that Harry Hamlin had no pen at all because Mrs Hamlin had just made him trousers and they were so tight - like a little girl's knickers. She was inordinately proud of them and that she always made his waistcoats. This was in the days when they lived opposite us (where Mrs Johnson lives now) and he worked in the Asylum [*Leavesden Asylum*] and she did dressmaking.

I do like your fawn coat-material, Marion, and I understand about your frock looking full in the bodice. I made my piece of navy stuff like that before I left home and I think I've only worn the garment three times. I'll write to Uncle Joe and Auntie Elsie, though I can only repeat my letters home. I love the snaps of you. I'm proud of my handsome son, daughter-in-law and bonny boy. Folks here say, "Oh isn't he cute". Can't you snip an infinitesimal piece of hair off and send it to me? Where were the snaps of Marion, Fred, Flora and Canadian Uncle (I presume) taken? [*Snaps of Marion Flint, Fred and Flora Botwright, and Flora's brother Roy Blake - uncle to Ken and Alan Botwright. Flora and Roy were from the family of 10 children of Fred and Lavinia Blake who lived at 75 (now 107) Primrose Hill, between Abbots Langley and Nash Mills. Flora was born in 1903 at the Booksellers' Retreat Lodge in Abbots Langley. The book "Abbots Langley, a Hertfordshire Village" by Scott Hastie includes a photograph "Railway workers, 1925". This was provided by Flora Botwright. Fred Blake, her father, is the ganger in the bowler hat in this photograph and he is standing on the Hunton Bridge to Apsley length of the LMS RAILWAY behind their home. Flora left school at 12 years of age to work in the JOHN DICKINSON & CO paper-mills at Nash Mills. Roy emigrated to Canada in the late 1920's, studied agriculture and served the Government initially under the Canadian Wheat Board, later overseas as a Trade Commissioner and, finally, as the Canadian Ambassador to Italy.*]

So William Timberlake [*JWT*] is home again. Has he left Rose [*JWT's wife*] in South Africa and has Harold [*JWT's son*] left his wife and children there also? Did I leave the gold half-sovereign in one of the little bureau drawers or in the wooden box in the medicine cupboard? I had an idea I gave it to Marion to keep for me but perhaps only intended to do so. I used to keep it in the box in the cupboard in a little twist of tissue-paper. So the garden looks lovely. I can see it in my mind's eye. My Topsy certainly did Teddy Beaumont over her kittens. A lady who keeps a cat here has a shop in Fillmore Street with an apartment and the animal can never go out - only in a little yard. The poor thing is in an awful state periodically - rolls and twists and sticks herself up. "She has no husband you see and we can't get her one." I laughed and thought of my poor Topsy and her train of followers.

Do hope you will get lots of apples, they are so good for the winter. There are tons of apricots and plums here now at 3lb for 10 cents and the finest at 5 cents a pound. Joe has no job yet and had something happen in the interior of his car engine. There was a bang and then a clap, clap, with every turn of the wheels when starting to pull - not when rolling level or going downhill. He took it over to Chester Noren's garage yesterday and they are taking all its inside out. He is helping, so that will reduce the cost of repair.

Poor old Joe, his pretty hair is gone from the top of his head and he does his hair across now. He had two queer lumps on top of his head (one large and one small) and it was a great embarrassment for him. He always kept them covered with hair. He'd had them years, well before he married. I at last persuaded him to go (whilst he has been at home) to a surgeon and have them removed. He would not consent for a long time but I paid for the operation ($25) much against his will and now he is quite glad. I fancy the hair will grow a bit and when the scars are healed it will be quite unnoticeable. Don't mention this at all when you write as he is most sensitive - both about the bumps and my paying for the operation.

Have you any Turkish or South African stamps, Fred, or can you get any? I have a bit of ironing to do and have to go out and get meat, etc, for tonight's dinner. Alta says I help her so much, but I've never had such leisure in my life. I shall never want to work hard when I return. I know that in one year from now I'll be with you all, please God.

My dearest love to you all, girls and boys, little and big,

From your loving Mother and Grandma

* * * * *

ANNIE sent a postcard (date-stamped 28 July 1938) showing the monument erected in 1897 to Robert Louis Stevenson in Portsmouth Square (in Chinatown where he liked to sit and watch passers by), San Francisco. On it is a quotation from his, "A Christmas Sermon" written in the Adirondack Mountains, New York State, and published in "SCRIBNER'S MAGAZINE" in 1888 during his second visit to the USA. The monument is crowned by a small, gilt statue of the ship "Hispaniola" from his story "Treasure Island". Annie remarked simply, "Isn't this a very beautiful inscription":

TO REMEMBER
ROBERT LOUIS
STEVENSON

TO BE HONEST, TO BE
KIND - TO EARN A LIT
TLE TO SPEND A LIT
TLE LESS - TO MAKE
UPON THE WHOLE A
FAMILY HAPPIER FOR
HIS PRESENCE - TO RE
NOUNCE WHEN THAT
SHALL BE NECESSARY
AND NOT BE EMBIT
TERED - TO KEEP A FEW
FRIENDS BUT THESE
WITHOUT CAPITULAT
ION - ABOVE ALL ON
THE SAME GRIM CON
DITION, TO KEEP FRIE
NDS WITH HIMSELF
HERE IS A TASK FOR
ALL THAT A MAN HAS
OF FORTITUDE AND
DELICACY

*

used to say she was very much like me in face. I had straight, red hair. Sister Marion's was yellow-gold. One can hardly tell from a snapshot, so I must wait until I see him. [*Annie's sister, Marion Dowse, died aged 3 in 1889 when Annie was 18. Annie probably named her daughter, Marion, after her young sister.*]

That snap of Roger is not good enough. Joe says he is like Bert, more so than David. Alta delights to show the shock-headed photo of David to people with, "Can you guess who this boy is?" Four out of five say it's some relation of Joe's, so he must look like him. I think it's the eyebrows - they are identical.

I expect Marion and Co are at Worthing this week. I wonder what the Sunday school is doing without them? It will soon be a year since I came to San Francisco. Last year I was just leaving Canada for Rochester, USA. It does not seem a year. Time flies and I'll soon be home again.

My dear love to you all,

Your loving Mother

PS. Tell David these are some teeth for his poor dad [*Bert Flint*]. I got them from a popcorn packet.

A little boy went to Sunday school. Asked how he got on, he said he liked it and his teacher also and said, "I think she must be Jesus's grandma for she talked about him all the time" (!!!)

* * * * *

AFTERMATH

GOLDEN GATE BRIDGE leads north to Marin County and the Point Reyes National Seashore. This is a region of some 150 square miles preserved in its natural state and inhabited by numerous species of birds. It embraces Drake's Bay where Sir Francis Drake is reputed to have landed in the "Golden Hind" in 1579. He claimed "Nova Albion" for England - the chalk cliffs reminding him of the Dover coastline. (Albion, a poetical term for England, comes from the Latin "albus" for white). Drake missed the Golden Gate and San Francisco Bay - probably because of sea-fog.

Annie Kimpton's friends, Winnie and Chester Noren, were building their new home near Point Reyes Station. Annie was offered a day-trip to the Point Reyes lighthouse and there were over 300 steps down to the lighthouse from the road. Annie's daughter, Marion Flint, was with her husband, Bert, and their two boys, David and Roger, on their summer holiday at Worthing when Annie made the journey to Point Reyes lighthouse. At Worthing a policeman brought a message to Marion from her brother, Fred, informing her that her mother had suffered a heart attack whilst visiting the lighthouse, probably after climbing the steps back to the road. Annie died shortly afterwards on Sunday, 28 August 1938. Bert Flint returned to Abbots Langley for a short while to help Fred Kimpton liaise with Joe and Alta Kimpton about the funeral arrangements. Marion and the boys, David and Roger, remained at Worthing.

The letters received by Marion Flint after her mother's death are reproduced here together with a poem on a redwood plaque and the details of Annie's Will:

[LETTER FROM JOE KIMPTON]

400 Duboce Avenue, San Francisco, California, USA
Monday, 29 August 1938

DEAR FRED AND MARION,

Was so sorry to have to send such a bald cable to you but Alta and I were nearly at our wit's end. Everything was so sudden. She seemed so well that we never dreamed that anything was wrong with her heart. On Sunday morning we went up to the Noren's place. Mother has no doubt mentioned them a lot. Mother was perfectly well and happy and was enjoying herself. In the afternoon she went for a ride with two friends to see the lighthouse. We stayed behind but she was so eager to go and was perfectly OK. They were so late in returning that we became a little alarmed and then the young fellow who was driving them came tearing back and said Mother had had a heart attack. We set out but met them almost immediately with a doctor.

It appears the Coastguard people did what they could for her and then, when she recovered a little, rushed her to the doctor. She was conscious and knew Alta and myself but was so weak she could not raise a finger. We got her to bed and the doctor gave two injections to get the heart going again but informed me quietly that it was hopeless. She lived about 20 minutes after she got back to us but towards the end passed into a coma. The doctor said it was a lesion of the heart valves. I don't know the medical term. Being a sudden death, of course, the coroner had to be called in. She died at about 5.45pm and we had to wait about two hours for the officials. They

[LETTER FROM JOE KIMPTON CONTINUED]
had to come from the county seat at San Rafael. They took her to an undertakers there, to await release. We had to come home and I immediately cabled you. She is being transferred to San Francisco today and I'm sure the formality of inquest and autopsy will be avoided as the doctor said he would certify without.

Your cable arrived this morning and I have the cash all right. I was forced to ask for it, Fred, for as you know I have been out of work and we are terribly short. [*Annie's Executors, Fred Kimpton and Bert Flint, sent Joe £40 towards the funeral costs in the USA.*] I have decided to cremate and ship the ashes home for internment at Abbots Langley and am calling to that effect tonight. We had never talked much about anything happening but I gathered she had no real feeling against cremation but she did have a fear of dying and being buried away out here, so she won't be buried. If we moved away she would be all alone with nobody to tend the grave or anything. I hope you and Marion can see this with me. I feel so bad about everything that I'm almost at my wit's end.

Poor dear old Mum. She was so happy here and enjoying everything and people thought so much of her. She was looking forward to seeing you all again and telling you about all the things she had seen and was so anxious to see baby Anthony. I can't write any more now, Fred. Will write again in a day or so and send a death certificate for the lawyer. Will also go more into matters affecting her.

Your loving brother and sister,
Joe and Alta

* * * * *

[LETTER FROM THE COASTGUARDS AT POINT REYES]

Point Reyes, California, USA
Wednesday, 31 August 1938

DEAR MR AND MRS KIMPTON,

I received a letter from Mrs Padden yesterday telling us the sad news of your mother's death and we want you to know how very sorry we are about it. It all happened so quickly and it was a terrible shock to you, I know. I want you to know that Mrs Padden and her son and each of us out here did the very best we knew how, to help her. I'm only sorry it wasn't possible for us to have done more.

I realized of course that she was terribly ill but I did hope for her recovery when we got her under a doctor's care. But try to be glad that she didn't have to suffer any longer, if she couldn't get well. I realize that words of sympathy are small comfort at such a time but Mr Powell and I and Mr and Mrs Zetterquist want you to know how sorry we are for you and for the other members of the family. We didn't want to hurry away on Sunday but Mr Powell had to go on duty at 6pm. If you come out to Point Reyes be sure to look us up.

Yours very sincerely,
Zelma Powell

* * * * *

A 1938 postcard view (probably bought by Annie Kimpton) looking down the steps to Point Reyes lighthouse. Point Reyes is 600ft high and it is the foggiest point on the Pacific Coast of the USA. The lighthouse was built in 1870 and was placed so that its light would shine below the fog. In 1975 a modern beacon replaced the original light but the lighthouse is still open to the public. There is also a visitors' centre in the old Coastguard keepers' quarters at the top of over 300 steps which lead down to the lighthouse.

[LETTER FROM ALTA KIMPTON]

400 Duboce Avenue, San Francisco, California, USA
Sunday, 4 September 1938

DEAR MARION,

The funeral services for dear Mother were held on Thursday. We got a hold of the minister who used to be at the little church Mother attended, the Rev Gustav Storaker, to conduct the services. Everyone told us how beautiful and utterly sincere his words were. He read a poem or hymn of which he is going to send us a copy and I shall send it on to you. (*This poem or hymn has not survived.*) The little chapel was a mass of flowers - roses, gladioli, gardenias, dahlias and many others. I am sending you the cards taken from the sprays and wreaths of those sent, both from the florists and the many more brought personally. All these have been acknowledged. She looked beautiful, just as though she was asleep. She wore the last little dress she made for herself, the blue with the pin spot. She was very fond of that one and we all admired it. She also wore a pretty little string of pearl beads which Kitty Hotchkiss had just given her and her wedding ring which we, of course, left on her finger.

[LETTER FROM ALTA KIMPTON CONTINUED]

After the service at the chapel the procession moved down to the Cypress Lawn Cemetery [*Annie had told of her visit to this Protestant Cemetery in South San Francisco in LETTER 32*] where the Rev Gustav Storaker conducted a short committal service in a little chapel all in white - the walls, the benches, the rostrum and even the organ. There were stained-glass windows high-up. There were potted plants and ferns and palms all around and the sun streamed through the windows. After the service the curtain was drawn and we left her there.

Joe has been terribly worried about his decision to have her cremated. He keeps saying, "I do hope I've done the right thing". We hope you will see our point of view and know that we couldn't have done anything else. As Joe told you in his letter to Fred, Mother once said she hoped she never had to be buried out here for if we should move, even to another city, she would be left all alone. Joe says things are bad here with the labor wars and depression and we may have to move if he is to get a job, maybe to Los Angeles where I have an uncle who is a manager of a large battery plant. So you see, if she was buried there might be no one but friends to care for her grave and they soon forget. Joe would like to send her ashes home to be put in his dad's grave. Fred's cable stopped us from doing this immediately, but he wants you and the rest of the family to think it over and try to see eye to eye with him in this matter. They will keep the ashes indefinitely at the crematorium in a little urn pending our arrangements.

I am enclosing a letter we received from the Coastguard people who were so kind in calling a doctor and bringing Mother back to us at the Noren's place. [*That letter has been included before this one, in its date order.*] We intend calling on them and thanking them personally. I am also enclosing a snapshot I took that very morning. [*This is included in the illustrated plates.*] Mother was so anxious that we take some of the house under construction to send to her Bert, to see what he thought of a frame-house. This is the only one she happened to be in. I'll send the others later. I shall also collect all the snaps our friends have taken of her and send them on.

As soon as we can make arrangements, we shall pack up all her things and send them to you - all her jewellery, letters, souvenirs and some of her clothes which are not too worn. Joe will give a full accounting of all financial matters to Fred. Joe has written to Aunt Lizzie in Canada and also to Mrs Hutchinson in London, Ontario, and to Mrs Stanton in Ottawa.

We never knew there was anything wrong with Mother's heart and I don't think she did either. She was always so well here and having such a good time. Now that we think back, once or twice since she was with us we noticed that she patted her chest and turned a little pale but when we asked her what was the matter she would say, "Oh, just a little indigestion. It will be all right in a minute," and it always was. So we thought that's all it was and I think she did too, but possibly it was her heart even then.

I can't begin to tell you how much we miss her; and I'm so glad she had that year with us. We've tried to show her a good time and take her to as many places as we could and show her as many things as we could and I think she thoroughly enjoyed it all. Her one regret was that her Marion couldn't be here to share it all with her and see the things she was seeing. She did so want to see her new little grandson, Anthony, and was so pleased with all the snaps and the little lock of his hair. She loved to talk about her little David and Roger. She loved everyone and everyone loved her. Our little appartment seems so empty without her and everytime we turn round we see evidence of her life with us and know it is just the same with you. However, we must try to remember that she is happy now and waiting for us all to be united with her again.

I forgot to tell you that we got a lovely spray of flowers for her with the words, "From Her Loving Children," which was meant to include all of you too. Well Marion, I must close now but will write again as soon as we hear from you.

Love to you all,
Alta and Joe

* * * * *

[LETTER FROM JENNIE STANTON]

Rivermead PO, Ottawa, Canada
Friday, 9 September 1938

MY DEAR FRED AND MURIEL,

Just to send you both and Marion our deepest sympathy on your terribly sad bereavement. It was an awful shock to us when we received Joe's letter yesterday. I could see it was from San Francisco and was so pleased as I had not heard from your dear mother for a long time and could not write to her as I did not have her address. So you can imagine how we felt when we read the sad news. We are so glad she was able to come and see us - if only for a few days - and I believe she enjoyed her visit. She certainly was very bright and cheerful all the time she was here which makes it seem all the more impossible that she has passed away. You will all miss your dear mother very much, we know. The only consolation you have is you know she did not suffer from a long illness and is now more happy than anyone here can possibly imagine. I have included Marion in this as I do not know her address. We all join in love to you all.

Yours affectionately,
Aunt Jennie

* * * * *

[LETTER FROM JOE KIMPTON]

400 Duboce Avenue, San Francisco, California, USA
Wednesday, 12 October 1938

DEAR MARION AND BERT,

Was very glad to get your last letter. I have been holding off writing hoping to hear from you so that I should know definitely just what to do. I guess, by this time, Fred has received the big registered package with all the bills, etc, in it and that you have got the enlarged snapshot all right. They are not very clear but the original was quite small. I'm more than glad to hear of your decision to have Mum's ashes sent home and will

[LETTER FROM JOE KIMPTON CONTINUED]

make the necessary arrangements this weekend. I shall probably have to get another death certificate from San Rafael and have it cleared by the Consul and lots of stuff like that, so it may be nearly a month from this date before they arrive. I knew that you would have a memorial service for Mum and I guess you will let us know about it. As for a burial service [*for Annie's ashes*] that is up to you at home, of course. I was glad that old Gustav Storaker could come over from Berkeley to take the burial service here. He was the only parson Mum liked. He is a very personable man and his diction is almost faultless for a Norwegian. I guess Mum wrote and told you all about him. She must have written some rare old epistles home to you all. There are lots of her papers left that she had collected which we shall send on to you.

We have been through all her stuff and made a preliminary sorting, Marion. Her clothes we have sent to a little old English lady in Haywood. She is very hard up and Mother knew her and liked her. Alta's mother, who feels the cold, took the heavy underwear. Mother had never used it as she never felt cold here. Alta would like to keep Mother's little crystal necklace but the rest we shall send home to you. I think we can discard the big old steamer-trunk (it's about done in anyway) and pack everything in the little blue suitcase. If old Mr Curtis is really making a trip in the spring he will bring it then which will save a lot of shipping costs, customs, etc. We found a redwood plaque in Mum's stuff addressed to you by her, probably for your birthday, so shall send that along by mail. She had saved all the letters she had received from the day she sailed, most of them were from you. We went through them carefully and took out all the snaps and burnt the rest. The snaps are mostly of you and Bert, the children, and Fred and Muriel. We shall keep them for ourselves if you don't mind.

I'm glad you asked old Britten about Mum's death. [*Dr Britten was Annie's doctor in Abbots Langley.*] It must have been coming on for years. Coronary thrombosis is the same as angina pectoris. I think she must have known a little herself but would never say, so we didn't have to worry about her. She seemed very happy here and we took her around quite a lot and she met dozens of people and they all thought the world of her. I'm glad we had our big old car to take her around in. She loved being driven and the old tank is so big in the back that she used to stretch out and take catnaps on a long drive. We drove her about six thousand miles in it and she did thousands of miles more in other peoples cars, so she saw quite a lot of California. Everywhere she went she said, "I wish my Marion could see all this," and I wish you could too. We miss her very much and I can't get settled down. We have only had about two real cooked meals in this place since Mum's been gone. All the rest have been scratch and eating out.

I haven't got a job yet but manage to pick up a dollar or two. Alta has her job and actually we are no worse off than when I lost my job. Of course we are no further ahead tho'. I have not yet turned in her passport to the Consul but once the ashes are shipped, I can do so. Poor Alta misses Mum. They used to go to shows together, broadcasts, skating and to the homes of the girls Alta worked with. If I thought I could get a job back home we would leave next year but I should probably be worse off than I am here. I am very tired of America and my luck has been out since I have

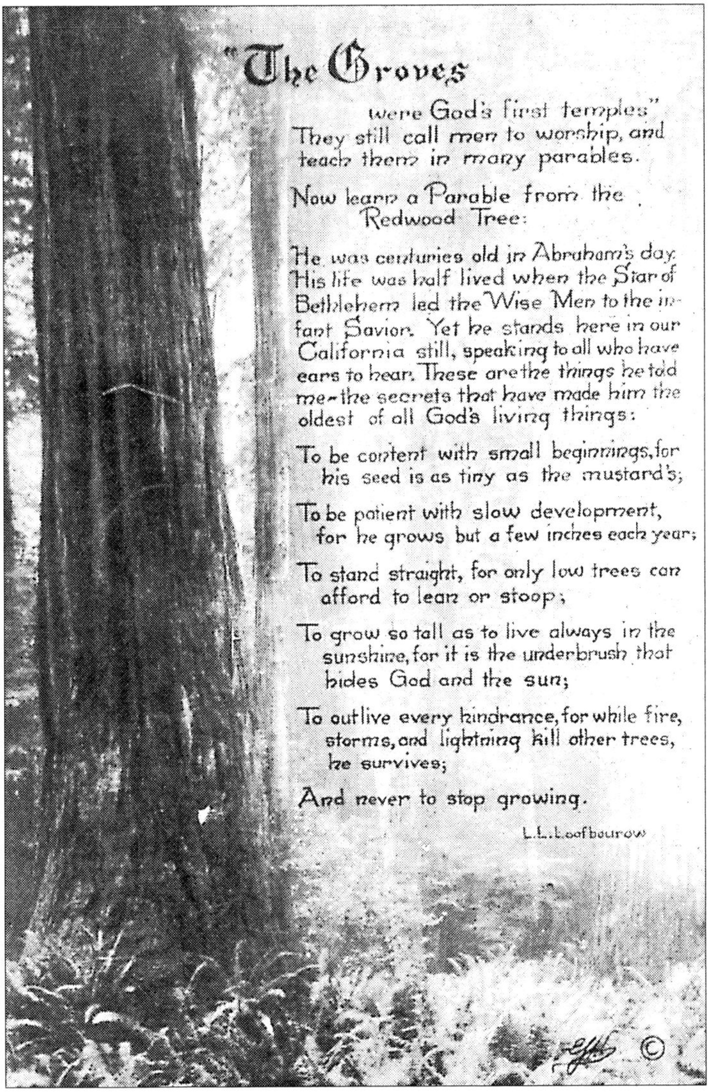

The 7in x 10in redwood plaque found in Annie Kimpton's effects (a birthday present for her daughter, Marion Flint) had a picture of a redwood tree and this poem by L L Loofbourow mounted on it.

been here but I guess I'll have to make the best of it. I had a letter from Uncle Will [*Joseph William Timberlake, JWT*] but haven't answered it yet. I guess I had better and get those letters of introduction even if they are of no use. Things are pretty rotten here now. The whole city is eaten up with strikes and we are seriously thinking of moving to Los Angeles where business is better, even if the wages are not. Alta has

[LETTER FROM JOE KIMPTON CONTINUED]
an uncle there who is boss of some place where they make batteries and he may be able to find me a job.

All of us here are mighty glad that the war scare is over at least for a time, tho' I think it will eventually come to a show-down with Hitler. Mussolini will, I think, shut his trap for a while. Ethiopia should keep him broke for years. Things looked pretty black for a while and I began to figure on a free trip home as did lots of English fellows out here. I suppose Hitler will want the colonies back next but Canada, South Africa, etc, will have something to say about that don't you think? [*Joe Kimpton is referring to the appeasement of Germany under Adolf Hitler by the Munich agreement on 29 September 1938 which ceded the German-speaking Sudetenland of Czechoslovakia to Germany - and the belief by the British Prime Minister, Neville Chamberlain, that he had obtained "peace in our time". Italy under Benito Mussolini had invaded Ethiopia in 1935 without effective opposition from the League of Nations, forerunner of the United Nations. Adolf Hitler had his eye on the former German colonies occupied by the Allies during World War I and still administered by some of them as mandates from the League of Nations.*]

The Norens are getting along swell with their home. I am going to put all the plumbing in for them. I have almost forgotten all I ever knew but hope it will come back. I work in Chester's garage for him occasionally when he has a big job in. It brings in a few dollars. He would give me a steady job tomorrow but the unions won't let him. You may be getting letters from some of the people out here who knew Mum - Kitty Hotchkiss, Mrs Carr and Mrs Balzar. If you do, I'll be glad if you would answer them as they are good friends of mine - and it only needs a line or two. I don't know what there is belonging to me in Mum's stuff at home but you might keep the brass idols, revolver and belt buckle for me. And if there are any pictures of India and Mesapotamia I should like them sent out - just the pictures, nothing else. She brought my spurs, etc, from Canada for me. I guess we can keep all the pictures she bought out unless there are any you would like back.

Poor old Mum. I wish she could have got back safely to tell you all about things. It seems so hard to go right in the middle of her one big holiday. How she did go for the books out here. We got, on average, a dozen per week and she read and read. We had a bedside lamp for her and it used to burn till 2am in the morning sometimes. One thing she loved was to stay in bed as long as she liked and it was only when we made a long trip that she got up early. She loved to go shopping even if it was just for the groceries up the street and got a big kick out of the dollars and dimes. She used to do a bit of sewing. Said she liked to keep her hand in. Said it was the first time she could quit sewing when she felt like quitting and sit and read. I am enclosing her last library card - she filled about three others. We shall send her bills and hymn-book home but I want to keep Grandad's old tuning fork that she bought out for her tonic sol-fa.

She learnt the Canadian national anthem, *O Canada!*, here and several other songs that she wanted to sing for you. We used to have little card parties in the evenings and she loved to play rummy and "Michigan", etc. I'm glad we got to see her again if only for a year. She was just the same old Mum as always, hadn't changed a bit. Alta loved her and I know she loved Alta. If I can only get a break we are certainly coming home sometime but it would be foolish to land broke with no prospects. I'm going to take a run over to Chester Noren's garage now and will write a bit more when I come back.

*

WELL there was nothing doing at Chester's except that he put a new set of high tension leads on the old Auburn. That ought to make her run a bit faster. I hope the address book I enclosed was the right one. It was all I could find. Alta has found some snaps to enclose. I have written on the backs. Alta says she will write to you pretty soon. I can't think of much more, Marion. Will write again soon. Love to you all and Fred, Muriel and family,

Yours, Joe

* * * * *

[LETTER FROM MRS CARR]

2198-15th Street, San Francisco, California, USA
Tuesday, 6 December 1938

DEAR MRS FLINT,

I have had it on my mind to write to you ever since your mother passed away. I felt I wanted you to know how very much my husband [*Tom Carr*] and I loved her. She was always so happy to come along with Joe and Alta and to spend an evening with her crochet. We used to sit and chat for hours together while our hands were busy with our crochet or knitting and while our husbands played darts and cribbage in the kitchen. I miss her so much and wish with all my heart that she was still here. My husband is a great joker and she was just right for him to tease. She used to smack his head and laugh at him so much, which of course was just what he liked. I called her up on the Wednesday before she died and asked her if she would like to come downtown with me and look at the shops. She came along and we went down and window-shopped and had a milk-shake and walked home. She enjoyed it so much and so did I. I am so glad I knew her and I am glad that she was able to come and see Joe. It made her so happy. She was always amused at how Joe and my husband spent their evenings together. It always started with darts and ended up with cribbage, every few evenings. They are doing it right now! Alta and I have to retire to the living room to be out of their way. Your Mother just loved Alta. Every time we were alone she used to say there wasn't a sweeter daughter-in-law in all the world and how pretty she is and how dainty she is and how much she loved her. It was the same with Alta too. They got along beautifully together. I'm afraid I haven't written the kind of letter I meant to when I started out but I hope you will understand just what I wanted to say. I hope your husband and sons are all well and wish you a merry Christmas.

Yours sincerely,
Winifred Carr

* * * * *

ANNIE KIMPTON'S Ashes were duly returned to England and arrived one morning through the letterbox at Conway, Marlin Square, Abbots Langley - the home of her daughter, Marion Flint. Marion remarked that her mother would have been "tickled pink" to think that her ashes had simply dropped onto the mat through the letter-box. Annie's ashes were interred above the remains of her husband, David Kimpton, in his grave in the parish churchyard at the church of St Lawrence, Abbots Langley. A new suitably inscribed marble headstone was erected in March 1939 by the Hemel Hempstead Marble and Stone Works at the cost of £6 7s 6d. This headstone stands a short distance from two others that stand side by side: that of Annie's father and mother, Matthew and Mary Timberlake; and that of their four children: Fanny Dorrofield Timberlake; Marion Dowse; Edith Marion; and Matthew Henry, who died whilst young. Photographs of both headstones are shown in the illustrated plates.

* * *

ANNIE KIMPTON'S Will was dated 11 June 1934. Her Residuary Account was drawn up by Sedgwick, Turner, Sworder & Wilson of Watford, Solicitors. Most of Annie's assets were in National Savings Certificates and a small amount in Keystone Trust Certificates. FURNESS LINES refunded £49 10s 9d for her unused return passage home from San Francisco. Annie's only debt was £16 18s 8d to Bert Flint, being the balance of expenses for repairs to 54 and 56 Adrian Road over rental income from 56. Annie left £25 to each of her three grandchildren, David, Roger and Anthony which was put in their Post Office Savings Bank accounts. Each of Annie's three children, Joe, Marion and Fred, received one third of the residue available for distribution after expenses had been paid, which came to £216 2s 11d each. Annie left both 54 and 56 Adrian Road to her daughter, Marion, on payment of £100 each to her brothers, Joe and Fred Kimpton, out of her share of the residue. The houses were vested in Marion Timberlake Flint on 31 December 1938, the agreement being signed by her Personal Representatives: Fred Kimpton, wireless operator, and Bert Flint, builder, and witnessed by Maurice (Moss) Harry Flint.

* * *

THE OLD TIME RELIGION

SOMEONE has said: "If we could get religion like a Baptist, experience it like a Methodist, be positive about it like a Disciple, be proud of it like an Episcopalian, pay for it like a Presbyterian, propogate it like an Adventist and enjoy it like a Negro - that would be some religion".

Dr Harry Emerson Fosdick

Annie Kimpton sent this quotation, written on a loose piece of paper.

EPILOGUE

IN SAN FRANCISCO, the Golden Gate International Exposition took place early in 1939. Joe Kimpton was never fully employed again. Alta continued to work until she retired but she changed her job and worked as a clerk in the City Hall in San Francisco. They had no children and remained all their married life in San Francisco (it was initially a condition of City Hall employment). The Second World War that Annie feared came in 1939. The United States entered the war in 1941 though President Roosevelt ensured aid to Britain before then. Alta and Joe sent food parcels to Marion Flint's and Fred Kimpton's families throughout the war via the agency CARE (Co-operative for American Remittances to Europe, a non-profit making organisation). The founding assembly of the United Nations was held in San Francisco as the Second World War ended in 1945. After the war they moved to a smaller apartment in a block on the corner of Duboce Avenue and Church Street.

*

IN ENGLAND in 1939 at the start of the Second World War, Arthur Flint was made responsible for local defence co-ordination. The first parade of the Home Guard volunteers was held on the Methodist Church tennis courts which were on his land. He also made the field he owned on the corner of Popes Road and Greenways, Abbots Langley, available to Methodist chapel families for allotments - to grow vegetables in the wartime "Dig for Victory" campaign. An ARP (Air-Raid Precautions) Report Centre was built in Popes Road next to Reg Cooper's coal yard on Arthur Flint's field which extended between Greenways and the end of Trowley Rise. Bert Flint, being a builder, was in a reserved occupation and was not called up into the armed forces but voluntarily ran an ARP rescue unit. The front room at Conway, Marlin Square, Abbots Langley, became an ARP post with a sandbag wall outside the front window and either Mr Bull or Tom Drake slept there on duty every night. An ARP lorry was kept in the adjacent FLINT BROTHERS builders' yard and the unit were called upon to dig out the injured and trapped from bomb-damaged buildings, including those hit by the V-1 flying bomb in Sandringham Road, Watford, in 1944.

Bert and Marion Flint took in two evacuee brothers from Eastbourne, Pat and Ken Hearn (their sister Pam went to another home in Gallows Hill Lane). Fred and Flora Botwright took in Terry Alexander, an evacuee from London. (Many years later, after Marion and Flora had been widowed, Marion was visited by Ken Hearn; and on another occasion, Terry Alexander visited Flora.) Bert Flint helped Fred Botwright build an air-raid shelter in the garden of 56 Adrian Road. Sunday school outings became picnics in the orchard of Verulam Farm on the corner of Bedmond Road and Harthall Lane, Bedmond. Arthur and George Flint bought this in 1929 and FLINT BROTHERS had built three houses on part of it.

After Annie's death, Jane and Teddy Beaumont moved into 54 Adrian Road and Fred and Muriel Kimpton moved to the Beaumont's old house, 75 Breakspear Road, Abbots Langley, where their second child, Frankie (Frances), was born in 1942. Fred

Kimpton was seconded from his job at CABLE & WIRELESS and given a commision to serve as a wireless operator with the armed forces, first in Malta and later in Italy. After the war, Fred and Muriel moved to Walmer Gardens in Ealing (where her mother's family originally came from) to be nearer Fred's work-place in London. Muriel Kimpton subsequently took up teaching again but was tragically killed in a plane crash at Heathrow Airport on 31 October 1950 when returning from a trip to Paris. She was one of 24 passengers and 4 crew that were on a BEA Vickers Viking aircraft, all of whom perished when the plane crashed into a pile of building materials beside the runway whilst landing in dense fog with zero visibility. Fred married Joan Sheppard, a colleague at CABLE & WIRELESS, in 1951.

When the Beaumonts died, Fred and Flora Botwright moved from 56 into 54 Adrian Road, Abbots Langley. Ben and Norah Taylor moved into No 56. Later, the Botwrights moved to their own house in Hazlebury Avenue, Abbots Langley. Arthur and Brenda Goodall from Langleybury moved into No 54. When Ben and Nora Taylor moved back to Norfolk, Walter and Daisy Greeves (Nora Taylor's sister) moved into No 56. Marion Flint sold the houses to their occupants in 1964 when Bert Flint retired. Bert and Marion Flint moved to a new bungalow, Lawrenny, which they built on part of the plot of land in Popes Road, Abbots Langley, that had once been used for the allotments in the Second World War.

*

IN 1954 Joe and Alta visited England. Joe (an illegal immigrant) obtained his United States citizenship because he was married to Alta and was dependant upon her. They joked that she used the procedure arranged for GI brides during the Second World War, many of whom married British girls. American Servicemen were nick-named GIs from the "GI" ("Government Issue") number on their uniforms.

David Flint visited Joe and Alta Kimpton in San Francisco in 1968 on his way to Brunei and again with his wife, Patsy (Patricia), and their children, Shani and Ria, on their return in 1970. He introduced Joe and Alta to his cousin Colin Flint who lived in San Mateo, he having emigrated initially with his wife, Jean (née Robins), and their children, Paul and Carolyn, to Vancouver, Canada, in the 1960's. David Flint found a photograph (taken by Marion Flint in the 1940's) in Alta's photograph album of Colin with David and Roger Flint (and other boys) on the Ovaltine Egg Farm gate (near to the railway bridge) in which Colin looked exactly like his son, Paul, who was now at a similar age. Alta gave the photograph to Jean.

After Joe Kimpton died in 1972, Alta brought Matthew Timberlake's tuning fork back to England and gave it to Marion Flint. Alta made several trips to England to visit Bert and Marion Flint and Fred and Joan Kimpton. Roger Flint with his wife, Mary, and their American friends, Carl and Nan Oster, also visited Alta in San Francisco in 1984 whilst on holiday in California and took her for a meal at her favourite restaurant on Fisherman's Wharf. Alta Kimpton died in 1989.

* * *

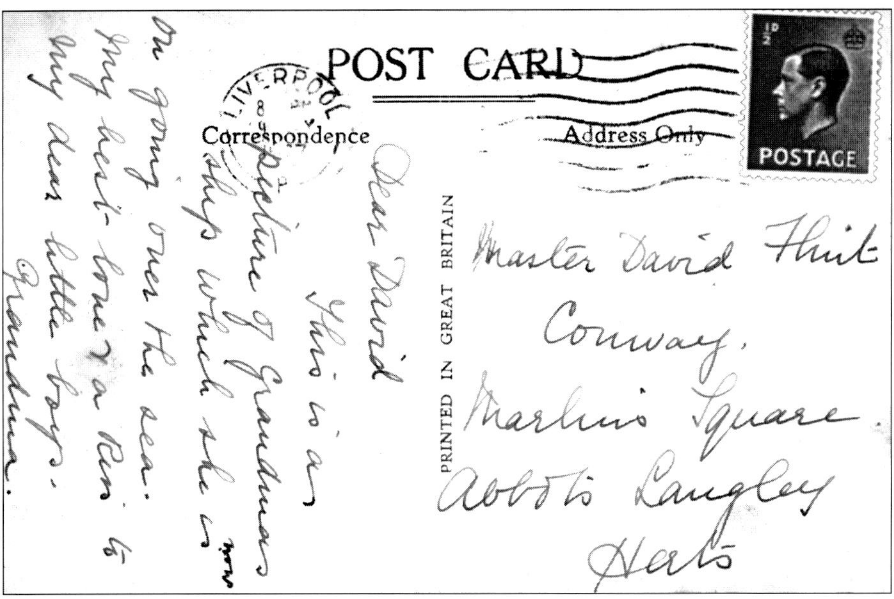

17a & 17b. Annie Kimpton's postcard of the SS "Manchester Regiment", sent in May 1937 whilst it sailed along the Manchester Ship Canal at the start of Annie's voyage across the Atlantic Ocean to Canada.

18. Ted (Edwin) Southam and his wife, Lizzie (Elizabeth), with Annie Kimpton sitting between them in May 1937 at the back of their house at 13 Ida Street, St Catharines, Ontario, Canada. Lizzie was born in Abbots Langley and had emigrated to Canada with Ted and her sister, Rose, in 1910.

19. Lizzie Southam née Hawkins and her brother, Jim Hawkins, with Annie Kimpton beside Jim's car in May 1937 at St Catharines, Ontario, Canada. Jim was born in Abbots Langley and had emigrated to Canada with his brother, Ben, in 1904.

Rose (Rosalind) Cherry née Hawkins — *Annie Kimpton* — *Lizzie (Elizabeth) Southam née Hawkins* — *Betty (Elizabeth) Outram née Cherry, Rose's daughter*

Mrs Buck — *Rose Cherry* — *Annie Kimpton* — *Mrs Shurz* — *Mrs -*

Betty Outram — *Lizzie Southam*

20a & 20b. Annie Kimpton with her cousins and other members of the Women's Auxiliary of "The Church of the Good Shepherd" at Niagara Falls, Ontario, Canada, in May 1937. Rose, Lizzie and Betty, were born in Abbots Langley and emigrated to Canada in 1910.

21. Alice Hawkins née Wicks with Annie Kimpton in Victoria Park, Niagara, Canada, in May 1937. Alice was married to Ben Hawkins who was born in Abbots Langley and had emigrated to Canada in 1904. They lived in Rochester, New York State, USA.

22. A studio wedding photograph of Joe Kimpton in 1932 aged 34. Joe emigrated to Canada in 1924 and "jumped" the border into the USA in 1925. Joe and Alta married on 6 August 1932 in San Francisco, California, USA, as mentioned in Annie's LETTER *66.*

23. A studio wedding photograph of Alta Kimpton née Farthing in 1932. Alta was born in Portland, Oregon, USA, and met Joe Kimpton who was staying at the same boarding house when she moved with her mother to live in San Francisco. Both photographs were taken by ROSHNELL, *San Francisco.*

24a & 24b. Alta Kimpton (above) sitting in Annie's favourite chair and Joe Kimpton (below) with the "denizens of the deep". Both photographs were taken at their home, Apartment 9, 400 Duboce Avenue, San Francisco, California, USA. Annie Kimpton crocheted the chairback cover during her stay there.

25. A pencil sketch of Annie Kimpton drawn by a young Italian or Mexican street artist on Olvera Street, Los Angeles, California, USA, on her visit in October 1937.

26a. The 1937 Christmas dinner with the Balzars in Oakland, California, USA. Around the table, clockwise from the left: Billie Balzar, Alta Kimpton, Joe Kimpton, Al Jones, Annie Kimpton, Cort Balzar and Mrs Balzar, Senior. Mrs Balzar was German.

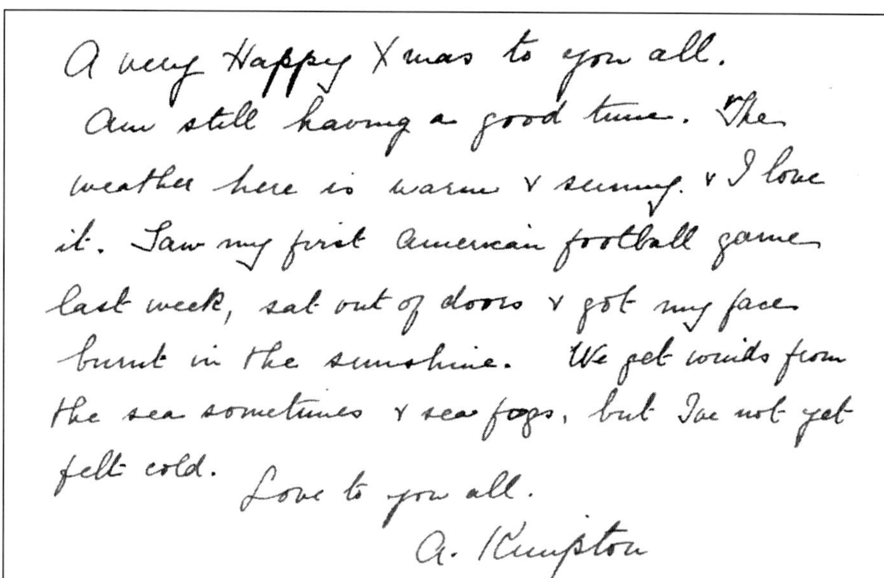

A very Happy Xmas to you all.
Am still having a good time. The
weather here is warm & sunny. & I love
it. Saw my first American football game
last week, sat out of doors & got my face
burnt in the sunshine. We get winds from
the sea sometimes & sea fogs, but I've not yet
felt cold. Love to you all.
A. Kimpton

26b. The message in Annie's 1937 Christmas card to the Botwright family at 56 Adrian Road, Abbots Langley. A picture of the Golden Gate Bridge was on the front. The card was found by Ken Botwright after his mother, Flora, died in 1998 aged 94.

27a. Joe Kimpton, Alta Kimpton and Wally Balzar picnicking on the beach at Russian River, California, USA, on their holiday in May 1938.

27b. Annie Kimpton, Alta Kimpton and Kitty Hotchkiss beside the table made from a section of a red wood tree, Sacramento Park, California, USA, in April 1938. Kitty was a Cockney who was courted by correspondence. She sailed out to San Francisco to marry Bob Hotchkiss, whom she had never met.

28. Constructing the Noren's new frame-house near Point Reyes, California, USA, taken on Sunday 28 August 1938. Annie Kimpton is framed in the window. Later that same day, Annie went on a drive to visit Point Reyes lighthouse where she suffered a heart attack and died.

29. An enlargement of the group of people framed in the window in Plate 28: Annie Kimpton is holding the Noren's dog, Patty. Winnie Noren and Joe Kimpton are standing beside her.

30. The last photograph together of Joe, Annie and Alta Kimpton taken on the visit to Chester and Winnie Noren's new house site near Point Reyes, California, USA, on Sunday 28 August 1938.

31. Annie Kimpton's bedroom during her stay with Joe and Alta Kimpton in 1937 and 1938. Annie would sometimes read her library books to 2am by the light of the bedhead lamp.

32. The headstone on the grave of David and Annie Kimpton in the parish churchyard of the Church of St Lawrence, Abbots Langley, Hertfordshire.

APPENDIXES

I : THE KIMPTON FAMILY

KIMPTON is a locative surname, one which originated in Hertfordshire. In the past, surnames were sometimes taken as identification by people moving to a new locality. The village of Kimpton is about 12 miles north-east of Abbots Langley, near the Bedfordshire border. The name Kimpton was grouped in the vicinity of the village in the earliest written records but had gradually spread well beyond by the 18th century. There are records of Kimptons living in Abbots Langley since 1619. During the 1700's and 1800's, the christenings and marriages of 13 Kimpton families were recorded in the parish of Abbots Langley. In 1802 a William Kimpton married a Sarah Flint at St Albans Abbey. William and Sarah had seven children who were christened at Abbots Langley: Abraham in 1804, James in 1806, Benjamin in 1808, David in 1810, Martha in 1813, Harriet in 1817 and Sophia in 1820. This marriage was some 130 years before the families were linked again when Annie Kimpton's daughter, Marion, married Bertram Flint at the Wesleyan Methodist chapel in Abbots Langley in 1931. In Annie's lifetime, there were a few Kimpton families left in Abbots Langley and the adjacent parish of Leavesden. By 1999 the name had almost disappeared from the locality.

*

DAVID KIMPTON, Annie's husband, was born on 22 December 1871 and was one of the 11 children of Alfred and Emma Kimpton née Sibley. Their father was an agricultural labourer, so the family were not well-off. The censuses of 1871, 1881 and 1891 recorded that they lived in Leavesden Green (the old name for Leavesden) near The Hare, about 2 miles south of Abbots Langley. After David left school at 14, he was apprenticed to the blacksmith at the smithy near Ganders Ash by the old junction of Langley Lane (now Forge Close) with Leavesden High Road. Forge Cottages still stand behind the site of the former smithy which was demolished in the early 1940s. He went to work as a blacksmith at the St Pancras Industrial Schools for orphaned children in Leavesden and later at Leavesden Asylum. Initially he was a strong man and fleet of foot. My mother (his daughter, Marion) would recall that on his way to work in the morning he would sometimes outrun a rabbit and flip it over with his cap, kill it and bring it home for dinner. He was also well known for feats of strength and for lifting considerable weights in competition with others. Reputedly, they included using his teeth to lift a bag of cement or raise a loaded wheelbarrow.

Yet there was a gentler side to him: in May 1908, Miss Phoebe Spencer aged 78 of Leavesden, who was crippled by rheumatism, made a Settlement which conferred the Power of Attorney and made David Kimpton and Matthew Timberlake her Trustees so that her capital and income were available to them for her maintenance and payment of debts (probably to her Doctor and Nurse). She provided that any residue on her death should go to David, to whom she acknowledged her "*indebtedness for kindnesses*". Phoebe Spencer died in November that year at Leavesden Green.

The Kimpton Family Tree is shown in Appendix II: *The Family Relationships*. In 1990 Joyce Willis née Fellows, daughter of Alice Fellows née Kimpton (one of David Kimpton's sisters) remembered the names of all David's brothers and sisters. Ciss Smith also had memories of William Kimpton, one of David's brothers, who lived at Trowley Bottom and drove the "Midnight Mail", emptying cesspits at night. Lois (Louisa), who used to visit Marion Flint hoping she would give her some money, was the daughter of another of the Kimptons. Lois was knocked down and killed by a car one night in about 1960 when walking from Abbots Langley to Leavesden along Langley Lane. Sibley (Gabriel Sibley), another of David's brothers, was a professional footballer and used to visit Marion and Bert Flint in Marlin Square. He used to tell them and their children about when he was trainer for a French football team, the Racing Club de Paris.

Jim Kimpton, a nephew of David Kimpton, and his wife Marie and their son, Robin (Robert Thomas), who lived at 19 Adrian Road were mentioned in Annie's letters. In 1978, when the Abbots Langley Methodist Church celebrated the centenary of its founding, Marie wrote from Taffs Well, near Cardiff, Wales, her homeland to which they had returned. Her words were quoted among other tributes in the commemorative booklet: "*About 40 years ago, I was a very happy member of your church. I recall with pleasure the Wesley Guild with various programmes that I myself took part in.*"

Doug Read was born at 19 Adrian Road and lived in it since Marie and Jim Kimpton left it in 1948. It was owned by his parents and rented to Marie and Jim whilst his family lived in a bungalow behind it, known as 19A Langley Road. When the old Scout Hut was demolished in 1970, 19A Langley Road was used for temporary accomodation until the new Scout Headquarters was completed. In 1999, Doug Read recalled Marie Kimpton cooking meals for him when he was a boy.

In 1982, Marion Flint recorded in a letter to her grandaughter, Ria Flint, that David Kimpton had, amongst others, a brother named Roger. There is no record of a Roger Kimpton so he was probably Alfred Kimpton, but called Roger to distinguish him from his father. I was probably named after him in the same way that my brother, David Flint, was named after David Kimpton.

One day in 1995, I received a telephone call from a previous Minister of the Abbots Langley Methodist Church, the Rev Morley Rattenbury, "Rats" as he was nicknamed. He was the Methodist minister in Abbots Langley from 1946-1950 and was now living in retirement at Silverdale, Cumbria. He said that he had met (at an Ecumenical House Fellowship meeting) a Robert Timberlake who was in his 90's and who was a relative of mine. Within a month, I had a telephone call from Robert Timberlake who explained that his father, Joseph Timberlake, was Annie Kimpton's brother.

Robert Timberlake was born in 1901 at Hastoe Farm near Tring in Hertfordshire on the Rothschild Estate and knew Abbots Langley quite well because his mother, Katie (Eunice Kate) was the sister of the village butcher, George Simons. Robert was educated first at Berkhamstead School like a number of other Rothschild dependents. He went to Cambridge University where he obtained a first class honours degree in classics. He taught at Stowe School and Rugby School and became headmaster of Lancaster Royal Grammar School in 1939. In the late 1990s, Michael Carpenter (the husband of Frances née Kimpton, Fred Kimpton's daughter) who then taught at Stowe School met Robert Timberlake at a school re-union and told him they were related, but was disbelieved.

I met Robert Timberlake and his second wife, Phyllis (née Kane), for the first and only time in the summer of 1997 at his home in Silverdale. He had retired there in 1961 and had served as a Justice of the Peace and had been awarded the OBE for services to the prison board of visitors at Lancaster Prison. He had been a lay Anglican reader for 50 years and when he retired from the parish council in 1994 was believed to be the oldest serving Parish Councillor in the country. Sadly, he died in 1998 not long after our meeting. At the time I met him he was physically infirm but of very clear mind. The first thing Robert Timberlake asked me was: what did I know about the reason for the disapproval, by the Timberlake family, of the marriage of Annie to David Kimpton? As Robert was very young when he first heard of the family's disapproval of the marriage between David and Annie (this having taken place some years before he was born) he wondered if I could shed any light on the matter? Robert was obviously very disappointed that I knew nothing. He said, *"Of course, you realise that David was a very rough man?"*

Copies of the Marriage Certificate and a Birth Certificate from the General Register Office gave the probable explanation. David Kimpton married Elizabeth Annie Timberlake on 14 August 1897 at the Wesleyan Church, Queens Road, Watford, Hertfordshire. They were married by the Rev William Timberlake, Annie's uncle - who must have returned from Canada by this time, and it was witnessed by Matthew Timberlake and Fanny Dorrofield, Annie's aunt. Annie and David's first son, Joseph Matthew, was born at 23 Victoria Road, Watford, on 28 December 1897.

Whatever qualms the Timberlakes had about David, they would appear to have been dispelled. About 13 years after Annie and David's marriage, Matthew Timberlake recorded a joint financial transaction in his diary: "*Cottages bought February 10th 1909 [from] Messrs R A & G Flint Bros by Messrs D Kimpton & M Timberlake - being nos 19 and 21 Marlin Sq, Abbots Langley. Conveyance fee £540.*" (But it seems unlikely that these two houses were built by FLINT BROTHERS, judging from their style.)

When David Kimpton died a few years later, Matthew Timberlake recorded in his diary: "*Thursday Nov 6, 1913 / Dave insensible / passed away 9.30pm / Mr Beaumont, Mother and Annie / I was just too late / his end was peace.*" After David's funeral, Matthew wrote in his diary: "*a good man*". Matthew also mentioned in his diary, a visit to *The Watford Observer* offices and a search of the copies of that local newspaper (kept at Watford Public Library) brought to light his notice of David's death. Besides details of all the floral tributes given, which included one from the Cadet Section of the Sons of Temperance, and another from Mr and Mrs Beaumont and Molly, it said:

> *"David Kimpton was well known and highly respected in the neighbourhood having been, for some 10 years, a steward in the Wesleyan Methodist church, a teacher at the Sunday school and*

an active worker in the Band of Hope; he was also an enthusiastic cricketer and footballer. There was a special service conducted by the Revs T B McCullagh and F G Howard in the Wesleyan Methodist chapel at which a large number of friends attended. Afterwards the body, borne by his fellow-workmen at the Leavesden Asylum and the members of the Sons of Temperance, was carried to the Parish Church where the Vicar, the Rev A H Parnell, officiated at the graveside. When this was concluded the Service of the Sons of Temperance was impressively read by Brother Hince (the deceased being a "Worthy Patron") after which the Rev T B McCullagh offered up a prayer. Besides the widow and children (to whom the sympathy of all goes forth), there were present a large number of relatives and friends of both families and the floral tokens of regard and sorrow were numerous. The undertaker was Mr Busby."

On the following Christmas Day, Matthew Timberlake wrote in his diary . . . "*miss David very much*".

Roger B Flint

* * *

A Victorian Valentine's Day card treasured by Phoebe Spencer and kept by Annie Kimpton with Phoebe's other papers.

II : THE FAMILY RELATIONSHIPS
with Family Trees

ANNIE KIMPTON mentioned early on in her letters that the relatives she met and stayed with during her time in Ontario, Canada, and in Rochester, USA, were cousins. However, the exact relationship between Annie and these cousins was not clear and the family had lost touch since the death of my mother, Marion Flint née Kimpton. I decided to write a letter requesting assistance to the two addresses in St Catharines, Ontario, Canada, where Annie spent most of her time in 1937, namely 13 Ida Street and 13 Sherbourne Street. It was appreciated that these places might not now exist or it was highly unlikely that the present residents would be related to the occupants in 1937.

The gist of the letters was that I was trying to trace relatives of mine who were resident at these addresses in May 1937. In that year my grandmother, Annie Kimpton, had spent some time with Lizzie and Ted Southam at 13 Ida Street and with Rose and Fred Cherry at 13 Sherbourne Street. I was interested in establishing the exact relationship between Annie Kimpton and these people. During my grandmother's time in Canada and America between May 1937 and August 1938 she sent over 60 lengthy letters back home to be kept by my mother, Marion Flint (Annie's daughter). I was now in the course of putting these letters into a format fit for publication. I should be most grateful if anyone could help me.

Well, much to my surprise, I received a reply within two weeks from Miss Robbie Craine who, in 1997, lived at 13 Ida Street in St Catharines: *"Just when I thought life was boring, I received your letter. Being a journalism graduate who enjoys research, I found your request intriguing and was determined to help, if possible."* Miss Craine then said how she headed for the public library where they keep copies of the local directories. She was able to trace the whereabouts of Irene Southam, Ben Southham's widow (Ben was the son of Lizzie and Ted Southam). She was in her late 80's and said she would be willing to help but had had little contact with the family since her husband died. Elizabeth Parker (Ben and Irene Southam's daughter) also expressed her willingness to help.

Some months after sending the two letters, I received the following reply from 16 Lombardy Avenue, St Catharines, Ontario, Canada: *"I am Betty Outram née Cherry. I received your letter in a very roundabout way. My sister-in-law, Shirley, Jim's widow (Jim Cherry) phoned me and read it to me. She received it from her papergirl's father who now lives at 26 Sherbourne Street. This is across the road from our former home at 13 Sherbourne Street. The papergirl is friends with my sister-in-law's granddaughter, Megan, and remembered her saying that her great-grandparents once lived at number 13. I remember your grandmother well, both from when she was here and when we stayed with her the winter we visited my father's people in 1923-24. The best way to tell you about relations is to include a Family Tree, as far as I have it."*

Betty Outram, was aged 89 when contact was made with her in 1997. Although she remembered the people and their names she was dependant upon her son, David

(Lawrence David) Outram, for doing all the research to produce the Family Tree. This confirmed that the cousins of Annie, both those at St Catharines, Ontario, and those at Rochester, USA, were from Annie's mother's side of the family by the marriage of her mother's sister, Esther Gates, to Benjamin Hawkins. It was a stroke of good fortune that Betty was still alive and able to remember her family history in such detail. The realisation that Betty Outram had visited Annie in England (though Annie does allude to it in her LETTER 11) was confirmed by reference to Matthew Timberlake's diary. The entry for 26 January 1924 states: "*Rose Cherry and family came / dinner after / Rose, etc, left about 8.30pm.*"

The Gates Family Connection is given overleaf showing the relationship between the Hawkins and the Timberlake families. The Family Tree of some of the members of the Hawkins family and their descendants in Canada (incorporating the details provided by Betty Outram) is also given. The Timberlake Family Tree is given and it shows that Jennie (Edith Jane) Stanton née Delafield of Rivermead, Ottawa, was a cousin of Annie Kimpton. Jennie was the daughter of Annie's father's sister, Elizabeth Delafield née Timberlake. The Kimpton Family Tree (that of Annie's husband) is also shown.

The Flint Family Tree (the family into which Annie's daughter, Marion, married) is given and shows the relationships of some of the people mentioned in these letters. It also includes Annie's descendants through her daughter, Marion. A surprising discovery made from the census returns was that, in addition to "Old" Reuben Flint's family, there were also those of his two brothers, William and Harry, living in Abbots Langley in the late 1890's. By the 1930's only Old Reuben's descendants were living in the village and it seems likely that the others had emigrated to Canada for that is where one of them, Nell Perry née Flint, had tried to meet Annie Kimpton in 1937. In 1900 the four sons of Old Reuben had established FLINT BROTHERS, builders and decorators, which would have provided them with a future in Abbots Langley. For their cousins, Canada would have presented a greater opportunity. All contact with the cousins' descendants in Canada has been lost since then.

Where a date is prefixed *c* in these Family Trees, it is a christening date obtained from the International Genealogical Index (the IGI) compiled by the Church of Jesus Christ of Latter-Day Saints (the Mormons) from the Parish Registers. Some dates of birth, marriage and death have been obtained from the General Register Office. Corroboration of the membership of families, their dates of birth, and their occupations have also been made by using the census returns. Particularly noticeable are the huge families of up to a dozen children.

Annie's "Grandma Gates", Mary Ann Gates née Coleman, is the matriarch of these families. Many of the characters mentioned in the letters and living in England, Canada and the United States were descended from her. Her photograph has been included at the start of the illustrated plates.

Roger B Flint

* * *

Family Trees

The names of people in the Family Trees who were born, christened, or married in the parish of Abbots Langley, or who lived in Abbots Langley for a period, are shown on a tinted background (though where they moved away on marriage their spouses would not necessarily have lived in Abbots Langley). Until the late 1800's, the parish of Abbots Langley was one of the largest in England covering about 12 square miles. Besides the village itself, it included Bedmond, Pimlico, Nash Mills, Langleybury, Hunton Bridge, Kitters Green and Trowley Bottom.

The tinted backgrounds are annotated in a right hand corner:

PARISH OF
ABBOTS LANGLEY

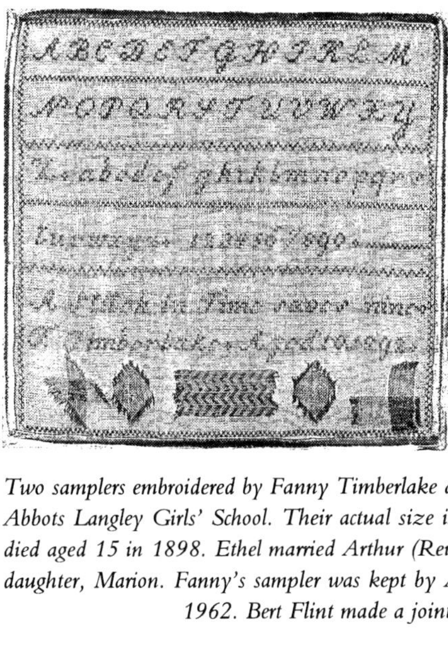
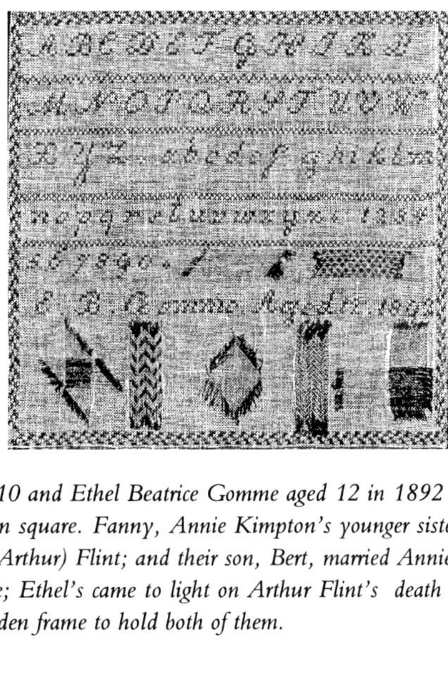

Two samplers embroidered by Fanny Timberlake aged 10 and Ethel Beatrice Gomme aged 12 in 1892 at Abbots Langley Girls' School. Their actual size is 13in square. Fanny, Annie Kimpton's younger sister, died aged 15 in 1898. Ethel married Arthur (Reuben Arthur) Flint; and their son, Bert, married Annie's daughter, Marion. Fanny's sampler was kept by Annie; Ethel's came to light on Arthur Flint's death in 1962. Bert Flint made a joint wooden frame to hold both of them.

The Gates Family Connection

Notes:

(1) *James and Mary Ann Gates' first child, James, was born at Aston Clinton. The family are recorded living at the hamlet of Astrope, by Puttenham (near Tring), Hertfordshire, in the censuses of 1851, 1861 and 1871. The 1881 census recorded them living alone in Aylesbury and James as a general labourer at the age of 75. Both James Gates' wife, Mary Ann, and James Hawkins' wife, Eliza (see the Hawkins Family Tree), were formerly Colemans of the same generation; they were probably related. James Gates, Mary Ann Gates and Eliza Hawkins all made their mark of an 'X' when reporting births to the Registrar. In the censuses of 1851 and 1861, all the young Gates children - both boys and girls - were described as straw plaiters from as young as 5 years old.*

(2) *In 1937 James (Jim) and Carrie Gates lived at Dover in Kent. The 1881 census shows that, as children, they lived at 29 and 25 Walton Street, Aylesbury.*

James Gates [*agricultural labourer*] (1) *m* Mary Ann Coleman [*straw plaiter*]
b 1806 at Aston Clinton, Buckinghamshire — *b* 1807 at Aston Clinton, Buckinghamshire

James (Jim) Gates
1828-1889
[*bootmaker*]
Sarah
b 1831 [*straw plaiter*]
Thomas Gates
b 1834 [*servant*]
Elizabeth
b 1837 [*straw plaiter*]

George Gates
1840-1902
[*bootmaker*]
m Mary A -

John Gates
b 1842
[*agricultural labourer*]

Mary Ann
1846-1912
m Mathew Timberlake
1845-1933

See the Timberlake Family Tree for further issue

Esther
1851-1933
m Benjamin Hawkins
1845-1911

See the Hawkins Family Tree for further issue

PARISH OF ABBOTS LANGLEY

Children of George Gates:

George Gates
b 1864

James (Jim) Gates (2)
b 1874
m Caroline (Carrie) Plested, *b* 1874

Further issue are not shown

The Timberlake Family Tree

Notes:

(?) *These links indicate possibilities only.*

(1) *John Timberlake and his family lived at Chesham, Buckinghampshire, when Thomas Timberlake was christened.*

(2) *Thomas and Ann Timberlake's family lived at Edlesborough, near Dunstable, Buckinghamshire.*

(3) *John and Marie Timberlake were married at Chenies, Buckinghamshire. They and the next two generations of Timberlakes lived at Sarratt, Hertfordshire.*

(4) *Richard and Jane Timberlake's family lived at Kings Langley, Hertfordshire.*

(5) *Joseph and Elizabeth Timberlake's family lived at Nash Mills, Hertfordshire.*

Nicholas Timberlake

(?)

John Timberlake (1)
c 1562
m Elizabeth -

and probably
other siblings

(?)

Thomas Timberlake (2)
c 1603
m Ann - *1632*

and probably
other siblings

Thomas Timberlake *c* 1633
William Timberlake *c* 1636
James Timberlake *c* 1638
Edward Timberlake *c* 1640
Christopher Timberlake *c* 1642

Sarah *c* 1644
Ann *c* 1647
Thomas Timberlake *c* 1649
Richard Timberlake *c* 1653

John Timberlake (3)
c 1655
m Marie Lewin *1684*

Joshua Timberlake
c 1660

John Timberlake *c* 1685
Marie *c* 1687
William Timberlake *c* 1688
John Timberlake *c* 1690
Alice *c* 1692

William Timberlake *c* 1694
Daniel Timberlake *c* 1696
Thomas Timberlake *c* 1698
(son) *c* 1700

Mathew Timberlake
c 1704
m Mary -

Susanah *c* 1704
(son) *c* 1707
Elizabeth *c* 1709

Matthew Timberlake
c 1726
m Elizabeth -

(son) *c* 1728
Thomas Timberlake *c* 1730
Mary *c* 1732

William Timberlake *c* 1736
Susanah *c* 1758

Ann *c* 1752
Mary *c* 1754

Richard Timberlake (4)
c 1756
m Jane Weedon

James Timberlake c 1760
Alice *c* 1764
Elizabeth *c* 1770
Thomas Timberlake c 1770

Jane *c* 1782
Sarah *c* 1784
Richard Timerlake *c* 1785
Elizabeth *c* 1789

Matthew Timberlake c 1790
James Timberlake *c* 1792
William Timberlake *c* 1794
Ann *c* 1797
Fanny *c* 1799

Joseph Timberlake (5)
1801-1882 [*paper maker*]
m Elizabeth Stratford Dowse

Continued overleaf

PARISH OF
ABBOTS LANGLEY

The Timberlake Family Tree, Continued

Joseph Timberlake *m* Elizabeth Stratford Dowse
1801-1882 [*paper maker*] *c* 1806

Joseph Timberlake
1834-1903 [*bricklayer*]
m Mary Emery
1830-1882

Fanny
c 1836
m Joseph Dorrofield

also married

Elizabeth
c 1838
m (i) George Delafield
m (ii) Joseph Dorrofield (2)

Joseph William Timberlake (3)
c 1866 [*manager*]
m Rose Slaughter

Albert Timberlake
1872-1936
[*bricklayer*]

married

Fanny Hannah (i)
c 1868

Elizabeth (Bessie) Dowse (i)
1870-1954
m Albert Timberlake

Harold Timberlake

Marjorie

Mary Elizabeth
b 1900

Bessie Emily
b 1903

Albert Ralph Timberlake
b 1906

Elizabeth Annie (Annie)
1871-1938 [*dressmaker*]
m David Kimpton *1897*
1872-1913

See the Kimpton Family Tree for further issue

Matthew Henry Timberlake
1873-1873

Joseph Timberlake
1874-1942 [*farmer*]
m Eunice Kate (Katie) Simons *1900*
1879-1929

Robert Raymond Timberlake
1901-1998 [*head teacher*]
m (i) Elsa Philippa (Pippa) Hickson, 1895-1979
m (ii) Phyllis Dorothy Kane, 1913-1999

Janet Elizabeth (Jane) (i), 1933-
m (i) Ronald Penhale *1959*
m (ii) Kenneth Everett *1974*

Jonathan Bruce (Bruce) Penhale (i)
1961-
m Danielle Esther Lowy

Sarah Elizabeth (i)
1962-
m Lorenzo Francesco Pieri

Andrew James Penhale (i)
1964-
m Lorraine (Lou) Bryan

Samuel Robert Penhale
1994-

Rebecca Jane
1993-

Jessica Maria
1995-

Daisy Rose
1998-

Oscar James Penhale
2000-

Notes:

(1) *William Timberlake went to Canada in 1871 and has descendants there and in the USA.*

(2) *Joseph Dorrofield was an original Trustee of the Abbots Langley Wesleyan Methodist chapel in 1879. This marriage would not have been permissible before the passing of the Deceased Wife's Sister Act in 1906 (the Brother's Widow's Marriage Act followed in 1921).*

(3) *Joseph William Timberlake (JWT) went to South Africa in 1893 and has descendants there.*

Sarah *c* 1840
[*died in infancy*]
Sarah 1841-1849

William Timberlake (1)
1844-1928 [*Wesleyan minister*]
m Emily Moore

- Mary *b* 1876
- Frances Balfour (Fanny) *b* 1877
- Alice Elizabeth (Tizzy) *b* 1878
- Ralph Moore Timberlake 1881-1949
- Elizabeth (Bessie) *b* 1883
- John (Jack) Timberlake *b* 1886
- Bowman Timberlake *b* 1889

Matthew Timberlake
1845-1933 [*bricklayer*]
m Mary Ann Gates *1870*
1846-1912

See the Gates Family Connection

Edith Jane (Jennie) *c* 1873(i)
m Robert (Bob) Stanton
[*emigrated to Canada*]

- Jack Stanton
- Muriel

Matthew Timberlake
1877-1934 [*clerk*]
m Elsie Venning
b 1886 [*no issue*]

Fanny Dorrofield
1881-1897

Edith Marion
1883-1884

Marion Dowse
1885-1889

PARISH OF ABBOTS LANGLEY

Eunice Mary
1904-1991

Kenneth Jack Timberlake
1909- [*farmer*]
m Barbara Thomas

Katherine Joy (Joy)
1934-
m Martyn Saunders

Keith Philip Saunders
1959-
m Gillian Ann Stairs (Gill)

- Benjamin Thomas Saunders 1988-
- Katie Philippa 1990-

Christopher Mark Saunders
1961-
m Angela Mary Vercoe (Ange)

- Emily Louisa Rose 1988-
- Lucy Alexandra Alice 1991-

Further issue are not shown except for Robert Timberlake's descendants

The Hawkins Family Tree

James Hawkins *m* Eliza Coleman (1)
b 1809 [*brewer*] *b* 1814

- Mary
  b 1833
  [*straw plaiter*]
- George Hawkins
  b 1835
  [*agricultural labourer*]
- Elizabeth
  b 1837
  [*straw plaiter*]
- Susanah
  b 1839
  [*bonnet sewer*]
- James Hawkins
  b 1841
  [*labourer*]
- Benjamin Hawkins (2)
  1845–1910
  [*Asylum attendant*]
  m Esther Gates *1875*
  1851–1933

  See the Gates Family Connection

  - James (Jim) Thomas Hawkins
    1876–1965
  - Elizabeth (Lizzie) Lydia
    1879–1953
    m (i) George Threader *1901*
    m (ii) Edwin (Ted) James Southam, 1887–1990
    - George Threader (i)
      b 1902
      m Nellie Gare
      - Jack (Jackie) Threader
      - Barbara
    - Benjamin (Ben) George Southam (ii)
      1911–1989
      m Irene Mary Croxall *1942*
      - Edwin Francis Southam
        1943–
        m Nancy Shutler (i)
        m Nancy Thompson (ii) *1976*
      - Mary Elizabeth Ann (Elizabeth)
        1949–
        m Ian Parker *1972*
        1947–
      - Janice Irene
        1946–
        m Calvin Leslie Graham
  - Benjamin (Ben) Hawkins
    b 1882 [*moved to the USA*]
    m (i) Mary Clapsadle
    m (ii) Alice Wicks
    [*no issue*]
  - Rosalind (Rose) Esther
    1885–1979
    m Frederick (Fred) Charle
    Cherry *1908*
    1885–1970
    - Elizabeth (Betty) Esther
      b 1908
      m (i) - [*not known*]
      m (ii) Lawrence (Larry) Bernard Outram *1936*
      1904–1968
      - Lawrence David (David) Outram (ii)
        1939–

Note:

(1) *In the 1851 census James and Eliza Hawkins and their family lived at the bottom of the Common at Redbourn, Hertfordshire, and James was an agricultural labourer. In the 1861 census they lived at Fair Tree Cottage, Redbourn, and James was shown as a brewer and Eliza as a "brewer's wife".*

(2) *Benjamin Hawkins and all his family emigrated to Canada in the early 1900's.*

Eliza
b 1848
[*straw plaiter*]

Amos Hawkins
b 1851

Lawrence Hawkins
b 1854

Agnes
b 1860

John Hawkins
b 1854
[*straw factor*]

Emma
b 1862

John Lawrence Hawkins
1888-1917
m Anna -

Harold Hawkins
1916-1917

May Mary
1891-1986
m (i) William Miles, 1898-1925
m (ii) Francis Love, 1883-1950
m (iii) Edwin (Ted) Southam, 1887-1990

George Arthur Hawkins
1893-1898

PARISH OF
ABBOTS LANGLEY

also married

Frederick (Fred)
Charles Cherry, Junior
1912-1992

James (Jimmy)
Thomas Cherry
1926-1990
m Shirley May
Alexander,
1925-

Megan [*grandaughter*]

Esther (i) 1913-1974
m Bruce Honsburger
1910-1989

Jeanne (i)
1913-1994
m Thomas Albert Boston
1921-1968

Elizabeth (ii)
m Jack Bryant

Patricia (Pat) (ii)
m - Luger

Further issue are not shown

THE KIMPTON FAMILY TREE

- John Kimpton *m* Ann Freeman *1755* (1)
  - Elizabeth *c* 1755
  - John Kimpton *c* 1757
  - Isaac Kimpton *c* 1761
  - Richard Kimpton *c* 1764
  - Mary *c* 1766
  - Sarah *c* 1768
  - Ann *c* 1769
  - Charlotte *c* 1771
  - Thomas Kimpton *c* 1773
    - Thomas Kimpton *c* 1801
    - William Kimpton (2) *c* 1803 [*agricultural labourer*] *m* Rosetta Shelton *1828*
      - Louisa *c* 1831 *m* William John Wiggs *1867*
      - Mary Ann *c* 1836 *m* Daniel Fenn *1864*
      - Alfred Kimpton *b* 1836 [*agricultural labourer*] *m* Emma Sibley *1862*
        - Adelaide (Addie) *b* 1863 *m* William Arthur Watts *1893*
        - William Kimpton *b* 1865 [*"Midnight Mail"*] *m* Mary Ann Thomas *1889*
          - William (Bill) Kimpton c 1895 [*bus driver*] *m* Alice Maud Shatter
          - Henry James (Jim) Kimpton *m* Mary Ellen (Marie) Hughes
            - Robert (Robin) Thomas Kimpton *c* 1931
            - and other siblings
          - Molly (Moggie) *m* – Wright
            - Barry Wright
            - (daughter)
        - Mary (Polly) *b* 1868 *m* – Eaton
        - Alfred (Roger?) Kimpton *b* 1870
        - David Kimpton 1871–1913 [*blacksmith*] *m* **ELIZABETH ANNIE TIMBERLAKE** *1897*
          - *See the Timberlake Family Tree*
          - Joseph (Joe) Matthew Kimpton 1897–1972 [*emigrated to the USA*] *m* Alta Farthing *1932* *d* 1989
        - John (Jack) Kimpton *b* 1873
      - Henry Kimpton *c* 1840 *m* Elizabeth Morson *1864*
    - Joseph Kimpton *c* 1804
    - Mary Ann *c* 1806

PARISH OF ABBOTS LANGLEY

The people mentioned in this book and their siblings are indicated, but further issue are not shown except for Annie Kimpton's descendants through her son, Fred.

Notes:

(1) *The earliest record of the Kimptons in the parish of Abbots Langley was the marriage of Mary Kimpton to Richard Carter in 1619. During the 1700's and 1800's, there were 13 male Kimpton marriages with 78 Kimpton christenings, and 8 female Kimpton marriages recorded in the parish of Abbots Langley.*

(2) *William and Rosetta Kimpton lived at Tanners Hill, Abbots Langley, at the time of the 1851 census.*

William Kimpton
c 1775

Timothy Kimpton
c 1780
m Mary Ewer *1801*

Isaac Kimpton
c 1781

William Kimpton
c 1788

Thomas Kimpton
c 1808

Eleanor
c 1810

Frederic Kimpton
c 1812

Harriet
c 1815

Emma
c 1844
[*died in infancy*]

Margaret Maria
c 1846

Kate
c 1850

PARISH OF ABBOTS LANGLEY

Kate (Kitty)
b 1876

Alice
b 1878
m James Henry Fellows *1889*

Joyce, *m* George Willis

Louisa
b 1881
m John Ashby *1889*

Henry (Harry) Kimpton
b 1883

Gabriel Sibley (Sibley) Kimpton
b 1887 [*footballer*]

Marion Timberlake
1902-1982 [*teacher*]
m Bertram Arthur Flint, 1904-1977

See the Flint Family Tree for further issue

Frederick (Fred) David Kimpton
1905-1984 [*wireless operator*]
m (i) Muriel Augusta Turner, *d* 1949
m (ii) Joan Sheppard, 1925-1987

Anthony David (Tony) Kimpton (i)
1938- [*emigrated to South Africa*]
m Uschi Boerhme
step children:
Tristam Boerhme
Zonia

Frances (Frankie) Mary (i)
1942-1998 [*teacher*]
m Michael Carpenter

Rachel Dorothy
1963-
m Owain Harries

Laura Frances Kim
1968-
m Harry Graham-Brown

Rhys Harries
1995-

Siân
1997-

Evelyn Frances Jane
1997-

Kimberly Jennifer Frances
1999-

THE FLINT FAMILY TREE

William Flint *m* Jane Mileman *1837* (1)
1808-1873 | 1815-1895

- Matthew Flint, *c* 1837
- Mahala, *c* 1840, *m* Jim Scalplehorn
  - Robert Scaplehorn
  - Eliza, 1866-1946
  - Sarah, 1869-1951
- Henry (Harry) Flint (2), *c* 1841 [*general labourer*], *m* Charlotte Dollemore [*bonnet sewer*]
  - Gertrude, *b* 1872
  - William Flint, *b* 1873
  - Harry Flint, *b* 1875
  - Charlotte (Lizzie), *b* 1878
  - Edith (Jane), *b* 1881
- Eliza, *c* 1849

- Florence, 1871-1952, *m* Arthur Lunnon, 1870-1948
  - Len Lunnon
  - Flory
- Kate, 1875-1880
- Reuben Arthur (Arthur) Flint, 1878-1962 [*builder*], *m* Ethel Gomme, 1878-1952
  - Bertram Arthur Flint, 1904-1977 [*carpenter*], *m* Marion Kimpton, 1902-1982

    See the Kimpton Family Tree

    - David Arthur Flint, 1932- [*civil engineer*], *m* Patricia (Patsy) Nobbee, 1940-1980 [*b in Trinidad*]
      - Shani Victoria, 1966-, *m* Stephen Walton
      - Ria Louise, 1968- [*b in Brunei*]
      - Matthew (Matt) David Flint, 1972-
    - Roger Bertram Flint, 1934- [*scientist*], *m* Mary Ellen Wise, 1935-
      - Christine Jane, 1960-, *m* Simon Richardson
        - Bejamin (Ben) John Richardson, 1991-
        - Suzanne (Suzie) Louise, 1994-
      - Andrew David Flint, 1963-, *m* Kirstie Watson
        - Isla Susan, 1996-
        - Lorna Elizabeth, 2000-
- Jeffrey George (George) Flint [*bricklayer*], 1881-1965, *m* Edith (Edie) Quebell, 1880-1968
  - Jeffrey Flint, 1906-1908
  - Harold Flint, 1908-1998, *m* Violet (Vi) Sleep
  - Nora, 1912-1995, *m* George Dunn
  - Donald F[lint], 1921-199[…], *m* Peggy [...] [*emigrated* … *Australia*]
- Margaret, 1883-1960, *m* Albert Filby, 1880-1970
  - (son)
  - Geoffrey Filby
  - Maurice Filby

Notes:

(1) *The earliest records of the Flint family in the parish of Abbots Langley were the christenings of Elizabeth Flint in 1756 and Fanny Flint in 1757. William and Jane Flint are buried at Leavesden.*

(2),(3)&(4) *Harry Flint, "Old" Reuben Flint and William Flint moved to Abbots Langley between 1879-1881. Harry Flint and William Flint probably emigrated to Canada with their families in the early 1900's.*

Reuben Flint (3)
1854-1925 [*stoker*]
m Emily Dollemore

William O Flint (4)
c 1859 [*bricklayer's labourer*]
m Hannah -

Owen Flint

Helen (Nell)
b 1884

Rainer Flint
b 1888

Arthur Flint
b 1890

James O Flint
b 1882

Jessie
b 1886

Ernest Flint
b 1887

Warren Flint
b 1889

William Flint
b 1900

Maurice Harry ("Moss") Flint
1885-1964 [*decorator*]
m Ellen Lawrence
1881-1967

Ethel Rose
1887-1934
m Alfred Blades
1882-1952

Fanny Maud
1890-1934
[*shop keeper*]

Leonard (Len) Flint [*painter*]
1892-1975
m Amy Waller
1892-1974

Edith Emily (Edie)
1895-1965
[*shop keeper*]

Hilda
1898-1974
m Arthur Hulett
1897-1964

(infant)

Eric Blades

Brian Blades

Walter Flint
b 1912 [*died in his 20's*]

Ivy
b 1914

John Hulett

Norman Flint
1914-
m Sheila McCarthy

Margaret
1916-
m Cyril Homans

Frank Flint
1918-1989
m Christine Pearce

Edna
1920-
m Charles Picket

Hilda
1922-1970
m Dennis Cook

Alan Flint
1923-2000
[*unmarried*]

Brenda
1927-
m Ivor Grout

PARISH OF ABBOTS LANGLEY

Colin Flint
1933-
m Jean Robins
[*emigrated to the USA*]

Jean
1934-
m Alan Pyke

Paul Flint

Carolyn

The people mentioned in this book and their siblings are indicated, but further issue are not shown except for Annie Kimpton's descendants through her daughter, Marion.

III : THE WESLEY GUILD

FOR MANY YEARS, from the early 1900's until the late 1940's, the Wesley Guild played a big part in the social life of the Methodist church at Abbots Langley. Marion Flint, Annie Kimpton's daughter, was Guild Secretary and made notes about the Wesley Guild events and kept copies of some of its programmes.

Meetings were held in the Abbots Langley Methodist church schoolroom on Wednesday evenings at 7.45pm, weekly from October to the end of April and fortnightly in the summer. A programme was arranged with a variety of topics. Among the local people invited to talk was "Kitch" (Geoffrey) Kitchingman, the blind musician and senior organist at the Church of Saint Lawrence, who lived at 102 Abbots Road. (Before Kitch became blind he was the deputy organist at St George's Chapel, Windsor.) The Guild programme included a "Magazine Evening" where members read original items for inclusion in an imaginary magazine. In October 1936 the best of these items were typed by Margaret Flint and Nora Flint and bound into the *Wesley Guild Magazine 1931-1936*. The original was kept by Marion Flint. The contributors were not named but some are identifiable, including Annie Kimpton who wrote an article on Bradford on Avon.

In November for many years, the Wesley Guild organised a *Lord Mayor's Banquet* - an opportunity for fun and quaint humour. *The Lord Mayor and Lady Mayoress of Chapel Alley* would be a local couple who the Guild wished to honour. *The Toast Master: The Company Sergeant Major* was always Stan Pratt who had a stentorian voice. Toasts (non-alcoholic, of course, on Methodist church premises) were made and replied to in a light-hearted manner. The Banquet Toast List would reveal some celebrated names because proposers and repliers were given a pseudonym - usually a play on words.

In 1931, Annie Kimpton proposed a toast to "THE VILLAGE" as *Countess Torkalotski*. The reply was by *The Right Honourable Justin Harniss BA* or Bertram Arthur Flint who had recently married Marion Kimpton. Jack Botwright (an Associate Member of the Institution of Electrical Engineers) whose son, Roy, had just been born became *Lord Heimer Parr AMIEE* and proposed the toast to "THE SUNDAY SCHOOL". In 1932, Mr Riddock (from Scotland) became *The Right Honorable Sir Titus Scott-Canby* and Billy Dunn (the chapel organist and choirmaster) became *General Octavius Playfair, Mus Bac ANAL*. In 1935, the toast to "THE LORD MAYOR OF CHAPEL ALLEY" was proposed by *The Ex-Lord Mayor: C Y Clone* (or Mr J R Gale, a lay Local Preacher and men's and boys' clothing outfitter who had a shop in North Watford). The reply was given by *The Lord Mayor: Viscount Brix A N Mortar* (or George Flint, the bricklayer). The Toast List for the 1936 Lord Mayor's Banquet is reproduced overleaf. *Charlie Chaplin* (or Bert Flint) proposed the toast to "THE SPCK" (The Society for the Propagation of Christian Knowledge) and it was replied to by *Greta Garbo* (or Annie Kimpton).

In 1937, *The Lord Mayor and Lady Mayoress* were Jack (Charles John) and Mabel Botwright. Mabel kept the hand-lettered *Proclamation* which Jack wrote and read as

ABBOTS LANGLEY WESLEY GUILD.

Syllabus 1936—1937.

Date, 1936.	*Subject.*
Oct. 7th	Opening Service, conducted by Rev. A. Jones. (Holy Communion)
,, 14th	Social — Social Committee.
,, 21st	"Spiritual Deafness." Speaker: Rev. B. C. Harris. Chairman: Mr. C. Miller.
,, 28th	Hymn Discoveries. Members. Chairman: Mr. W. Flegg.
Nov. 4th	"Stars." Speaker: Miss V. Belsher. Chairman: Mr. C. J. Botwright.
,, 11th	"X = O" Five Members. Chairman: Mrs. B. Flint.
,, 18th	Sectional Guild Rally. Hatfield Road, St. Albans. Speaker: Rev. J. Edwin Reding.
,, 25th	"The Seven Lamps" (Lantern Lecture). Lecturer: Miss L. L. Moxey. Chairman: Mr. D. Flint *(Collection for N.C.H.O.)*
Dec. 2nd	"An Anthology of Beautiful Thoughts." Chairman: Mr. E. Coles. Members.
,, 11th	Discussion. Members.
,, 16th	Xmas Party. Social Committee.
,, 23rd	Carolling.
,, 30th	"India and Irak." Lantern Lecture. Lecturer: Rev. A. Jones. *(Collection for Home Missions)*

NOTE:-Annual Lord Mayor's Banquet, Fri., Nov. 13th.

Meetings held in Methodist Schoolroom on Wednesdays, at 7.45 p.m.

Date, 1937.	*Subject.*
Jan. 6th	"Spheres of Christ" Readings by Members. Chairman: Mr. G. Taylor.
,, 13th	"Stories of the East End" Speaker: Rev. B. C. Harris. Chairman: Mr. Miller. *(Collection for London Mission)*
,, 20th	Wireless Evening Members. Chairman: Mr. Stanley Pratt.
,, 27th	Visit of North Watford Choir. Chairman: Mr. W. Dunn.
Feb. 3rd	"A Portrait Gallery of Pilgrims." Speaker: Mrs. Brown. Chairman: Mrs. Kimpton.
,, 10th	"The Naturalness of the Supernatural." Speaker: Rev. G. F. W. Knifton. Chairman: Mr. B. Taylor.
,, 17th	Visit of Kings Langley Guild.
,, 24th	"Worship" Speaker: Mr. L. Huddy. Chairman: Mr. Waites.
Mar. 3rd	"China" (Overseas Mission) Speaker: Rev. H. B. Sutton. Chairman: Mr. J. R. Gale.
,, 10th	Visit to Hemel Hempstead. Chairman: Mr. E. Coles.
,, 17th	"Round-about Jerusalem & the Sea of Galilee" Speaker: Rev. A. S. Hallah. M.C. Chairman: Mr. C. J. Botwright. *(Collection for Timberlake Memorial)*
,, 24th	"Wilson of the Antactic." Speaker: Mrs. B. Flint. Chairman: Mr. G. Dunn.
,, 31st	Gents' Evening. Bachelors and otherwise.
Apr. 7th	"Say it with Music" Mr. W. Dunn.
,, 14th	Closing Social. Social Committee.
,, 21st	General Meeting.

Secretaries : Mrs. B. Flint, Miss I. Flint.

This Syllabus for 1936-1937 was printed inside the Abbots Langley Wesley Guild annual membership card; it is reproduced from Jack Botwright's membership card which was kept by Mabel Botwright. Annie (Mrs Kimpton) chaired the Wesley Guild meeting on 3 February 1937, not long before setting sail for Canada on 7 May 1937. Note the coming annual Lord Mayor's Banquet for 1936 and the many names that have been referred to before:

> *The Rev A (Alfred) Jones; The Rev B (Benjamin) C Harris; Mr C (Charlie) Miller; Mr C J (Jack) Botwright; Mrs B (Marion) Flint; Mr Stanley Pratt; Mr W (Billy) Dunn; Mrs Brown; Mr J R Gale; Mr G (George) Dunn; and Miss I (Ivy) Flint.*

And some other chapelgoers, not previously mentioned:

- *Mr W (Wilf) Flegg came from Norfolk and worked at Leavesden Asylum; he and his wife, Doreen, lived at Holcumbeech, Bell Lane, Bedmond, which was built for them;*
- *Mr D (Don) Flint (son of George and Edie Flint and brother of Harold Flint and Nora Dunn) who served as a navigator in the RAF in the Second World War and emigrated to Australia in the late 1940's, with his wife Peggy née Boley;*
- *Mr E (Ted) Coles who lived in Marlin Square; he was given the pseudonym "Admiral Sir Crysastor Gardener" at the 1932 Lord Mayor's Banquet because of his hobby;*
- *Mr G (George) Taylor who also came from Norfolk and worked at Leavesden Asylum;*
- *Mr B (Ben) Taylor (brother of George) from Norfolk who also worked at Leavesden Asylum.*

LORD MAYOR'S BANQUET 1936.

TOAST LIST.

THE KING.		
THE RETIRING LORD MAYOR.	Proposer	LORD C. HARIS LORT. O.N.
	Reply	The Late Lord Mayor....LORD C.H.R'ISTOF ERSTOW, N.E.
THE TOWN PLANNING COMMITTEE	Proposer	SIR F. REDASTA, I.R.E.
	Reply	LORD W. I. LE'HEY.
THE S.P.C.K.	Proposer	VISCOUNT C. HARLE CHAP, Lin.
	Reply	LADY G.R.E. TAGAR, B.O.
THE LOCAL PLAYING FIELD ASSOCIATION	Proposer	ADMIRAL C.L.ORDHULBE, R.T.
	Reply	MAJOR S.T.VENKIN GHAUL, M.C.C
THE LORD MAYOR and LADY MAYORESS	Proposer	HIS EXCELLENCY U.N.CLEMAK, N.W.
	Reply	THE LORD MAYOR..LORD R.O.NALDOLE, M.A.N.
THE SOCIETY OF FRIENDS	Proposer	SIR T. O'.MIHAND, L.E.
	Reply	RT. HON. H. E. N. RIHALLS GEST.
THE GIRLS FRIENDLY SOCIETY	Proposer	LORD ST. A. INSLESTEP, H.E.N.
	Reply	MARCHIONESS L. C. C. ARLIS, L.E.

TOASTMASTER SIGNOR USGEORGI PLANK.

The Toast List for the 1936 Lord Mayor's Banquet at the Wesley Guild in Abbots Langley. This was the last Banquet attended by Annie Kimpton. The celebrities - and the "stand-ins" - recorded by Jack Botwright on his copy of the Toast List were:

Film Actor:	*Charles Laughton*	-
Radio Music Presenter:	*Christopher Stone*	-
Film Dancer:	*Fred Astaire*	-
Film Comedian:	*Will Hay*	-
Film Actor:	*Charlie Chaplin*	*[Bert Flint]*
Film Star:	*Greta Garbo*	*[Annie Kimpton]*
Film Comedian:	*Claude Hulbert*	*[Ted Coles]*
Radio Broadcaster:	*Stephen King-Hall*	*[George Dunn]*
Children's Hour Broadcaster:	*Uncle Mac (Derek McCulloch)*	-
Film Star:	*Ronald Coleman*	-
Radio Comedian:	*Tommy Handley*	-
Dance-Band Leader:	*Henry Hall*	*[Mr J R Gale]*
Radio Comedian:	*Stainless Stephen (Arthur Clifford)*	*[George Taylor]*
Radio Singer:	*Elsie Carlisle*	*[Mrs George Flint]*
Music Hall Artist:	*Wee Georgie Wood*	*[Stan Pratt]*

Lord Mayor on 5 November 1937 (a change of date from the programme). Jack was probably commenting on local controversy about the lack of street lighting. Leslie Hore-Belisha, Minister of Transport 1934-1937, had introduced Belisha beacons in 1934 but they would not come to Abbots Langley until the 1970's:

> "IN ACCEPTING THE OFFICE OF MAYOR OF THE ANCIENT BOROUGH OF CHAPEL ALLEY, I DO SOLEMNLY DELCARE, NAMELY AND TO WIT, THAT I WILL AT ALL TIMES UPHOLD THE RIGHTS AND PRIVILEGES OF THE BURGESSES TO WALK IN THE MIDDLE OF THE ROAD, CYCLE ON THE FOOTPATHS, EXERCISE THEIR CHILDREN ON THE TENNIS COURTS, GROW CABBAGES ROUND THE PUBLIC BUILDINGS AND DO ALL MANNER OF THINGS AS HERETOFORE AND NOTWITHSTANDING.
>
> I WILL MAINTAIN IN A CLEAN AND RECOGNISABLE CONDITION THE BELISHA BEACONS IN THE HIGH STREET.
>
> ANY PERSON FINDING A STREET LAMP AND DULY REPORTING THE SAME TO THE RIGHT DEPARTMENT WILL BE APPOINTED CAPTAIN OF THE FIRE BRIGADE.
>
> AS CHIEF MAGISTRATE I WILL ADMINISTER JUSTICE AT REASONABLE RATES, SPECIAL TERMS TO REGULAR CLIENTS. MOTORISTS CHARGED WITH ANY OF THE 5728 OFFENCES ON SALE, WILL BE ALLOWED 5 PER CENT FOR PROMPT PAYMENT, THE FREE USE OF THE BOROUGH STARTING HANDLE AND ONE GALLON OF PETROL TO REMOVE THE STAINS FROM THEIR LICENCES.
>
> THIS I DO PROMISE, PROVIDING I AM FORTHWITH AND WITHOUT PREJUDICE, IPSO FACTO OR MALICE AFORETHOUGHT, GIVEN A GOOD SQUARE MEAL."
>
> *Proclamation read when installed as Lord Mayor, C J Botwright, Nov 5th, 1937*

In *The Abbots Langley Wesley Guild Magazine 1931-1936,* under "Childrens Corner - Nursey Rhymes for Guilders" and "Who's Who", there were rhymes and limericks. Their author is not named but it was probably Marion Flint. The Guilders' identities can be deduced and some have been mentioned in Annie's letters:

Dickory, dickory dock
This lady has no clock,
And sure as fate
If she's not late,
She gives everybody a shock.
[*Annie Kimpton*]

★

A person once said with concern,
"I really don't know where to turn,
I've my wireless and bees
And my dear wife to please
And my encyclopedia to learn".
[*George Flint*]

A genial person named Coles
Said, "I really must start to dig holes!
My seeds I must dust
Or they'll never bust,"
Quoth that genial person names Coles.
[*Ted Coles*]

★

Bertie, Bertie up so far
How I wonder what you are,
Up above us, Oh so high
Like a pylon in the sky.
[*Bert Flint*]

Marie, Marie
So Soprani,
How do your high notes go?
Like Silver Bells
When I sing of Wales,
And my, ain folk long ago.
[*Marie Kimpton*]

There was a little man
And he had a little choir,
And he wagged his little stick to and fro, fro, fro.
And he said if they can't sing
When I've had my little fling,
I'll stand upon a wall and I'll crow, crow, crow.
[*Billy Dunn*]

⋆

There were once two mischievous boys
Who delighted in making a noise,
They said you've no notion
What kind of commotion
We'd make if we weren't such good boys.

[*Basil and Bernard Funnell*]

There was once a young person called Fred
Who was daring enough to get wed,
When he said, "Here's my Flora,
Oh, how I adore her!"
"Why, where? - We can't see her," they said.

[*Fred and Flora Botwright. Flora was very small. This limerick was read at her funeral at the age of 94 in the Abbots Langley Methodist church on 15 October 1998 - to the delight of all her family.*]

⋆

Until the late 1940's, the Wesley Guild provided the social life for chapel people and the opportunity for youngsters to further their courting. In the 1940's, a Youth Club and, subsequently, a Young Wives' Club deprived it of young blood. The Methodist Guild (as it was renamed) became the province of the older men where they played table tennis and chin-wagged. The advent of television led to its final demise at Abbots Langley Methodist Church. Another of Marion Flint's rhymes in *The Wesley Guild Magazine 1931-1936,* summed it up:

Sing a song of Guilders
Nearly sixty strong,
When there is a Banquet
How they flock along,
When there's something highbrow,
Or a rainy day,
Or the wireless calls them,
How they stay away.

⋆ ⋆ ⋆

IV : ANNIE'S ABBOTS LANGLEY
with Maps, 1867-1938

ABBOTS LANGLEY is in Hertfordshire about three miles north of Watford. The name of the village derives from AD1045 when a Saxon thegn, Ethelwine the Black, and his wife, Wynfleda, gave "Langelei Abbatis" (which is the name recorded in the Domesday Book in 1086) to the Abbot and monks of the Abbey at St Albans. The village then had 19 families, a priest, 300 swine and two water mills for grinding corn in the Gade Valley - one at Nash Mills ("Assemille") and another at Apsley. Henry VIII took Abbots Langley away from the Abbey in 1539. The same Saxon, recorded as Aegelwine le Swarte, also gave the water mills of Redbourn, Hertfordshire, to St Albans Abbey. The two mills at Abbots Langley were converted to paper-making in the eighteenth century and bought by John Dickinson in the early nineteenth century. Several members of the Hawkins family were millers at one of the Redbourn water mills, Redbournbury Mill. Probably they were related to Ben Hawkins (Senior) who came from Redbourn, which is about 6 miles north-west of Abbots Langley.

In 1868 when the Estate of Sarah Smith was sold, her farm stood adjacent to the Abbots House and a pond stood on the site of the old Bricklayers Arms. An Elizabethan barn, The Old Maltings (now a cottage) and an oasthouse which belonged to Sarah Smith's farm still survive behind the present-day High Street shops. The Declaration, The First Schedule and the Plan given in the Abstract of the Title of the BRITISH LAND COMPANY to Sarah Smith's estate are reproduced at the end of this Appendix.

When Matthew Timberlake brought his family to the village in 1872, the population of the parish was around 2,500. By 1937 when Annie Kimpton left for Canada it would have been nearer 6,000. When Annie first lived in Adrian Road (named after Nicholas Breakspear, Pope Adrian IV, who was born in the parish of Abbots Langley) the High Street cottages stretched from Langley House to the Kings Head on the eastern side. On the other side they extended from the Abbots House to the Bricklayers Arms though these were newly built on Sarah Smith's former farm. Before the construction of the Wesleyan Methodist chapel in 1881, Matthew Timberlake preached from 1874 on Chapel Green. At one time, the landlord of the Bricklayers Arms on the High Street offered a room - and some Sunday services were held there. Adrian Road, Breakspear Road, Garden Road, Popes Road and Abbots Road had been laid out by the BRITISH LAND COMPANY but very few houses had been built on them. Building plots were auctioned off and houses were constructed by the local builders.

Construction of the Leavesden Asylum and the St Pancras Industrial Schools brought an influx of families from the surrounding villages. Many of the families were already related and new relationships blossomed. Charlotte Dollemore who married Harry Flint and Emily Dollemore (the sister of Charlotte Dollemore) who married Reuben Flint, both came from Redbourn. Arthur (Reuben Arthur) Flint said that his father, Old Reuben, used to walk to Redbourn and back from Abbots Langley when he was courting. In Abbots Langley in the 1890's there were the interrelated families of the three Flint brothers, the two Gomme brothers from Bledlow, the two Gates sisters from Astrope, and Harry Dollemore from Redbourn - probably a brother of the Dollemore sisters who married two of the Flint brothers. There were probably many more similar links in this new community. And then, in the early 1900's, the attractions and opportunities of the New World led to the emigration of several generations of three out of these eight families. Probably many other villagers emigrated too.

By 1937 only The Crescent was lit, a few lamps having been installed by the house builder. But in earlier days, the High Street of Abbots Langley was bathed in gaslight on winter evenings from at least nine lamps. In 1870 the owner of Cecil Lodge had a gas pipe laid from the gasworks at Hunton Bridge to light his house. The Parish Council and some private owners were permitted to tap this main. By 1916, there was a lamppost at the schools' entrance; a lantern hung from a bracket on the builders' shop next to George Simons the butcher; a lantern hung from a bracket on the Rose and Crown; there was a very ornamental lamppost at the entrance to the Vicarage Drive; a large lantern hung from a bracket on the Abbots Langley Supply Stores (later Dazely's); there was a lamppost at the Village Hall; another on the corner of Abbots Road oposite Chapel Green; another at the corner of Adrian Road; and another on Kitters Green. Except for the one at the school (removed when the War Memorial was built) and the one opposite Chapel Green, these can be seen in the old photographs in *Abbots Langley, A Hertfordshire Village* by Scott Hastie. Fred Dobson (now an antique dealer at his father's old barbers' shop, 53 High Street), remembers that as a boy he climbed up the lamppost on Kitters Green. By the 1920's none of these were functioning because of the unwillingness of the private owners or the Rate payers to fund them. Electric street lighting did not arrive until the 1950's.

The expansion of Abbots Langley from 1867 to 1938 is shown at the end of this Appendix by the reproduction of extracts from the Ordnance Survey maps. In 1937 the way to the village from King's Langley and Abbots Langley Station (as it was named then) led under the railway bridge and past the Booksellers' Retreat (where Flora Botwright was born in 1904) and up Gallows Hill Lane to its junction with Hazelwood Lane. Hazelgrove Farm, where Mrs Aves lived, was sited here together with Hazelgrove Cottages (once the home of Mrs Turner and her daughter, Muriel) which still exist though they are now sited on Kindersley Way. Further up the lane was Kitters Green opposite the Manor House. On one corner of Kitters Green (at the end of Garden Road) stood the village laundry behind Yew Tree cottage which had washing-lines on the Green. This cottage was formerly part of Sarah Smith's Estate and Sue Simons née Collins lived at Yew Tree cottage before she married George Simons the butcher. The first turning on the right, past Kitters Green, was Adrian Road where Annie lived. Opposite Adrian Road was Causeway House occupied by Mrs Iris Neish (whose meadow on the corner of Abbots Road was used for the Methodist Church Fête and also by visiting fairgrounds). At the cross roads, facing Chapel Green was the Methodist chapel and the schoolroom.

As a dressmaker, Annie Kimpton would have made frequent visits to William Hill's Drapery, Clothing and Boot Store at 12 High Street, near the Abbots House. The propri-

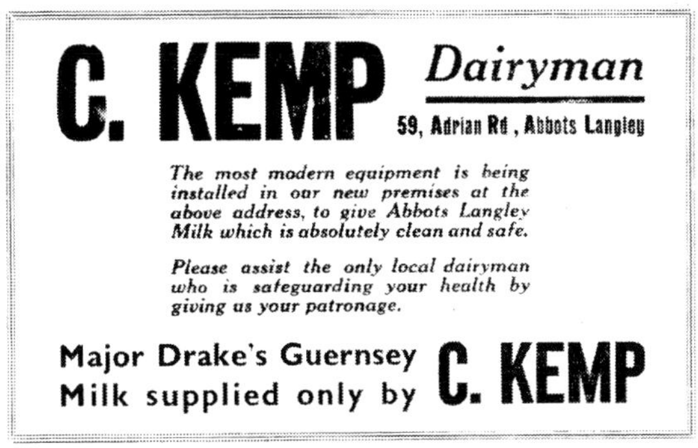

An advert from the 1937 Methodist Church Fête programme. Major J H Drake (who liked to sport a Golden Hind ensign on his car) was the last resident of the Manor House from 1922 to 1938. The Manor Farm has since been built upon but the Manor grounds became the cricket field and open space for Abbots Langley.

was Miss E H Honess who dispensed packets of pins as an alternative to a farthing change (when prices were quoted at one farthing short of a round shilling). Annie would also go to George Simons the butcher for fresh meat (killed on the premises) because they were related by marriage.

Over the years, there were a series of local builders with yards who all built houses in the village: Homer Busby in the High Street next to the old Kings Head; Joseph Chalk at the crossroads who sold part of his land to the Wesleyan Methodists; Teddy (Edwin) Glenister in Adrian Road opposite Annie's home; Bill Buckoke in Breakspear Road; and FLINT BROTHERS in Marlin Square.

There were ponds in the village - one opposite the Cricket Meadow, another in the school playing field and several in the grounds of Cecil Lodge and Langley House. The meadow lands between Trowley Rise and Greenways (belonging to Arthur Flint) and between Trowley Rise and Tanners Hill were open space for children to play in. The half-demolished Cecil Lodge with its overgrown grounds and Cog Dell were for the adventurous to explore. When snow fell, the slopes now occupied by Kindersley Way could be reached from Causeway Alley and were used by children for sledging.

Before the First World War the roads were unsurfaced. By 1937 there was a frequent local bus service to Watford and Hemel Hempstead; and a Green Line bus left the centre of the village every hour to London. By 1937 many more villagers were commuting daily by rail to London. Nevertheless, it was an enormous step that Annie Kimpton took in May 1937, aged nearly 66, to go alone across the Atlantic Ocean to Canada; and then take two trains a further 3,600 miles across the United States to San Francisco to see her son. She certainly went a long way.

★

The Abstract of the Title of the BRITISH LAND COMPANY to Freehold land situated at Abbots Langley dated 1867 was a 23-leaf document prepared by Russell and Davies, Solicitors, and a copy is in the possession of the Flint family. It includes details of the land inherited in 1797 by Thomas Smith, Mealman, from his uncle, John Smith, in the Manor of Abbots Langley alias Lees Langley. It also has details of the subsequent inheritance of this land by Sarah Smith upon the death of her husband, Thomas Smith, in 1805. Curiously it includes this Declaration, dated March 14, 1867; perhaps Sarah Smith's paper title to ownership was thought not sufficient:

***Declaration** of William Easy of Hemel Hempstead County of Hertford, Tailor, as follows–*

> *"I am seventy-two years of age and was born at Abbots Langley Herts and resided there till I was twenty-two years of age. My father was a Baker there and I assisted him with his trade and used to go out with his cart and deliver the bread to his customers. After I left Abbots Langley I went to reside in the adjoining Parish of Hemel Hempstead where I lived for about ten years and then went to live at Leverstock Green which is about two miles form Abbots Langley where I resided about six years and then returned to Hemel Hempstead where I have resided ever since. I have never lived more than five miles from Abbots Langley and I have always kept up my acquaintance with Abbots Langley and its inhabitants by going there at different times every year and for two years during my residence at Leverstock Green I used to go to Abbots Langley every Sunday to conduct the Sunday School there under the Vicar. From my earliest days down to the time of her death I knew and was acquainted with Mrs Sarah Smith late of Abbots Langley aforesaid Widow who died there on the 6th day of August last. I was in the habit of calling upon her at different times when I went to Abbots Langley and she occasionally used to make me stop and dine with her. I also recollect her husband Mr Thomas Smith who died when I was about ten years old. From the time of his death the said Sarah Smith resided in the house near the Church at Abbots Langley aforesaid where she died and which house is part of Lot 1 mentioned in the Particulars of Sale now produced to and marked by me and is numbered 1 in the Sale Plan annexed to said Particulars and she was always reputed and known to be the owner of said house and of all the farm and lands held therewith and of other cottages and premises at Kitters Green which farm and lands cottages and premises are particularly described in said Plan and Particulars under which said estate and properties were sold by auction at the Auction Mart London on the 19th day of November last in several lots. I knew said farm and lands cottages and premises well. Said Sarah Smith occupied and cultivated said farm and all the lands thereto belonging which are numbered 3, 4, 5, 6, 7, 8, 9, 10, 13 part of 15 and 16 and 17 from her said husband's death until she let them to Mr Benjamin Toovey the present occupier of the farm who has occupied the same for about 35 years now last past as tenant to said Sarah Smith. Said Sarah Smith from the time of her said husband's death was also always reputed and known to be the owner of the two cottages now in the respective occupations of John George Chalk and Mrs Brandom which formed part of her homestead and are numbered 2 on said Plan and of the two cottages and gardens on the respective occupations of Isaac Collins and Mrs Chandler which form part of number 15 on said Plan."*

***The First Schedule** referred to by abstracting Indenture—*

No on Plan	*Color on Plan*	*Names and Descriptions of Lands and Premises*	*State of Cultivation*	*Quantities in Statute Measure*			*Names of Tenants*
				a	*r*	*p*	
1	*Pink*	*Residence Gardens and Buildings*	—	0	2	14	*Unoccupied*
2	*Pink*	*Two Cottages and Gardens* - -	—	0	0	13	*John George Chalk* *Mrs Brandom*
3	*Pink*	*Farmstead Buildings and Malting*	—	0	1	3	*Benjamin Toovey*
4	*Pink*	*The Paddock* - - - - -	*Meadow*	11	2	30	*Ditto*
5	*Light Green*	*Church Dog Dell* - - - -	*Arable*	17	0	23	*Ditto*
6	*Yellow*	*Six Acres* - - - - - -	*Arable*	7	2	20	*Ditto*
7	*Dark Purple*	*Dell* - - - - - -	*Wood*	0	2	25	*Ditto*
8	*Light Purple*	*Twelve Acres* - - - - -	*Arable*	12	3	24	*Ditto*
9	*Light Brown*	*Seven Acres* - - - - -	*Arable*	7	0	23	*Ditto*
10	*Dark Green*	*Eight Acres and Bottom Fields* -	*Arable*	11	0	31	*Ditto*
11	*Light Blue*	*Maudlins or Marlins* - - - -	*Meadow*	8	3	33	*Ditto*
12	*Dark Blue*	*Two Cottages and Gardens* - -	—	0	0	19	*Isaac Collins* *Mrs Chandler*
13	*Brown*	*Land* - - - - - -	*Meadow*	2	1	38	*Benjamin Toovey*
14	*Red*	*Wood Barn and Garden Ground*	—	0	0	28	*Isaac Collins* *Mrs Chandler*
15	*Olive*	*Land* - - - - - -	*Meadow*	2	1	29	*Benjamin Toovey*
16	*Crimson*	*Land* - - - - - -	*Meadow*	2	3	3	*Ditto*
				86	1	10	

The First Schedule and its accompanying hand-coloured Plan (which is reproduced overleaf) indicates the lands bought by the BRITISH LAND COMPANY from Sarah Smith. The Abstract of the Title refers to the names by which these lands were known in Abbots Langley in 1867 and also to their former names when inherited by Thomas Smith from his uncle, John Smith, in 1797. It is not possible to correlate these former names precisely with the fields shown in the First Schedule:

The residence of Thomas Smith, which was also referred to as the farm house, was called The Great House (now the Abbots House);

Church Cogdell Field was formerly called Little Cogdell Field (of 7 acres);

The pastures called Home Mead and Roundabout (totalling 8 acres) were formerly called Roundabouts;

Rick Meadow (2 acres) was formerly called Long Slipe;

Marlins Meadow or Marlins Mead (4 acres) was formerly called Little Marlins or Little Marlings;

A field of 15 acres was formerly called Great Cogdell Field;

The field below Cogdell (6 acres) was formerly divided into Great Wood Field and Little Wood Field;

A field of 9 acres was called Great Gallows Field;

A field of 2 acres was called Little Gallows Field.

★

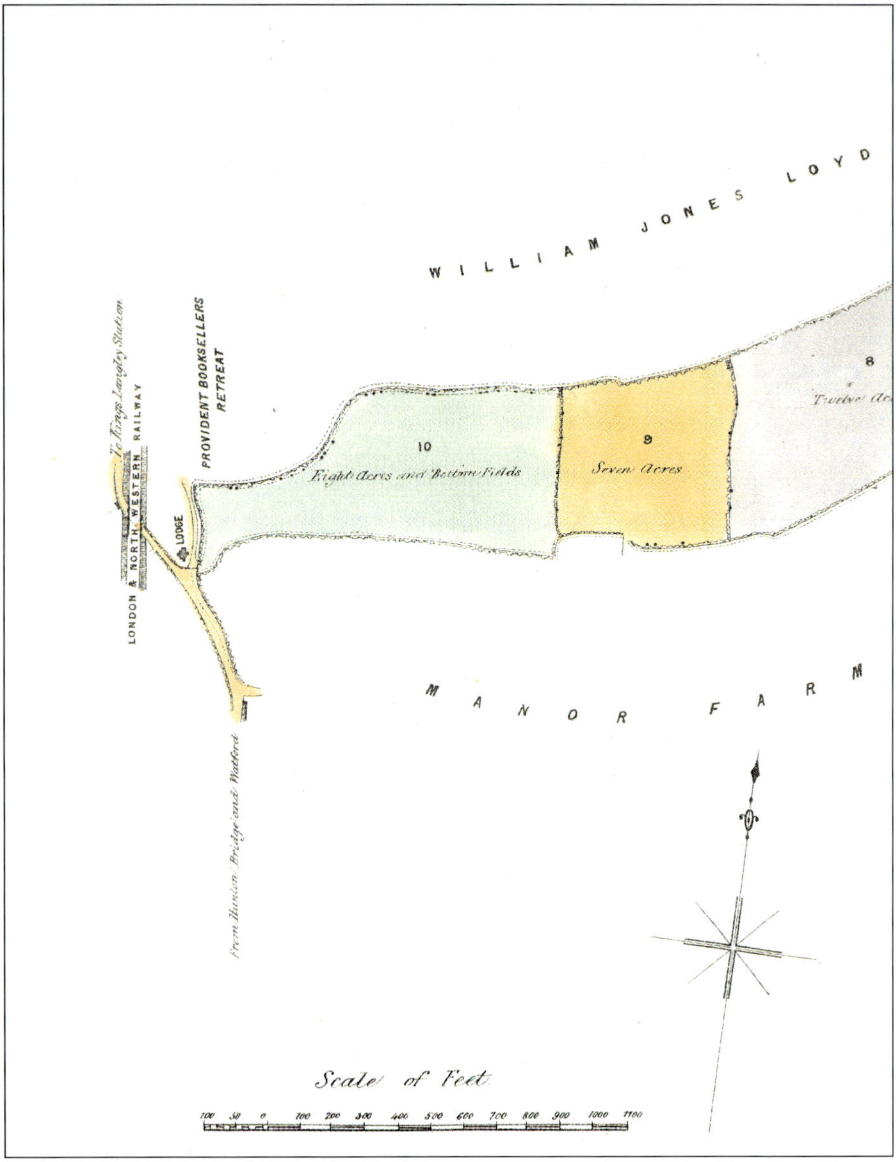

The layout of the roads of Abbots Langley and the later property boundaries were shaped by the former field pattern of Sarah Smith's land:

Abbots Road was threaded through the middle of fields 4, 5, 6, 8, 9 and 10. (Cog Dell, field 7, is the purple patch between fields 5 and 6.) Adrian Road (where Annie Kimpton's home of houses number 54 and 56 would be built) was laid down the middle of field 11. Breakspeare Road was laid through the middle of fields 13, 15, and 16. Garden Road was laid between fields 13 and 15. Popes Road was laid along the boundary of field 16. Lot 5 was sold to another purchaser who was given a right of way and was required to maintain a hard road along the strip of land coloured brown and marked

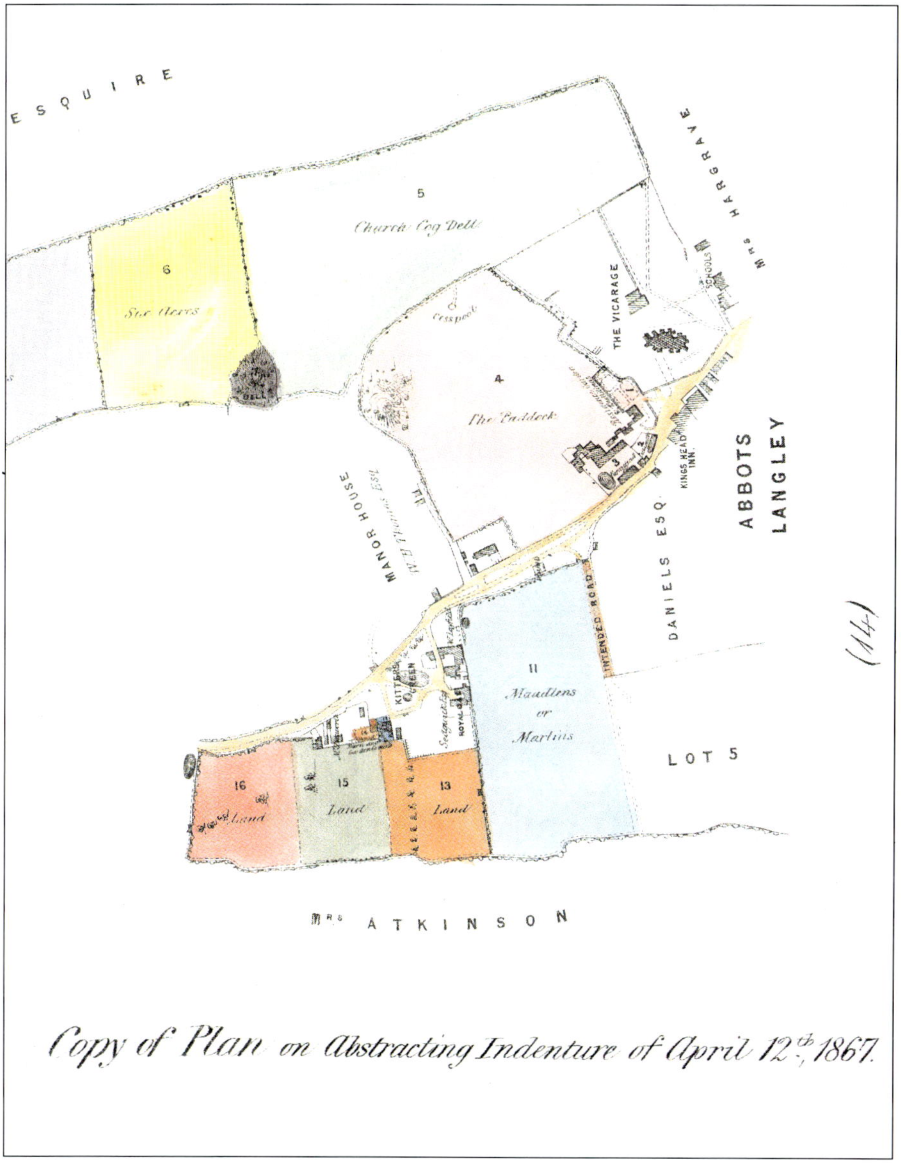

"intended road" which became Langley Road. Lot 5 later became Marlin Square which was the most compact way of developing this field. The spot marked "cesspool" in field 4 "The Paddock" which is now in the garden of Half Dome (the home of the publisher of this book) is one of the lowest points on the hilltop of Abbots Langley and still can flood on occasions.

The Plan of Sarah Smith's Estate at Abbots Langley included in the Abstract of the Title, 1867.

Note: The Plan is reproduced at two thirds of the original size and is shown divided into two parts; the title and the scale have been re-positioned.

Note: This map and the following maps are each shown divided into two parts.

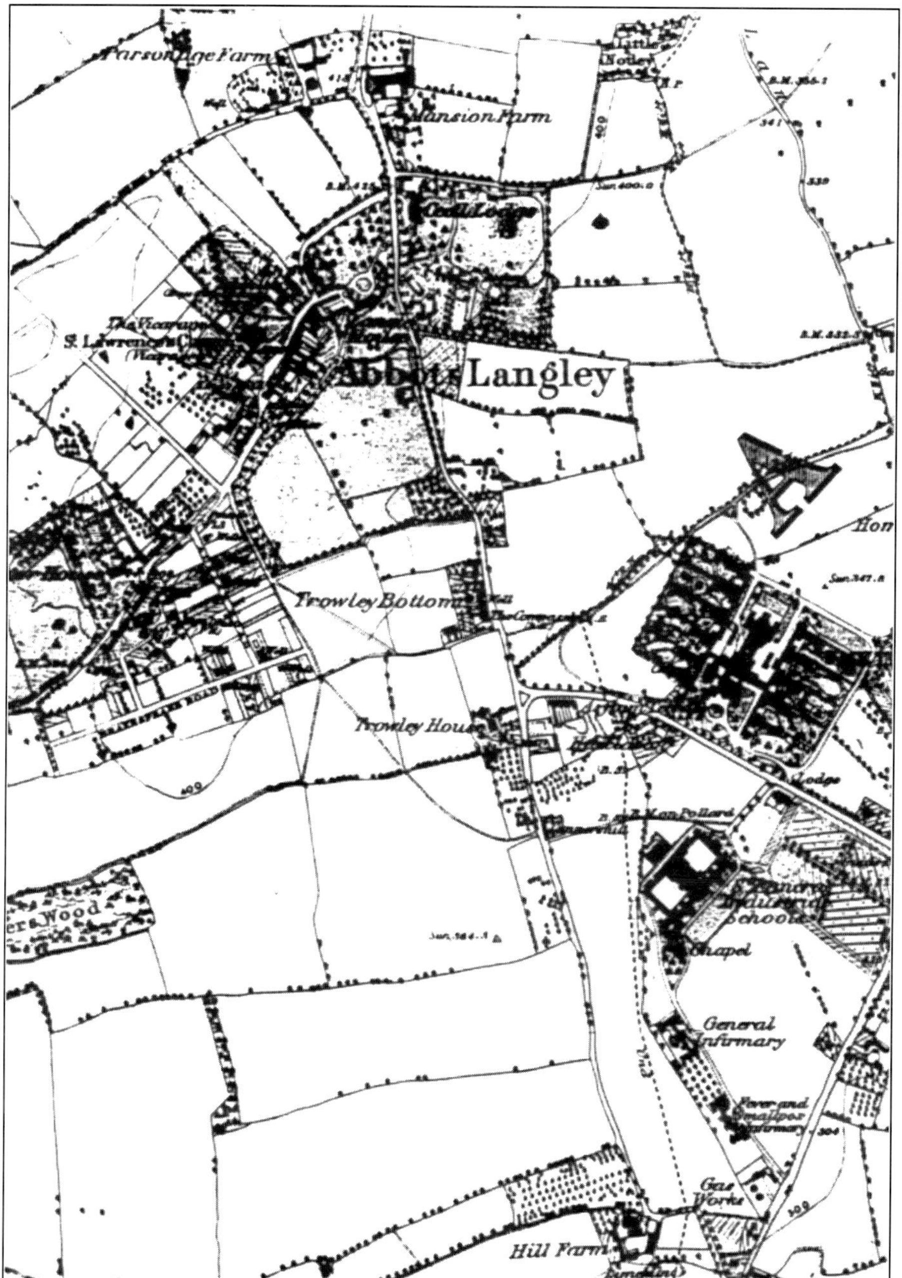

Ordnance Survey map of Abbots Langley in 1873, scale 6 inches to the mile or 1:10,560, reproduced true to scale from the HERTFORDSHIRE SHEET 39 NW: FIRST EDITION published 1883 (surveyed 1871-1873).

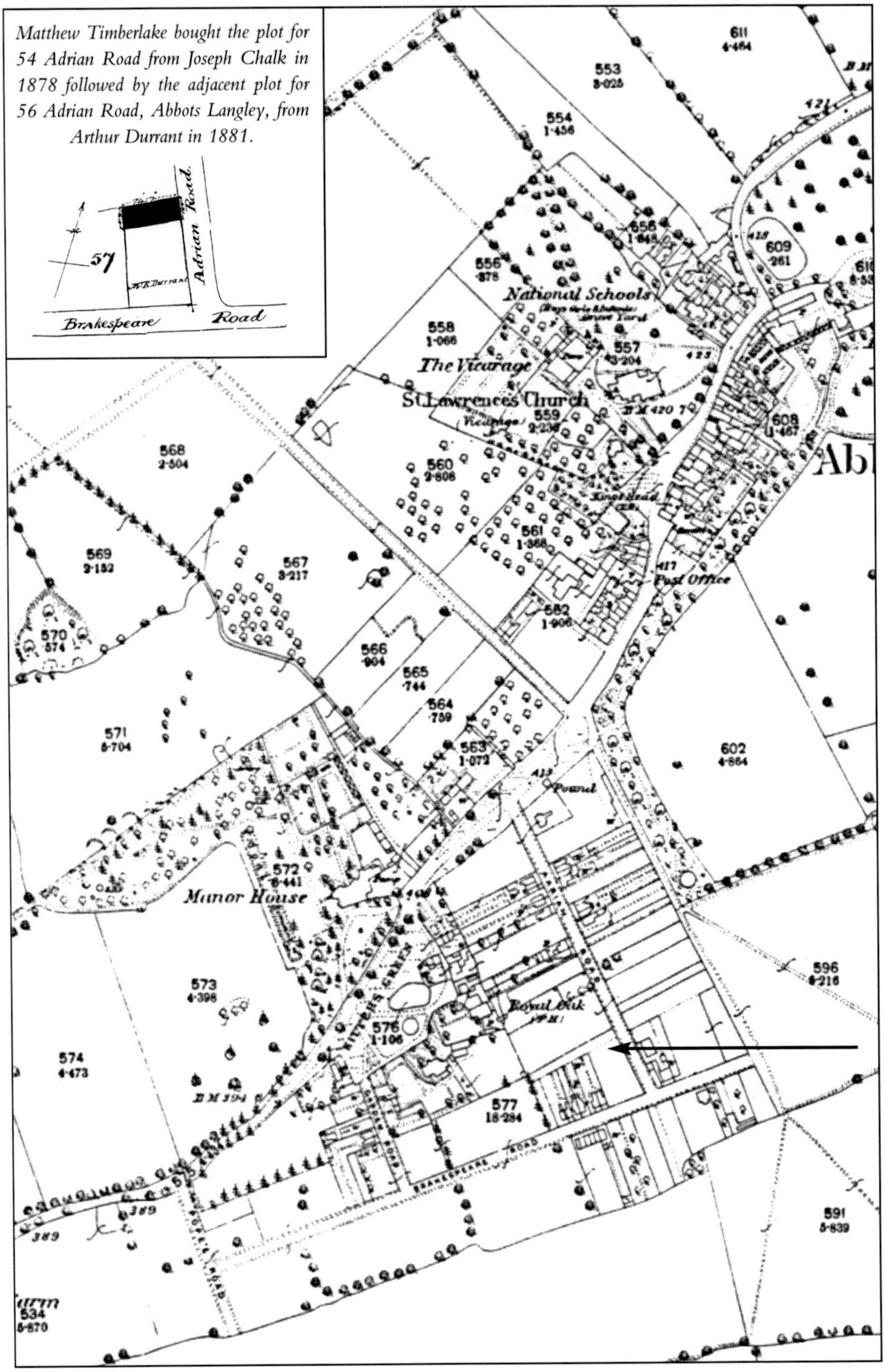

Matthew Timberlake bought the plot for 54 Adrian Road from Joseph Chalk in 1878 followed by the adjacent plot for 56 Adrian Road, Abbots Langley, from Arthur Durrant in 1881.

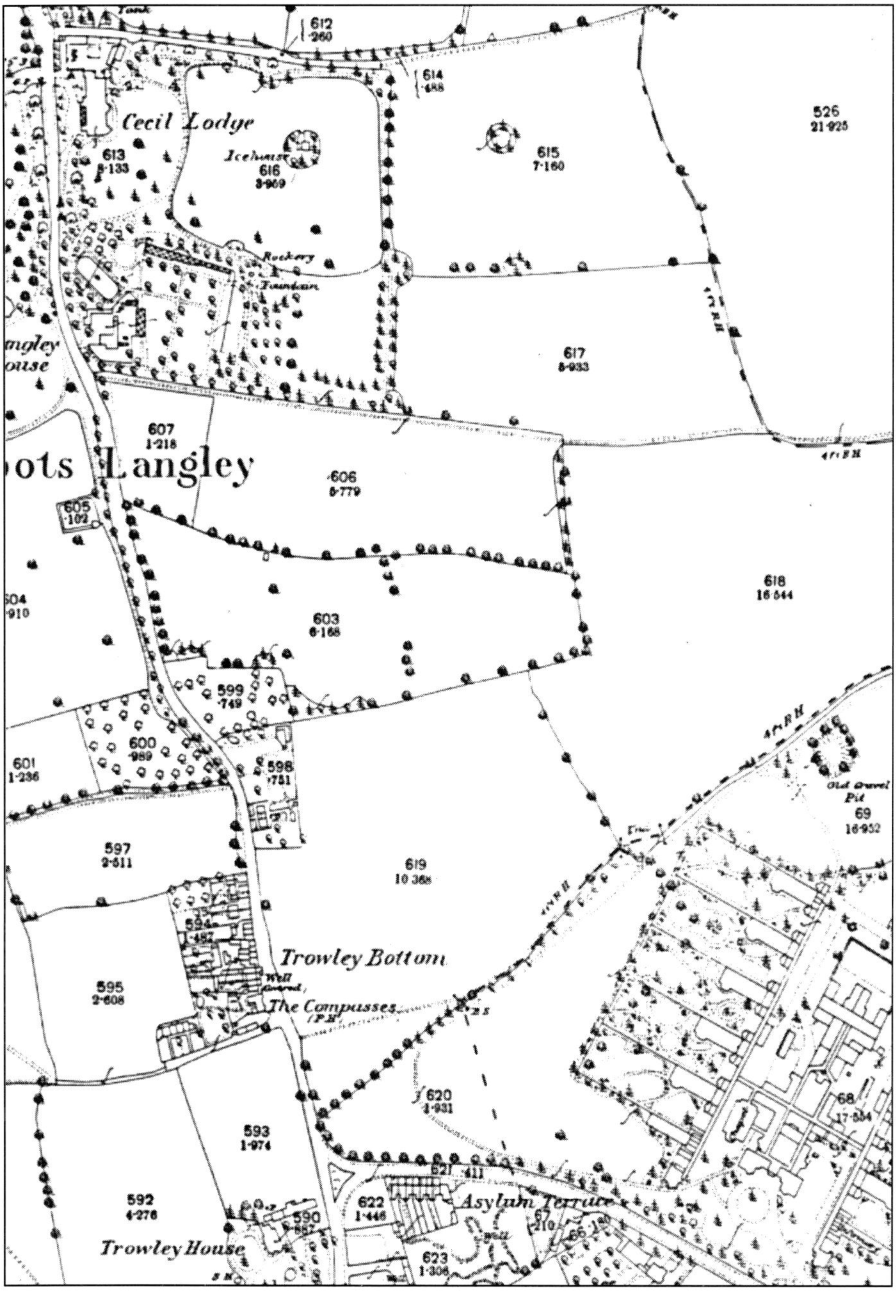

Ordnance Survey map of Abbots Langley in 1873, scale 25 inches to the mile or 1:2,500, reproduced at half size from the HERTFORDSHIRE SHEET 39.5: FIRST EDITION 1874 (surveyed 1871-1873).

Note: The arrow opposite indicates the location of the plot plan insert.

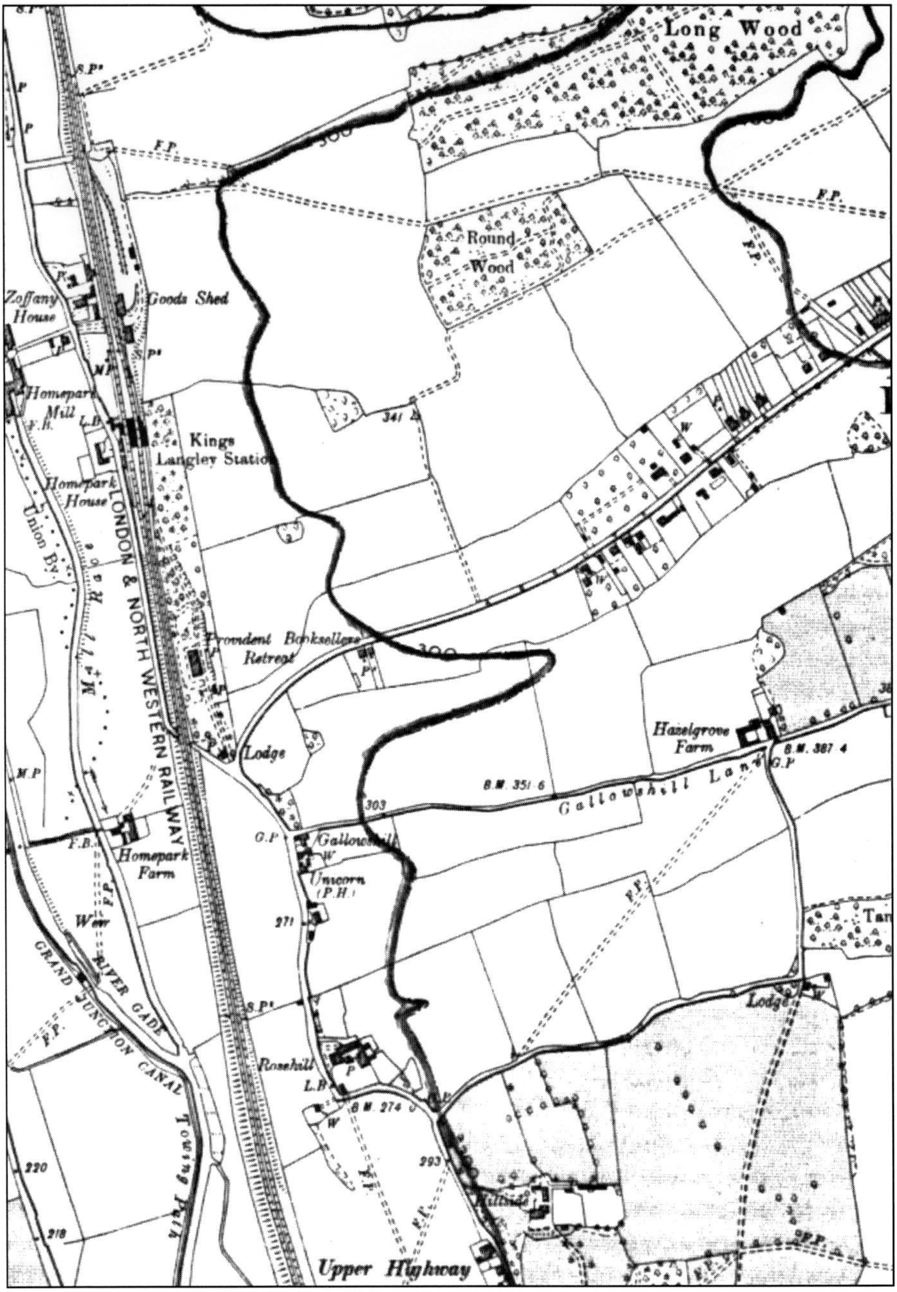

Note: The 300 and 400 foot contour lines have been outlined on this copy of the map.

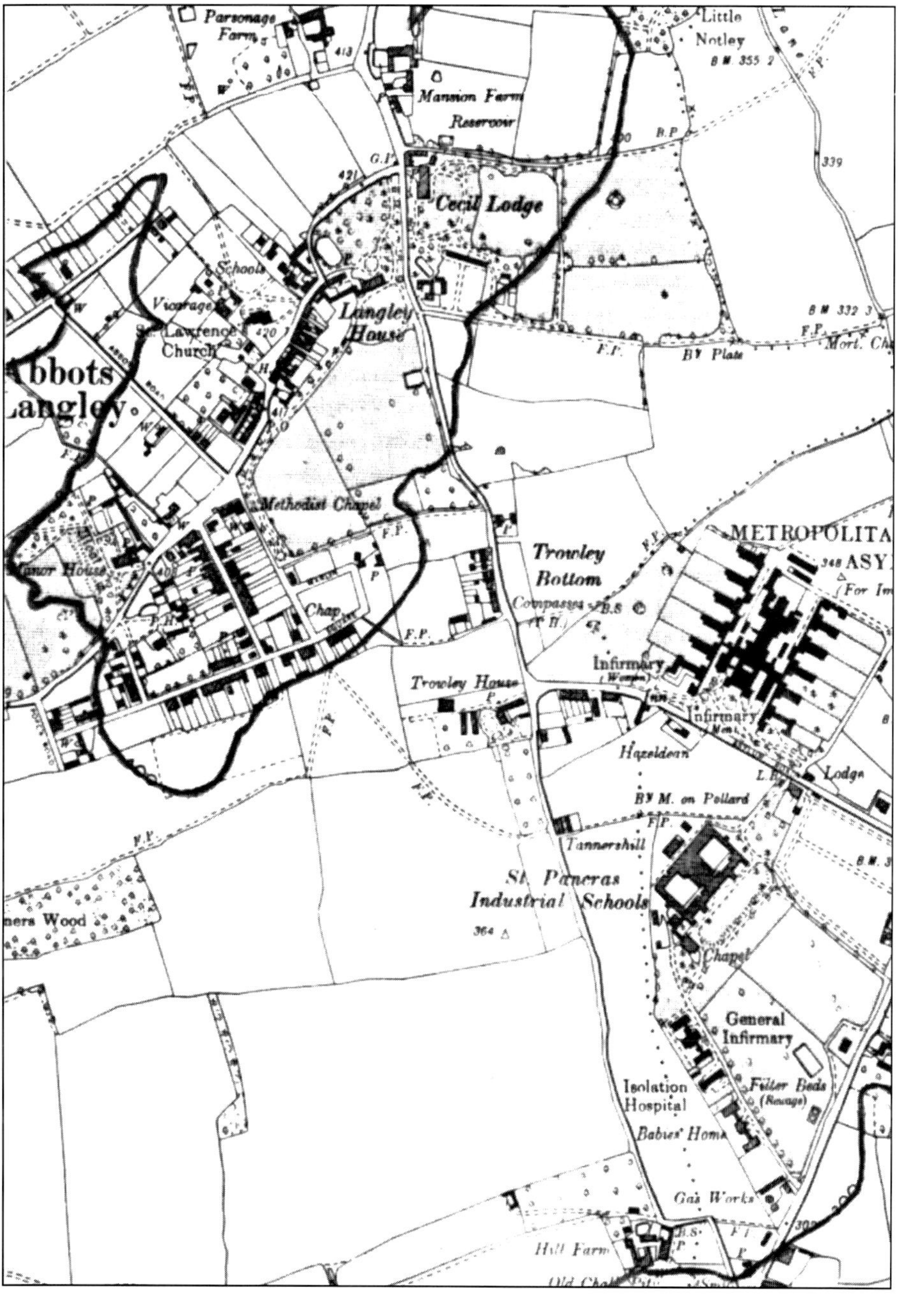

Ordnance Survey map of Abbots Langley in 1896, scale 6 inches to the mile or 1:10,560, reproduced true to scale from the HERTFORDSHIRE SHEET 39 NW: SECOND EDITION 1899 (revised in 1896).

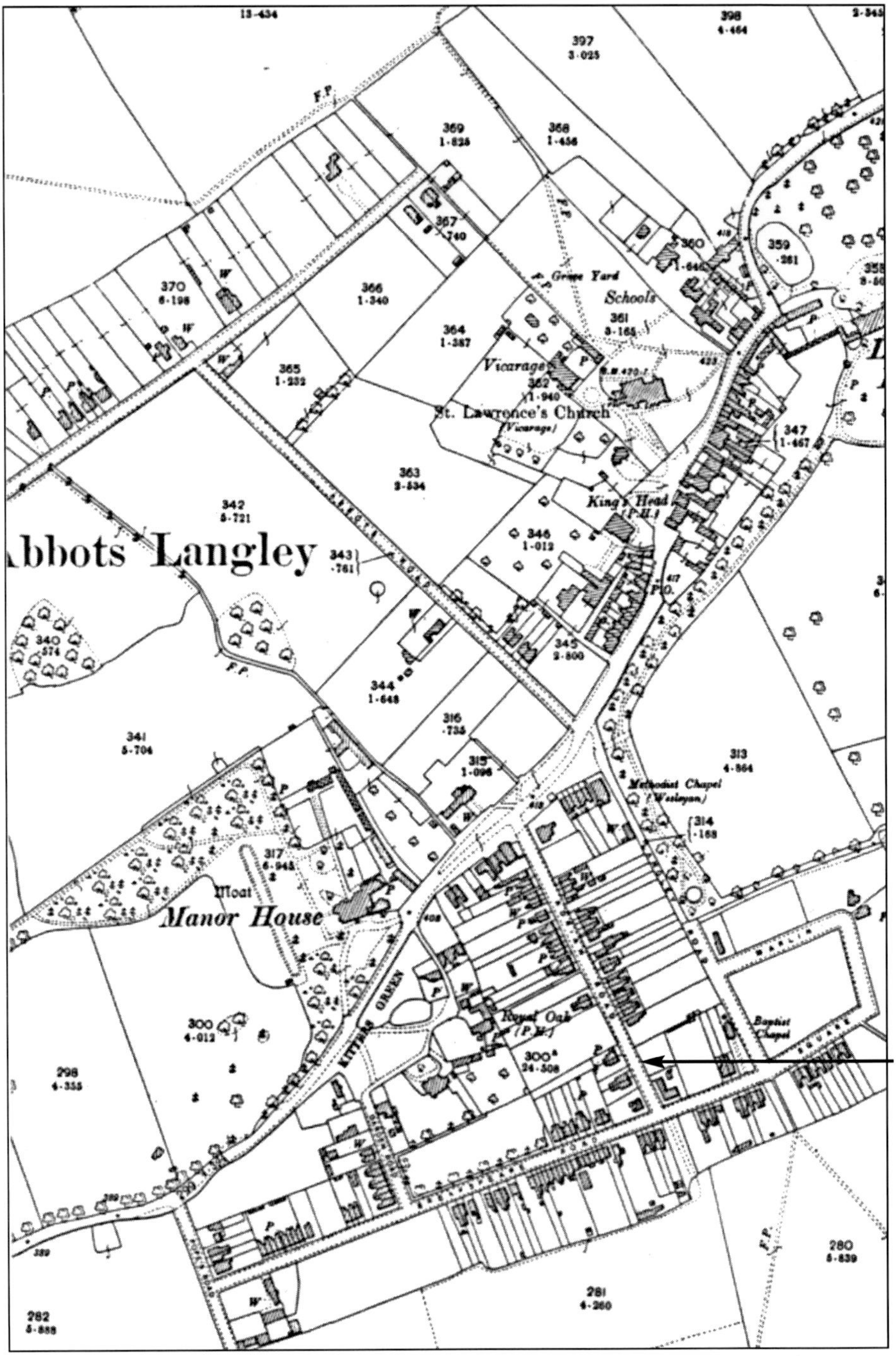

Note: The arrow above indicates Annie Kimpton's home, 54 & 56 Adrian Road, first shown on this edition.

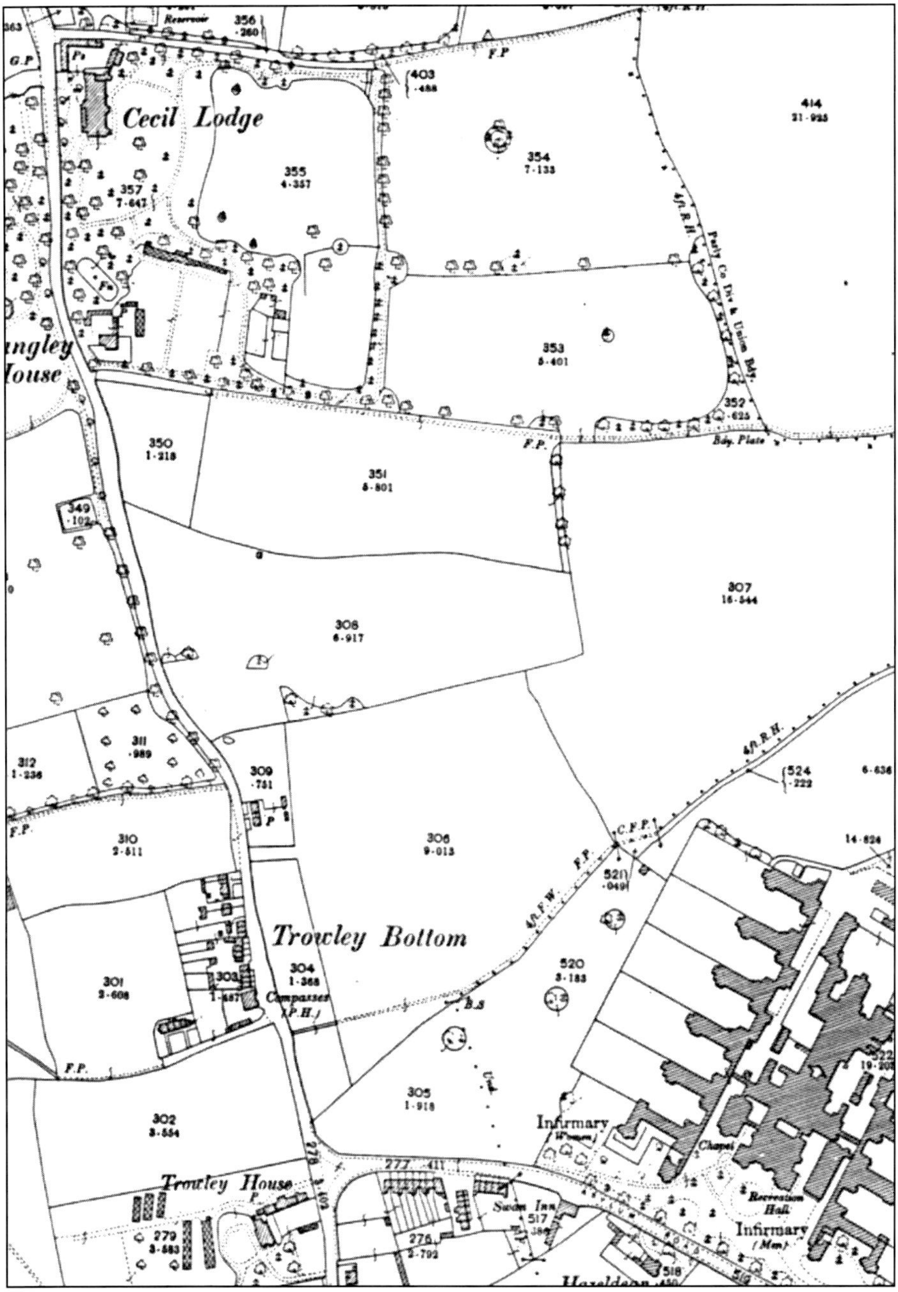

Ordnance Survey map of Abbots Langley in 1896, scale 25 inches to the mile or 1:2,500, reproduced at half size from the HERTFORDSHIRE SHEET 39.5: SECOND EDITION 1899 (revised in 1896).

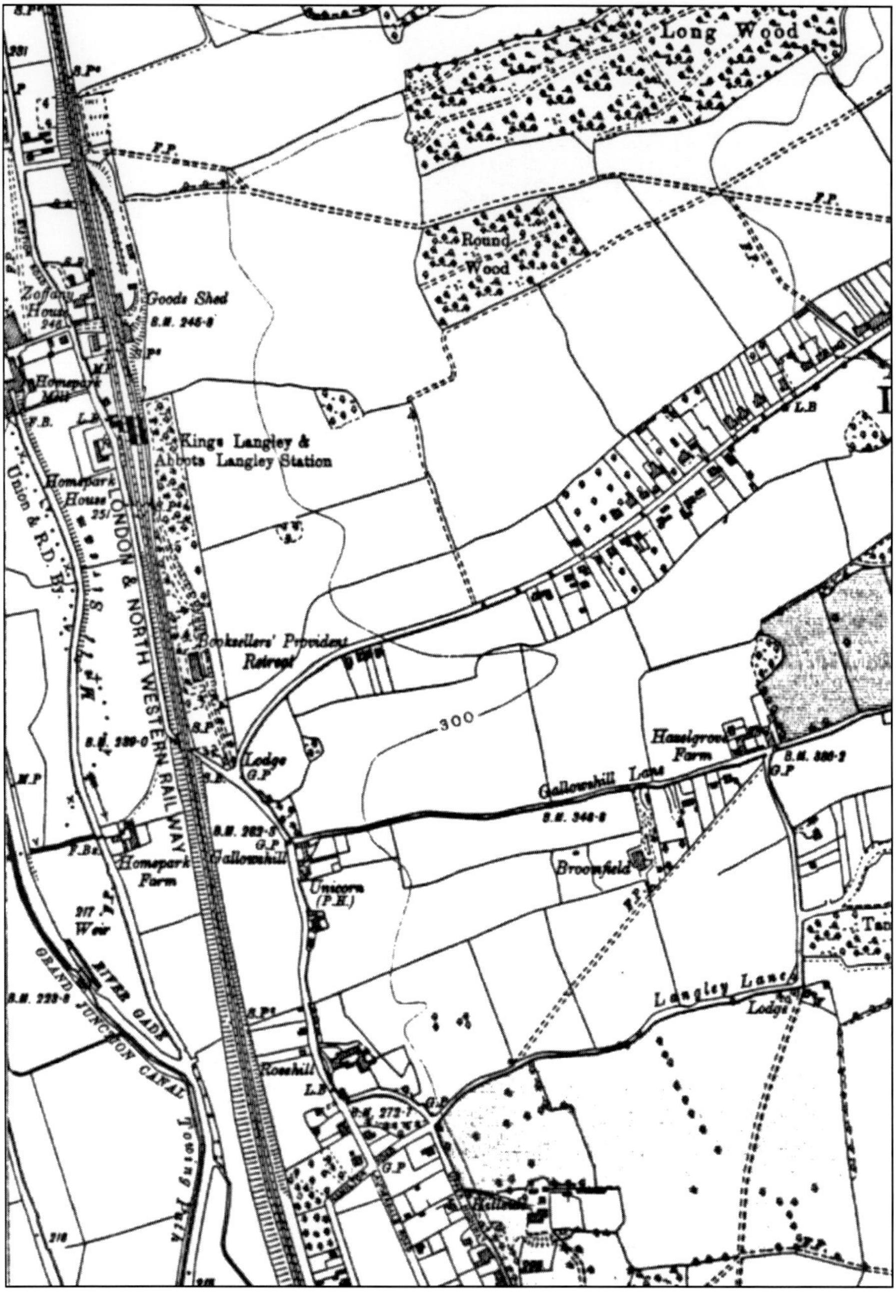
Long Wood
Round Wood
Goods Shed
Zoffany House
Homepark Mill
Kings Langley & Abbots Langley Station
Homepark House
Union & R.D. By.
LONDON & NORTH WESTERN RAILWAY
Booksellers' Provident Retreat
300
Lodge
Gallowshill Lane
Hazelgrove Farm
Broomfield
Gallowshill
Unicorn (P.H.)
Homepark Farm
Weir
RIVER GADE
GRAND JUNCTION CANAL
Towing Path
Langley Lane
Lodge
Rosehill

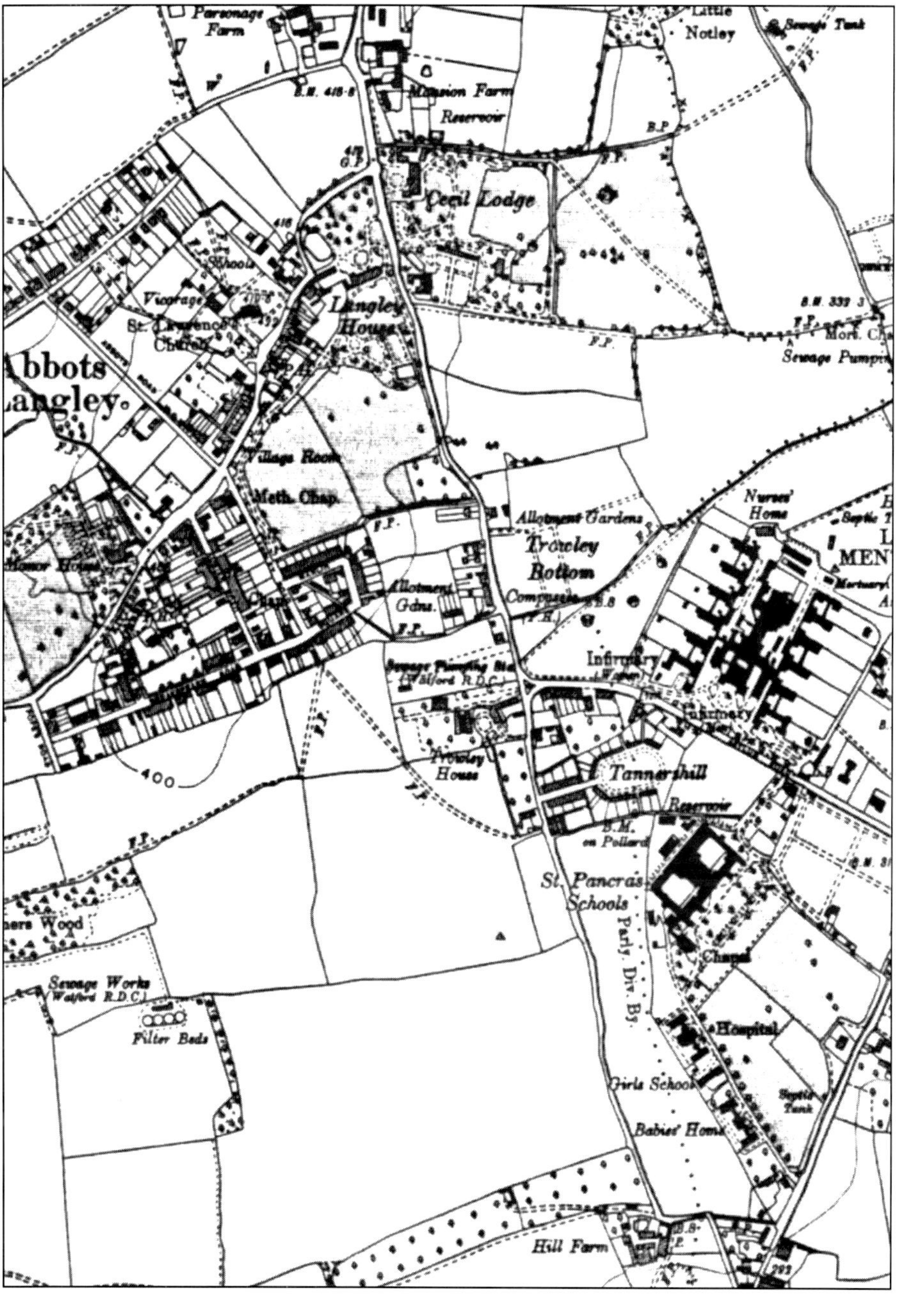

Ordnance Survey map of Abbots Langley in 1923, scale 6 inches to the mile or 1:10,560, reproduced true to scale from the HERTFORDSHIRE SHEET 39 NW: EDITION OF 1925 (revised in 1923).

Note: The National Grid lines which were added to this edition are not parallel to the edges of the map.

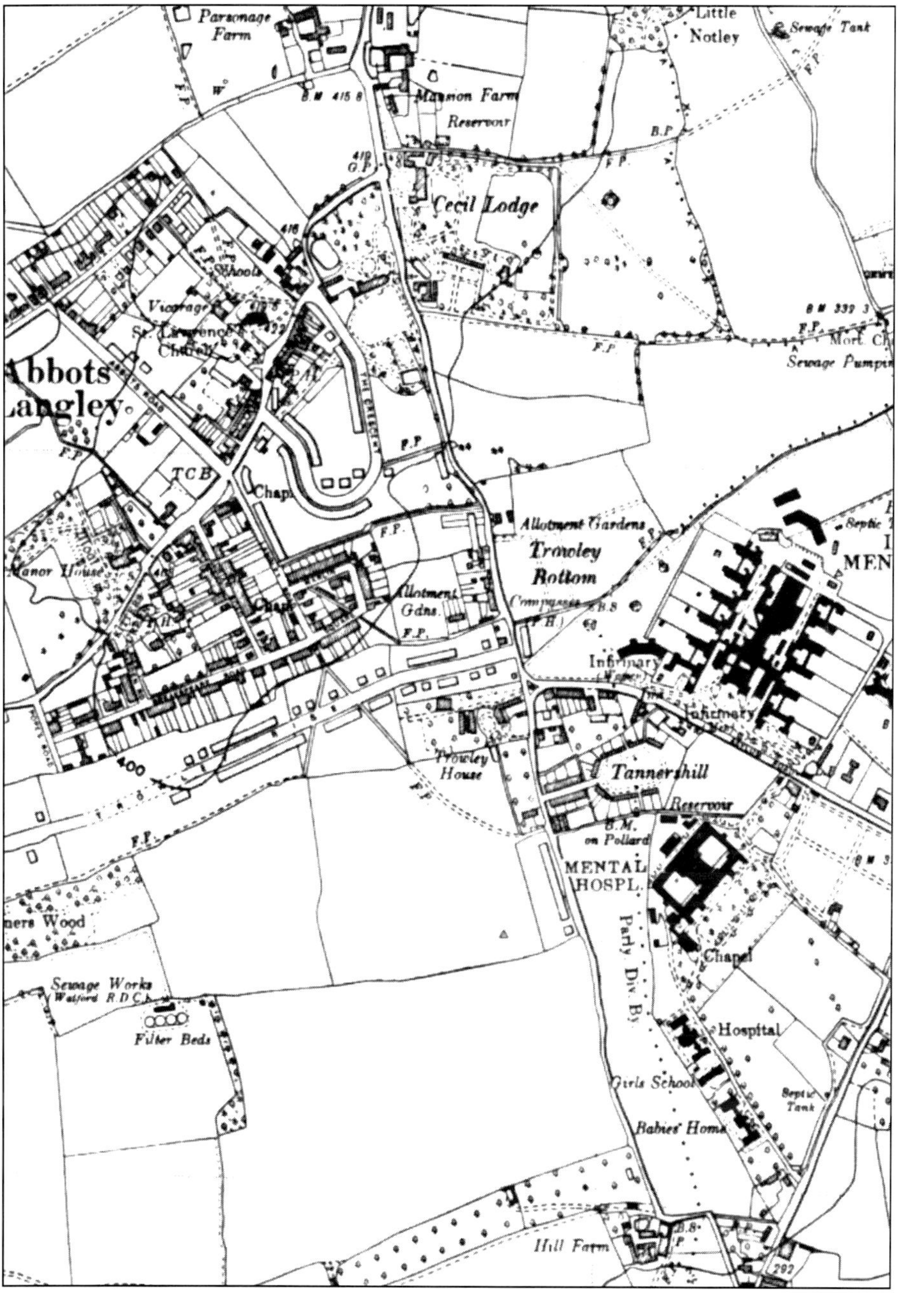

Ordnance Survey map of Abbots Langley in 1938, scale 6 inches to the mile or 1:10,560, reproduced true to scale from the HERTFORDSHIRE SHEET 39 NW: PROVISIONAL EDITION with addtions in 1938.

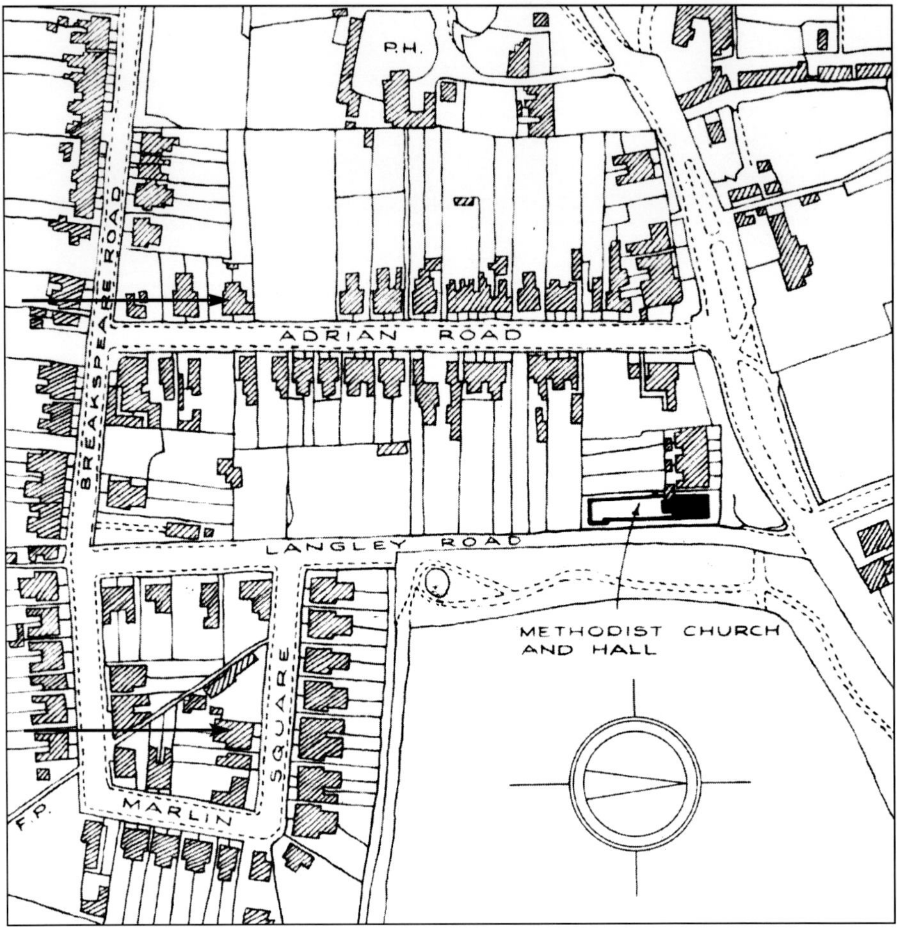

The Location Plan for the proposed Abbots Langley Methodist Church and Hall, scale 1:2,500 based on the 1923 Ordnance Survey map. This was included amongst the blueprints for an extended church submitted in 1938 by Harrison and Stevens, Architects and Surveyors. (The plan was not updated to show the new houses built in 1928 on the opposite side of Langley Road nor those built in The Crescent.) Due to the interruption of the Second World War, this first scheme was not implemented. Another scheme was implemented in 1962.

Note: The upper arrow indicates Annie Kimpton's home, 56 and 54 Adrian Road, Abbots Langley, where the recipients of her letters, Fred and Muriel Kimpton, lived whilst Annie was away during 1937-1938.

The lower arrow indicates Conway (adjacent to FLINT BROTHERS' builders yard), Marlin Square, Abbots Langley, where the other recipients of Annie's letters, Marion and Bert Flint, lived from 1931-1964.

INDEX OF NAMES

THE NAMES of all the people mentioned by Annie Kimpton in her letters or incorporated in the editorial matter are listed herewith the exception of those which occur only in the Family Trees. When names are frequently mentioned, only the relatively important entries are listed. The numerals in *italics* prefaced *P* refer to the illustrated plate number between pages 64-65 and 240-241:

POSTSCRIPT

In September 2000, whilst this book was with the printer, an e-mail was received by the "Visitors' Book" of the Abbots Langley Local History Society internet web site, launched earlier in the year:

> "*Great Site! I am interested in researching my family history and in all likelihood there are folks in your Society who may be able to help me. My grandmother was from Abbots Langley and her name was Helen Perry née Flint and I am interested in any replies with which I can further my research as far back as possible. Thank you, Don Perry, Castleton, Ontario, Canada.*"

This meant that Don Perry was the grandson of Helen (Nell) Perry née Flint who Annie Kimpton had tried to meet in Toronto in 1937. They missed each other on two occasions as Annie described in LETTER 20. A reply was sent immediately by e-mail to Don and a copy of the Flint Family Tree (which had been prepared for this book) was posted to him. Don knew of Nell Perry's father, Harry Flint, and had a yellowing photograph of Nell Perry's mother, Charlotte Flint née Dollemore. But Don was not aware of Harry Flint's brothers who lived in Abbots Langley at that time, William Flint and Old Reuben Flint who had married Emily Dollemore from Redbourn. Don asked, "*Have I got it straight that two Dollemore sisters married two Flint brothers?*"

Don Perry had fond memories of his grandmother, Nell Perry, and his grandfather, Charles Walter (Walter) Perry. Walter Perry's father, Old Walter Henry Perry from Fordingbridge in Hampshire, was a gardener on the Cassiobury estate at Watford. Walter Perry's mother was Ellen Lucy Perry née Eames from Great Missenden in Buckinghamshire. Don believed that Walter Perry emigrated to Canada and Nell followed soon afterwards in 1914 with their two children Doris and Don's father, Bert. Their third child, Fred, was born in Canada. Nell and Walter Perry prospered and Walter owned and operated an engraving company, RELIANCE ENGRAVERS, in downtown Toronto. They later brought his parents out to Canada.

Nell Flint's birth certificate showed that she was born in 1884 at Kingsfield Cottages, Abbots Langley. These are the five cottages behind the Compasses public house at Trowley Bottom, formerly a row of four cottages. Nora Dunn née Flint (1912-1995) used to recite the names of the families in the order they once lived there: "FLINT, SWALLOW, MUTTON, QUICK". This saying must date from the time of Nell Flint's childhood, for in 1881 Harry Flint and his family lived at Rose Cottages, Asylum Road, but by the time of the 1891 census they had moved to Adrian Road. Nora Dunn probably learnt it from her father, George Flint.

Both Don Perry and his daughter, Martha Macleod (who discovered the Abbots Langley Local History Society web site whilst browsing on the internet), have visited England. They and their families stayed at the Two Brewers, Chipperfield, whilst looking for the old Perry addresses in Watford. Don was pleased to discover that he had a distant cousin, Roger Flint, in Abbots Langley and said: "*I have cousins in all parts of Canada. Nell and Walter Perry did their small part to populate the New World.*"